The publisher gratefully acknowledges the generous contribution of this book provided by Joan Palevsky.

Epic Traditions
in the Contemporary World

Epic Traditions in the Contemporary World

The Poetics of Community

EDITED BY

Margaret Beissinger,
Jane Tylus, and
Susanne Wofford

UNIVERSITY OF CALIFORNIA PRESS
Berkeley   Los Angeles   London

University of California Press
Berkeley and Los Angeles, California

University of California Press, Ltd.
London, England

Library of Congress Cataloging-in-Publication Data

Epic traditions in the contemporary world : the poetics of community /
  edited by Margaret Beissinger, Jane Tylus, and Susanne Wofford.
    p.   cm.
  Includes bibliographical references and index.
  ISBN 0-520-21037-9 (alk. paper).—ISBN 0-520-21038-7 (alk. paper)
  1. Epic literature—History and criticism.   2. Literature and society.
  I. Beissinger, Margaret H.   II. Tylus, Jane, 1956– .   III. Wofford,
  Susanne Lindgren, 1952– .
  PN56.E65E665   1999
  809.1'32—dc21   98-49047
                                                                      CIP

Printed in the United States of America
9 8 7 6 5 4 3 2 1

To Our Families

CONTENTS

SECTION THREE · THE BOUNDARIES
OF EPIC PERFORMANCE / 153

SECTION FOUR · EPIC AND LAMENT / 187

SECTION FIVE · EPIC AND PEDAGOGY / 237

ACKNOWLEDGMENTS

Like many epic works, this project has had a lengthy gestation, and in the process we have incurred numerous debts. Colleagues at the University of Wisconsin-Madison were particularly instrumental in the early stages of this book, including James Bailey, Alger Nicholas Doane, and Denis Feeney. The comments from Seth Schein and the two anonymous readers for the University of California Press were invaluable to us in making necessary revisions. Thanks are also owed to Cathlin Davis, our graduate assistant at the University of Wisconsin, for her superb work as a manuscript and computer editor. At the University of California Press, we would like to thank Mary Lamprech for her initial interest and encouragement, Kate Toll for her enthusiasm and constant support, and Rosana Francescato for her help with publication. Special thanks in addition to Lawrence Millman for permission to reprint "The First Loon" and "The Origin of Robins" and to the Department of English at the University of Wisconsin-Madison for helping to cover the permissions fee. We are also grateful to Dr. Giovanna Lazzi, Director of the Biblioteca Riccardiana in Florence for her permission to use for our cover the color photograph from the Riccardiana's beautiful 1472 manuscript of Virgil's *Aeneid*. We also thank Cornell University Press for permission to republish Joyce Flueckiger's essay in a revised form.

Finally, as the dedication of this book attests, we would like to thank our families, especially our husbands—Mark Beissinger, William Klein, and Jacques Lezra—for their careful reading of the manuscript and their support and encouragement throughout the project.

Introduction

Margaret Beissinger, Jane Tylus, and Susanne Wofford

"I have always heard
your voice in that sea, master, it was the same song
of the desert shaman, and when I was a boy

your name was as wide as a bay, as I walked along
the curled brow of the surf; the word `Homer' meant joy,
joy in battle, in work, in death, then the numbered peace

of the surf's benedictions, it rose in the cedars,
in the lauier-cannelles, *pages of rustling trees.*
Master, I was the freshest of all your readers."

DEREK WALCOTT, Omeros

Much as the narrator of Walcott's poem seeks to fashion a bridge between the canonical works of Western literature and the vibrant poetry of the contemporary Caribbean, this volume aims to provide an interdisciplinary dialogue between verbal art genres that have rarely been in dialogue: literary and oral epic. It presents the work of leading scholars of written and oral epic poetry, ancient, Renaissance, and contemporary, from a wide variety of disciplines, including anthropology, classics, Slavic studies, comparative literature, folklore, and English. Epic poetry now stands at the center of an intense debate concerning the relevance and cultural significance of the works that have helped to define Western culture. Using examples of epic poetry from *Gilgamesh* to Walcott's *Omeros*, and of performance traditions from places as different as the Central Himalayas and the Balkans, we propose a new way of considering the position of the epic in cultural and intellectual life in the United States (where many of these debates have been fought most fiercely), in Europe, and in many other areas with living epic traditions. The position of epic is especially vexed in those countries involved in postcolonial debates about the relation of their national literatures to the canons of Western and classical literature, which, as part of a colonial educational policy, often were imposed on school curricula.

The juxtapositioning of these disciplines reveals new and sometimes surprising connections between contemporary performed epic poetry from

1

around the world and epic of the traditional Western canon. It places the epic poetry of Homer, Virgil, Ovid, Spenser, Tasso, and Milton in the context of performances of epic poetry in contemporary Egypt and India, and it sets current fieldwork and ethnographic research about the political and poetic complexities of epic performance in the context of studies of the densely self-referential Western literary epic. We make these juxtapositions in the hope of accomplishing three ends: (1) to provide a new interpretive frame for the literary epic that will help to revitalize interest in the Western canon, though in a way that will require not the exclusion of other literary traditions but a stimulating connection to them; (2) to strengthen the links between studies of narrative, politics, and performance in both fields, and thus to place contemporary work in oral epic within a broader poetics; and (3) to provide a source for teachers, scholars, and readers that will make important work now being done in each of these areas of study accessible to those with training in only one. The epic has been an object of study for two millennia, in part because the great classical epics and their modern counterparts continue to inspire cultural definition and self-definition. The epic is also a vital contemporary art form, both in writing and in performance. With this volume we hope to reshape understanding of epic so as to keep both of these aspects of the epic in sight, and to inspire a greater degree of comparative understanding, both of the form and of the related cultures in which each individual poem is embedded.

What is the epic? This book compels its readers to grapple with this question. A first reaction of many scholars of the classical or Renaissance epic to an account of contemporary performed oral poetry might be to argue that it is not really the epic as they know it. Similarly, scholars doing fieldwork who can measure their epics by the number of days it takes to perform them might question whether strict formal limits can produce an adequate definition of the genre. Our working definition for this volume itself has a polemical or at least limiting edge: the epic is defined here as a poetic narrative of length and complexity that centers around deeds of significance to the community. These deeds are usually presented as deeds of grandeur or heroism, often narrated from within a verisimilitudinous frame of reference. We exclude from the arena of study myth and other kinds of tales that depend largely on magic (many epics include briefer magical episodes), and we also exclude epics in prose, although in historical perspective it is clear that the novel, for one example, is a form of the epic.[1] Emphasizing poetry helps to delimit the field of contemporary performance but does not signal that the issues posed by the contributors to this volume are disconnected from prose genres that have epic qualities. The epic also has a peculiar and complex connection to national and local cultures: the inclusiveness of epic—the tendency of a given poem to present an encyclopedic account of the culture that produced it—also explains its political potency. This political explosiveness is evident in the charged contemporary performances of epic (several examples of which are described in this volume), in the intense reimagining of epic undertaken by most emerging European nations as a means of coming to self-knowledge as a nation, and in the bitterness of accusations today about the dangers of abandoning canonical study in the academy. We hope to show that knowledge of this traditional arena of cultural definition is extended, not limited, by the kind of cross-cultural context constructed here.

The essays in this volume argue strongly, then, for the value of comparative literary study and do so in the context of an intellectual climate in which study of traditional genres sometimes is seen as rather old-fashioned. The challenge to cross-cultural study of a particular literary form has come especially from those (whether old or new historicists) who emphasize the importance in literary study of historical and political particularities. This challenge has its base in an accurate and productive skepticism about both the idealizations of culture so characteristic of late nineteenth- and early twentieth-century studies in myth and comparative religion (exemplified by James George Frazer's *Golden Bough*) and about the idealizations of form characteristic of the close poetic analyses put forward by the American New Critics and others in the middle decades of the twentieth century. One critique of both these idealizations is that they each in different ways obfuscate precisely the political effects of epic poetry—whether the potentially propagandistic effect of glorifying the current rulers or the more complex cultural imperialism evidenced in many epic poems. The work in this volume seeks to avoid some of the pitfalls of generalized generic comparison by rooting the analyses in the political culture of the societies at issue. Thus to look at the function of lament in classical and later Western epic, we include one broader cross-cultural study by a leading scholar of the epic who argues for the centrality of lament in most major Western epics from *Gilgamesh* to Milton's *Paradise Lost*, and two more culturally focused studies of, respectively, Greek and Latin epics. Each of these examines the positioning of this female genre within a characteristically male form while considering the culturally distinct role of women (and of lament) in archaic Greek society and Roman culture. Similarly, the political role of epic performance is the central focus of several of the essays that rely on fieldwork in India. We propose, then, that comparative literary study can and should make the political and the culturally specific more visible, rather than hiding cultural contest and debate behind an idealized or essentialized mask. To look at the position of epic in the contemporary world is to pose, not to evade, the question of epic ideology and its relation to nationalism, national identity, and the politics of gender.

EPICS AND CONTEMPORANEITY

To those trained in the traditional canon of Western letters, any discussion of contemporaneity is virtually anathema in regard to epic poetry, which, as though it were a living organism, is said to experience birth, maturity, and death. One might argue that on numerous occasions, announcements of the death of Western epic have in fact been premature. Even though Francesco Petrarca, whose name is usually synonymous with the Renaissance, failed miserably in his own attempts to resuscitate classical epic, it was not long before Camões, Tasso, Spenser, and Milton succeeded. But in the twentieth century in particular, despite and perhaps partly because of the epic strivings of novelists such as George Eliot, Thomas Mann, Marcel Proust, and of course James Joyce, the Western epic has been theorized as being, like the wicked witch in *The Wizard of Oz*, really and sincerely dead.

Two critics who have been extremely influential in the past several decades might be said to epitomize much current thinking about the trajectory of Western epic—a rubric that is often used as a facile substitute for epic itself. These are the Soviet critic Mikhail Bakhtin and the German essayist Walter Benjamin. Their writings reflect strains of thought that, though not entirely new, are certainly characteristic of much modern criticism of the literary epic and its tendencies to oppose the terms "modern" and "epic."

On the one hand, Bakhtin can be said to have inherited the attitude of those Renaissance writers who busily rehabilitated epic in the name of a cultural and political privilege they were trying to claim for themselves. In a period that worried immensely about its origins, and one that was increasingly marked with the urgent need for a master discourse that could rival Christianity, Trissino, Ariosto, Tasso, Spenser, Camões, Milton, d'Aubigné, and again, Petrarca reinvented epic as a genre of and for the elite communities in which they not only wanted to partake but which they wanted to define—whether that community was the sophisticated court of Tasso's Ferrara or the "fit audience though few" of Milton's post-Cromwellian England. Bakhtin's comments on epic in the first essay from *The Dialogic Imagination* likewise privilege the genre as of and for an elite. Bakhtin regards epic as the master discourse par excellence, which he opposes to the popular and open-ended novel that necessarily overtook the earlier genre, impervious as it was to change. For Bakhtin, the epic is monologic. It has only one word, one tongue, one point of entry: the aristocracy's or ruling people's, who want to maintain a status quo and idealize a past that is "utterly different and inaccessible."[2] It is the novel that thrives on contemporaneity, on "contact," on multiplicity; the epic is based on memory, on distance, and on an absolute unity that defies the act of questioning and communal participation.

Yet although Bakhtin adapts the Renaissance's posture toward epic's privileges, he fails to see Renaissance writers themselves as true epic writers, and in fact the only epic poetry that really fits his definition is—virtually by his own admission—Homer's, and only the *Iliad* at that. The fact that the *Iliad*'s supposedly profound inimitability becomes a criterion for distinguishing an epic poem is thereby problematic, particularly given what we know now to have been the performative conditions for that work. Moreover, by denying to the *Iliad* the right to contemplate and question itself, Bakhtin denies to this splendid archaic Greek text its profound reflections about human agency and its only tentative attempts to articulate an ethos that might outlast the fragility of its own always impermanent performances. In effect, Bakhtin mistakes the belated *desires* for epic's authority and canonical status—by fifth-century rhapsodes, by Virgil and his Renaissance imitators—for epic's immediate *effect*. In so doing, he monumentalizes Homer before Homer has finished singing. But he also forces us to be attentive to the processes through which epic—which has typically claimed to narrate the recovery of an originary identity of a group bound by linguistic ties (the Homeric epics), tribal bonds (the African poem *Sun-jata*), religion (the Pentateuch), nationality (Camões's *Lusiades*), or empire (Virgil's *Aeneid*)—is canonized and rendered necessarily authoritative over time.

But if epic was rekindled by early modern writers as an "elite" genre, the nationalistic and romantic tendencies of Johann Gottfried von Herder and other late eighteenth-century figures wanted to find in it more of a "popular" spirit, and one sees in Herder's "Origins of Hebrew Poetry" the attempt to locate in Greek and Hebrew writings the influence of the "Volk."[3] This is where Benjamin's musings on epic in his classic essay on the Russian short-story writer Nikolai Leskov essentially fit. In "The Storyteller," Benjamin envisions epic not as Bakhtin does, as an antiquated and outmoded form which of necessity yielded to the popular novel, but as itself a genre that reflects a "popular" spirit: it is the product of a community and is thereby ever-changing, insofar as it is told by a storyteller whose manner of presenting tales is oral and alive. Benjamin's writing is strikingly contemporaneous with the work of Milman Parry, who demonstrated that the formulas in Homer attested to oral composition and who may have been inspired by the romantics' formulation of epic and national origins. But unlike Herder and others who initiated the study of folklore in the late eighteenth century—many of whom, one is well reminded, were long taken in by the bogus poetry of Ossian—Parry was able to demonstrate epic's oral roots philologically, given his close work with nonliterate South Slavic bards. For Parry and later for Albert Lord, of course, this contemporary phenomenon served largely to verify their theses regarding the performative dynamics of Homer's poetry. For Benjamin, probably unaware of Parry's work, the phenomenon of oral storytelling can provoke only a sense of nostalgia. Epic performance belonged to an irrecoverable past when tales were not distanced from their audience and their sources, before art lost its "aura," before it was hardened, congealed, into an object.[4]

Benjamin's essay is essentially an act of mourning for the loss of a tradition that once gave communities their identity, a tradition no longer possible in an age defined by technology. Still, there is something paradoxical about "The Storyteller." Its ostensible subject is not the days of Homer—as is the case in the opening pages of Gyorgy Lukacs's *The Theory of the Novel*, likewise nostalgic for the organic wholeness of illiterate communities[5] —but the recent feudal, highly class-based society of late nineteenth-century Russia, supplanted in Benjamin's own time by the classlessness of a Marxism with which Benjamin long flirted. He is also discussing a writer, one whose own highly nuanced sense of style was often laced with the kind of laconic irony that is also a hallmark of Benjamin's prose. For both Bakhtin and Benjamin, there is the tendency for the categories supposedly so necessary to epic's definition to weaken if not collapse, a tendency that is yet not so marked as to prevent the many literary critics who read them from insisting rather simplistically that the epic has no value for the contemporary moment. By the same token, despite the ultimate intermingling of supposedly opposed categories in the two essays, both writers fundamentally believe that epic is a legacy of the past because the circumstances that enabled or necessitated its production are no longer present.

In this volume, Bakhtin and Benjamin are challenged directly as the various pressures of the contemporary are brought to bear on a genre that they have declared is either a dead letter or a vital oral phenomenon that is simply no more. Indeed, the essayists in this volume directly address the contemporaneity of epic by taking into consideration one or more of the following: *(a)* contemporary performances and anthropological research regarding epics' functions in communities, and the resultant attentiveness to stylistic innovations and audience, and thus to how epics shift in regard to political, social, and performative conditions; *(b)* contemporary theoretical stances deriving from feminism, psychoanalysis, poststructuralism, and cultural studies that have resituated epics in their relationship to cultures and communities, forcing scholars to be more attentive to epics' margins, their silences and acts of silencing; *(c)* contemporary discussions of what constitutes the canon, and the canon's relevance to current heterogeneous classrooms in the United States. Such discussions have compelled many to question the assumption that epic is a purely textual phenomenon that began with Homer and ended with Milton, and to see epics existing in societies that have been denied the "right" to have epic (such as North African societies, as Joseph Farrell notes in his essay).

Yet the form in which this challenge is cast does not overlook Benjamin's and Bakhtin's readings and concerns. On the one hand, essayists in this volume who specifically consider the nuances of performance are attentive to the impact not only of political and social pressures on the production of epic, but of technological developments as well. Although they might not embrace Benjamin's nostalgia for an irrevocably lost communal *Geist* as embodied in oral poems, they are concerned with the "invasion" of the local by the cosmopolitan even as they are aware of the pressures that the local exerts on the cosmopolitan in turn. Such attentiveness necessarily extends to those contributors, such as Sheila Murnaghan, who consider the roles of ritual and that archaic form of storytelling known as the lament. Lament could consolidate community, but it could also threaten the other stabilizing bonds that held groups and epic poems together. On the other hand, the terminology invoked by Bakhtin regarding Homeric epic—its monologism, its closure, its authority—is likewise invoked by a number of scholars not so much in regard to single epic poems as in regard to an epic tradition and a desire found in numerous cultures to grant authority to epic tales of origins and political legitimation. Bakhtin's version of epic has never existed—indeed, as a theory it ignores what has always been present in epic's dialogic voices—but the desire for his version of epic have long existed, as attested by the allegorists whom Andrew Ford discusses.

The "contemporary," then, is in fact immediately relevant to discussions of epic. The essays that follow alert us to the *ongoing* function of epics in various parts of the world today. They articulate how current theoretical initiatives and debates about the canon are critical for an understanding of the hold of epic on the imagination in antiquity as in the present.

At least part of the attraction of epic poetry consists in the skill and imagination of those who create, revise, and recite it. It is to this critical question that we turn next: What makes an epic poet?

THE EPIC POET

When oral epic or literary epic are examined, they are generally treated as separate and distinct verbal narrative art forms, each with its own concept of authorship and its own array of characteristics, both formal and thematic. Oral traditional epic is understood as orally composed and orally transmitted. It is, very importantly, a genre that is performed before an audience. While individual performers of epic (each with varying levels of creativity) are appreciated, anonymity and collective involvement surround authorship per se. Oral epic is typically marked by compositional devices that facilitate performance and transmission, as well as by content that is regarded as deeply traditional, at times even mythic (bringing with it an identification of oral epic with story patterns that are both ancient and widespread).

From the perspective of scholars of folklore, literary epic, unlike oral traditional epic, is usually seen as the creation of a single author, immersed in literacy and everything that literacy brings with it. Literary epic is created with artistic perfection in mind, not expediency of performance. It is imagined as an art form crafted by someone with the leisure to chisel phrases, verses, and sentences, to develop and refine artistic expression with the author's best as the desired outcome. Furthermore, literary epic allows for (and even expects) the author's original and creative expression in narratives that adroitly challenge readers with their well-designed tropes and innovative uses of textual conventions and themes.

If the creative processes of the oral epic poet and the writer of epics thus remain significantly different, it is worth considering more specifically what defines the poetic work of the oral poet. Much has been written on the apprenticeship of oral epic poets.[6] The art of the oral epic poet is not randomly developed nor casually perfected, for it is a complex art that entails years of training and practice. Furthermore, traditional performers of oral epic are often characterized by gender and are not only artistically and at times professionally marginalized within the larger community but also situated on the periphery ethnically and socially.

The art of oral epic singing is by and large—though not always—an art perpetuated by men for public performance. Customarily, young boys begin to cultivate the art of epic singing at a young age, first by learning to play an instrument. This is usually followed by mastering the art of singing and stringing metrically appropriate verses together. Finally, they assemble entire narrative songs and begin to perform in public. The instruction process is predicated on the young singer's knowledge of the repertoire, gained customarily through repeated attendance at epic performances. In some cultures, the art of epic singing is passed from older male relative to young boy, such that the child's mentor is typically from within his own family; thus the milieu for this learning surrounds him perpetually. Frequently, epic singing is also performed for remuneration (at traditional weddings, birth celebrations, at market or in cafés, and so on), such that it becomes a profession. In certain cultures, epic is even perpetuated by a "class" of singers who are effectively on the margins, both ethnically and socially, of the community. They are what Susan Slyomovics has called the "poet outcasts" in an example from the Egyptian oral epic tradition.[7] A similar phenomenon is found among traditional Romanian epic singers, who are typically Gypsies— spurned within the context of mainstream society, yet highly venerated as verbal artists for the community.[8]

This way of highlighting the differences between the role of the poet in written epic and the performer's embodiment of a more or less collective voice helps to illustrate a central tension in the written epic as well. Like the oral epic poet, the writer of epic poetry has generally been male (though this has begun to change in the last two centuries) and is immersed in a tradition that takes years of training to master. The art of the epic poet depends centrally on imitation—on being able to reproduce, but in a new cultural register or in a new language, images, events, plot motifs, and whatever other textual details give the form its generic authority. In *The Anxiety of Influence,* Harold Bloom suggests that English poets who wrote after a Milton regarded as largely inimitable struggled in a variety of ways to master and usurp their great precursor. Yet in many senses, to begin with the romantics is to begin 2,000 years too late. Moreover, while the psychoanalytic vocabulary Bloom invoked is enlightening for our own era, it is not an essential theoretical rubric for understanding Virgil's wrangling with Apollonius Rhodius or Callimachus's challenge to archaic epic in writing an epic of fragments (or to go back even farther and to expand momentarily our definition of epic, Plato's attempts to have Socrates surpass Homer and the rhapsodes as an oral poet in his *Ion*). Indeed, written epic often twists uncomfortably on the dilemma of whether the poet should emphasize submersion in a collective voice or an individual poetic voice and authority. When Virgil writes "Arma virumque cano" (Of arms and a man I sing), his use of the first-person verb form stands out in contrast to the more anonymous invocations of the Homeric bard: "Sing, Muse . . . " The contrast with the living oral epic performances described in this book thus helps to expose a latent tension in the written epic. It also makes more apparent where the literary epic poet's immersion in tradition approaches a more collective voice and where the individual reshaping or challenge to tradition becomes most pointed.

It is in going back to Homer and the tangled origins of written epic in the West that one finds potentially similar circumstances to those present in the shaping of oral poetry, and arguably they have impinged on the production of written epic itself. And it is also in Homer that we find the image of the marginalized poet, subject to the whims of patronage (such as Phemius, who is told now by Telemachus, now by Penelope, and now by the suitors, what to sing) or physically marked by the sign of his outcast and yet privileged status (such as the blind bard Demodocus, who performs for Odysseus and the Phaiakians).[9] It is perhaps only historical accident, but again and again one encounters poets in the tradition of literary epic who likewise write from the margins and whose poems thereby hinge on the thematics of exile and estrangement: Dante writing his *Commedia* in exile from Florence, Milton writing *Paradise Lost* during the Restoration, the composer of the *Chanson de Roland*—perhaps—in figurative exile at the English court. In such ways, the social and economic vulnerabilities to which oral poets continue to be subject have left their mark, however mediated, on the legacy of written epic as well.

WRITTEN VERSUS ORAL

It is with such crossovers and concerns that we now engage more directly in the questions of orality and literacy that have been so central to the issue of

epic in the past century or so. Walter Ong has been, perhaps, the most elo-
quent spokesperson for the impact of literacy on culture and literature, tracing various developments from orality to literacy and mass dependence on
the printed word. Along with others, Ong has argued persuasively for a recognition of the profound changes that literacy has engendered in human history. Indeed, polemics surrounding orality and literacy among scholars of
oral poetry frequently focus on texts that are not unquestionably either oral
or literary, or on transitional texts—those that fall somewhere between oral
and literary for any number of reasons. Similarly, the role of literacy in the
creative process of oral poets (and determining which features point to either orality or literacy in their poetry) has been a matter of controversy.
Nonetheless, it is rare when critical readings of oral and literary verbal art
are truly exchanged; the distinction between "us" and "them" still tends to
dominate scholarship, from whichever perspective.

The essays in this volume challenge the current understanding of orality
and literacy as opposed categories. By putting aside strict boundaries of genre
and methodology, they enable an exchange between literatures and between
scholars that confronts the very idea of what epic is and how it can be read.
And this exchange proves effective because, put simply, those who study oral
epic and those who study literary epic have much to learn from each other.
Epic conceived as a poetic narrative of length and complexity that centers
around deeds of significance to the community transcends the oral and literary divide that has long marked the approach to the genre. In transcend-
ing that divide, epic emerges as a larger genre within which comparative study
becomes more dynamic and broader in scope. By addressing authorship,
readership (or "listenership"), form, and meaning in the "other" (be it oral
or literary epic), scholars in this volume have been challenged to see how
they have constructed the "other" as opposed and separate, and are thus encouraged to reexamine the epic tradition they know best.

Because of their "literary" nature, written texts have engendered a level
of theorizing that cannot yet be assumed by scholars of oral literature. The
tangible written text in itself generates complex theoretical systems of approaching literature—systems that can also provide exciting tools for the understanding of oral literature. For instance, readings of ambiguity in poetic
language and studies of the literary poet's manipulation of metaphor and
allegory suggest powerful models for ways in which figurative language might
be examined in oral epic. Philip Hardie's treatment of rhetoric in Latin epic
and Andrew Ford's essay on early Greek allegoresis are particularly evocative in this regard.

From the literary side, the ethnographic criticism of oral epic also furnishes
means by which the study of literary epic may be given a sharper political and
cultural focus. Emphasis on the performativity of oral epic poets, who compose and transmit their art before an audience and who function as discrete

figures wielding a type of mythic knowledge within the community, provides a challenge to students of written epic, where concerns about performance and performative genres have recently taken the forefront. The essays by Susan Slyomovics and Dwight Reynolds on Egyptian oral epic poets provide especially rich examples of this detailed analysis of performativity. The immediate politics of oral epic performance—how a traditional genre can be interpreted, say, as a potent political statement to the community—is explored in the essays on the Indian epic by Joyce Flueckiger and William Sax. It is precisely through the juxtaposition of oral and literary epic in cases like these— and the recognition of a larger concept of epic that transcends orality and literacy—that a more complex sense of the interactions of form, genre, politics, and culture may be brought to the interpretation of the genre.

Studies of oral epic similarly suggest that interpretation of written epic could be directed more toward study of the tension between the local and the national or universal. Oral epic continues in general to be more attuned to the indigenous or local traditions that inform epic poetry. This focus can be a productive one for scholars of written epic. Jane Tylus explores the cultic resonances that inform Virgil's and Tasso's "universalizing" poems. And in their feminist reappraisals of Greek and Roman epic, Sheila Murnaghan and Elaine Fantham demonstrate how the oral tradition of female lament threatens to subvert the heroic functions of literary epic. Students of oral epic can be more attentive, in turn, to ambiguity, linguistic nuances, and the extent to which oral texts, like written texts, construct themselves as theoretical systems. Several of the essays in this volume that give detailed accounts of performances suggest the virtues of this approach. Dwight Reynolds's study, for example, is a bracing account of the multivalent strategies and variety of speech acts to which the poet has access in any given performative situation.

In the exploration of various forms of verbal art, there is a point at which one can speak of a larger aesthetic that embraces both the oral and the literary. In so doing, one is liberated to speak of language elevated from the pedestrian to the realm of higher poetic diction, not only among the "lettered" poets, but among the "unlettered" as well. Ultimately, epic poets, be they oral or literary, all create. They all manipulate devices and techniques by which their art is revealed, whether those devices are orally transmitted or rooted in literacy. They all seek to tell a good story: to relate a narrative that, it is hoped, will light a fire, touch a soul, entertain for an evening (be it with book in hand or grouped around a singer), or even change the destiny of a nation.

CROSSING BOUNDARIES

The thematic kernel of this volume is the idea that the dynamics of epic, both oral and literary, are created and sustained through the challenging of boundaries—boundaries of genre, gender, locality, and language. The intellectual inquiry undertaken in most of the essays presented here turns on questions of genre, gender, and trope. Moreover, the volume is organized to cross and re-cross that most fundamental of boundaries, namely, that between oral and literary epic. Gregory Nagy's comparative reading of genre in oral and literary epic and Joyce Flueckiger's argument for the role of regional and social identity in Indian epic both complicate and challenge the concept of genre. Genre definitions are similarly challenged and expanded in discussions of the boundaries of epic and the interplay and overlapping of genres, both in oral performances (explored in Egyptian and Indian epic) and in literary works (Joseph Farrell's discussion of Walcott's *Omeros* and Susanne Wofford's consideration of Native American tales alongside the "classical" works of Ovid and Spenser). Lament, deeply embedded in the genre question, provides striking examples of the prominence of genre within genre, or countergenre within genre, once again challenging the boundaries of epic.

The appropriation of gender roles or crossing of gender boundaries in epic is examined also as it reflects regional, cultural, and political concerns. Tracing the role of Balkan epic in the development of nineteenth-century literature, Margaret Beissinger illustrates the use of an oral genre for political purposes, revealing how gender is appropriated in literary epic as an instrument of nationalism. Sheila Murnaghan also theorizes the role of gender boundaries and the crossing of those boundaries in epic in her study of the role of lament in Homer. She argues that female laments are more subversive of the epic than laments spoken by men, not just because they dwell on grief and suffering attendant upon heroic action, but because they ignore the death-defying *kleos* that provides compensation for heroic sacrifice, a major function of epic. Elaine Fantham explores in Roman epic a similar problem—how much does lamentation disrupt the capacity of a poem to function as an epic? She sees the balance as tipping from public lament (with its typically male response of provoking desire for revenge) to the more disruptive private laments (often spoken by female characters) in the course of the development of Roman epic.

Another kind of boundary crossing at issue in many of these essays concerns the crossing from one meaning to another achieved by verbal ambiguity. The concern in written epic with wordplay, image, and trope is matched in the oral epic (such as in the Egyptian genre) by the marked use of punning, as well as the interplay between overlapping levels of verbal performance. Punning and linguistic ambiguity are linked to other modes of language play found in literary epic, such as the use of allegory and metaphor as strategies for subverting boundaries, in the essays by Hardie and Ford.

· · ·

The essays in this volume are divided into five sections. The volume's organization speaks to the shared concerns of scholars of oral and written epic, as well as to the methodologies and strategies that distinguish the two forms. Appropriately, the book opens with an essay by the noted classicist and folklorist Gregory Nagy, one of very few scholars whose work marks out the interface between performance and scribal traditions that the volume as a whole aims to expand. The first section, entitled "On the Margins of the Scribal: From Oral Epic to Text," is devoted to the examination of what happens in the lively process of transforming an oral poem into a written text, and in interrogating the etymologies and contexts of several words used consistently in epic poetry. Nagy begins by critiquing the dominance of generic norms established by written epic. Drawing on the important work of Richard Martin on the relation of speech act theory to the theory of oral performance, Nagy argues that our concepts of performance can be rendered more complex by understanding what is performed by the spoken or sung words.

The other essays in the first section of this volume likewise interrogate ways in which performative content has been either obscured by the scribal tradition or compromised by the exigencies of catering to increasingly elite audiences. In an essay on the origins of allegoresis in ancient Italy, Andrew Ford discusses how the horizons of an epic genre once invoked to define a people (*laos*) were gradually narrowed so as to accommodate only "initiated" audiences who became the preeminent users of a new cultural construction of literature. Despite the fact that Susan Slyomovics is dealing with a radically different narrative tradition, the oral epic of northern Egypt, she nonetheless offers a strikingly similar reading of the transformation of epic poetry into a genre that indulges an increasingly selective audience— primarily, in the case of the Egyptian poetry she is discussing, because of the epic performer's subtle negotiations of his outcast status. Her reading of epic puns, which float, like the poet, "between acceptability and rejection," becomes a way of reading epic itself as a negotiation between popular and elite culture. Finally, Margaret Beissinger analyzes the interconnections between oral epic and orally inspired literary epic in Balkan culture as she interprets gender roles in the different traditions and exposes the way in which they were appropriated for political and nationalistic purposes, particularly within the developing "scribal" tradition of the nineteenth century. While women play significant roles in South Slavic oral epic, their relevance to the written epic that mirrored the oral genre and defined the beginning of national literatures in the Balkans was radically diminished. She argues that this occurred because the male-dominated political climate of nineteenth-century nations emerging from centuries of Ottoman rule found the female voice effectively unnecessary to the political statements expressed in their burgeoning literatures.

Whereas the first section largely focuses on the gradual canonization of epic as it veers between the popular and the elite, the second section of essays, entitled "Epic and Authority," explores the challenges to epic's presumed canonicity as embodied within the process of epic making itself. Jane Tylus's essay examines the cultic resonances in Virgil's *Aeneid* and Torquato Tasso's *Gerusalemme liberata* in light of what T. S. Eliot condemned as the provincialism that "true" masterpieces of Western literature, beginning with the *Aeneid,* have supposedly managed to escape. Tylus suggests that far from escaping from the provincial, epic must necessarily contend with the authority that local customs and traditions can grant, even when epic is written in the service of an imperial agenda that presumes to be universal. Particularly in classical and medieval epics, the leap from the provincial or local to the universal was facilitated through allegory. The essay by Philip Hardie nonetheless exposes the instability and often unintentionally subversive function of allegoresis. Focusing on Virgil and Ovid, Hardie demonstrates that allegory in fact threatens the rigid classificatory system that had been at work in Homer, challenging the important distinctions between human and animal, the winners and the losers, a monumental text and a permeable, amorphous text that changes over time. Joyce Flueckiger also focuses on the destabilizations evident in epic texts, particularly the destabilizations of gender categories, in her study of regional performances of northern Indian epics. Her fieldwork suggests that local pressures result in very different epic poems, and whereas one region faithfully produces epic as an authoritative, unchanging tale of origins and legitimation, another performs an epic poem in ways that reflect the diverse and changing communal and social realities within it.

This attentiveness to performative variabilities is especially apparent in the third section, "The Boundaries of Epic Performance." Both essays in this section consider contemporary epic performances and question how performance itself challenges notions of canonicity and generic boundaries. In an essay that will interest readers of books 9–12 of the *Odyssey,* where Odysseus tells his own heroic tale to the avid Phaiakians, Dwight Reynolds shows how the performer of Arabic oral poetry makes his own speech act equivalent to that of the hero. Incorporating the audience into the story's plot in what Reynolds suggestively terms a kind of "Russian roulette," the epic poet moves fully into the role of the hero by the end of his performance, thereby exaggerating his own function and in effect diminishing that of the hero and the tradition that he supposedly serves. William Sax's essay on the epics of northern India discusses, like that of Reynolds, the participatory nature of contemporary epic. For Sax, however, the recent changes in performed epics are due largely to the ongoing pressures of nationalism and the disappearance of the "local"—a reading that suggests both that the dynamics of individual communities are not necessarily apparent in epic performance and that the poet is not so much the shaper of his performances as he is shaped by larger political forces beyond himself. Like Tylus's account of Virgil and Tasso, then, Sax's study of epic exposes powerful antagonisms between the more local and the national or imperial impact of the form.

This nexus of concerns—the extent to which epic poets perceive themselves or can be perceived as the makers of their songs—defines the next section, "Epic and Lament." Moreover, in many ways, the essays in this section bring together the issues of performance, authority, and the transition from oral to written poems broached in the first three sections by looking specifically at a public, largely female-centered tradition that has had an ambivalent relationship with epic since its inception. As she traduces the ground between Greek and Roman epic, Elaine Fantham charts the uncomfortable dynamic between lament and heroic action. With the Latin poet Statius, this struggle ends with the "triumph" of the former, as the bitter world of civil war renders heroic action finally incapable of attaining the level of glorification. Sheila Murnaghan produces a more explicitly gendered and theoretical reading of lament, seeing in it (like Fantham) a subversive element that challenges the epic ideology of Homer, predicated on fame untainted by suffering. Murnaghan suggests that the laments by women in the *Iliad* offer a different reading of the origins of epic from those commonly rehearsed: *kleos* begins with grief for one's friends and enemies before it is converted into the "pleasant song" celebrated by the Phaiakians in the *Odyssey*. Finally, Thomas Greene's magisterial reading resolves what Fantham and Murnaghan would unsettle, in his exploration of the extent to which epic tears are in fact the true Aristotelian *telos* of the genre. Weeping becomes a constant and necessary element of epic from *Gilgamesh* through *Paradise Lost*, after which the act of lament becomes a private rather than a public affair. For Greene, there is no dissonance between the lament proper—shared by women and men alike—and the goal of the epic poem; the tragic ritual is that which leads us to "shared stillness within tremendous ruin," a stillness that is valuable as a marker of cultural identity and integrity.

The essays in the final section of the volume—"Epic and Pedagogy"—ask directly what many of the other essays imply. If we are to accept the interdisciplinarity of so many of the pieces, with their challenges to a highly traditional epic canon and its separation of the scribal and the performative, then how do we go about teaching epics in the here and now? The poet on whom Joseph Farrell focuses, the contemporary Caribbean writer Derek Walcott, himself asks such questions in the course of his own contentiously epic poem. In *Omeros*, the narrator travels, like Walcott, from the isle of Santa Lucia to Portugal, to Boston, and back again, only to meet up with the ghost of Homer himself when he returns to his beloved island. Farrell's sensitive treatment of Walcott's poem, which hovers between dialect and "canonical" English and thereby asks difficult and unanswerable questions about epic's roots, insists that the debate concerning what is meant by the word *epic* must be an ongoing one. Farrell demonstrates how the reading experience of *Omeros* is a challenge both to critics who deny the experience of epic poetry to non-European people (relevant here is an assertion of V. S. Naipaul's that the Caribbean can only mimic, never create anew)[10] and to critics who insist that taking up the epic canon at all is an insult to a native people for so long enslaved by those who professed the ideology of that canon. The political issues of multiculturalism that Farrell—and Walcott—raise are also addressed by Susanne Wofford, who proposes that the canonical Western epic might best be taught in the context of living oral traditions of heroic song and tale, including most notably Native American traditions. She takes as her case in point the use of the origin tale in Virgil, Ovid, and Spenser, contrasting the political and poetic functions of these short narratives with "epic" and reexamining the political telos of "epic" in an effort to define a New World reshaping of the canon.

Taken as a whole, the essays in this volume challenge us to think about epic as a genre that is an ongoing attempt to tell the stories of things past in such a way as to make them relevant and even necessary to the present. It is precisely epic's—and epics'—subscription to the principle of contemporaneity that makes it such an powerful art form for us to grapple with today, as we not only come to understand more fully but are ourselves caught within the very social, political, and cultural forces that at once influence the production of epics and are shaped and directed by them.

NOTES

1. As Cervantes, often described as the author of the first novel, has his Canon of Toledo in *Don Quijote* explain, "La épica tambien puede escribirse en prosa como en verso" ("The epic, moreover, can be written in prose as well as in verse"). The date of this comment, with which many Renaissance writers would have been in sympathy, is 1605.

2. Bakhtin 1981, 14. For Bakhtin's most definitive statement on epic's refusal of contemporaneity, see pp. 13–14: "In its style, tone and manner of expression, epic discourse is infinitely far removed from discourse of a contemporary about contemporary issues addressed to contemporaries."

3. "Vom Geist der ebraischen Poesie" (1782); English translation available in Simpson 1988.

4. See both "The Storyteller" and, for Benjamin's comments on a work's "aura," "The Work of Art in the Age of Mechanical Reproduction," in Benjamin 1969, 83–110; 217–254.

5. Lukacs 1971, chap. 1.

6. See Lord 1960, chap. 2 ("Singers: Performance and Training").

7. See Slyomovics 1987.

8. See Beissinger 1991. Indian oral epic is also performed typically by men who

are from the lower strata of society and are even untouchables in many cases; see Blackburn et al. 1989.

    9. See Ann L. T. Bergren's suggestive essay (1983), particularly her comment on p. 93 on "blindness and mutilation (with the suggestion of castration) as marks of the male poet" in Greek epic.

    10. See Derek Walcott's response to Naipaul's criticism (which he quotes in full) in "The Caribbean: Culture or Mimicry?" (1974), reprinted in Hamner 1993, esp. pp. 52–54.

WORKS CITED

Bakhtin, Mikhail.
    1981.   *The Dialogic Imagination.* Edited by Michael Holquist. Translated by Caryl Emerson and Michael Holquist. Austin: University of Texas Press.

Beissinger, Margaret H.
    1991.   *The Art of Lăutar: The Epic Tradition of Romania.* New York: Garland Publishing.

Benjamin, Walter.
    1969.   *Illuminations.* Edited by Hannah Arendt. Translated by Harry Zohn. New York: Schocken.

Bergren, Ann L. T.
    1983.   "Language and the Female in Early Greek Thought." *Arethusa* 16: 69–95.

Blackburn, Stuart, Peter Claus, Joyce Flueckiger, and Susan Wadley, eds.
    1989.   *Oral Epics in India.* Berkeley: University of California Press.

Cervantes, Miguel de.
    1968.   *Don Quijote de la Mancha.* Edited by Martín de Riquer. Barcelona: Editorial Juventud.

Hamner, Robert D., ed.
    1993.   *Critical Perspectives on Derek Walcott.* Washington, D.C.: Three Continents Press.

Lord, Albert B.
    1960.   *The Singer of Tales.* Cambridge: Harvard University Press.

Lukacs, Georg.
    1971.   *The Theory of the Novel: A Historico-Philosophical Essay on the Forms of Great Epic Literature.* Translated by Anna Bostock. London: Merlin Press.

Simpson, David, ed.
    1988.   *The Origins of Modern Critical Thought: German Aesthetic Literary Criticism from Lessing to Hegel.* Cambridge: Cambridge University Press.

Slyomovics, Susan.
    1987.   *The Merchant of Art: An Egyptian Hilali Oral Epic Poet in Performance.* Berkeley: University of California Press.

Walcott, Derek.
    1990.   *Omeros.* New York: Farrar, Straus and Giroux.

. . .

On the Margins of the Scribal

From Oral Epic to Text

1

• • •

Epic as Genre

Gregory Nagy

One of very few scholars who can speak authoritatively of both oral and written epic traditions, Gregory Nagy confronts the supposed divide between these traditions in this brief and suggestive exploration into the origins of the epic genre. In the spirit of his earlier work, such as *The Best of the Achaeans,* which demonstrated the impact of religious and political rituals on the Homeric poems, Nagy demonstrates that *epos* was even for the Greeks an elusive form whose generic expectations and demands changed considerably from archaic to classical Greece. In this rigorous philological reading of the term *epos* and its relationship to other terms such as *muthos,* Nagy cautions us to be sensitive to the varying cultural conditions that produce heroic poetry, arguing against a fixed definition of epic as such in order to encourage more flexible and inclusive models of genre.

In order to speak of epic as genre, we need a set of working definitions for three not two concepts: besides genre and epic, we need to define the concept of Homer as a prototypical exponent of epic as genre. This essay develops such a set, arguing that our received idea about epic results primarily from a narrow understanding of Homer as the author of the *Iliad* and the *Odyssey,* to the exclusion of other ancient Greek traditions, such as the so-called Epic Cycle. As we will see, it is Aristotle's *Poetics* that ultimately made this idea prevail, just as it is Aristotle who has been most influential in shaping the concept of genre in general. In his essay "Epic and Novel," Mikhail Bakhtin goes so far as to say: "Aristotle's *Poetics,* although occasionally so deeply embedded as to be almost invisible, remains the stable foundation for the theory of genres."[1]

A problem more fundamental than the definitions of genre and epic is the definition of poetry itself in social contexts where the technology of writing is involved in neither the *composition* nor the *performance* of any given poem or song. My invocation of the two factors of composition and performance implies a derivation of ancient Greek poetry from oral poetry, as defined through the comparative fieldwork criteria developed by Milman Parry and Albert Lord.[2] From Lord's empirical study of living oral traditions, especially those of South Slavic heroic song, it becomes clear that composition and performance are aspects of the same process in oral poetry. In order to achieve a more accurate taxonomy of the earliest phases of the Greek song-making tradition culminating in "Homer" and, ultimately, in our received notions of epic as genre, the two factors of composition and performance must be kept in mind. Only then may we arrive at a basis for considering the utility of a concept such as genre—and of a related concept, occasion.

In addressing these two factors of composition and performance, I propose to bring into play a crucial work that has taken them both into account, Richard P. Martin's *The Language of Heroes* (1989). Martin has pioneered an explicit connection between Lord's empirical observations about performance in living oral traditions and J. L. Austin's theories about the performative uses of language, as articulated in his book *How to Do Things with Words* (1962).

As Martin demonstrates, Austin's formulation of the performative, where you *do* something when you *say* something, meshes with Lord's formulation of performance as the key to bringing the words of a song to life. To use Austin's wording, song is a speech act, as Martin shows in detail with reference to Homeric poetry. Ironically, Austin himself resisted the idea that poetry could count as a speech act, and we can see clearly the reason for his reluctance: for Austin, poetry is a matter of writing, not speaking. For Austin, the dimension of oral tradition is utterly removed from his own conceptualization of poetry.

Martin's book demonstrates not only the self-definition of Homeric song as a speech act. It shows also that this medium is capable of demonstrating the function of song as "quoted" within its overall frame of song. That is to say, Homeric song dramatizes, as it were, the performative aspects of songs that it quotes. Ironically, the performative aspects of Homeric song itself are shaded over while the performative aspects of the songs *contained* by it are highlighted, including pronouncements of praise or blame, laments, proverbs, and so on. To put it another way, Homeric song specifies the occasion of songs that it represents, or even presents, while it leaves vague any potential occasion for its own performance.

I have used the word *occasion* here in referring to the contexts of speech acts "quoted" by Homeric song. In fact, I am ready to define occasion as the context of a speech act.[3] Further, I define genre as a set of rules that produce a speech act. In offering this definition of genre, I follow Tzvetan Todorov in chapter 2 of his *Genres du discours;* for him, genres are "principles of dynamic production" of discourse in society.[4]

Here I propose to build on this most useful formulation in three ways.

First, I hope to tighten up the notion of speech act, correlating it with the specific interweavings of myth and ritual in traditional societies and dissociating it from purely philosophical considerations that center on individual judgments concerning when a speech act is a speech act. For purposes of this presentation, a speech act is a speech act *only when it fits the criteria of the community in which it is being used.* To determine the validity or invalidity of a speech act is to observe its dynamics within the community in question.

Second, I would observe that the genre, the set of rules that generate a given speech act, can equate itself with the occasion, the context of this speech act. To this extent, the occasion *is* the genre.[5] For example, a song of lament can equate itself with the process of grieving for the dead. A case in point is the Homeric use of the words *akhos* and *penthos*, both meaning "grief," as programmatic indicators of ritual songs of lament.[6]

Finally, I would note that if the occasion is destabilized or even lost, the genre can compensate for it, even recreate it.[7]

In view of these criteria for defining the concept of genre, are we ready to say that epic is a genre? Or that Homeric song is epic? I would suggest that the answer is "Not yet." Granted, we may say that Homeric song dramatizes genres such as pronouncements of praise or blame, laments, proverbs, and so on, but we can recognize those genres *only because their performative aspect is represented by Homeric song.* By contrast, Homeric song does not directly refer to its own current performative aspect, and so we cannot easily recognize it as a genre in and of itself. Further, we are as yet far from being able to identify Homeric song as epic.

For Albert Lord, in fact, the term "epic" is far too vague to be useful in his description of Homeric song-making—or of its counterparts in the South Slavic traditions:

> The word "epic," itself, indeed, has come in time to have many meanings. Epic sometimes is taken to mean simply a long poem in "high style." Yet a very great number of the poems which interest us in this book are comparatively short; length, in fact, is not a criterion of epic poetry. Other definitions of epic equate it with heroic poetry. Indeed the term "heroic poetry" is sometimes used (by Sir Cecil M. Bowra, for example) *to avoid the very ambiguity in the word "epic" which troubles us.* Yet purists might very well point out that many of the songs which we include in oral narrative poetry are romantic or historical and not heroic, no matter what definition of the hero one may choose. In oral narrative poetry, as a matter of fact, I wish to include all story poetry, the romantic or historical as well as the heroic; otherwise I would have to exclude a considerable body of medieval metrical narrative.[8]

Despite the imprecision of the term "epic," we may still say with confidence that there are many oral traditions strikingly comparable to what we find in the "epic" of Homer. There has been a wealth of comparative evidence about oral "epics" collected over recent years in Eastern Europe,[9] central Asia,[10] the Indian subcontinent,[11] Africa,[12] and so on.[13] In this context, I cannot stress enough the abiding importance of the comparative evidence provided by the South Slavic tradition of "epic": although it is different in many ways from what we see in the Homeric poems, this tradition, as Martin argues, "still has a claim to being one of the best comparanda."[14]

But the point is, what leads us to persist in referring to the South Slavic tradition as "epic" is the influence of received notions about Homeric poetry. My further point is that the classical Greek idea of epic, as presupposed by these received notions, needs to be situated in its own historical context. Once we see it in that light, this idea of epic may continue to serve as a useful point of comparison, but it cannot any longer be imposed as some kind of universal standard.

Applying comparatively the classical Greek idea of epic, one Africanist has developed a working definition, based on his experience with living oral traditions of Africa and elsewhere:

> An oral epic is fundamentally a tale about the fantastic deeds of a man or men endowed with something more than human might and operating in something larger than the normal human context and it is of significance in portraying some stage of the cultural or political development of a people. It is usually narrated or performed to the background of music by an unlettered singer *working alone or with some assistance from a group of accompanists.*[15]

Although there is no need to impose classicist models like the classical concept of epic on indigenous African oral poetic forms,[16] and although Lord himself, as we have seen, has explored the inherent difficulties of defining epic in terms of living oral traditions,[17] the fact remains that there are striking empirically observable analogies in a wide range of African oral poetic forms to what any classicist would indeed classify as epic.[18] As one Africanist puts it, "The burden of explanation therefore rests with those scholars who, for reasons best known to themselves, bandy about phrases like 'epic poetry in the normal sense of the word' and contend that on the whole the heroic narrative traditions in Africa yield little more than 'certain *elements* of epic.'"[19]

What is needed, then, is an understanding of epic that accommodates comparative perspectives:

> What is epic according to one definition may be excluded according to another. And, most important, a general definition of a genre will often violate the internal definition of genres inside a given society. Ideally, if oral epic were to be directly comparable from one society to another, it would not be enough that the epic genres themselves were similar; their place in the general spectr[um] of literary forms of the society in question ought to be similar too.[20]

Further, it is not enough to say that "epic" may or may not exist as a genre in the oral traditions of a given society. For epic to be a "genre," it has to have a functional relationship of interdependence or complementarity with another "genre" or other "genres." The principle of complementarity is key to Laura Slatkin's formulation of genre in oral traditions:

Genres can be viewed, like other cultural institutions, as existing in *a relationship of interdependence*, in which they have complementary functions in conveying different aspects of a coherent ideology or system of beliefs about the world. The crucial point about these distinctions or differentiations is their *complementarity*: they exist within, and serve to complete, a conception about the way the world is ordered.[21]

Thus genre is not an absolute.[22] We may apply the classical Greek model of epic for comparative purposes only after we succeed in defining epic as a genre in relation to other genres within the historical context of classical and pre-classical Greece.[23]

The earliest available evidence is the usage that we find in Homeric song, where the word *epos* is regularly used as a complement to *muthos*: as Martin has argued, *muthos* is a marked way to designate speech, whereas *epos* is the unmarked way—at least with reference to an opposition with *muthos*.[24] Martin defines the terms "marked" and "unmarked" as follows: "The 'marked' member of a pair carries greater semantic weight, but can be used across a narrower range of situations, whereas the unmarked member—the more colorless member of the opposition—can be used to denote a broader range, *even that range covered by the marked member:* it is the more general term."[25] The Homeric sense of *muthos*, in Martin's working definition, is "a speech-act indicating authority, performed at length, *usually in public*, with a focus on full attention to every detail."[26] This is the word used by Homeric song in referring to genres that are dramatized *within* Homeric song, such as pronouncements of praise or blame, laments, proverbs, and so on.[27] To this extent, *muthos* is not just any speech act reported by song: it is also the speech act that is the song itself, the "epic" of Homer.[28] The Homeric counterpart *epos*, on the other hand, is "an utterance, ideally short, accompanying a physical act, and focusing on message, as perceived by the addressee, rather than on performance as enacted by the speaker."[29]

As the unmarked member of the opposition, *epos* or its plural *epea* can occur even in contexts where *muthos* would be appropriate.[30] On the other hand, "one can never simply substitute the semantically restricted term *muthos*—meaning authoritative speech-act, or 'performance'—for the ordinary term *epos*."[31]

Whereas *epos* can be found in place of *muthos* in Homeric diction, the reverse does not happen: "In Homer, a speech explicitly said to be an *epos*, and not also represented as *epea* (the plural), is never called a *muthos*." Further, "*epea* can co-occur to refer to a *muthos*, but *muthoi* in the plural is never correlated with the singular form *epos*, to describe a speech."[32]

Even if *epos* designates "ordinary" speech when early Greek epic refers to speech, we must keep in mind that the unmarked category of "ordinary" speech is a "default" category: "'Ordinary' is a variable concept, depending on whatever is being perceived as 'special' in a given comparison or set of comparisons."[33] Further, "the perception of plain or everyday speech is a variable abstraction that depends on the concrete realization of whatever special speech . . . is set apart for a special context."[34] In the case at hand, if it were not for the opposition to unmarked *epos* by way of marked *muthos*, the word *epos* need not designate speech that is "ideally short," nor need it be perceived as merely "focusing on message."[35] Even an adjective added to the plural of unmarked *epos* can achieve a marked opposite of *epos* in Homeric diction: as Martin shows, *epea pteroenta*, "winged words" is a functional synonym of *muthos* in denoting certain kinds of marked speech.[36] If *muthos* can designate song as performed, then so too can *epos*, provided that *muthos* is not contrasted with it.

We may see in the Homeric term, *epea pteroenta*, "winged words," a poetic expression that recognizes the semantic potential of the word *epos* to designate, in its own right, song as *performed*. This potential gets activated as soon as *epos* gets detached from its complementarity with *muthos*. Such a detachment, I suggest, is made historically permanent by the eventual semantic destabilization of the word *muthos*. In post-Homeric contexts, as I have argued elsewhere, the words *alēthēs*, "true," and *alētheia*, "truth," evolve in explicit opposition to the word *muthos* in contexts where true speech is being contrasted with other forms of speech that are discredited, that cannot be trusted (e.g., Pindar *Olympian* 1.29–30).[37] As the word *alēthēs*, "true," or *alētheia*, "truth," becomes marked in opposition to *muthos*, which in turn becomes unmarked in the context of such opposition, the meaning of *muthos* becomes marginalized to mean something like "myth" in the popular sense of the word as it is used today in referring to the opposite of truth.[38]

The marginalization of *muthos*, resulting from its relatively later opposition to *alēthēs*, "true," or *alētheia*, "truth," may be pertinent to the earlier opposition of marked *muthos* and unmarked *epos*.[39] We may allow for the possibility that the unmarked member of this earlier opposition had once been the marked member in still earlier sets of opposition.[40] The semantic markedness of *epos* reemerges in post-Homeric contexts: as Martin points out, this word begins to appear in the specialized sense of "poetic utterance" and even "dactylic hexameter verse."[41] In other words, the semantic specialization of *epos* in post-Homeric contexts suggests that it had once been a marked word in opposition to some other unmarked word for "speech," and that "it had served as an unmarked word in Homeric diction only within the framework of an opposition with *muthos*."[42] In our own contemporary usage of the English words *epic* and *myth*, we see indirect reflexes of the later semantic specialization of *epos*, and of the later semantic specialization of *muthos*. As parallels to English *epic* and *myth*, we may look back and compare Aristotle's use of *epē* (the Attic form of *epea*) in the sense of epic and of *muthos* in the sense of myth as "plot."[43]

Mention of Aristotle brings us full-circle, finally, to his own concept of "epic," which he regularly designates as *epē*. Near the beginning of the *Poetics* (1447a14–15), he says: "The making of *epē* [*epopoiía*] and the making [*poiēsis*] of tragedy, also comedy, and the making [*-poiētikē*] of dithyrambs, and the [making] of reed songs and lyre songs—all these are in point of fact forms of *mimēsis*, by and large" <u>ἐποποιία δὴ καὶ ἡ τῆς τραγῳδίας ποίησις</u>, ἔτι δὲ κωμῳδία, καὶ ἡ διθυραμβοποιητική, καὶ τῆς αὐλητικῆς καὶ κιθαριστικῆς πᾶσαι τυγχάνουσιν οὖσαι μιμήσεις τὸ σύνολον. For Aristotle, as we can see from the underlined portions of the passage, there exists a basic complementarity between epic and tragedy, as also between tragedy and comedy. If we follow Slatkin's formulation of genre in oral traditions, it is the principle of complementarity here that defines epic as genre, in opposition to the genre of tragedy. Analogously, it is the principle of complementarity that defines tragedy as genre, in opposition to the genre of comedy, and so on.

In the historical context of classical Athenian traditions, it seems preferable to specify that these genres are a matter of *performance* traditions, not so much oral traditions in a looser sense of the term "oral." In Athens, during a period starting roughly from the middle of the sixth century and running through the fourth, tragedy and comedy can be viewed as two complementary genres evolving side by side and becoming mutually assimilated as *performance media* within the framework of a major Athenian state festival, the City Dionysia. In the same historical context, we can see taking shape an analogous complementarity between tragedy and epic, evolving side by side and becoming mutually assimilated as performance media within the two complementary frameworks of the City Dionysia and the Panathenaia respectively, subsumed under the larger framework of the overall cycle of Athenian state festivals.[44]

Applying Aristotle's point of view, we may justifiably describe the Homeric *Iliad* and *Odyssey* as the genre of epic—but only in the historical context of Athens during the period just noted, starting roughly from the middle of the sixth century and running through the fourth. In a separate work, I have argued extensively that this particular phase in the evolution of Homeric song making represents but one of at least five distinct periods, "Five Ages of Homer."[45] During this particular phase, the equivalent of "period 3" within an evolutionary scheme of five periods, the very idea of "Homer" as author became restricted to the *Iliad* and the *Odyssey*, to the exclusion of a vast reservoir of additional or alternative material known as the Epic Cycle.[46] For Aristotle, the "authors" of the Epic Cycle are clearly distinct from the Homer of the *Iliad* and the *Odyssey* (*Poetics* 1459b1–7). As we read the words of the fourth-century Athenian statesman Lycurgus (*Against Leocrates* 102) declaring that only the *epē*—which we may now confidently translate "epic"—of Homer could be performed at the Feast of the Panathenaia in Athens, we can be sure of what he means: for Lycurgus, only the *Iliad* and the *Odyssey* can be considered true epic.[47]

In sum, we may expect the criteria for determining the status of epic as genre to vary from culture to culture, even from period to period within a culture. When Bakhtin speaks of "epic" in his essay "Epic and Novel," he obviously has in mind the taxonomy of Aristotle. And yet, as valid as Aristotle's criteria may be from a classical and postclassical Greek point of view, they cannot be universalized or absolutized.

Even in the ancient Greek epics that we have, the *Iliad* and the *Odyssey*, we may detect patterns of complementarity that point to the need for genre distinctions that require subdivisions of Aristotle's notion of "epic." I would go so far as to say that Bakhtin's hermeneutic model of "epic," if we follow through on his criteria for distinguishing it from "novel," fit the *Iliad* only, to the exclusion of the *Odyssey*, which actually seems more appropriate to Bakhtin's hermeneutic model of "novel," not "epic."

If we take a broader view of ancient Greek civilization, there are still further possible criteria to consider. For example, in light of typological evidence for oral "epics" transmitted by women in various cultures,[48] we may see in song 44 of Sappho, "The Wedding of Hektor and Andromache," the traces of earlier Greek "epic" traditions that could cross back and forth between female and male performative conventions.[49]

In this connection, I invoke a distinction made by Joyce Flueckiger and Laurie Sears in their general formulation of epic: "Epic narratives exist both as oral and as performance traditions."[50] In terms of these shorthand designations "oral traditions" and "performance traditions," we may in effect distinguish between "a general knowledge of the 'whole story' (as summary) that many in the folklore community would be able to relate and the epic as it is performed in a marked, *artistic* enactment of that oral tradition."[51] That is to say, there is a gap between the notional totality of epic as oral tradition and the practical limitations of epic in actual performance:

> Thus, although scholars have spent considerable energy recording epic stories "from beginning to end," counting the number of hours and pages required to do so, this is not how the epic is received by indigenous audiences. Further, certain episodes of the epic are performed more frequently than others; and there may be episodes that exist only in the oral tradition and not in performance at all.[52]

This insight may prove to be a key to understanding the inclusiveness of "epic" as a form, or even as a genre: if indeed epic can be realized informally as well as formally, it becomes the ideal multiform, accommodating a variety of forms. I draw attention to the inclusiveness, the notional wholeness, of Homeric poetry. Here is a genre that becomes a container, as it were, of a vast variety of other genres, realized in varying forms of performance and in varying degrees of formality in performance. Here is a repertoire shared by men and women, replete with stories suitable for a broad spectrum of different performances, ranging from the songs of Sappho to the declamations of rhapsodes who claim, at the very start of their performances, to be Homer himself.[53] Here, finally, is a medium of discourse that sees itself as all-embracing of the society identified by it and identifying with it.

NOTES

1. Bakhtin 1981, 8.
2. See Parry 1971; Lord 1960, 1991, 1995.
3. Cf. Nagy 1990, 31.
4. Todorov 1990, 20.
5. See Nagy 1990, 362; Flueckiger 1996, 21.
6. Cf. Nagy 1979, 79–93.
7. See Nagy 1990, 9 and 362 n. 127.
8. Lord 1960, 6 (my emphasis).
9. Lord 1991.
10. Reichl 1992.
11. Blackburn et al. 1989.
12. Okpewho 1979.
13. See in general the valuable bibliography of Foley 1985.
14. Martin 1989, 150.
15. Okpewho 1979, 34 (my emphasis).
16. See Edwards and Sienkewicz 1990, 187–189, esp. p. 188: "The epic is considered so important and such a quintessential art form that, if epic performances did not evolve in a particular society, that society was considered to be somehow deficient."
17. Lord 1960, 6.
18. See Okpewho's summary (1979, 240–243).
19. Okpewho 1979, 241, with reference to Finnegan 1970, 109–110. In fairness to Finnegan, I should note that I consider her book, *Oral Literature in Africa* (1970), a veritable treasure-house of comparative evidence. Okpewho (p. 242) praises Finnegan's book for its reliance on "the relevance of African oral literature for comparative literature in the wide sense" (Finnegan, p. 518).
20. Jensen 1980, 18.
21. Slatkin 1987, 260 (my emphasis); cf. Smith 1974 and Ben-Amos 1976.
22. Absolutist notions of genre can be traced back to Plato: *eidos*, a word used by Plato in the sense of "genre" (Nagy 1990, 87, 109), is also used in the sense of "form" in his Theory of Forms.
23. Cf. Flueckiger 1996, 132.
24. Martin 1989, 10–26.
25. Ibid., 29 (my emphasis).
26. Martin 1989, 12 (my emphasis).
27. Ibid., 12–42.

28. Cf. Nagy 1996a, 132–133.
29. Martin 1989, 12.
30. Ibid., 26–30.
31. Ibid., 30.
32. Ibid., 30.
33. Nagy 1996a, 121.
34. Nagy 1990, 30.
35. Nagy 1996a, 121.
36. Martin 1989, 30–37.
37. Nagy 1996a, 122.
38. Ibid., 122–128.
39. Ibid., 127.
40. Cf. Nagy 1990, 68 n. 84.
41. Martin 1989, 13. For further details and bibliography, see Nagy 1996a, 128, esp. n. 68.
42. Nagy 1996a, 128.
43. Ibid., 128.
44. Nagy 1990, 388, 390–391; 1996b, 81–82.
45. Nagy 1996b, 110.
46. Nagy 1996a, 37–38.
47. Nagy 1996b, 71.
48. Flueckiger 1989, 40; see also Flueckiger 1996, 131–155, esp. p. 146.
49. Nagy 1996a, 56–57.
50. Flueckiger 1996, 133, summarizing Flueckiger and Sears 1991, 6.
51. Flueckiger 1996, 133, with reference to Bauman 1977, 3.
52. Flueckiger 1996, 133–134). For more on the notion of "episodes," see also Nagy 1996a, 77–82.
53. See Nagy 1997.

WORKS CITED

Austin, J. L.
1962.   *How to Do Things with Words.* New York: Oxford University Press.
Bakhtin, Mikhail M.
1981.   "Epic and Novel: Toward a Methodology for the Study of the Novel."
             In *The Dialogic Imagination: Four Essays by M. M. Bakhtin,* edited by M.
             Holquist and translated by C. Emerson and M. Holquist, 3–40. Austin:
             University of Texas Press.
Bauman, R.
1977.   *Verbal Art as Performance.* Rowley, Mass.: Newbury House Publishers.
Ben-Amos, D.
1976.   "Analytical Categories and Ethnic Genres." In *Folklore Genres,* edited
             by D. Ben-Amos, 215–242. Austin: University of Texas Press.
Blackburn, S. H., P. J. Claus, J. B. Flueckiger, and S. S. Wadley, eds.
1989.   *Oral Epics in India.* Berkeley and Los Angeles: University of Califor-
             nia Press.

Edwards, V., and T. J. Sienkewicz.
1990.   *Oral Cultures Past and Present: Rappin' and Homer.* Oxford and Cambridge, Mass.: B. Blackwell.
Finnegan, R.
1970.   *Oral Literature in Africa.* Oxford and London: Clarendon Press.
Flueckiger, J. B.
1996.   *Gender and Genre in the Folklore of Middle India.* Ithaca, N.Y.: Cornell University Press.
1989.   "Caste and Regional Variants in an Oral Epic Tradition." In *Oral Epics in India,* edited by S. H. Blackburn et al., 33–54. Berkeley and Los Angeles: University of California Press.
Flueckiger, J. B., and Sears, L. J., eds.
1991.   *Boundaries of the Text: Epic Performances in South and Southeast Asia.* Ann Arbor: University of Michigan Press.
Foley, J. M.
1985.   *Oral-Formulaic Theory and Research: An Introduction and Annotated Bibliography.* New York: Garland Publishing.
Hainsworth, J. B.
1991.   *The Idea of Epic.* Berkeley and Los Angeles: University of California Press.
Jensen, M. Skafte.
1980.   *The Homeric Question and the Oral-Formulaic Theory.* Opuscula Graeco-Latina, Supplementa Musei Tusculani 20. Copenhagen: Tusculanum Press.
Koller, H.
1972.   "Epos." *Glotta* 50: 16–24.
Lord, A. B.
1995.   *The Singer Resumes the Tale.* Edited by M. L. Lord. Ithaca, N.Y.: Cornell University Press.
1991.   *Epic Singers and Oral Tradition.* Ithaca, N.Y.: Cornell University Press.
1960.   *The Singer of Tales.* Cambridge, Mass.: Harvard University Press.
Martin, R. P.
1989.   *The Language of Heroes: Speech and Performance in the "Iliad."* Ithaca, N.Y.: Cornell University Press.
Nagy, G.
1997.   "An Inventory of Debatable Assumptions about a Homeric Question." *Bryn Mawr Classical Review* 97.4.18.
1996a.   *Homeric Questions.* Austin: University of Texas Press.
1996b.   *Poetry as Performance: Homer and Beyond.* New York: Cambridge University Press.
1990.   *Pindar's Homer: The Lyric Possession of an Epic Past.* Baltimore: Johns Hopkins University Press. Paperback, with corrections, 1994.
1979.   *The Best of the Achaeans: Concepts of the Hero in Archaic Greek Poetry.* Baltimore: Johns Hopkins University Press. 2nd ed., with new foreword, 1999.
Okpewho, I.
1979.   *The Epic in Africa: Toward a Poetics of the Oral Performance.* New York: Columbia University Press.

Parry, Milman.
  1971.   *The Making of Homeric Verse: The Collected Papers of Milman Parry.* Edited by Adam Parry. Oxford: Clarendon Press.
Reichl, K.
  1992.   *Turkic Oral Epic Poetry: Traditions, Forms, Poetic Structure.* New York: Garland Publishing.
Slatkin, L.
  1987.   "Genre and Generation in the *Odyssey.*" *MHTIC: Revue d'anthropologie du monde grec ancien* 2: 259–268.
Smith, P.
  1974.   "Des genres et des hommes." *Poétique* 19: 294–312.
Todorov, Tzvetan.
  1990.   *Genres in Discourse.* Translated by C. Porter. Cambridge and New York: Cambridge University Press. Originally published as *Les genres du discours* (Paris, 1978).

2

• • •

Performing Interpretation

Early Allegorical Exegesis of Homer

Andrew Ford

Ethnographic accounts of living epic traditions show that "context" is a very complex thing that can extend to providing a social frame for the reception and evaluation of poetry as well for its performance. Andrew Ford's essay explores how far we may discern such traditions of performing epic interpretation behind the texts of Homer. Ford's focus is epic's very ancient connection with allegory, and he shows that even such an apparently textual affair as allegoresis can be fully understood only in the light of social and political contexts of interpretation. Ford turns to pre-Socratic evidence to argue that allegoresis becomes a part of the Homerist's arsenal a full century before the early sophists and two centuries before Aristotle's *Poetics*. Especially in the context of the archaic Greek city, the use of allegorical commentary allowed performers to constitute a select, elite audience, giving those with pretension to cultural leadership in the city a claim to authority based on having access to an exclusive meaning intended for an exclusive audience.

The study of living epic traditions valuably reminds readers of Homer that an oral poem is never presented to an audience "in itself" but always in the context of performative conventions, which can powerfully determine its significance.[1] Because the Homeric poems have for so long exerted their influence on Western criticism and poetry in the form of canonized texts—scrupulously reconstructed in Hellenistic academies and minutely examined in Greek and Roman classrooms—it may be difficult fully to appreciate that in their case, too, performative context was not something "extra" added to the "pure" text but was inextricable from epic as a social and cultural object. Among the ways in which context may shape a poem on a given occasion is by providing a structured forum for the evaluation and interpretation of epic as well for its performance. Some measure of what a text of Homer cannot give to modern readers is suggested by Dwight Reynolds's recent ethnographic account of Arabic epic poets in the Nile Delta:

> In al-Bakātūsh one attends a performance of epic first of all to participate in
> and share a social experience and only secondarily to attend to the "text." In
> essence, the social action within the event is, in this indigenous "reading," the
> *text*. . . . The sarha [epic performance] is a stage for social interaction; though

epic singing may form the focus of an evening's activities, the accompanying discussions, evaluations, arguments, and storytelling constitute, in a very real sense, the heart of the event.[2]

Plato's *Ion* confirms the importance and antiquity of such commentary in Greek traditions of epic performance. Ion, a professional expert on Homer, has a double professional competence: not only can he give dramatic recitations from the poems, but he has also labored to acquire a stock of ennobling observations on their meanings or "thoughts" (*pollai kai kalai dianoiai, Ion* 530D). Indeed, he says, this has cost him more effort than mastering the poems themselves (530C). This aspect of Ion's practice is traditional and not decadent, for he claims to interpret Homer better than a host of contemporaries and "*anyone who ever lived.*" Yet the *Ion* also neatly shows that in the fourth century B.C.E. exegesis and commentary were regarded as detachable from a notional text-in-itself: with some comic irony, Socrates politely but repeatedly declines the rhapsode's offers to perform (530D, 536D). All the philosopher wants from the rhapsode is that he reproduce pieces of Homer's text for Socratic analysis, and the dialogue ends with Ion's show of "embellishing" (*kosmein*) or "praising" Homer (*Ion* 536D) indefinitely postponed.

The present study aims to recover more fully some of the interpretative practices and traditions that surrounded Homeric poetry when it was still circulating primarily in oral performances. Specifically, I will focus on a time when it appears that the exegesis of Homer underwent a radical change: histories of literature report that allegorical interpretation in the West can be traced back to Greek readings of Homer in the last quarter of the sixth century B.C.E.[3] A certain Theagenes from Rhegium in southern Italy is recorded as the first to have interpreted Homer in a way that, for example, would see beneath the battles between gods in the *Iliad* a coded description of the natural strife that prevails among the physical elements composing the world. In this he is supposed to have been defending the traditional gods against contemporary rationalizing critiques. I revisit this episode both because I believe that current accounts of this key moment in the construction of the Western epic tradition should be revised, and more generally to urge that purely rhetorical analyses of textual traditions remain inadequate to the extent that they do not consider criticism and interpretation as what Reynolds calls a "social act."

I shall first review the evidence for Theagenes, considering contemporary influences and possible precursors for his allegoresis (by which I mean allegory as an interpretative mode). In order to understand the scope and purport of his project, I shall reconsider the history of terms for allegory, focusing on a stunning example of allegorical exegesis from the fourth century B.C.E. This text will suggest that in its earliest phase epic allegory was understood on the model of a widespread and significant mode of speech in archaic Greece, the riddling *ainos*. Clarifying the relationship between epic and *ainos* at this time will allow me to redescribe the aims of early epic allegoresis by considering it not abstractly as a problem of theology or signification, but functionally as a way of expanding the uses of epic and of discourses about epic in particular social contexts.

THEAGENES AND HIS TIMES: SOURCES OF ALLEGORESIS

Although the "extra-textual" discourses that situated Greek epic for its earliest audiences were not preserved when oral performance was converted into text, some of what rhapsodes, littérateurs, and schoolmasters said in explaining Homer made its way into early written treatises on Homer's life and poetry and eventually into ancient commentaries. These commentaries, being kept physically apart from the poems, were themselves lost, but a number of specific interpretative observations survived and fought their way back into the texts of the poems in the form of marginal comments and interlinear glosses preserved in medieval manuscripts. Hence it is that the late note of a scholiast is often our only link to ancient traditions of "embellishing" the Homeric poems with commentary.

The prime piece of evidence for Theagenes comes from one such scholiast on the *Iliad*. The passage to be commented upon is *Iliad* 20.67ff., in which the Olympians are set free by Zeus to descend to the Trojan Plain and fight each other for the fate of the city. When the poet begins to catalogue how Poseidon lined up against Apollo, the War God against Aphrodite, Hera against Athena, and so on—the scholiast remarks:

> In general, [Homer's] account of the gods tends to be worthless and unsuitable, for the myths he tells about the gods are inappropriate. To such charges as this, some reply on the basis of Homer's way of speaking [*lexis*], holding that everything is said by way of allegory [*allēgoria*] and refers to the nature of the elements, as in the passage where the gods square off against one another. For they say that the dry battles with the wet, the hot with the cold, and the light with the heavy. Moreover, water extinguishes fire while fire evaporates water, so that there is an opposition between all the elements composing the universe, which may suffer destruction in part but remains eternal as a whole. In setting out these battles Homer gives fire the name Apollo, Helius, or Hephaestus, he calls water Poseidon or Scamander, the moon Artemis, the air Hera, and so on. In a similar way he sometimes gives names of the gods to human faculties: intelligence is Athena, folly is Ares, desire Aphrodite, speech Hermes, according to what is characteristic of each. Now this kind of defense is very old and goes back to Theagenes of Rhegium, who first wrote about Homer.[4]

A good deal of caution is required in evaluating such information. This note has been traced to Porphyry, the Neoplatonist philosopher and commentator on Homer of the third century C.E. His account is thus some eight centuries after the time of Theagenes, who is placed by another source in the last quarter of the sixth century B.C.E.[5] Porphyry depends on intermediary sources now unknown,[6] and it is these sources who may be responsible for the specific allegorical equivalencies listed; to Theagenes, Porphyry only ascribes the method of apologetic allegoresis of Homer as a whole. In addition, there are prima facie problems with this piece of history. Greek scholars had a penchant for "discovering" founding figures for any significant cultural practice, and one may doubt on its face any claim that allegoresis had a single founder or a definite starting point. After all, Homer and Hesiod offer allegories in their poems,[7] and Homer's characters even exhibit an aptitude for the allegoresis of divine and heroic names.[8]

If it is scarcely credible that Theagenes could have invented epic allegoresis single-handedly, it becomes difficult to specify what he did that was remarkable, especially if, as Denis Feeney suggests, he did nothing more than etymologize a few names of Homeric gods along the lines of equating "Hera" with "Air."[9] His fame may be due simply to the fact that he managed to leave an example of his interpretative practice in a written text, the one remembered as the first treatise on Homer.[10] Still, the text Theagenes expounded and wrote on was Homer's, and no one else was remembered to have done so earlier. Our sources then may be taken as indicating that in the later sixth century the traditions in which Greek epic were handed down and commented upon changed in the sense that at that time allegorical exegesis became prominent and was incorporated into the repertoires of recognized authorities on epic. The question is, Why?

Histories of criticism have understood Theagenes' allegoresis as a response to late sixth-century rationalist attacks on epic myth by the likes of the philosophers Xenophanes, Heraclitus, and perhaps Pythagoras.[11] Xenophanes in particular provides a suggestive context; this poet, performer, and savant spent a good part of his life in cities very near Theagenes' Rhegium and has left us remarkable poems that propound a new vision of divinity while criticizing the traditional representations of gods to be found in Homer and Hesiod. Declaring that "there is one god greatest among gods and men, / resembling mortals neither in bodily form nor in thought" (B23 DK), he issued biting critiques of Greek anthropomorphism, saying that if animals could paint and sculpt, then horses would fashion gods that looked like horses and cows like cows (B15 DK). Devotees of Homer could hardly have enjoyed all this, and they may have felt rebuked when Xenophanes condemned those who sing about the battles of Titans, Centaurs, and Giants, the "fabrications of men of old in which there is nothing of value" (B1.21–23 DK).

Juxtaposed with the activities of this nearby contemporary, Theagenes' practice becomes comprehensible if we view him as a rhapsode or at least an expert on Homer. Evidence for Theagenes as a "Homerist" may be found in one other scholium that attributes to an unspecified "Theagenes" a variant form of an Iliadic half-line.[12] If this is Theagenes of Rhegium, he seems to have been capable of performing or reproducing epic lines himself, and so we may think of him as something of a rhapsode-cum-explicator who, like Plato's Ion, both performed epic texts or parts of them and offered observations on the poet's "fine thoughts." As such, he would have been strongly moved to reaffirm the poet's authority. On this view, allegory in its earliest phases would have functioned as it often has later, as a defensive measure for sustaining the authority of aging narrative traditions whose literal interpretation is becoming inadequate to new ways of thinking. By the end of the sixth century some recognizably stable form of the *Iliad* would have been getting on to 200 years old.

Xenophanes and Theagenes seem to make a neat historical fit as prosecution and defense, yet viewing the rise of Homeric allegoresis so abstractly no doubt oversimplifies the situation, for to explain the rise of epic allegoresis as a response to philosophical critiques of the poems says nothing about the basic and most intriguing questions of why allegoresis should have been hit upon as the way to meet criticism of Homer, and why such an outlandish method should have been deemed credible. Even if we can assume that Theagenes' motives were defensive, allegoresis does so by what is surely a very bold hypothesis that the poems are about something quite other than what they declare themselves to be on their face. One can hardly suppose that allegoresis was the only or inevitable option available to the challenged Homerist; the ancients developed, after all, many other, less radical ways of defending Homer against critical attacks, as can be seen from the résumé of such defenses in chapter 25 of Aristotle's *Poetics*.[13]

Moreover, our scanty evidence can as well be taken as indicating that allegoresis was originally a *positive* strategy, exegetical rather than defensive, and that it had already been developed among the early Greek philosophers, who "appropriated for their own use some at least of the mythical traditions which they could not help venerating."[14] A precursor for Theagenes has been claimed in Pherecydes around the middle of the sixth century: he is reported to have read Homer allegorically, and his own prose cosmogony includes a few passages that may readily be read as allegorical.[15] Others have pointed to the Pythagoreans flourishing in southern Italy at the time: at least at a later period, Pythagoreans certainly practiced allegorical exegesis of Homer, and with a moralizing slant very similar to the one in Porphyry's note.[16] There is in addition a strong resemblance between some allegorical equivalencies and the use of folk etymology among early Pythagoreans to derive cosmic truths from the sounds of certain words: the Pythagorean belief that the truth of incarnation can be glimpsed in the closeness between the words for "body" (*sōma*) and "tomb" (*sēma*)[17] seems not far from the notion in Porphyry that "Hera" (*Hēran*) in the Iliadic theomachy conceals the element "Air" (*aera*).[18] But magical etymology was by no means confined to Pythagoreans in archaic

Greece, and on such grounds it has been claimed that Theagenes also had precursors in early Orphic circles.[19] Indeed, as noted above, one can go yet further and find the sources of Theagenes' practice in the epic poets themselves, since Homer often plays upon the names of gods and heroes such as Zeus or Odysseus and, unwittingly or not, provides a paradigm for the popular Hera etiology as Air in a suggestively phrased line from his theomachy: "A deep mist of *air Hera* / spread before [the Trojans] to check their flight."[20]

In view of the above, it seems prudent to put aside the quest for a single source of allegoresis and to stipulate that Theagenes' approach must have had wider roots and ramifications, not all of which can we hope to trace in full. The significance of the tradition about Theagenes is that it points to a time in which heroic narratives (we should probably not yet speak of "literary" texts) were subjected to a new kind of exegesis not traditional in that form, though one that was perhaps already developed in certain philosophical or religious circles. We can posit that there was in the later sixth century, particularly in southern Italy, an environment in which mystical texts and language itself were being plumbed for hidden depths of meaning; it was here that the Homeric poems, now being regarded from a number of new angles, were first subjected to a kind of exegesis that had thitherto been used with esoteric poetry. Before we can understand the motives that led epic expounders to adopt or adapt such a method, we must clarify what it was exactly that they claimed to be doing. We can do so by turning to consider the vocabulary in which early allegoresis was conducted.

LEXICAL EVIDENCE: "ALLEGORY" AND *AINOS*

Writing around 100 C.E., Plutarch says that the term *allēgoria* is not very old and that what is called *allēgoria* in his day had formerly been called *huponoia*.[21] Plutarch is borne out by our evidence. We do not find the noun *allēgoria* securely attested until the first century B.C.E., though it is possible that it and related words go back to the Hellenistic period.[22] As for *huponoia*, "a thought or intention that lies below the surface," it is attested in a special sense of "under-meaning" in two significant texts of the fourth century B.C.E. describing exegetical practices of the fifth. In the first, Plato uses it to refer to allegoresis of the type attributed to Theagenes: Socrates rejects from his city stories about "the binding of Hera by her son, the casting out of Hephaestus from Olympus when he went to defend his mother from his father [cf. *Iliad* 1.591–3, 15.23–24], and all the battles among gods Homer has composed [e.g., *Iliad* 20.67ff.], regardless of whether they are composed with or without allegorical meanings [*en huponoiais, aneu hupnoiōn*]" because the young can't tell the difference (*Republic* 378D). The term is also significantly used in Xenophon's *Symposium* when Socrates and some sophisticates are discussing the value of Homeric poetry in education. The well-bred Niceratus has been compelled by his father to learn the *Iliad* and the *Odyssey* by heart so as to become a gentleman (3.5). But the company agree that being able to recite Homer by heart is no worthy accomplishment in itself; rhapsodes, after all, can do as much, and this company is unanimous in viewing them as the most stupid of men because they "do not know the *huponoiai*." Niceratus therefore is to be congratulated because he has "paid a good deal of money to Stesimbrotus and Anaximander and many others so as to miss out on nothing of their valuable learning" (3.6).[23]

These texts establish that in the fifth century *huponoia* was in use in intellectual circles for the distinctive and subtle interpretations of poetry offered by certain Homerists and sophists, though not by rhapsodes. If a rhapsode expounded on the "fine thoughts" of Homer (*kalai dianoiai*), an education in poetry could still be called incomplete without an acquaintance with the "under-meanings" (*huponoiai*) available from a different class of experts. The etymology of *huponoia* suggests a rather intellectualist and even text-based conception of poetic meaning: *hupo-* puts the meaning in a depth and thus implies a surface, and the root *-noia* is the most important fifth-century word for "thought" as intellection and calculation rather than mere perception or recognition.[24] *Huponoia* is thus a good name for implicit philosophical or ethical theses that may be derived from a poem in the course of a sophistic discussion. Allegories belong to the class of *huponoiai* because *huponoiai* were by definition subtle and unapparent meanings. The term demarcated economic and social distinctions more precisely than rhetorical ones: in pointing out the noble thoughts the poet intended (*dianoiai*), rhapsodes could win crowns and prizes from poetic guilds or state festivals; sophists, on the other hand, could sell to select students at considerable prices the unexpected *huponoiai* known only to a few.

In the fifth century, then, allegorical readings of epic could be offered as an intellectual commodity under the term *huponoia*. But we can reconstruct a yet earlier phase of this history by considering a piece of evidence that has not so far been adduced in this connection. This is our earliest preserved specimen of extended allegorical interpretation, the Derveni papyrus, discovered in 1962 and still not yet fully published.[25] This papyrus itself is dated archaeologically to the fourth century B.C.E., but its text may be earlier by as much as a century and in any case clearly derives from the ambit of pre-Socratic thought. The text is a commentary on an Orphic cosmogonic poem, a half-rationalizing, half-mystical exegesis that repeatedly resorts to allegoresis. Although many of these passages are only partially preserved, it is nevertheless clear that the proper term for allegorical writing in this author is *ainittesthai*, "to speak in hints" or "to speak enigmatically," and his word for "allegorically" is *ainigmatōdēs*, "in the mode of an *ainos* or *ainigma*."[26]

In the clearest passage—a textbook example of defensive allegoresis—our commentator puzzles over an Orphic phrase he misconstrues to mean

"Zeus ate the god's genitals."[27] He is quick to say that "since through the whole poem [Orpheus] is speaking allegorically [*ainizetai*] about things in the world, it is necessary to consider each word [or verse] individually."[28] This assumption allows him to allegorize "genitals" as the sun, since the sun is the source of generation; Zeus's alleged meal turns out to mean that the governing power of the universe also controls generation. This interpretation uses as its operative verb for "allegorize" *ainittesthai*, a word that occurs twice more in the same sense. In a more scrappy fragment the target phrase from Orpheus is the anthropomorphic expression "he [i.e., Zeus] took in his hands," and our commentator says the poet "uttered this as an allegory [*ēnizeto*]."[29] Precisely what these hands signified must now be a matter of conjecture,[30] but the author is clearly proposing a hidden, nonliteral meaning, one to be distinguished from the construction put on that phrase by "those who do not understand" mentioned a few lines before.[31] Finally, he uses an adverbial form, *ainigmatōdōs*, perhaps to say that certain goddesses are described "allegorically"[32] and, in a very broken piece from the early and possibly introductory portion of the work, speaks of "allegorical" (*ainigmatōdēs*) poetry.[33] Neither *huponoia* nor any of its cognates is used in the twenty-four columns so far available.

The Derveni papyrus thus shows that, outside the philosophical-rhetorical tradition of the later fifth century, which sought the *huponoia* of poets, *ainittesthai* and its cognates supplied the standard set of terms in which to discuss what was eventually called *allēgoria*. Since this is our only direct pre-Socratic evidence for the early practice of allegoresis, we must hold that the operant term for expressing oneself allegorically was *ainittesthai* before it became *huponoiein* and then *allegorein*.[34] A passage from the late archaic poet Theognis places this vocabulary back in the time of Theagenes: Theognis concludes a fairly extensive allegory of the "ship of state" by saying: "Let these things be riddling utterances [*ēinikhthō*] hidden by me for the noble. / One can be aware even of future misfortune if one is skilled."[35]

The fact that the technical term for allegory changes is of more than philological interest. Recovering the language in which allegories were discussed before they were called *huponoiai* or *allēgoriai* allows us to locate early allegoresis in relation to other contemporary forms of interpretative and expressive activity. The root of both *ainittesthai* and *ainigmatōdēs* can be traced to the word *ainos*, which named an important mode of riddling discourse in the archaic and early classical period. The *ainos* was a polymorphous but quite distinctive and important mode of speech, and one that interacted in significant ways with nearly all the major forms of Greek literature. It is my contention that the use of *ainittesthai* in the Derveni author, and presumably in his predecessors going back to the time of Theagenes and Theognis, indicates that early allegoresis involved a shifting of generic boundaries so that epic could be viewed as a specimen of the *ainos*. Thus, whatever the debts of early epic allegorists to mystical traditions or to the epics themselves, their procedure announced itself as assimilating epic to this familiar form of ambiguous speech. We are thus obliged to look more closely at the archaic *ainos.*

Although the *ainos* assumed too many forms to be thought of as a genre, it is often used of animal fables such as we find in Archilochus[36] or Aesop. The prototypic example may be Hesiod's tale (called "an *ainos* kings will understand" at *Works and Days* 202) of a hawk that holds a nightingale (*aēdōn*) in its clutches; this seems to refer in some way to the power the king has over the singer (*aoidos*). Other early examples of *ainoi* refer more generally to any "fable or other story with an implied message in it for the hearer,"[37] such as the story Odysseus tells Eumaeus in the *Odyssey:* in need of covering for the night, the beggar-Odysseus tells the swineherd a story about a ruse the "real" Odysseus had once used to secure a cloak on a cold night watch. Eumaeus is quick to perceive the point of the story and, commending the *ainos,* offers his guest a cloak.[38] Whether it takes the form of an animal fable or a pointed story, the *ainos* should be regarded as a mode of speaking rather than identified with any particular kind or form of narrative.[39] Gregory Nagy defines *ainos* as an "authoritative speech: an affirmation, a marked speech act made by and for a marked social group,"[40] highlighting the fact that the selective audience may serve to rein in the polysemy of *ainos:* an *ainos* is decoded by those the speaker considers "wise" or "good," and so "akin" to himself (the *sophoi* or *philoi* commonly addressed in ainetic poetry). This select audience is thought to be capable of this decoding not through linguistic expertise but through an innate gift presumed to mark the truly noble, the *agathoi.* Thus, though an *ainos* may be analyzed thematically as an allusive tale or structurally as a coded message, in its Greek context it was defined as a message that had a special meaning for a special audience; it was a socially rather than rhetorically constructed riddle.

Another dimension of the *ainos* is brought out in Thomas Cole's fascinating *Origins of Rhetoric,* which suggests that the hinting *ainos* was an especially appropriate use of language in a context of social inequality. Cole notes that tradition recorded the slave Aesop as the inventor of the *ainos,* and points to a passage in Aristotle's *Rhetoric* in which *ainos* is associated with what Aristotle calls the "slavish" habit of talking around a point when addressing a superior.[41] On this view what is essentially ainetic about the fable of the hawk and the nightingale in Hesiod is that the subordinate singer tells an *ainos* "the *kings* will understand"; so too the cloak story of Odysseus qualifies as an *ainos* because a suppliant castaway must be circumspect in making demands on his host. The marked, oblique speech act known as *ainos,* then, may take the form of allegory when the situation calls for the most discreet self-presentation on the part of the speaker. Such occasions are reflected in the verse *ainoi* that were commonly sung within aristocratic coteries such as those addressed by Archilochus, Alcaeus, or Theognis. In such *ainoi* the encoding allowed discretion in times of political uncertainty all the while reinforcing the solidarity of close-knit aristocratic groups.[42] But *ainoi* of course would also have been useful in wider contexts too, as in stories of Stesichorus's using animal fables to dissuade his fellow citizens from giving the strongman Phalaris a bodyguard: in predicting a tyranny one doesn't dare be too offensive to a powerful man.[43]

The significance of all this for epic allegorists depends on an important point, stressed by Nagy, that Greek epic is *not ainos:* though epic may incorporate *ainoi,* such as Odysseus's tale of the cloak, and though it may give us a portrait of a master of *ainoi* in "Odysseus *poluainos,*" it does not refer to itself as *ainos,* nor does it ever declare it has a hidden meaning for the cognoscenti. Pindar will often characterize his odes to Olympic victors as *ainoi,* but not Homer.[44] In this case, it seems that for an allegorizing critic to say that the epic poet *ainittetai* this or that was to assimilate narrative epic to another form of discourse with its own special rules and ethos. In view of our lexical evidence, then, the rise of epic allegoresis may be reinterpreted as the assimilation of the Homeric poems to the *ainos.* It was not so much that the sixth-century allegorists concocted a bizarre new method of reading epic as that they transferred epic to a special and well-established form of speech act, one in which discreet self-expression requiring expert decoding was the norm. With this closer view of what allegoresis amounted to in the archaic period, we can turn to suggesting why the *ainos* might have appealed to Homerists as a model for their favored poetry.

THE USES OF HIDDEN MEANINGS

In assimilating epic to *ainos* allegorists would have done more than appeal to a readily intelligible model of encoded speech or verse. The *ainos* defined not simply a special kind of message but also a special relation of speaker to audience and so brought in its a train a series of social implications that made possible a new use for epic poetry in the city. For a professional Homerist like Theagenes, the most important function of *ainoi* may have been that it was the customary way for poets, councilors, and wise men generally to address their most powerful and lavish patrons in the West. The tyrants and dynasts of Sicily whom Pindar served a generation later are repeatedly praised as "wise," "skilled" (*sophos*), or "discerning" (*sunetos*), and part of this ideal image of the tyrant involves being skilled in interpreting *ainoi.*[45] In this respect the situation at the Sicilian courts where Xenophanes performed in the late sixth century or where Pindar sent songs in the fifth had changed very little by the time Plato was trying to advise the unpredictable tyrant Dionysius. Plato's Seventh Letter says that he and his friends thought it best to communicate their doctrines about ruling justly "not by expressing them straight out—which was not safe—but through riddles [*ainittomenoi*]" (332D).

Like the poet before the king in Hesiod, or the beggar before his host in the *Odyssey,* the Homerist addresses the sixth-century tyrant or aristocratic coterie as a master of oblique discourse. To adopt this mode of address was thus both to respect one's proper station and also to adopt the ideology of the great ruler that depicted him as at once powerful and perceptive (*sunetos*). To sustain a position of authority in this politically tumultuous period required not only force of arms but the ability to read signs aright so that one could, in the classic allegory of the time, steer the "ship of state" through the tempestuous waters of politics.[46] That the discernment needed to rule extended to the decipherment of obscure symbols may be illustrated in Herodotus (4.131–2). He tells us that when the Scythians were being attacked by Darius, they sent him messengers bearing a bird, a mouse, a frog, and five arrows. The messengers challenge the Persians—"if they are wise [*sophos*]"—to "recognize" what the gifts mean. Darius optimistically interprets the objects as symbolizing complete submission, "likening" (*eikazōn*)[47] the mouse and frog to earth and water—traditional tokens of fealty—and the birds and arrows to the Scythian cavalry and arms, all of which he thinks are being handed over to him. But one of his advisers proposes a different reading: unless the Persians can fly like a bird, burrow like a mouse, or dive like a frog, they will not escape Scythian archers. The upshot, designed to warm the heart of any professional wise man, is of course that Darius read this allegory wrong, and he is soon planning a hasty retreat. The distance between Darius faced with such symbols and a Greek potentate who may hear about the air, water, and fire underlying the text of Homer may be not so great as appears at first glance. The Greek king or prince striving to catch the political import of every shifting wind is well advised to cultivate courtiers—his *xenoi* or *philoi* as everyone would politely put it—of equal discernment.

The first epic allegorists of the West, then, found their place in this culture of competitive interpretative expertise. A model for their role was afforded by the tyrant's circle of advisers-companions or, more distantly, by the Eastern king's viziers. Yet the allegorists seem not to have interpreted epic in terms of current events. Different book-bearing *sophoi* exploited these veins, such as the oracle-monger Onomacritus, whose readings of ancient prophetic texts he edited (and interpolated) led him in and out and back in favor with the ruling Peisistratids at Athens (cf. Herodotus 7.6). If we can judge from the kinds of allegory Plato rejects, with Theagenes or soon after, allegorists rather focused on epic scenes of theomachy and struggle between gods (as they long continued to).[48]

That allegorists should have been drawn to passages such as theomachies may be explained along standard lines as stemming from a desire to assuage outraged piety; but it is also worth noting that theomachy could serve as a mythic paradigm for destructive infighting among the nobility, as in Xenophanes, who rejects not only mythic accounts of fighting Titans, Centaurs, and Giants but also songs of civil strife, *stasis* (B1.23 DK).[49] Hence to discourse about theomachy may be to speak about the management of strife, the cosmic principle and social force that Hesiod's *Works and Days* had taught could be both beneficial and harmful. Allegorized along these lines, Homer presents a world in which both hierarchy (Zeus commanding the Olympians, the Olympians far greater than mortals) and conflict are naturalized. The tyrant who reads Homer this way may find an image of his own power, identifying himself with Zeus who sits atop a pyramid of battling that ranges from his own divine lords down to pathetic mortals. Hence if allegorists preferred timeless verities of cosmology and general ethics, their readings in context were yet themselves *ainoi* pointing to, without naming, the pervasiveness of social tension and the need for a stable hierarchy among aristocrats.

Allegoresis had another function apart from the particular coded message conveyed. In making Homer ainetic allegorizing critics gave a new and special use to the poetry. The very strategy of repositioning these stories as coded messages allowed allegorists to constitute a select audience who could distinguish themselves by their subtle understanding. This was all the more valuable in the sixth century, when rhapsodes were crossing the entire length of the Aegean giving public performances of Homeric epic, and some states were incorporating such performances into their city festivals, such as the Panathenaia at Athens. References to Homer, which begin to crop up at this time, take special note of the breadth of his appeal:[50] when Simonides says that "Homer and Stesichorus sang to the people," he implies a wide and perhaps undiscriminating diffusion of the poetry by using for "people" an epic term (*laos*) for the army or citizen body as a whole as distinct from its generals.[51] Homer's critics concede something to the widespread respect in which he is held, as when Xenophanes says that "all men have learned from Homer" (B10 DK) or when Heraclitus calls Homer "wiser than all other Greeks" before going on to deflate that reputation (B56 DK). Heraclitus's rejection of the poets' doctrines is mingled with contempt for the witless *dēmos* who use them as teachers (B104 DK), and he would ban poets from public contests (B42 DK).[52]

In the context of many archaic cities, then, allegorical readings of epic enabled certain experts to proffer and certain audiences to obtain an elite purchase on a kind of poetry that was increasingly becoming the possession of all Greece. Allegoresis of epic did for audiences with pretensions to cultural leadership in the city what the recherché interpretations of Orphic poetry or Pythagorean sayings did for those desiring to form exclusive communities at the city's margins: these groups too cherished and collected "texts" in which they found subtle meanings intended for the elect. Such were Pythagorean watchwords or *symbola* and the Orphic poems, one of which begins: "I will sing for the discerning."[53] Whether at court or in a conventicle, allegoresis confers a nimbus on a body of poetry that is to be penetrated only by the wise or initiated. Applied to Homer, it forms inside the larger community within hail of a passing rhapsode's voice a smaller group of those who rightly understand.[54]

This use of allegoresis to create distinctive audiences became more extensive in the fifth century, when, as is indicated in the passage from Xenophon, some Homerists professed to offer invaluable *huponoiai* that were not available from the scorned rhapsodes. Then, as in the sixth century, traveling experts in traditional song could well have an interest in presenting themselves as possessing a hidden knowledge of poetry, one that was not so public as the declamation of a rhapsode, that was not controlled by guilds on Chios or Samos or broadcast by the Athenian state. In this vein we may understand the sophists' portraying Homer as one who "covered up" and "veiled" his wisdom so that only they are able to disclose it, even if they did not allegorize the texts at great length.[55] Suspicions about the method are voiced by Plato, as we saw, who found allegories dangerously ambiguous and regarded as trivial the games played by "those who are so clever about Homer" (*Cratylus* 407C). After him the way was clear for Aristotle to treat poetry as a problem of form and structure rather than one of theology or hermeneutics, and the tradition of formalist and rhetorical analysis of literature flourished at Alexandria, where "interpreting Homer from Homer" meant reading him in his own terms and not those of another system. Of course there were always competing views and backsliding, as in the allegoresis favored by Crates of Mallos and to some extent among the Stoics.[56] Epic's affinity with allegory both as an expressive and as an interpretative mode endured through the eighteenth century and formed a basic frame for conceiving the genre for such poets as Vergil, Spenser, Tasso, and Milton.[57] Since then, allegory has gone in and out of favor but has never been absent from the range of techniques deployed in Western literary, and especially epic, interpretation.

If we consider Theagenes' practice in the history of epic performance in its full sense, including the performance of commentary, he appears to stand not for the origin of allegoresis but for a change in the traditions of epic interpretation: however old allegoresis may be as an interpretative strategy, it came to cultural prominence only when it intersected with the wider Greek history of epic reception. Though epic had long called for and been accompanied by many kinds of exegesis, when allegoresis became available to the Homerist's arsenal—a full generation before the early sophists and nearly two centuries before Aristotle's *Poetics*—expertise in poetry could not only boast a command of the texts and of a tradition of lore about them and their author but also distinguish itself by offering wholly unexpected accounts of what these old and familiar poems really said. It seems that it was in only in the later sixth century that certain Greek readers and their audiences found that epic could begin to say something of value only when it began to say something other.

Throughout this long history, that protean thing called allegory always has involved social practices and institutions that define literature and criticism as well. I reaffirm this point in concluding, since to discuss allegory historically is problematic from certain points of view today, especially theories that would identify allegory with the workings of language itself. If one defines *allēgoria* etymologically as "saying one thing and meaning something other,"[58] allegory may appear not simply as one mode of speech among others but as the figure of speech that most directly exemplifies the fundamental arbitrariness of language, its lack of any firm bond between signifier and signified. Allegory may then be said to attend any and every type of speech: all texts may be called allegorical,[59] and all interpretations insofar as they state the meaning of a text in other terms than those of the text.[60] These lines of analysis suggest that to give an account of allegory in historical and social terms is only to offer yet another allegory of allegory while evading its ubiquitous and uncontrollable character. After all, a recovery of true but concealed early meanings has been one of the favorite promises of allegoresis.

One might argue in turn that conceiving allegory solely as a trope rather than as the act of an interpreter is itself an interpretative strategy, which can be situated historically within the late and postromantic revival of allegory as a symbolic mode.[61] But the issue is whether it is adequate to define allegory solely as an affair of diction or reference. In my view, reducing allegory to operations on a linguistic plane cannot account for the extremely varied uses allegoresis has had, uses ranging from defensive recuperation of threatened traditions to their radical reevaluation. To attempt to historicize allegory need not be to quest after its chimerical origins but may allow us to see it as a practice whose semantic dislocations always take place within a culturally and historically specific context. I side then with ethnographers like Reynolds:

> In seeking reactions to and interpretations of the epic, I found again and again that I was listening to evaluations not of an individual performance or event, but of larger social patterns and of the epic as a symbolic catalyst. To a great extent, evaluations of the epic were only extensions of the speaker's position vis-à-vis the social forces he or she saw the epic as representing.[62]

Viewed in this way, the ancient allegorist Theagenes suggests that we may understand epic allegoresis not only as a philosophical, theological, or hermeneutic position, but as a social performance within the cultural construction of "literature" in its time.

NOTES

1. On the ethnography of commentary and its inseparability from text in performance, see Tedlock 1983; for a tradition of exegesis in Indian epic, see Lutgendorf 1989.

2. Reynolds 1995, 210–211. See also Slyomovics 1987 for an analysis of a single poet's improvisatory adaptations of his text in a constant negotiation over social status.

3. For a concise overview with bibliography, see Whitman 1994. The ancient material is excellently surveyed in the first chapter of Feeney 1991.

4. Porphyry apud schol. B ad *Iliad* 20.67. My translation is based on the text of Schraeder (1880, 240.14–241.12, reprinted in chap. 8.2 of Diels and Kranz 1952 [hereafter DK]).

5. Tatian *In Graecos* 31 (= 8.1a DK): "Those responsible for the most ancient researches into Homer's poetry, birth, and time are Theagenes of Rhegium, at the time of Cambysses [529–522 B.C.E.], Stesimbrotus the Thasian, Antimachus the Colophonian, Herodotus of Halicarnassus. . . . "

6. Certainly Stoic, but perhaps Neopythagorean too: see Wehrli 1928, 89–91, and Cantarella 1967.

7. Cf. Pfeiffer 1968, 4–5.

8. Most (1994) persuasively argues that when Patroclus upbraids Achilles for his heartlessness by saying: "Your parents were not Thetis and Peleus, but you were born from the sea and the cliffs" (*Iliad* 16.33–35), this is an allegoresis of Achilles' parentage—Thetis as sea goddess and Peleus as connected to Mt. Pelion. I thank Philip Hardie for drawing this article to my attention.

9. Feeney 1991, 9. So too Tate 1927, 215 n. 5.

10. That Theagenes *wrote* about Homer is specified in Porphyry (8.2 DK, quoted above) and the Suda (8.4 DK).

11. Cf. Feeney 1991, 8–14, and Svenbro 1984, 101–121.

12. Schol. A ad *Iliad* 1.381 (= 8.3 DK). For Theagenes as rhapsode, see Wilamowitz-Moellendorff 1932, 219 n. 2. Often this evidence is adduced in support of an ancient interpretation (cf. 8.2 DK) of Theagenes as a protophilologist, downplaying his interest in allegory: see Pfeiffer 1968, 10; Svenbro 1984, 111; Wehrli 1928, 91; Detienne 1962, 65–67. But N. J. Richardson (1975, 65–81, esp. 68) has well shown that grammatical, "philological," allegorical, and other practices coincided in many of these early figures.

13. Such defenses seemed to have flourished in sophistic circles of the fifth century; see Carroll 1895.

14. Tate 1934, 108.

15. Tate 1927, citing B5 DK, on which see Schibli 1990, 100 n. 54.

16. Delatte 1915, 114–115; Wehrli (1928, 90) compares a philosopher often associated with Pythagoreanism: Alcmaeon of nearby Croton (B4 DK). For reservations, see Burkert 1972, 291 n. 67; cautious acceptance: Lamberton 1986, 31–40. See also the following note.

17. Cf. Philolaus (?) 44 B14 DK; first cited in Plato *Gorgias* 493A and assigned to "a certain wise mythologer from Sicily or Italy," on which see Dodds 1959 ad loc. and pp. 296–299.

18. Indeed, allegoresis and etymology may be seen as two sides of the same coin, as in Burkert's concise formulation: allegory is an etymologized narrative while etymology allegorizes an individual word (1970, 450). Plato plays on such traditions in *Phaedrus* 252B when he allegorizes passion (*eros*) as "winged" (*pteros*) based on an esoteric hexameter couplet ascribed to Homeric rhapsodes.

19. Nestle 1942, 129–130.

20. *Iliad* 21.6–7: *ēera d' Hērē.* Cf. note 9 above.

21. *Moralia* 19E. The history of terms for allegory is surveyed with bibliography in Whitman 1987, app. I. Cf. Pépin 1958, 87–92.

22. In 60 B.C.E.: Philodemus *Rhetoric* 1.164.22, 174.24–25, 181.25 (Sudhaus); Cicero *Orator* 94, *De Oratore* 3.42, 166–167. Making matters uncertain are passages in Demetrius *On Style* (99–102, 151, 243), which is dated variously from the third to the first century B.C.E.: see Whitman 1987, 264, and Kennedy 1989, 86, 196.

23. Stesimbrotus comes second to Theagenes in Tatian's catalogue of Homeric allegorizers (see note 5 above); Anaximander is probably the Anaximander the Younger from Miletus who at the end of the fifth century wrote *Exegesis of Pythagorean Symbola* (58C6 DK = *FGH* 9T1; cf. 59A1.11 DK); this work appears to have applied to Pythagorean sayings the same kind of allegorical explanation that had been used on Homer: cf. Burkert 1972, 166–175.

24. LSJ s.v. Cf. Pépin 1958, 85–88.

25. On the Derveni papyrus, see now Laks and Most 1997. Pending official publication, I use small Roman numerals for columns of the text printed in *Zeitschrift für Papyrologie und Epigraphik* 47 (1982) after p. 300. I hope to discuss elsewhere the specific problems of interpretation that the Greek presents.

26. West (1983, 78 n. 14) and Feeney (1991, 22) note in passing that *ainittesthai* bears the sense "allegorize" here.

27. For the interpreter's error, see West 1983, 85, and, somewhat differently, Rusten 1985, 125.

28. ix.6–7. For a discussion of this ambiguous sentence, see Rusten 1985, 133–134.

29. v.10–11. Cf. too xiii.13, where the poet's mention of Zeus as "head" is taken as "expressing something else" (*ainizetai*), probably sovereignty.

30. Discussion in Rusten 1985, 128–130.

31. v.2–4. Cf. the distinction in xix.2 between what is "unclear to the many" but not "to those who rightly understand."

32. iii.5. The word *sēmainein,* "to indicate by signs," is used for what the poet means by his obscure expression in xix.7; cf. xxi.13.

33. iii.4, on which see West 1983, 78 n. 14. In the *Republic* Plato equates speaking "poetically" with "speaking in riddles" (*ēinixato, Republic* 332B9–C1).

34. Note that Porphyry uses *ainittesthai* in introducing Pherecydes (B6 DK); cf. Schibli 1990, 99 n. 54 and 117 n. 30, and, more generally, Reinhardt 1960, 35–39, and Whitman 1987, 4.

35. Theognis 681–682: *tauta moi ēinikhthō kekrummena tois' agathois, ginōskoi d' an tis kai kakon an sophis ēi.* For text and translation, see Nagy 1985, 26ff.; 1990, 149.

36. Frags. 174, 185 in West 1992.

37. Pfeiffer (1968, 5) defines the *ainos* as a fictional *story* that has special significance in the present circumstances.

38. *Odyssey* 14.508. Cf. Nagy 1979, 234–237.

39. Nagy 1985, 22–30; cf. Edmunds 1985, 105–106.

40. Nagy 1979, 222–241, esp. 235–238; 1990, 148 and index s.v. *ainos.*

41. Aristotle *Rhetoric* 3.14 (1415b23–24). Cole 1991, 48–49; cf. pp. 55–68.

42. Gentili 1988, 43–44, 197ff., 212–213.

43. Aristotle *Rhetoric* 2.20 (1393b8–22); cf. 2.21 (1394b34–1395a2), 3.11

(1412a22–26); Nagy 1990, 427. Some apparently meteorological passages from Solon's poetry were, at least later, read as political allegories: he was said to be predicting the tyranny of Peisistratus to the Athenians when he sang: "Just as the force of snow and hail comes from a cloud, thunder comes from bright lightning," so the city should recognize in advance the destruction that threatens when some men become too great. Cf. Diogenes Laertius 1.50 and others cited by West 1992 on Solon frag. 9; cf. frag. 12.

44. Nagy 1990, 149, 192–194, 196–198.

45. See discussion in Cole 1991, 49–54; Cole cites (p. 164 n. 7) Pindar *Olympian* 2.82ff., 11.10; *Nemean* 7.12–19; *Pythian* 2.72 and 3.80ff. (where it is a question of the addressee being wise enough to appreciate the import of *Iliad* 24.527ff.). Cf. Battisti 1990. I thank Lowell Edmunds for this reference and other suggestions.

46. Alcaeus frag. 6 in Campbell 1982, 239; note too that Theognis's lines on "riddling for the wise" quoted above conclude an allegory of the ship of state.

47. Used similarly in the Derveni papyrus xv.8, where Orpheus "likens" Zeus to Air to express the intelligent and universal ruling principle.

48. Cf. "Longinus" *On the Sublime* 9.6, 7; Buffière 1956, 105.

49. Cf. Babut 1974, 83–117, esp. 102–103.

50. See further Ford 1997.

51. Simonides frag. 564 in Campbell 1991, 452.

52. Hesiod is sometimes paired with Homer (Xenophanes 21B11 DK) and attacked as an ignorant "teacher of the multitude" (*didaskalos pleistōn Hēsiodus*, Heraclitus 22B57 DK).

53. *aeisō xunetoisi* (frag. 334 Kern); West 1983, 110 n. 82, compares Heraclitus's scorn for the "undiscerning" (*axunetoi*, B1; cf. B34 DK) and Pindar's excursus into Orphic eschatology, figured as arrows that "speak to those who are discerning" (*phōnaenta sunetoisin, Olympian* 2.85).

54. A suggestive analysis of the parables of Jesus in this regard is Kermode 1979. Just before Plato rejects the impious myths of epic, he essays that such tales ought to be buried in silence or at least kept to a "very small audience, bound by pledges of secrecy and requiring extraordinary sacrifices," not the mere sacrifice of a little pig, so as to be heard by "as few people as possible" (*Republic* 378A). The rejection of the piglet as the price of initiation is a cutting allusion to the Eleusinian mysteries, which, like Homer, were available to anyone, Greek or foreigner, slave or free.

55. Cf. Plato *Protagoras* 316D, with the discussion of Richardson 1975, 68–69. The regrettable democratizing implications of their teaching are spelled out at Plato *Theaetetus* 180D: Socrates ironically contrasts the way the ancients concealed the truth of universal flux from *hoi polloi* by expressing it (allegorically) through the story that Ocean and Tethys are parents of the gods (cf. *Iliad* 14.201, 302) with their "wiser" successors who spell out everything in their presentations (*anaphadnon apodeiknumenōn*) so that even cobblers can share their wisdom.

56. On Alexandria, see Dawson 1992; for Stoic allegoresis, Long 1992.

57. See the excellent studies of Murrin (1980).

58. So defined in Heraclitus the Rhetor *Homeric Questions* 5 (*ho gar alla men agoreuōn tropos, hetera de hōn legei sēmainōn*). Accounts of the rise of Greek allegoresis often begin with this late rhetorical definition: e.g., Buffière 1956; Svenbro 1984, 119–121.

59. E.g., de Man 1979, 1983. On de Man's challenge to the possibility of literary history, see Bush 1991, 35–59.
60. Frye 1957. Useful discussion in Bruns 1992, esp. 83–86.
61. Importantly begun in works like Honig 1959 and Fletcher 1964.
62. Reynolds 1995, 211.

WORKS CITED

Babut, Daniel.
1974.   "Xénophane, Critique des poètes." *Antiquité classique.* 45: 83–117.
Battisti, Daniela.
1990.   "*Sunetos* as Aristocratic Self-Description." *Greek, Roman and Byzantine Studies* 31: 5–25.
Bruns, Gerald.
1992.   *Hermeneutics: Ancient and Modern.* New Haven: Yale University Press.
Buffière, F.
1956.   *Les mythes d' Homère.* Paris: Belles Lettres.
Burkert, W.
1972.   *Lore and Science in Ancient Pythagoreanism.* Translated by E. L. Miner, Jr. Cambridge, Mass.: Harvard University Press.
1970.   "La genèse des choses et des mots: Le papyrus de Derveni entre Anaxagore et Cratyle." *Les études philosophiques* 25: 443–455.
Bush, Ronald.
1991.   "Paul de Man, Modernist." In *Theoretical Issues in Literary History,* edited by David Perkins, 35–59. Cambridge, Mass.: Harvard University Press.
Campbell, D.
1991.   *Greek Lyric.* Vol. 3. Loeb Classical Library. London: Heinemann.
1982.   *Greek Lyric.* Vol. 1. Loeb Classical Library. London: Heinemann.
Cantarella, R.
1967.   "Omero in occidente e le origini dell'omerologia." *La parola del passato* 22: 5–28.
Carroll, M.
1895.   *Aristotle's Poetics c. XXV in the Light of Homeric Scholarship.* Baltimore: John Murphy.
Cole, T.
1991.   *The Origins of Rhetoric in Ancient Greece.* Baltimore: Johns Hopkins University Press.
Dawson, David.
1992.   *Allegorical Readers and Cultural Revision in Ancient Alexandria.* Berkeley: University of California Press.
Delatte, Armand.
1915.   *Études sur la littérature pythagoricienne.* Paris: Champion.
de Man, Paul
1983.   "Literary History and Literary Modernity." In *Blindness and Insight,* 187–228. 2d rev. ed. Minneapolis: University of Minnesota Press.
1979.   *Allegories of Reading.* New Haven: Yale University Press.

Detienne, M.
    1962.   *Homère, Hesiode et Pythagore: Poésie et philosophie dans le pythagorisme an-cien.* Collection Latomus 57. Brussels: Universa.
Diels, H., and W. Kranz.
    1952.   *Die Fragmente der Vorsokratiker.* 6th ed., 3 vols. Berlin: Weidmann.
Dodds, E. R.
    1959.   *Plato: Gorgias.* Oxford: Oxford University Press.
Edmunds, Lowell.
    1985.   "The Genre of Theognidean Poetry." In *Theognis of Megara: Poetry and the Polis,* edited by T. J. Figueira and G. Nagy, 96–111. Baltimore: Johns Hopkins University Press.
Feeney, D. C.
    1991.   *The Gods in Epic.* Oxford: Clarendon Press.
Fletcher, Angus.
    1964.   *Allegory: The Theory of a Symbolic Mode.* Ithaca, N.Y.: Cornell University Press.
Ford, Andrew.
    1997.   "The Inland Ship: Problems in the Performance and Reception of Early Greek Epic." In *Written Voices, Spoken Signs: Tradition, Performance, and the Epic Text,* edited by E. Bakker and A. Kahane, 83–109. Cambridge, Mass.: Harvard University Press.
Frye, Northrup.
    1957.   *The Anatomy of Criticism.* Princeton: Princeton University Press.
Gentili, B.
    1988.   *Poetry and Its Public in Ancient Greece: From Homer to the Fifth Century.* Translated by A. T. Cole. Baltimore: John Hopkins University Press.
Honig, Edwin.
    1959.   *Dark Conceit: The Making of Allegory.* Evanston: University of Illinois Press.
Kennedy, G., ed.
    1989.   *The Cambridge History of Literary Criticism.* Vol. 1, *Classical Criticism.* Cambridge: Cambridge University Press.
Kermode, F.
    1979.   *The Genesis of Secrecy.* Cambridge, Mass.: Harvard University Press.
Laks, André, and Glenn Most, eds.
    1997.   *Studies on the Derveni Papyrus.* Oxford: Clarendon Press.
Lamberton, R.
    1986.   *Homer the Theologian: Neoplatonist Allegorical Reading and the Growth of the Epic Tradition.* Berkeley: University of California Press.
Long, A. A.
    1992.   "Stoic Readings of Homer." In *Homer's Ancient Readers,* edited by R. Lamberton and J. J. Keaney, 41–66. Princeton: Princeton University Press.
Lutgendorf, Philip.
    1989.   "The View from the Ghats: Traditional Exegesis of a Hindu Epic." *Journal of Asian Studies* 48: 272–288.
Most, Glenn.
    1994.   "Die früheste erhaltene griechische Dichterallegorese." *Rheinisches Museum* 136: 209–212.

Murrin, Michael.
   1980.   *The Allegorical Epic.* Chicago: University of Chicago Press.
Nagy, G.
   1990.   *Pindar's Homer: The Lyric Possession of an Epic Past.* Baltimore: Johns Hopkins University Press.
   1985.   "Theognis and Megara: A Poet's Vision of His City." In *Theognis of Megara: Poetry and the Polis,* edited by T. J. Figueira and G. Nagy, 22–82. Baltimore: Johns Hopkins University Press.
   1979.   *The Best of the Achaeans.* Baltimore: Johns Hopkins University Press.
Nestle, Wilhelm.
   1942.   *Von Mythos zum Logos.* 2d ed. Stuttgart: Kröner.
Pépin, J.
   1958.   *Mythe et allégorie.* Aubier: Montaigne.
Pfeiffer, R.
   1968.   *History of Classical Scholarship: From the Beginnings to the End of the Hellenistic Age.* Oxford: Clarendon Press.
Reinhardt, K.
   1960.   "Personifikation und Allegorie." In *Vermächtnis der Antike,* edited by C. Becker. Göttingen: Vandenhoeck und Ruprecht.
Reynolds, Dwight F.
   1995.   *Heroic Poets, Poetic Heroes: The Ethnography of Performance in an Arabic Oral Epic Tradition.* Ithaca, N.Y.: Cornell University Press.
Richardson, N. J.
   1975.   "Homeric Professors in the Age of the Sophists." *Proceedings of the Cambridge Philological Society* 21: 65–81.
Rusten, J.
   1985.   "Interim Notes on the Papyrus from Derveni." *Harvard Studies in Classical Philology* 89: 121–140.
Schibli, H.
   1990.   *Pherecydes of Syros.* Oxford: Clarendon Press.
Schraeder, H.
   1880.   *Porphyrii Quaestionum Homericarum ad Iliadem pertinentium reliquias.* Leipzig: Teubner.
Slyomovics, Susan.
   1987.   *The Merchant of Art: An Egyptian Hilali Oral Poet in Performance.* Berkeley: University of California Press.
Svenbro, J.
   1984.   *La parola e il marmo: Alle origini delle poetica greca.* Turin: Boringhieri.
Tate, J.
   1934.   "On the History of Allegorism." *Classical Quarterly* 28: 105–114.
   1927.   "The Beginnings of Greek Allegory." *Classical Review* 41: 214–215.
Tedlock, Dennis.
   1983.   *The Spoken Word and the Work of Interpretation.* Philadelphia: University of Pennsylvania Press.
Wehrli, F.
   1928.   "Zur Geschichte der allegorischen Deutung Homers im Altertum." Diss., Basel.

West, M. L.
   1983.   *The Orphic Poems.* Oxford: Clarendon Press.
   ———, ed.
   1992.   *Iambi et Elegi Graeci.* 2d ed. 2 vols. Oxford: Clarendon Press.
Whitman, Jon.
   1994.   "Western Allegory." In *The New Princeton Encyclopaedia of Poetry and Poetics,* edited by A. Preminger and T. V. F. Brogan, 31–36. Princeton: Princeton University Press.
   1987.   *Allegory: The Dynamics of an Ancient and Medieval Technique* Oxford: Clarendon Press.
Wilamowitz-Moellendorff, U. von.
   1931–1932. *Die Glaube der Hellenen.* Berlin: Weidmann.

3

The Arabic Epic Poet as Outcast, Trickster, and Con Man

Susan Slyomovics

The heroic deeds of the Bani Hilal tribe—a tribe of Bedouin Arabs who migrated from the Arabian peninsula into North Africa during the tenth and eleventh centuries—are preserved throughout the Arabic-speaking world in a diverse cycle of narratives (both prose and poetry), including the oral epic of *Sīrat Banī Hilāl.* The epic is perpetuated in Upper Egypt by a class of poets who perform in public and are simultaneously regarded by the community as social and ethnic outcasts, as well as respected verbal artists and transmitters of cuture. Susan Slyomovics maintains that Hilali oral epic poets excel in rhetorical devices during performance, most typically puns or wordplays. She suggests that puns, the trope par excellence of Egyptian epic, serve as a poetic challenge to audiences to negotiate the ambiguities inherent in the outcast-poet of performance, the outcast-poet-hero of the narrative, and the discourse of both.

Across the folklore of virtually all cultures, the figure of the trickster stands out as a convergence of deception, disguise, and verbal ambiguity.[1] The trickster acts and speaks in a paradoxical fashion, one that Roger Abrahams characterizes as "combin[ing] the attributes of many other types that we tend to distinguish clearly. At various times, he is clown, fool, jokester, initiate, culture hero, even ogre."[2] Claude Lévi-Strauss has described the trickster as the expression of both sides of any binary opposition—life against death, chaos versus order, the sacred and the profane.[3] Such clownlike personalities are often culturally sanctioned characters, allowed, either in narrative or in performance, to reverse the rules of both language and society.

This essay explores several levels of the use of the trickster figure in the Arab epic *Sīrat Banī Hilāl,* a cycle of heroic tales recited throughout the Arabic-speaking world in the specific version I collected in Upper Egypt in 1983. What are the interconnections between the role of the Upper Egyptian outcast-poet in his society and the Arab trickster-epic hero in the epic narrative, and how do these connections mediate the relationship between the storyteller and his story in an enacted performance? I claim that at the heart of this configuration is an outcast-poet, on the one hand, a trickster-culture hero, on the other, with a third equally ambiguous and polyvalent feature

54

of Upper Egyptian performance, namely, the proliferation of puns embedded and improvised in live performance. I begin with a brief description of the life of a contemporary performer and reciter, the Upper Egyptian epic poet ʿAwaḍallah ʿAbd al-Jalīl ʿAli, in order to relate the ambiguous, outcast position of this epic poet to the rich, multivocal role of the trickster-epic hero, Abū Zayd the Hilali.

THE EPIC POET, ʿAWAḌALLAH ʿABD AL-JALĪL ʿALI

ʿAwaḍallah ʿAbd al-Jalīl ʿAli is an epic poet from the province of Aswan in Upper Egypt. He sings in the surrounding southern Egyptian marketplaces, in cafés, during public ceremonies, and at people's homes to celebrate births, weddings, circumcisions, a return from the hajj to Mecca, and Ramadan breakfasts. I have described elsewhere the complex status of the epic poet in southern Egypt—his role as an outcast yet at the same time the artistic bearer of his group's cultural history. In Upper Egypt, epic poets own no land, are ethnically designated as gypsies (everywhere an outcast group), and do not possess ʾaṣīl, the Upper Egyptian term for honorable character aligned with good, "clean" lineage. All these characteristics disqualify them from respectable social standing. But both audiences and poet see the poet at the moment of performance as the bearer of tradition and not as an individual, let alone an individual creative artist.[4] In performance, ʿAwaḍallah's epic story is respected, though ʿAwaḍallah the epic poet is not.

THE EPIC HERO, ABŪ ZAYD— OUTCAST, TRICKSTER, AND EPIC POET

Abū Zayd the Hilali is the hero of the Arab folk epic *Sīrat Banī Hilāl,* the epic sung by ʿAwaḍallah and the many poets of Egypt and the Arabic-speaking world. The epic hero Abū Zayd is in part a trickster figure, a characterization that is closely linked to the black skin he owes to a single word that almost accidentally governed his origin. In "the birth of the hero" sequence that is the first part of the traditional tripartite division of the epic, the hero's mother, Khaḍra Sharīfa, has been barren for eleven years.[5] In hopes of conceiving a son, she goes down to a magic spring in the Arabian peninsula. There she wishes upon a black bird, fierce and combative. She says:

Give me a boy like this bird,
black like this bird.
I swear to make him possess Tunis and Wadi Hama!
I swear to make him possess Tunis by the blade of the sword![6]

Her wish is granted, but divine interpretation of it is absolutely literal: her son is born with a black skin. When the Hilali Bedouin Arabs discover her son's skin color, mother and son are banished to the desert. Abū Zayd is therefore of noble birth, but also black-skinned, in Arab epic a sure sign of servile status; he is a warrior by definition, but also by definition an outsider or outcast. The childhood and youth of this exiled hero are marked by the most approved occurrences and exploits.[7] He combats authority figures: he begins by killing his Koranic teacher, then he annihilates the Arabs responsible for humiliating his mother, and almost slays his own father. Eventually he manages to win reinstatement with the tribe, marry, father children, and acquire a great reputation as a warrior.

It is Abū Zayd's destiny to unite the warring Bedouin tribes for the battle for Tunis and the conquest of the Maghrib, the centerpiece of the epic narrative.[8] However, before embarking on the grand westward migration, as if to rehearse for the exploits ahead, the hero Abū Zayd must defend his tribe and his religion in the Arabian peninsula against two local enemies: first, a Jewish leader named Khaṭfa, and second, the evil Arab and Muslim king Ḥanḍal, who has raided the holy city of Mecca, captured the Hilali women, and wounded the hero's father. It is the latter tale that will be examined more closely in this essay.[9]

THE PUN AS OUTCAST, THE OUTCAST AS PUN

According to Jonathan Culler, who called his introductory essay on puns "The Call of the Phoneme," puns are a reality of the language "where boundaries—between sounds, between sound and letter, between meanings—count for less than one might imagine and where supposedly discrete meanings threaten to sink into fluid subterranean signifieds too undefinable to call concepts."[10] Puns show how language, literature, and even social relations work by forging unexpected connections. Beyond serving as obvious linguistic wordplay and artistic ornamentation, the pun can expand into the narrative to generate plot, episodes, and even protagonists. Because of the ready availability of homophones in Arabic in particular and the ambiguous nature of language in general, frequent punning is a hallmark of much Upper Egyptian performance of epic poetry,[11] and the tale of king Ḥanḍal versus the Hilali Bedouins, as it is told before Egyptian audiences, is a narrative in which deceit, trickery, and disguise propel the plot, and puns seem not only to govern the way it is articulated by the poet but also to generate the events and the substance of the plot itself.

We begin with the fact of a black hero whose black skin causes him to float between acceptability and rejection, much like the pun. He is accused of bastard origins, but puns are too. As will be seen, the black hero plays with identity the way puns play with language. This essay describes what unites (1) the black epic hero, (2) the outcast Upper Egyptian epic poet who sings about the black outcast-epic hero, and (3) the language of the Arab epic song. I claim that because the black outcast-epic hero disguises himself in the narrative as an epic poet, who in Egyptian society is coded as a social outcast, he therefore uses the language of the outcast, the double-talk and double meaning of puns, all of which points to the potential deceptiveness of language itself.

THE TWO-FACED HERO, THE DOUBLE-TONGUED POET

The Arab epic hero Abū Zayd is two-faced, the Egyptian epic poet ʿAwaḍallah is double-tongued. This points to a countertradition, an antirhetoric in the literary history of rhetoric. Indeed, Roland Barthes speaks of deliberate transgression, calling the use of puns "'a black rhetoric [une rhetorique noire],' of games, parodies, erotic or obscene allusions . . . , where two taboos are circumvented, language and sex."[12] In other words, wordplay suits texts and characters that are not straightforward. Certainly, the Arab epic Sīrat Banī Hilāl frequently pronounces, in oral formulaic fashion, lines that speak to the hero's triumphs over the world. Some examples to describe the hero and his actions are taken from texts cited below: "Abū Zayd worked his trickery, / he mixed lies, he brought falsity"; "The hero Abū Zayd, who but him deceives the defenseless?" (ilbaṭal abū zĕd mīn g̣īru yikīd ilʿuzāl) and "I know him, Abū Zayd, the man of lies" (btāʿilahyāl)—frequent epithets for the hero scattered throughout the epic.

In the episode of the evil Arab king Ḥanḍal against the Hilali Bedouin, the range of punning and deceit has much to say about the role of epic poets in society and epic heroes in narrative. One device within the tale, for example, not only comments on the social status of the epic poet at the king's court but also exemplifies multiply embedded frameworks of disguise. The Ḥanḍal tale turns on the witty syncopation of the hero Abū Zayd's disguising himself first as an epic poet and then as an old man who is also black. He assumes the poet's disguise in order to wander freely in the enemy court to entertain, to seek information, and to free his kidnapped womenfolk by slaying the enemy ruler Ḥanḍal. (An important advantage of this disguise is that epic poets in Upper Egypt are permitted to associate freely with women strangers, another instance of the characteristics of the trickster converging to invert and subvert social beliefs.)[13] Thus ʿAwaḍallah, the Upper Egyptian epic poet sings about a hero disguising himself as an epic poet (who presumably sings about an epic poet who sings about an epic poet and so on). The second disguise is that of a black slave who is the jailer of the black epic poet.

It is also noteworthy that the Ḥanḍal story itself is introduced by an episode in which a mother and son meet in disguise and attempt to deceive each other. The hero Abū Zayd, while traveling through mountain and desert disguised as an epic poet with his musical instrument, the rabāba, slung over his shoulder, encounters his mother Khaḍra Sharīfa. As if to prove that ambiguity and disguise are hereditarily acquired through the maternal line, Abū Zayd's mother has also put on a disguise; she too is dressed in the clothes of a despised black slave, the easier to flee Mecca with her wounded husband, the hero's father. Mother and son greet each other disguised as blacks and as slaves, assuming the precise trangressive characteristics that caused their original traumatic expulsion from the Bedouin Arab confederation. Abū Zayd, who is truly black-skinned, is able to pierce his mother's fake blackface, whereas the mother cannot recognize her own son disguised as an epic poet, even though one of the son's many formulaic descriptions declares that the hero is yoked, paratactically and genetically, both to his trickster status and to his mother: "(Abū Zayd), son of Sharīfa, the trickster" (*ibn sharīfa btāʿ ilaḥyāl*), where the description "trickster" can apply, by zeugma, to either or both of them. The mother has merely changed superficial attire, the first and basic level of disguise and trickery; but the son can both alter and divine appearances. He is even trickier than the mother: he deceives her for no apparent reason by announcing his own death to her in language full of ambiguities, as though to underline that the pun is the realm of the oblique, the sly, and the teasing. Then he laughs as she weeps and laments (56–65):

56: min ahd abu zēd mitwaffa
57: tammit-lu sabʿa -ttiyām
58: šūfī -ddunya -lkaddāba
59: la dāmit li-baša wala sulṭān
60: bakit xaḍra bi madmaʿ ilʿen
61: ana fann ilʿarāyib ḤOZIN(A)
62: bakit xaḍra bi madmaʿ ilʿēn
63: ya ma fan ilʿarāyib ḤOZIʾANA
64: owʿani -zzamān w -ilbēn
65: ʿala kabdi ʾannawaḥ ḤAZINA[14]

56: "From the day Abū Zayd died,
57: seven days have passed.
58: See the world of deceit;
59: it does not last for a pasha or sultan."
60: Khadra cried tears from her eyes.
61: I, the art of Arabs, my possession / sorrowfully.
62: Khadra cried tears from her eyes.
63: Oh, how the art of Arabs is my possession / sorrowfully.
64: Fate and separation torment me.
65: Over my beloved [literally "my liver"] I mourn sorrowfully / my possession.

The word for "sorrowfully" (*hazana*) can split into two words (*hozi ana;* "my possession" is *hozana*) that are puns, cross-coupling the notion of art as full of sorrow even as the mother's beloved son is her possession and his death is to be mourned in sadness. The multiple puns in this line also render the speaker indeterminate, allowing for ambiguity in line 61 about the art of the Arabs: do these sentiments belong to the epic poet ʿAwaḍallah or to the epic hero Abū Zayd disguised as an epic poet, or are they the words of the mother? This pun recognizes that any of the three may be the speaker, thereby illustrating the instability not only of sounds to which different meanings can be assigned but also of meanings to which different nuances can attach in the mouths of different speakers.

Puns are about the deliberate cultivation of overlap, mess, and struggle; they emerge from language like the hero's laughter in response to his mother's laments. Laughter, a nonverbal physical reaction to one's own or another's puns and disguises, causes Abū Zayd to bare his front teeth to reveal his one unconcealable descriptor, the famous gap-teeth that forever mark the identity of the hero Abū Zayd in folk memory. His true identity is thereby revealed to his mother. While a dominant motif of this black Arab hero-trickster is his superiority of verbal wit and intellectual cunning, it is also the case that laughter, like disguise, resides in the body in an ephemeral way. Laughter acoustically emerges from the gap-toothed grin. Abū Zayd responds to this mother's laments at his supposed demise not with duplicitous punning words that exit from the hero (perhaps the poet's mouth); instead there is laughter, a nonverbal physical reaction to puns and disguises. Laughter resolves its owner's identity. Indeed, in this epic all products of the mouth are viable: the hero's laughter is revelatory and happily reunites the family. The hero's spittle, the magical liquid of his mouth, cures his father's wound. Finally, the hero's words, a vow to his father to return after twenty nights with the ninety captured Hilali maidens, set the action of the tale in motion.

THE PLOT OF KING ḤANḌAL

The tale of Abū Zayd against the Arab king Ḥanḍal properly begins when Abū Zayd arrives in Ḥanḍal's orchards. There, he finds the Hilali maidens dressed in sackcloth and bearing the heavy waterskins (*girba*) usually carried by men. The Hilali maidens are forced to attend the *diwans*, the public assemblies or gatherings of Arab men where females on public display are fair game for insults by passing Arabs. Abū Zayd, in his disguise as an epic poet, addresses in turn each of his beautiful maidens. In this way we, the audience, are introduced to the famous heroines of the epic, Jāz the woman warrior and herself a trickster; Rayya, Abū Zayd's daughter; Diyya, his niece; Naʿsa, his wife, and so on. To each he insultingly addresses the epithet *Jammasiyya*. The Jammasa are an outcast tribe of Upper Egypt; to be associated with them is an insult. Yet they are in fact the modern lineal descendants of the same Bani Hilal who are the heroes of the Arab epic. In the rest of the Arabic-speaking world, descent from the Hilali tribes is a marker of noble Arabian Bedouin heritage,[15] but in Upper Egyptian society, these subjects of heroic song are as ostracized and outcast as the poets who sing about them. In southern Egypt not just epic poets and epic heroes, but even membership in the Hilali tribe, there known as the outcast Jammasiyya tribe, reinforce the conflation and attribution of outcast status to tale, teller, and even topic.

Rayya, Abū Zayd's daughter, objects strongly to this abusive language by her father, though, in fact, he has named her what she is, a Hilali, but he has used Upper Egyptian pejorative terms. Rayya's reply yokes the identity of poet and warrior, a link altogether absent in Upper Egyptian ascriptions of social status to their epic poets. In lines 240–243 Rayya says to the epic poet who, unknown to her, is her father, the hero Abū Zayd:

> My father is a poet like you—
> he conceals himself, he pretends he's an artist,
> he comes concealed, he pretends he's a poet,
> —a bold valiant man, a horseman.

She urges Abū Zayd in his role as epic poet to make poems and give news about their predicament wherever he travels. Rayya's views of her father Abū Zayd resembles a dual-purpose metaphor of mobility: he is both epic poet and its social opposite, a horseman and a warrior whose contrasting epithets provide simultaneous, though competing, references in the same unit.

Abū Zayd then presents himself at Ḥanḍal's court, where he is rudely ignored. Ḥanḍal, who has heard of Abū Zayd, his black skin and his penchant for disguises, becomes the recipient or audience to Abū Zayd's multilayered characterizations. Ḥanḍal instinctively recognizes the equation black outcast equals epic poet equals brazen liar as in lines 269–274:

> He [Ḥanḍal] feared he was the hero Abū Zayd,
> lest he pretend to be an artist,
> lest he with his *rabāba*
> open the doors of destruction
> and take the Zoghba daughters:
> "I know him, the man of lies [*btāʿ baḥtān*]."

Abū Zayd begins by rebuking Ḥanḍal for his ignoble treatment of visiting epic poets, and Ḥanḍal apologizes. He asks Abū Zayd to play music while the Hilali maidens dance for his men. Abū Zayd fears such public display would insult his women. To delay, he insists that Ḥanḍal arrange for the women to be bathed, perfumed, and beautifully attired before being presented to the Arab men. The Egyptian epic poet ʿAwaḍallah describes in detail their enticing dress, which renders men delirious. Rayya, the hero's daughter, leads the other women. She describes their predicament in a pun: it is "bitter," the extended meaning of *ḥanḍal* (derived from its literal meaning, "bitter colocynth"), and bitter due to a human cause, a king called Ḥanḍal. This appears to be the simplest way to pun: an identity of sound that proposes complementary denotations according to a bifurcated but related context of a name and its meaning. Ḥanḍal means "bitter," and the tyrant who bears this name exemplifies bitterness, thanks to a justifiable etymological basis. The relationship of a person to his or her proper name is taken up in order to draw out the important pun on the meaning or import of a personal name that also specifies the content, as in the following sequence where the words in parentheses propose the secondary meaning (11: 12–22):[16]

> The young maidens, the daughters of Hilal,
> women of kohl-darkened eyes,
> they went out of the baths,
> they have roses on their cheeks, glowing.
> Rayya says: "O women,
> my heart from sorrow is BITTER [ḤANḌAL];
> when he comes he brings hypocrisy,
> he says to the maidens, that ḤANḌAL [BITTER],
> he says: 'Dance, O maidens.'
> Beware of agreeing to any word:
> the sword before the dance."

> xaragu -ṣṣabāya banāt hilāl
> ʾummāt alʿuyūn ilkaḥāyil
> xaraju min ilḥammām
> lihum ward ʿalxadd I sāl
> rayya -tgūl ya niswān
> galbi min ilhamm ḤANḌAL
> lamma yāji yijīb dihān
> yigūl -ṣṣibāya da ḤANḌAL
> yigūl argiṣu ya ṣabāya
> iʿwa -tmašu-lu kilma
> issēf awla min irragaṣān

Rayya tells Ḥanḍal his very name will not only forever stand for "bitterness" but will also be the linguistic sign for ignominy among the Arabs when word circulates via the epic poet that Ḥanḍal dishonors Arab women by forcing them to dance and display themselves publicly. Ḥanḍal strikes Rayya, and she falls to the ground. Her father, Abū Zayd, still disguised as the epic poet, is forced to witness violence against his beloved daughter; only then does he reveal himself to her in the secret language, the Najdi Arabic dialect they share. Until now, the Arab maidens' refusal to expose themselves and their bodies to strange men has been matched by Abū Zayd's insistence on concealment even from his closest family members. Only when the inviolate female seclusion is threatened by dishonoring public display does

Abū Zayd seek refuge in the play of secret language, where he can safely reveal himself. The suggestion is of secret subculture, set apart linguistically,
perhaps on a higher level, and based on those few initiates who decode meanings. The trickster not only shifts among various human identities, but he
is also the master of linguistic register (11: 84–95):

> Abū Zayd the bold one saw her,
> And his sound reason was lost.
> Abū Zayd said: "This is folly.
> I put difficulties behind, and I find them ahead."
> His reason says unsheathe your sword.
> His reason says patience is the model.
> He spoke gibberish to the Hilali women
> in the Najdi tongue, a foreign tongue;
> he said: "Dance, O Rayya,
> You whose lot is darkness.
> Come, dance a little.
> I am myself the Hilali, your father."
> He said: "Dance, O Rayya,
> Woman of earrings and coquettish.
> I am myself the chief of war,
> My father Rizg, my grandfather Nāyil."
> He said: "Dance, O Rayya.
> I am myself your father, Salama."
> (11: 84–95)

> wi'i -lha -lmigdim abu zēd
> aglu -ssalīm indār
> abu zēd gāl di balāwi
> afūtha warā w-alġāha giddām
> aglu yigūl ashab sēfak
> aglu yigūl issabr istimtāl
> ratan banāt ilhilāliyya
> bi -lsā najd ġarīb ya lisān
> yigūl argusi ya rayya
> ya -lli layāli nabūki
> ta'āla 'argusi šwayye
> bi zāt ilhilāli abūki
> gāl liha argusi ya rayya
> ya -mm ilhalag wa -ddalāyil
> bizāti rayīs ilgomāya
> abūya rizg wi jadd I nāyil

In the end, Abū Zayd is unmasked by Handal's daughter, 'Ajāja, who is a
sand-diviner. She is able to penetrate his disguise as an epic poet and singer
because her power resides not in the identity transformations of a trickster
but in her ability to read the truth about the present and the future in the

sands. Abū Zayd tries to forestall ʿAjāja's exposure of this identity by claiming that according to Arab custom women have no right to be present, let alone speak in Arab male assemblies; to deflect attention from her accurate reading of his form, he reproaches her with unveiling her own. This leads the evil king Ḥandal, ʿAjāja's father, to accuse his own daughter of loving the epic poet, a dishonorable passion that leads to her dishonorable presence among men. Nonetheless, she speaks, connecting all Abū Zayd's disparate disguises and social meanings. Her words send him to prison.

In prison, Abū Zayd continues to proclaim he is merely an innocent wandering epic singer. Ḥandal proposes to Johar, his black jailer, that he, Johar, travel to the Hilali homeland in Najd to verify whether the real Abū Zayd is there: a man, unlike a pun, cannot be present in two places, distant Arabia and Ḥandal's jail, at one time. Johar's reward is to be Jāz, one of the Hilali heroines. Marriage to her would ennoble a black slave's children: Johar enunciates a rule of class and color (ʿabīd ma ʿawwiz ʿabīd), "a slave does not want a slave," 13: 248). After a journey of seven nights, Johar arrives in the Hilali territory, enters their diwan, and pretends to be the sultan of Sudan. Jews have attacked his city, he relates, and he seeks help from the hero Abū Zayd to defend his people.[17] In other words, the black slave pretends to be a prince in order to investigate the identity of the black prince in his custody, who is pretending to be an epic poet and will soon—as will be seen shortly—pretend to be a slave. The two are even described in identical oral formulas, for example (xalaṭ izzūr wi jāb ilbuhṭān, "Johar mingled lies and brought untruths/slander," 13: 268).

The Hilalis truthfully inform him that Abū Zayd is at Ḥandal's court on another mission—namely, to rescue the Hilali maidens. Johar returns successfully from his mission to inform Ḥandal that the black epic singer locked in his prison is in truth the hero Abū Zayd. Ḥandal resolves to kill Abū Zayd and again promises his slave Johar marriage to a Hilali maiden of his choice once Abū Zayd is dead.

At this point in the complicated crossing of class and color, cross-dressing, duplicity, and false identities, there is one character in the tale who voices a critique of puns, obliqueness, and also presentation. The imprisoned Abū Zayd had called for help from al-Khiḍr, his magic protector since he was born.[18] A figure with magical powers, al-Khiḍr insists Abū Zayd renounce disguise—in other words put an end to puns, ontological confusions, and attendant catastrophes. It is as if he insists: let there be uncomplicated likenesses, everyone be who they are, names fit their owners, and human behavior based on action not wordplay. He delivers his plea clearly, repetitively, and without any punning. Moreover, he insists, Abū Zayd must replace himself in prison with the character in the narrative (the black slave Johar) whose disguise Abū Zayd has donned, so that all actors are in their appropriate place for the ensuing events (11: 332–341):

> al-Khiḍr said to him: "I bid you, O Prince Abū Zayd,
> Come reveal yourself to people,
> O Abū Zayd, come to me, revealed,
> And I will make you victorious in every place."
> He said to him: "The slave who brings you a tray,
> shackle him in chains.
> If you shackle him in your place,
> your life continues till now.
> If you don't shackle him in your place,
> go dwell in a grave of sands."

Nonetheless, al-Khiḍr performs his magic on Ḥandal's daughter, ʿAjāja: she becomes inexplicably stricken with concern for Abū Zayd's welfare. She orders the same black slave, Johar, to bring Abū Zayd a tray of food. Johar demands nights of passion in her bed as his price, and she agrees. Then Johar delivers food to the imprisoned Abū Zayd. By playing upon a shared black identity, Abū Zayd asks Johar to release one hand so he can eat from the tray. With only a single arm, Abū Zayd pounds Johar to the ground, shackles him, and escapes.

As this point in the performance, the Upper Egyptian epic poet ʿAwaḍallah comments in an understated aside that again Abū Zayd "begins his trick anew" (*jaddad aḥyāl*, 12: 8), "mixing lies with untruths." Abū Zayd now disguises himself as Johar, Ḥandal's black slave, and returns with the tray of food to Ḥandal. Ḥandal asks "Johar" (remember this is Abū Zayd in disguise) to bring Abū Zayd before him. In a rhetorical mode, it could be said that Abū Zayd is faced with the crisis of the pun forced to be put into explicit words, to disambiguate the uncontrollable in language.

Abū Zayd, alias Johar, calls for King Ḥandal's ninety horsemen to enter the prison. Then, Abū Zayd, still as Johar, stations himself outside the prison entrance, sending the ninety horsemen into the dungeon in search of himself. When they emerge again, they encounter not Abū Zayd disguised as Johar but Abū Zayd the Hilali warrior, who proceeds to slaughter all ninety of them. Abū Zayd then returns to Ḥandal, reverting to his disguise as Johar, to announce that Abū Zayd has escaped from prison. Ḥandal goes to the prison and finds the real Johar, but at this point he no longer knows if the black man before him is Johar or Abū Zayd disguised as Johar. In the manner of tyrants, Ḥandal kills the black man who is really Johar, reasoning thus: if the black man in his presence is indeed his slave Johar, then he, Johar, failed in his mission and deserves to die, and if it is Abū Zayd the enemy, he must be killed instantly.

There is a dead black body. The ninety fair Hilali maidens approach it, they see no identifying gap-tooth, and they rejoice in the knowledge that Abū Zayd still lives. In the meantime, Abū Zayd grabs a horse and takes refuge

in Ḥanḍal's garden, where the Hilali maidens find him. Despite their urg-
ings to escape, Abū Zayd stays to fight Ḥanḍal. Abū Zayd sends two letters:
one to Ḥanḍal, announcing Abū Zayd's imminent arrival, and a second to
the Hilali tribe encampment in Arabia. In his second letter to his Hilali kinsmen, Abū Zayd signs his missive with yet another identity, that of his enemy
Ḥanḍal. Again he repeats an earlier trick from other episodes in the epic:
he writes to his fellow tribesmen in Ḥanḍal's name that Abū Zayd has died,
and they now owe tribute and wealth. His point is twofold: to test again his
worth among his tribesmen and to ensure their presence in the final battle.
Though his tribesmen weep and lament at Abū Zayd's death, the Hilali warriors quarrel over the need to rescue the maidens still imprisoned at Ḥanḍal's
court. They finally arrive thirty days later, engage the real Ḥanḍal in battle,
and are defeated. Only when the hero's own mother, Khaḍra Sharīfa, prepares to join battle because she believes yet again that her son is dead, does
Abū Zayd comes forward to stop her.

Finally, only in the last section of the Ḥanḍal tale, do Abū Zayd and Ḥanḍal,
hero and villain, engage in the bloody, descriptively detailed, set battle piece
on horseback so beloved of the epic genre. Ḥanḍal is killed, and the tale
concludes when ʿAjāja, Ḥanḍal's daughter, a sand-diviner who saw through
Abū Zayd's disguise, is, at her own request, brought under Hilali authority
and protection.

CONCLUSION

Disguise, metamorphosis, multiple meanings, and the variety of effects
achieved by the use of linguistic puns serve, I claim, to reestablish a serious
hierarchy. Abū Zayd can play with becoming a black slave, but the corresponding reversal cannot be so readily effected; Johar, the genuine black
slave, can never become a hero. So too puns have limits: they can uncover
truths, and they can serve as cover-ups, but you cannot invent puns that are
not already potential in the language. For this reason, Abū Zayd can disguise
himself as an epic poet. He can add meaning, gain identities (even with a
temporary loss of status in the narrative), and he can celebrate ambiguities.
He can trick or mix with evil yet lose no honor. Punning can extend to a
whole narrative and even misread an entire situation. Epic poets, whether
they are Abū Zayd in the epic narrative or ʿAwaḍallah in his southern Egyptian milieu, possess a high conception of poetic vocation. Though epic poets prefer multiple visions and meanings in the universe, nonetheless the
everyday circumstances of social life in Upper Egypt ensure that, like Johar
the black slave and unlike the black hero Abū Zayd, the epic poet ʿAwaḍallah
ʿAbd al-Jalīl ʿAlī of Upper Egypt can never be seen as an epic hero—certainly
never in his own society, but then not even in performance.

NOTES

1. For a historical and bibliographical overview of the trickster figure, see Doty and Hynes 1993.

2. Abrahams 1968, 170–178.

3. Lévi-Strauss 1963, 224–226.

4. For additional material on Upper Egyptian epic singers, see Slyomovics 1988, 1987a and b, 1986, and "Praise of God, Praise of Self, Praise of the Islamic People: Arab Epic Narrative in Performance" (forthcoming).

5. ʿAwaḍallah divided the epic into three parts: (1) "the Birth of Abū Zayd" (*milād abū zēd*); (2) "the Reconnaisance" (*al-riyāda*); and (3) the "Journey Westward" (*tagrība*). For a discussion of the epic's divisions according to oral Egyptian poets, see Reynolds 1995, 16 n. 30.

6. For a translation of the birth sequence according to ʿAwaḍallah, see Slyomovics 1997. The text of ʿAwaḍallah's Ḥanḍal story is based on my unpublished fieldwork tapes recorded in 1983 in Upper Egypt. A complete set of ʿAwaḍallah's version of *Sīrat Banī Hilāl* is available in the Folk Arts Center, Tawfiqiyya, Cairo, Egypt. For text and analysis of a Ḥanḍal tale collected in a northern Egyptian Nile Delta village by Dwight Reynolds, see Reynolds 1995, 79–87 and 214–215.

7. Abū Zayd has many exploits following the hero patterns described by Lord Raglan, Otto Rank, and Alan Dundes; see Raglan 1934, 1956; Dundes 1980; Rank 1959.

8. Some historians interpret the epic as a literary analogue to the religious and political Islamicization of North Africa: see, for example, Brett 1982.

9. ʿAwaḍallah places Ḥanḍal's tale in part 1, the "Birth of the Hero." This tale appears in printed versions: the 1948 Cairo "yellow book" edition, *Qiṣṣat al-Haydabi wa-al ʿUqayli Ḥanḍal*, pp. 181–198.

10. See Culler 1988, 3.

11. Parenthetically, concerning the history of pun-making in Egyptian folklore, so prevalent was the practice of Egyptian punning that a ninth-century Arab rhetorician, al-Ṣafadi, remarked on this propensity: "The poets of Egypt, he writes, excelled in the use of this difficult figure" (the pun, which he called *tawriya*). The reason for this, according to al-Ṣafadi, "is that the water of the Nile in Egypt is of an excellent quality so that poets living in these regions are endowed with both delicacy and intellect" (cited in Bonebakker 1966, 74).

12. Barthes 1970.

13. On the ambiguous sexuality of the Upper Egyptian poet, see Slyomovics 1988, chaps. 1 and 2. See also Reynolds 1995, 84.

14. Transliteration protocols for Ṣaʿīdī (or Upper Egyptian) Arabic follow Slyomovics 1988, 269–273 ("Appendix A: Notes on Translation and Transliteration").

15. Baker 1978 discusses Tunisian pride in Hilali descent. For a survey of Arab countries where Hilali genealogy is proudly claimed, see Mukhlis 1964, 80–98.

16. For descriptions of punning possibilities, see Redfern 1984 and Brown 1956.

17. For the structural role that Jews and blacks play in ʿAwaḍallah's narrative of the Hilali cycle, see Slyomovics 1988, 60–64.

18. al-Khiḍr frequently functions as a fairy godmother-like figure; see, for example, Slyomovics 1988, 12.

WORKS CITED

Abrahams, Roger.
1968.   "Trickster, the Outrageous Hero." In *Our Living Tradition: An Intro-
            duction to American Folklore*, edited by E. Tristram P. Coffin, 170–178.
            New York: Basic Books.
Baker, Catherine Anita.
1978.   "The Hilali Saga in the Tunisian South." Ph.D. diss., Indiana
            University.
Barthes, Roland.
1970.   "L'ancienne rhétorique." *Communications* 16: 174.
Bonebakker, S.
1966.   *Some Early Definitions of the Tawriya*. The Hague: Mouton.
Brett, Michael.
1982.   "Ibn Khaldoun and the Invasion of Ifriqiya by the Banu Hilal, 5th Cen-
            tury AH / 11th Century AD. *Actes du Colloque International sur Ibn Khal-
            doun, Alger, 21–26 juin, 1978*. Algiers: Société National d'Edition et
            Diffusion.
Brown, J.
1956.   "Eight Types of Puns." *Publications of the Modern Language Association*
            71.
Culler, Jonathan, ed.
1988.   *On Puns: The Foundation of Letters*. London: Blackwell.
Doty, William G., and William J. Hynes.
1993.   *Mythical Trickster Figures: Contours, Contexts, and Criticism*. Tuscaloosa,
            Alabama: University of Alabama Press.
Dundes, Alan.
1980.   "The Hero Pattern and the Life of Jesus." In *Interpreting Folklore*,
            223–262. Indianapolis: Indiana University Press.
Lévi-Strauss, Claude.
1963.   *Structural Anthropology*. New York: Basic Books.
Mukhlis, Faiq Amin.
1964.   "Studies and Comparison of the Cycles of the Banu Hilal Romance."
            Ph.D. diss., University of London.
Raglan, Lord.
1956.   *The Hero: A Study in Tradition, Myth, and Drama*. New York: Vintage.
1934.   "The Hero of Tradition." *Folklore* 45: 212–231.
Rank, Otto.
1959.   *The Myth of the Birth of the Hero*. New York: Vintage.
Redfern, Walter.
1984.   *Puns*. Oxford: Oxford University Press.
Reynolds, Dwight Fletcher.
1995.   *Heroic Poets, Poetic Heroes: The Ethnography of Performance in an Arabic
            Oral Epic Tradition*. Ithaca, N.Y.: Cornell University Press.
Slyomovics, Susan.
Forth-   "Praise of God, Praise of Self, Praise of the Islamic People: Arab Epic
coming.   Narrative in Performance." In *Classical and Popular Medieval Arabic Lit-*

erature: A Marriage of Convenience? Festschrift in Honour of H. T. Norris, edited by Farida Abu-Haidar and Jareer Abu Haidar. London: Curzon Press.

1997. "'The Birth of Abu Zayd': The Epic of the Hilali Tribe in Upper Egypt." In *Oral Epics from Africa: Vibrant Voices from a Vast Continent,* edited by John William Johnson, Thomas A. Hale, and Stephen Belcher. Indianapolis: Indiana University Press.

1988. *The Merchant of Art: An Egyptian Hilali Oral Epic Poet in Performance.* Berkeley: University of California Press.

1987a. "The Death-Song of Amir Khafaji: Puns in an Oral and Printed Episode of Sirat Bani Hilal." *Journal of Arabic Literature* 18: 62–78.

1987b. "Methodes de transcription et traduction d'une performance de geste orale arabe." In *Le conte,* edited by Pierre Lyon and Paul Perron, 127–139. Montreal: Didier.

1986. "Arabic Folk Literature and Political Expression." *Arab Studies Quarterly* 8: 2: 178–185.

4

· · ·

Epic, Gender, and Nationalism

The Development of Nineteenth-
Century Balkan Literature

Margaret Beissinger

Epic poetry has been a vibrant oral tradition in the Balkans since at least the fourteenth century and was perpetuated through centuries of Ottoman and other foreign rule. It provided a main source of entertainment in the courts of the local aristocracy as well as among the folk. Although the first published heroic songs were included in a Croatian literary poem from the mid-sixteenth century, the systematic collecting of epic among Serbs, Croats, Bulgarians, and Romanians did not begin until the nineteenth century, coinciding with the rise of nationalism, aspirations for liberation, and the formation of national or revival literatures. Oral epic—a genre that, for the "nation builders," had come to exemplify the heroic resistance of the people—thus became a model for poetic masterpieces, such as Petar Petrović Njegoš's *Mountain Wreath*. As Margaret Beissinger argues, however, these early literary epics, while inspired by the folk genre, also evoked strong nationalistic messages that served the political agenda of the male public.

The male-dominated political milieu of the nineteenth-century Balkan world—in which nations were asserting their own identities after centuries of Ottoman authority—was unsympathetic, if not indifferent, to the female voice for the dissemination of the nationalistic messages expressed in their burgeoning discourse. While *oral* epic recognized women in substantial ways, *written* epic—a genre that mirrored the oral genre and initiated the cultural revivals of the nineteenth century—ignored them. Instead, literary epic, which became an important means for forging a sense of nationhood in the Balkans, embraced a social construction of reality created effectively by men. As nation building developed in various communities in eastern Europe, gender became an objectified issue in the creation of culture and shaping of literatures. Women were subjected in this process to reified roles, particularly in the early literary epic of the nineteenth century. The female voice in this literature, emanating from the private and personal sphere, was actually more often than not the thinly disguised voice of the more public and collective male, ardently constructing culture and nation.

This essay explores the intersection between gender roles and nationalism in nineteenth-century Balkan culture.[1] It examines gender and nationalism in oral literature versus orally inspired literature, and in particular how women were represented in epic poetry. Although women were rarely central figures in traditional Balkan Christian oral epic,[2] they were often cast in significant roles that were clearly necessary and vital to the integrity of the narratives. By contrast, the first modern literary works of the nineteenth-century Balkan world were nationalistic poems that relied heavily on oral epic and yet virtually ignored women in their narratives. These were works that—despite whatever judgments we may make today of their literary merits—played very important roles in the making of Balkan national consciousness. In this early literary epic, unlike in oral epic, women played very minor roles (or no roles at all) precisely because the authors of literary epic, acting in their role as "cultural entrepreneurs,"[3] crafted a literature that sought to appeal primarily to men, the main participants in nineteenth-century nationalist movements. This contrasts sharply with the art of oral epic poets, which reflected women's varied roles in society and whose intended audiences were multigender in character.

Romantic nationalism profoundly affected the cultural and literary revivals that mushroomed in the Balkans in the modern period. Johann Gottfried Herder's notion of the "Volk" was central to the larger currents of cultural nationalism that swept both western and eastern Europe. "Volk" was conceived of as a social collective or nation that was a patriarchal construction—much like a traditional nuclear family—where history, language, and culture are interrelated and shared. Implicit in this thinking was the authority of the "fathers" and other males of society.[4] Those who espoused romantic nationalism equated much of the perpetuation of society with the transmission of tradition and folklore. The "voice of the people," as found in their folklore, was considered the core of national culture. The desire to preserve the precious oral traditions of the folk resulted in an intense interest in the collection of oral poetry throughout the eastern European world during the nineteenth century. It also fostered—in its patriarchal discourse—national literatures that developed with necessarily male topics and agendas at the forefront.

Folklore played a central role in the formation and development of Balkan national literatures in the nineteenth century. Oral tradition, viewed as a cultural treasure that survived centuries of foreign (both Ottoman and Austro-Hungarian) domination, was seen as a source of expression of struggle against foreign influence. It was a vehicle through which ideals of liberation and national identity were expounded and promoted. Fully exploited in the creation of national consciousness, folklore was manipulated for political purposes.

Throughout the nineteenth century, folklore provided ideal ingredients for what Benedict Anderson has termed "narrative[s] of 'identity'"[5]—narratives that validate the convictions and aspirations of nation building and that are, in fact, necessary in the creation of national culture. Folklore—as embraced by the literary public—exemplified an idealized past that became a vital component in the formation of national narratives, literature, and culture. As Roger Abrahams has pointed out, "The folk and their lore were enlisted in the nation-building cause." The manipulation of both folk and lore in this drive to create national culture was "the result of elitist social and cultural constructions."[6]

The first broad stage in the development of modern Balkan literatures was the composition of literary epic. The genre drew heavily from oral epic that was extant at the time. Examples of such works include *Gorski vijenac* (The mountain wreath, 1847) by the Montenegrin Petar Petrović Njegoš II, *Smrt Smail-Age Čengića* (The death of Smail-Aga Čengić, 1846) by the Croat Ivan Mažuranić, *Gorski pŭtnik* (Woodland traveler, 1857) by the Bulgarian Georgi Rakovski, and *Dumbrava roşie* (The red oak grove, 1872) by the Romanian Vasile Alecsandri. Each of these works was inspired by Balkan oral epic: each reflects aspects of the style, language, and narrative content of the oral genre. All of these epics were key in the development of national literatures in their respective societies.

Njegoš, Mažuranić, Rakovski, and Alecsandri were all major literary figures in their respective communities, as well as keenly involved in the collection and dissemination of oral traditions. Furthermore, all of them were significant political actors in the nationalist dramas of the nineteenth century, some even holding formal political offices. The educated public of the Balkans during the nineteenth century had extensive contact with oral poetry. Major collections of oral poetry became influential among those who constructed national culture (including political activists) and shaped literary development. These were collections of folklore with which the writers of early national literature were familiar and which, in fact, inspired them.

The most prominent cultural figure in nineteenth-century Serbia was Vuk Stefanović Karadžić, often referred to as Vuk. Vuk was the most important champion of folklore, collecting and publishing voraciously throughout his lifetime (1787–1864). Vuk also was an eminent grammarian. He standardized the Serbian literary language and orthography, thereby providing the context for the development of the modern Serbian language and a national literature. Vuk published his first collection of oral poetry in 1814. His continuing efforts to record and publish oral literature culminated in a four-volume anthology entitled *Srpske narodne pjesme* (Serbian folk songs), which was published in Leipzig between 1823 and 1833 and later expanded and reissued in Vienna between 1841 and 1862. His collections were popular and widespread in the South Slavic world, not to mention known and appreciated by Jakob Grimm, Goethe, and others in western Europe. As Svetozar Koljević has pointed out, "Owing to the work of Vuk Karadžić, [who] gained international recognition, the folk traditions became the objects of literary cult and inspiration."[7] Vuk's publications of oral poetry were instrumental in the nineteenth-century development of literature in Serbia, Croatia, and Montenegro. Indeed, as Albert Lord noted, "The popular poetry, especially the Vuk collection, . . . was widely imitated, and its form was influential in shaping the style of literary poetry, both narrative and lyric, throughout the century and even later."[8]

In the oral epics collected by Vuk, women play a variety of roles that are not trivial and even often instrumental in the narratives told. This analysis focuses on what Vuk termed the oldest heroic songs, that is, the contents of his second volume of *Serbian Folk Songs* (100 in all).[9] By and large, these epic songs are heroic and therefore are concerned with "male" narratives. They represent a deeply patriarchal way of life. Within this context, however, women frequently figure in remarkably significant and requisite ways.

Most of the female (as well as male, for that matter) figures fit into established patterns that are stereotypical throughout the tradition—a hallmark of oral literature. The most common female roles in South Slavic oral epic are helpers, clever or wise maidens, mothers, sisters, and wives of heroes, spirited women, otherworldly creatures resembling fairies, and victims. The female helper is an ancient figure, found in world epic from antiquity to the present. Female helpers typically facilitate the hero's passage. Sometimes they aid in the release of prisoners. Such helpers, often termed the jailor's daughter type, are widespread in the larger Balkan and Turkic continuum.[10] Other female helpers include the innkeeper's wife, who drugs the enemy while he is drinking and then releases the hero—also a widespread Balkan epic figure.[11] Clever and wise maidens also form a type. Sometimes they judiciously advise heroes; at other times they outwit the hero in a triumph of brains over brawn.[12] Mothers also surface frequently and are portrayed as noble figures who provide counsel to their heroic sons. The advice of the hero's mother takes on a near-sacred quality because of the wisdom that it reflects.[13] Accordingly, the proverbial "curse of a mother" is seen as the least desirable fate for a son. Sisters typically are seen as honorable and faithful to their heroic brothers.[14] Wives of heroes fall into two broad stereotypes: the relatively passive but eternally loyal mates, and the treacherous, unfaithful ones. Both are influential insofar as they propel the narrative forward in important ways. The quintessential faithful wife steadfastly awaits her absent husband in the traditional return songs that are widespread throughout the Balkans.[15] Her opposite, the deceitful wife, is found at times betraying her heroic husband in the interests of another man. She is usually punished, at times brutally.[16]

Other female figures in oral epic in a sense break out of the patriarchal mold and are what I term spirited women. They include both maidens and wives. Though stereotypical in profile, they nonetheless defy the patriarchal conventions or requirements imposed on them (for example, in refusing to marry the husband chosen for them).[17] Yet another class of women in the epic songs are the "vilas," otherworldly female figures who inhabit forests and live near streams. They are beautiful, physically powerful, seductive, easily angered, naughty, or helpful.[18] Finally, female victims are utilized as a form of tax or are forced to marry against their will, to name a few of the most common types.[19] In other words, women played significant roles in the South Slavic oral epic from which literary epic drew inspiration. Indeed, many of the figures in Vuk's collection are found throughout the other Balkan traditions.

Female figures played significant roles in oral epic, but not always positive roles. Extolling the noble character of the oral poems that he collected, Vuk himself referred to the "masculine Serbian spirit" that they mirrored.[20] Indeed, one might ask how the various female characters in Balkan oral epic reflected nineteenth-century social reality. The women presented in these epics portrayed a variety of female roles in society, albeit within a highly patriarchal framework. To be sure, the oral traditional culture—unlike the more urbane, literary culture—acknowledged more fully the various roles that women naturally played in society. This implicit recognition is reflected in the diverse roles that women occupied in oral epic. In relating stories of relevance to the community, oral tradition embraced figures—both male and female—who represented a wide array of roles. It was the goal of oral epic poets to compose engaging narratives that resonated in the community, not to disseminate political messages. Furthermore, their audiences were—in the case of the Balkan Christian epic—multigendered.

Gorski vijenac (The mountain wreath), by the Montenegrin Petar Petrović Njegoš II (1813–1851),[21] provides an excellent illustration of literary epic that was inspired by oral epic yet served—unlike oral epic—to establish a burgeoning national literature and foster a sense of nation. Published in 1847, it is considered Njegoš's greatest work and occupies a venerable position in the Serbian canon. It played an integral role in the forging of Serbian nationalist culture, serving as a sacrosanct text that formed a literary basis of the nationalist ideology.

Njegoš met Vuk in Vienna in 1833, at which point a lifelong friendship and meeting of minds was established (Njegoš saw Vuk for the last time shortly before his own death in 1851). Njegoš avidly supported Vuk's various activities—from collecting oral literature to linguistic and orthographic reforms. Furthermore, Njegoš, a native of rugged and isolated Montenegro, was steeped in the oral literature that was a part of everyday life there. The oral traditional milieu that characterized village life in Montenegro had a profound influence on him. As a youth, Njegoš learned the art of oral epic singing to the *gusle* (a one-stringed folk instrument), continuing in the tradition that his father had also mastered. He later collected folk poems and published several volumes of them; he also wrote "folk" poetry.[22] In other words, Njegoš was constantly in contact with oral poetry. But Njegoš was not only a cultural figure. Beginning in 1833, he was also the prince-bishop of Montenegro; holding firm to a nationalist agenda, he wielded considerable political power.

Loosely modeled on an oral epic that recounted the same subject, the literary epic *The Mountain Wreath* focuses on the theme of Turkish oppression and Slavic (Montenegrin) resistance. It powerfully moved nationalists in the nineteenth century. *The Mountain Wreath* depicts a meeting of Montenegrin clan leaders who must decide what to do with the Montenegrins who have converted to Islam. After much deliberation, it is finally agreed that extermination of the Muslim converts is the best method of combating the Turkish menace. Although the poem is constructed in dramatic form (complete with "stage directions"), there is virtually no action, only discussion of the problem and possible solutions. Bishop Danilo ("Vladika Danilo")—the bishop and Christian ruler of Montenegro—is the main character (and mirrors the person of Njegoš himself, similarly torn between expedient and righteous postures in the mediation of the many Christian-Muslim and other tribal disputes in Montenegro).[23] He takes counsel with his various clan leaders throughout the poem, weighing the question of whether violence should be used as a solution in the desired "extermination of Islam," or whether other modes of reconciliation might be preferable. This all culminates in a decision by the Christians to proceed with a massacre of converts—an event that the reader does not witness per se, but that takes place and is reported on, after which the poem concludes. The parallels with ethnic cleansing in the former Yugoslavia today are obvious.

The Mountain Wreath begins with the short "Dedication to the Ashes of the Father of Serbia," which is written in sixteen-syllable meter. It is followed by the narrative itself, a dramatic epic poem of 2,819 lines, composed in decasyllabic meter, with a word break after the fourth syllable—that is, the meter of South Slavic oral epic. Njegoš turned to spoken and vernacular linguistic forms in the poetry. The poetry abounds with proverbs, incantations, and sayings taken "from the folk." A folk round dance is employed as a type of chorus. Furthermore, oral literary genres (especially wedding song and lament) are embedded in the narrative at various points, as are numerous references to oral tradition, such as traditional Serbian weddings or family feasts (the "slava").[24] Finally, Njegoš repeatedly utilized devices of oral composition—repetition, parallelism, pleonasm, and parataxis. In this way he created a poetic rhythm that imitated oral epic, thereby seeking to stir his readers. *The Mountain Wreath* reflects many of the characteristics found in oral epic, a genre with which nationalism identified more than any other because of its reflection of the "folk"—perceived as the soul of the nation—as well as its invocation of the glorious past and heroic ideals. Indeed, Vuk—the "father" of Serbian folklore—time and again called attention to the "sacred" nature of Serbian oral tradition and the profound linkage between it and the Serbian nation and its history.[25] Njegoš put these same powerful symbols to equally powerful political use.

Forty individual characters figure in *The Mountain Wreath*. Of these, only two are women.[26] The poetry relates a male story, with men as the central actors and speakers. The first woman in *The Mountain Wreath* appears about two-thirds of the way through the poem. She is the "sister of Batrić," a young woman who grieves over the recent treacherous death of her brother at the hands of the Turks. Batrić was a heroic ideal to his fellow Montenegrins. Batrić's sister laments in poignant oral traditional style, employing the typical meter of death lament in the South Slavic tradition (an eight-syllable line followed by a four-syllable refrain). She addresses her deceased brother:

> Where have you flown away from me, O my falcon,
> away from your most noble flock, my dear brother?
> Didn't you know the faithless Turks? May God curse them!
> Didn't you know they'd deceive you, O lovely head?
> My world is gone, forever lost, my brother, my sun!
> My deep wounds can never be healed, my bitter wound!
> My very eyes are plucked from me, light of my eyes!

> Kuda si mi uletio, moj sokole,
> od divnoga jata tvoga, brate rano?
> Da l' nevjerne ne zna Turke, Bog ih kleo!
> e će tebe prevariti? divna glavo!
> Moj svijete izgubljeni, sunce brate!
> moje rane bez prebola, rano ljuta!
> moje oči izvadjene, očni vide![27]

She mourns for fifty verses, then seizes her grandfather's knife and kills herself. The sister of Batrić and her lament serve to underscore the tragedy and futility of young Batrić's death. The sister does not have a name, nor an identity beyond her role as sister. Indeed, after she has expressed her lament, she surrenders herself to the world that has already snatched away her brother. Joining him, she denies her own existence. After mourning, she is no longer needed in this drama, so Njegoš literally removes her from the scene in a gesture that reflects not only a sister's sentimental love for her brother (providing a quintessential depiction of the cult of the sister), but perhaps even more significantly an objectification of one of the only female characters in the work. Her role in Njegoš's poem is primarily to articulate her brother's identity.

Why should Batrić's sister exemplify the tragedy of the dead hero? In the traditional Balkan world, it is women, not men, who perform death rites. It is they who are the caretakers of the dead, from dressing and guarding the corpse to performing laments. Death rite is a female function and a female social duty. Women alone have the license to lament and communicate with the dead in this traditional world. Thus, by the conventions of ritual, Batrić's sister is the only person who *can* perform this function with the intensity that Njegoš intends. The death rites in Montenegro traditionally have been particularly prominent among the life-cycle rituals. Laments that glorify dead heroes—sung by female kin—are especially rich. The lament sung by Batrić's sister is an exemplary poem in this regard, bridging oral poetry and literary imitation of oral poetry.[28] Furthermore, her lament epitomizes the Balkan cult of the sister—a potent metaphor through which the tragedy of Montenegro is expressed.

The only other female figure in *The Mountain Wreath*, an old woman (the "prophetess-witch"), makes her appearance about 200 verses later in a gathering of the men. She forms part of a brief incident. After claiming that she is a witch and then answering a series of questions posed by the clan members, the old woman confesses that she was sent by the vizier (who has learned that the Christian Montenegrins plan to do away with their Muslim brothers). She claims that she was ordered to bewilder the men: "He sent me to confuse you," she tells the chieftains, "so you would be busy with your troubles." ("Pa me posla da vas ja pomutim, da se o zlu svome zabavite.")[29] The woman is saved from being stoned to death by the intervention of the chieftains.

The old woman is clearly an outsider. She is past childbearing age and thus is in some senses a symbolic male. She is "betwixt and between,"[30] neither fully female (because she no longer represents fertility) nor fully male (she is, after all, a woman). Furthermore, she is not from central Montenegro, but rather from Bar (on the Adriatic coast), and thus is very literally a stranger. A prophetess-witch was a perfect ploy for the assembled men—a figure who could pose as someone who deals in otherworldly matters. Furthermore, this "ploy" had to be someone who was vulnerable and easily duped. No better candidate could exist than an old woman—perceived as weak and vulnerable, as a result of both age and gender. In her confession, the old woman tells how the vizier threatened to imprison and burn her sons and grandchildren if she did not play his game of confusing the Christians. She herself says to the men:

It was this threat that did force me, brothers,
to sow discord 'mong you Montenegrins.

Ta me sila, braćo, naćerala
te pomutit hoćah Crnogorce.[31]

Because women were associated with powerlessness (and men with power), to succumb to such threats would be considered female, something that only women would do. The old woman from Bar became the vizier's puppet because of her twofold outsider status (both as a person not from central Montenegro and as a symbolic male—thus permitted to mingle in male public space) and because of her powerlessness as a woman.[32]

In addition to these two female characters, women are alluded to or mentioned on occasion by men in various dialogues in the poem. These references describe a number of female roles. Women are regarded as lamenters (such as the sister of Batrić, who is herself a close parallel to the faithful sisters of oral epic). They mourn dead heroes—husbands, brothers, brothers-in-law, and sons. One male character, for example, declares to the bishop that "men bravely bear what women lament about" ("Ljudi trpe, a žene nariču")—an observation that pointedly juxtaposes the martial strength of men and the ritualized weakness of women.[33] Lamenters are often compared to the cuckoo bird (kukavica); the bishop, for example, is said to be "wailing just like some cuckoo bird" (kukaš kao kukavica); the simile is meant to underscore his weakness (and thus femaleness).[34] Women are alluded to as having otherworldly connections (recall the old woman from Bar. Most notably, they are described as "vila"-like (bewitching) in their seductive powers: "She is prettier than any white vila!" ("Ljepša mu je od vile bijele!").[35] Women are often also portrayed as seers of the future:

Why do you talk magic like old witches
or like some old women reading their beans?

Što bajete kao bajalice
ali babe kad u bob vračaju?[36]

"Reading beans" is a reference to a traditional means of foretelling the future in the Balkans, typically performed by women.

Women are also referred to in perhaps their most important role in the nationalist cant—as those who give birth to Serbian heroes. They are seen as vessels that serve to bear male heroes. As Bette Denich has noted, in the Balkan context, "the only enduring social units are formed through the male descent line, and women are exchanged among these units to procreate future generations of males. . . . [W]omen serve merely as links between fathers and sons, and between male in-laws." Indeed, "only as the mother of sons does a wife secure a place in the group."[37] Speaking of one of the Montenegrin heroes, a group of male voices in Njegoš's poem cries out:

Serbian woman has never borne his like,
since Kosovo or even before it!

Srpkinja ga jošt radjala nije
od Kosova, a ni prijed njega.[38]

The mothers mentioned in *The Mountain Wreath* of course find parallels in the noble and wise mothers of oral epic. A mother's curse is also, as in oral epic, anathema:

The mother's curse thus fell upon her son,
and massacred was his entire army.

Stiže sina materina kletva,
pogibe mu vojska svakolika.[39]

Finally, women are depicted as victims captured and violated by the enemy. For example, referring to the rape of Christian maidens by the Turks, a Montenegrin chieftain tells one of the Muslim leaders:

If there is a garland of flowers
to decorate the heads of lovely brides,
you harvest it at the peak of flowering.

Ili imah kitnoga vijenca
koji kruni čelo nevjestama,
požnješ mi ga u cv'jetu mladosti.[40]

"Harvest" has a sexual meaning here; the sense extends also, of course, to the "rape" and "harvest" of Montenegro. The symbolic meaning of rape in this context is as powerful as the act itself. As Virginia Sapiro has pointed out, "The control over women's sexuality has often been played out in inter-group conflict through the dynamics of rape. . . . What we might call the 'politics of honor' [is] played out between groups through the medium of women's sexuality. The assault on the enemy involves a wide range of physical and psychological tactics, but one of the most notable means of assaulting the honor or pride of a nation or community is to assault the 'honor' of its women through rape."[41] Obviously, this continues to remain an important dimension of nationalist politics in the Balkans today. Rape is (and has been throughout the ethnic conflicts in the former Yugoslavia) a particularly powerful mode of warfare, because it not only attacks the honor of its female victims, as Sapiro notes, but it also shames and thus dishonors their husbands, brothers, fathers, and sons.[42] Such men are humiliated in the face of other men. As Denich has remarked, the "prescriptions for male behavior" in the Balkans involve a "public image of warrior courage . . . linked with a self-image of indomitable virility and elaborated ideologically in terms of the value codes of 'honor.'"[43] Male honor is deeply connected to power and control over females. Thus, references to rape in *The Mountain Wreath* are in some senses a male symbol. As Cynthia Enloe has noted, "In the context of nationalist struggles, . . . the abuse of women often seems recast as more a problem for men than women." Through rape, she notes, "the honor of the community's *men* has been assaulted."[44]

Of course, the works of Njegoš represent the use of literary epic, inspired by and drawn from oral epic, for national and political expression. There were other contemporaries of Njegoš throughout the Balkans whose literary epics were related to oral epic in meter, style, language, and content and were powerful statements to the male public, imbued with the nationalist spirit of the nineteenth century. In Croatia, the most outstanding writer of the romantic literary movement during the first half of the nineteenth century was Ivan Mažuranić (1814–1890), whose literary epic *Smrt Smail-Age Čengića* (*The death of Smail-Aga Čengić*) was published in 1846.[45] Mažuranić was from a peasant family and had been fully exposed to traditional poetry. He was, like Njegoš, thoroughly knowledgeable about Vuk's collections. Also like Njegoš, he held a political office: "ban" (governor) of Croatia. *The Death of Smail-Aga Čengić*, Mažuranić's most famous work, is a poem of 1,134 lines that relates one event in the continuing struggle between Turks and Montenegrins—the ambush of a Muslim champion, Smail-Aga, and his slaying by a band of Montenegrins in revenge for his slaughter of some Christians. Unlike the incident that Njegoš related, the event that formed the basis for Mažuranić's epic actually occurred, and news of it was disseminated in the press. It created an immediate frenzy and became a type of popular metaphor for Muslim-Christian hostilities.[46]

In *The Death of Smail-Aga Čengić*, Mažuranić turned to oral epic for inspiration, frequently employing decasyllabic verse, as well as oral poetic and stylistic devices such as patterned repetition, parallelism, and fixed epithets. The narrative, like that in *The Mountain Wreath*, is about liberation and national identity. There is not a single female character in Mažuranić's poem. A few "vilas," a faithful wife, and Christian maidens who are regularly taken "for the night" by the Turkish tax collectors are mentioned in passing by men in the text. Stereotypes who are simply background are the token female "appearances," and once again the reference to rape is effectively a male statement. As passive victims, women provide a pretext for male discourse on warfare and honor; rape challenges men's power.

Georgi Rakovski (1821–1867) was an ardent Bulgarian nationalist who collected folk songs, issued newspapers, wrote literature, and in general devoted his entire life to the Bulgarian nationalist cause. Rakovski's *Gorski pǔtnik* (Woodland traveler) was first published in 1857. The poem (928 verses) centers on Bulgarian freedom fighters ("hajduti") and their stories of struggle against the "Turkish yoke." It was a clear statement on nation and liberation and has been called "the first revolutionary epic poem of Bulgarian literature."[47] Although now generally viewed as minor literature, its impact on the Bulgarian public of its day was considerable. It was one of the most popular literary works of the Bulgarian national revival. The work idealizes the Bulgarian past and invokes it as a symbol of the power and liberation that was desired in nineteenth-century Ottoman-dominated Bulgaria. Rakovski, like his South Slavic brothers from Montenegro and Croatia, was an advocate of oral poetry and found inspiration in it for his own epic. Like Njegoš and Mažuranić, Rakovski composed a narrative in which a political message dominated—a political message characterized by nationalist sentiment and a call to arms. Women do not figure in any significant way in Rakovski's poem.

A final example further illustrates the point. The Romanian folklorist and poet Vasile Alecsandri (1821–1890) wrote *Dumbrava roşie* (*The red oak grove*) in 1872. It is a literary epic that narrates a struggle in the late fifteenth century between the ruler of Moldavia—Stephen the Great—and the Polish king. The message of liberation at the core of the epic was highly pertinent in the nineteenth-century context as the Romanian principalities (Walachia and Moldavia) sought to be released from all ties with the Ottoman empire, still a suzerain power at the time. The 859-line poem was an important work in its day. Alecsandri—renowned not only for his own poetry, but also for his pioneering work in the collection of Romanian oral poetry (especially epic) and his political involvement in Romanian nationalist activities—drew from oral epic in the creation of what he considered a Romanian national epic. Stephen the Great—a historical figure who was embraced in folklore and nationalist culture in the rhetoric of emancipation—embodies heroic resistance to foreign invaders in Alecsandri's poem. Other male heroic figures also sing of liberation; however, the role of women in the epic is negligible.

Remarking on the gendering of nationalism among Romanians, Katherine Verdery has suggested that in the construction of a "national self" it has been a collective, implicitly male "self" that has dominated. This "entity" is characterized by "heroism, triumph, victimization, and sacrifice" and represents not only a "collective [male] individual," but also the avowed "nation that unites" this collective.[48] Prominent "individuals" of this "collective" who epitomize this heroic concept have been invoked throughout Romanian history and include figures such as Stephen the Great, viewed as a sacrosanct emblem of the "nation." Alecsandri exploited this forceful symbol—male, heroic, defiant—as he constructed his epic of Romanian nationhood, *The Red Oak Grove*. Women were entirely dispensable, because the epic expressed a theme that was intended to resonate among the *men* who formed the elite of nineteenth-century Romanian society. As Verdery has noted, "The image of a collective Romanian nation" was "reproduced without women's intervention."[49]

Speaking of the profound "linkage between gender and cultural identity," Sapiro has remarked that in some societies "the struggle for liberation has been termed a struggle for 'manhood.'" Furthermore, "the loss of manhood is culturally understood to mean one is being turned into a naturally weaker and less significant being: a woman."[50] I suggest that if the centuries-long state of foreign domination (be it Ottoman or Austro-Hungarian) in the Balkans in the nineteenth century is viewed as a state of powerlessness, or, by extension, femaleness, then the struggles for liberation were effectively struggles to gain or regain maleness (manhood) and power. Thus, in order to move from powerlessness and oppression (the state of being female) to power and independence (being male), one strategy was to objectify women and femaleness and elevate men and maleness to the center of the various narratives that aided in generating "identity." This is precisely what Njegoš, Mažuranić, Rakovski, and Alecsandri did. In their literary pleas for liberation and independent national identity, they constructed male worlds that were free of the emblems of oppression and emasculation, peripheralizing female symbols. Their epics spoke to the ardent romantic nationalist desires and beliefs that men held and espoused—liberation, regaining of power, authority, and control—all concepts or states that were seen as antithetical to the status of women. Men were the main audience of this literature in the nineteenth century because they were the principal participants in the nationalist movements in the Balkans. It followed then that men also had to be the main actors and mouthpieces in this literature.

As Enloe has pointed out, "Women haven't had an easy relationship with nationalism."[51] Nineteenth-century writers of literary epic in the Balkans were asserting a nationalism in their writing that lauded the liberation and removal of foreign oppression. These ideals were equated almost exclusively with male identity. The various literary epics discussed here were narratives primarily about manhood. When women did surface in them, they were token representations that furthered the male nationalist message: women as lamenters for dead heroes, mothers as receptacles for the birth of national heroes, women as objects in the potent national symbol of rape, and women as representatives of otherworldly connections, such as witches or "vilas." By contrast, the various roles women held in oral epic were not politically motivated in this way. Indeed, both oral and literary epic included—either actively or passively—female roles and references. Female kin, female victims, and otherworldly women all functioned in various ways, large and small, in these narratives—whether to propel the narrative forward (especially in oral epic) or to embellish the message of male-centered nationalism (as in literary epic). By comparison, the female helpers, clever maidens, and spirited women that figured (sometimes quite prominently) in oral epic were not present in the early literary epic of the Balkan world—precisely because they were not seen as effective vehicles for promoting or elaborating the nationalistic agenda.

Oral epic, as opposed to its literary imitations, reflected the greater diversity of roles that women played in traditional society and thus offered a multifaceted portrayal of womanhood. Literary epic had, after all, a political subtext. It either presented or alluded to women who could aid in the advancement of this subtext or neglected them altogether. Athough oral epic was used by nineteenth-century romantic nationalists to further their cause, it did not arise, as literary epic did, out of a need to advocate national and political convictions, but rather out of a need to relate the cherished stories in which the deep mythic convictions of the community were expressed. By objectifying femaleness in the literary epics that they consciously constructed, writers such as Njegoš, Mažuranić, Rakovski, and Alecsandri were able to embrace maleness—the essence of nationhood, liberation, and power.

NOTES

1. Reference will be made to Serbian, Croatian, Bulgarian, and Romanian literatures.

2. Balkan Christian epic is a term used to distinguish the oral epic sung by Christian singers as opposed to Balkan Muslim singers, the most well-known being those who performed in Bosnia-Hercegovina and who served as many of the informants for Milman Parry and Albert Lord in the earlier twentieth century. In a broader sense, it also refers to the oral epic traditions among the Bulgarians and Romanians. The singing of oral epic, though it continued well into the twentieth century, has gradually been in decline, especially since the Communist period. Epic singers were still performing in Yugoslavia and Bulgaria (to some extent) during the 1960s. In Romania, where the singing of epic is perpetuated by professional traditional Rom (Gypsy) musicians, the genre still continues (though it is definitely dying out). On South Slavic oral epic, see Lord 1960; see also Coote 1978. On Romanian oral epic, see Beissinger 1991.

3. See Young 1976, 28ff.

4. For a discussion of gender issues and Herder, see Fox 1993.

5. See Anderson 1991, 205.

6. See Abrahams 1993, 10, 11.

7. See Koljević 1991, 5.

8. See Lord 1974, 105. On the influence of Vuk's collections of Serbian oral epic on the developing concepts of nation, see Koljević 1980.

9. See Karadžić 1969. For an English translation of some of these poems, see Pennington and Levi 1984.

10. Examples of the "jailor's daughter" type of female helper from the Vuk collection include Vuča's wife in "Marko Kraljević and General Vuča" (who, upon the hero Marko's request, takes "the keys of the dungeon" and releases three heroes, after which she and Marko negotiate and come to terms). In "Marko Kraljević and the Daughter of the Arab King," the jailor's daughter "opened the door of the dungeon" and led Marko forth, thereby releasing him. In this and all future references to the Vuk collection, see Karadžić. See also the jailor's daughter figures in "The Story of Bamsi Beyrek of the Grey Horse" from the Turkic epic *The Book of Dede Korkut* in Lewis 1974.

11. The innkeeper's wife is Janka the alewife in "Marko Kraljević and Djemo the Mountaineer" (Vuk collection). For the Romanian tradition, see the innkeeper's wife in "Doicin the Sick Man" in Amzulescu 1964.

12. Examples from the Vuk collection include Jerina as a counselor to the hero in "The Wedding of Djuro of Smederevo." Clever maidens also figure in "The Wedding of Marko Kraljević" and "A Maiden Outwits Marko."

13. Examples of the wise and noble mother abound in the oral epics of the Balkans (in the Vuk collection, for example, see "Marko Kraljević and Mina of Kostur"). This stereotypical image of the mother fits what might be called the Balkan (or larger Slavic) "cult of the mother."

14. In "The Wedding of King Vukašin" (Vuk collection), for example, a hero's faithful sister (Jevrosima) is juxtaposed to his wife as he offers his sister in marriage to the king.

15. In the Vuk collection, the most striking example is found in "Marko Kraljević and Mina of Kostur." The *Odyssey* is, of course, the most obvious and well-known version of this narrative.

16. Vidosava in "The Wedding of King Vukašin" (Vuk collection) is such a traitorous wife. "Banović Strahinja" also includes a treacherous wife, but she is spared.

17. "Marko Kraljević and the Arab" (Vuk collection) presents an unconventional woman—the sultan's daughter, who refuses to marry "the Arab," thus challenging her father's orders. Another example is found in Rosanda (who is both beautiful and proud) in "The Sister of Leka Kapetan." When Rosanda is told to choose a husband from among a group of heroes, she rejects the idea of marriage to any of the men assembled and debunks her brother. Her spirit does not go unpunished; she is cruelly injured.

18. See, for example, the powerful "vila" who prohibits singing in her territory in "Marko Kraljević and the Vila" (Vuk collection).

19. See "Marko Kraljević Abolishes the Marriage Tax" (Vuk collection).

20. See Nedić 1965, 362.

21. See Njegoš 1986.

22. See Njegoš's *Srpsko ogledalo* (*The Serbian mirror*), first published in 1845. It includes Njegoš's own collections of oral poetry in Montenegro, as well as poems written in the "style" of oral epic. For more on the various stages of Njegoš's poetic output, see "The Transitional Text" in Lord 1995 and chapter 6 in Lord 1960.

23. One of the themes of the poem concerns the warring factions within the state, which could not unite in the face of the Turkish threat. For a fuller discussion of this, see Koljević 1991.

24. "Slava" refers to the traditional celebration and feast among Serbian Orthodox families for their patron saint.

25. See Nedić 1965. For a discussion of Vuk and his reflections on history, see also Milošević-Djordjević 1994.

26. Njegoš wrote two other literary epics in which women play no roles at all: *Luča mikrokozma* (The ray of the microcosm, 1845) and *Lažni Car Šćepan Mali* (The false czar Stephen the Small, 1851).

27. See Njegoš 1986, ll. 1913–1919.

28. For a discussion of lament in Montenegro, as well as collected examples, see Džaković 1962.

29. See Njegoš 1986, ll. 2203–2204.

30. See Turner 1967, 93ff.

31. See Njegoš 1986, ll. 2216–2217.

32. Speaking of men and social structure in Montenegro, Bette Denich has noted that "property and power are vested exclusively in men" (1974, 244). Furthermore, as for male activity and the external world, "since all public arenas have the poten-

tiality for combat, they are designated as male. The household's external environment is exclusively a male domain" (p. 248).

33. See Njegoš 1986, l. 108.
34. Ibid., l. 91.
35. Ibid., l. 1265.
36. Ibid., ll. 1718–1719.
37. See Denich 1974, 246, 251.
38. See Njegoš 1986, ll. 393–394. Kosovo here refers to the decisive battle in 1389, which heralded the beginning of centuries of Ottoman rule.
39. Njegoš 1986, ll. 706–707.
40. Ibid., ll. 979–981. Mihailovich's translation of "vijenac" in the first verse of this excerpt as "garland" obscures its connection to the noun in the title of the epic ("vijenac," otherwise rendered as "wreath").
41. See Sapiro 1993, 40.
42. On the use of rape in the civil war in the former Yugoslavia see Olujić 1995; see also Feldman 1993.
43. See Denich 1974, 250.
44. See Enloe 1989, 62.
45. For an English translation, see Mažuranić 1969a.
46. See Koljević 1991.
47. See Matejić 1981, 104.
48. See Verdery 1996, 73.
49. Ibid.
50. See Sapiro 1993, 38.
51. See Enloe 1989, 42.

WORKS CITED

Abrahams, Roger.
  1993.   "Phantoms of Romantic Nationalism in Folkloristics." *Journal of American Folklore* 106: 3–37.
Alecsandri, Vasile.
  1974.   "Dumbrava roșie: Poem istoric." In *Poezii alese,* 184–208. Bucharest: Editura Minerva.
Amzulescu, Alexandru I., ed.
  1964.   *Balade populare romînești,* Vol. 2. Bucharest: Editura pentru literatură.
Anderson, Benedict.
  1991.   *Imagined Communities: Reflections on the Origins and Spread of Nationalism.* London: Verso.
Beissinger, Margaret H.
  1991.   *The Art of the Lăutar: The Epic Tradition of Romania.* New York: Garland Publishing.
Coote, Mary P.
  1978.   "Serbocroatian Heroic Songs." In *Heroic Epic and Saga: An Introduction to the World's Great Folk Epics,* edited by Felix J. Oinas, 257–285. Bloomington: Indiana University Press.

Denich, Bette.
1974. · "Sex and Power in the Balkans." In *Women, Culture, and Society,* edited by Michelle A. Rosaldo and Louise Lamphere, 243–262. Stanford: Stanford University Press.

Džaković, Vukoman.
1962. *Narodne tužbalice: Antologija.* Belgrade: Narodna Knjiga.

Enloe, Cynthia.
1989. *Bananas, Beaches, and Bases.* London: Pandora.

Feldman, Lada Čale, Ines Prica, and Reana Senjković.
1993. *Fear, Death, and Resistance—An Ethnology of War: Croatia 1991–1992.* Zagreb: Matrix Croatica X-Press.

Fox, Jennifer.
1993. "The Creator Gods: Romantic Nationalism and the En-genderment of Women in Folklore." In *Feminist Theory and the Study of Folklore,* edited by Susan T. Hollis, Linda Pershing, and M. Jane Young, 29–40. Urbana: University of Illinois Press.

Karadžić, Vuk Stefanović.
1969. *Srpske narodne pjesme.* Vol. 2, *U kojoj su pjesme junačke najstarije.* Belgrade: Nolit.

Koljević, Svetozar.
1991. "Folk Traditions in Serbo-Croatian Literary Culture." *Oral Tradition* 6: 3–18.
1980. *The Epic in the Making.* Oxford: Clarendon Press.

Lewis, Geoffrey, ed. and trans.
1974. *The Book of Dede Korkut.* Middlesex, England: Penguin Books.

Lord, Albert B.
1995. *The Singer Resumes the Tale.* Edited by Mary Louise Lord. Ithaca, N.Y.: Cornell University Press.
1974. "The Nineteenth-Century Revival of National Literatures: Karadžić, Njegoš, Radičević, the Illyrians, and Prešeren." *Review of National Literatures: The Multinational Literature of Yugoslavia* 5: 101–111.
1960. *The Singer of Tales.* Cambridge, Mass.: Harvard University Press.

Matejić, Mateja.
1981. *A Bibliographical Handbook of Bulgarian Authors.* Edited by Karen L. Black. Columbus, Ohio: Slavica Publishers.

Mažuranić, Ivan.
1969a. "Smail-Aga Čengić's Death." Translated by Charles A. Ward. *The Bridge* 17: 5–34.
1969b. *Smrt Smail-Age Čengića.* Edited by Milorad Zivančević. Belgrade: Srpska književna zadruga.

Milošević-Djordjević, Nada.
1994. "The Poetics of the Serbian Oral Tradition of Vuk Karadžić." In *The Uses of Tradition,* edited by Michael Branch and Celia Hawkesworth, 51–67. London: School of Slavonic and East European Studies.

Nedić, Vladan, ed.
1965. *Sabrana dela Vuka Karadžića: Pjesnarica 1814–1815.* Vol. 1. Belgrade: Prosveta.

Njegoš, Petar Petrović.
  1986.   *Gorski vijenac* (The mountain wreath). Edited and translated by Vasa
             D. Mihailovich. Irvine, Calif.: C. Schlacks, Jr.
  1967.   *Srpsko ogledalo.* Edited by Radosav Bošković and Vido Latković. Bel-
             grade: Prosveta.
  1851.   *Lažni Car Šćepan Mali.* Trieste: Andrija Stojković.
  1845.   *Luča mikrokozma.* Belgrade: Knjažestva srbskoga knjigopečatnja.
Olujić, Maria.
  1995.   "Women, Rape, and War: The Continued Trauma of Refugees and
             Displaced Persons in Croatia." *The Anthropology of East Europe Review*
             13 (Spring): 40–43.
Pennington, Anne, and Peter Levi, trans.
  1984.   *Marko the Prince: Serbo-Croat Heroic Songs.* New York: St. Martin's Press.
Rakovski, Georgi.
  1952.   "Gorski pŭtnik." In *Arhiv na G. S. Rakovski,* edited by M. Arnaudov, 1:
             133–163. Sofia: Bŭlgarska akademija na naukite.
Sapiro, Virginia.
  1993.   "Engendering Cultural Differences." In *The Rising Tide of Cultural Plu-
             ralism,* edited by Crawford Young, 36–54. Madison: University of Wis-
             consin Press.
Turner, Victor W.
  1967.   *The Forest of Symbols: Aspects of Ndembu Ritual.* Ithaca, N.Y.: Cornell Uni-
             versity Press.
Verdery, Katherine.
  1996.   "From Parent-State to Family Patriarchs: Gender and Nation in Con-
             temporary Eastern Europe." In *What Was Socialism, and What Comes
             Next?* 61–82. Princeton: Princeton University Press.
Young, Crawford.
  1976.   *The Politics of Cultural Pluralism.* Madison: University of Wisconsin
             Press.

SECTION TWO

· · ·

Epic and Authority

5

Metamorphosis, Metaphor, and Allegory in Latin Epic

Philip Hardie

Philip Hardie focuses here on the ways in which metamorphosis can serve as a guide to understanding the differing kinds of figurative meanings in epic narrative. Using Ovid's *Metamorphoses* as his principal example, Hardie explores the relation between metaphor, personification, allegory, and metamorphosis and argues that metamorphoses in Ovid's epic create an unresolved and shifting exchange of literal and figurative meanings that precludes identifying heroic essence as something stable or certain. Hardie shows that earlier epic, including especially Virgil's *Aeneid* and Homer's *Odyssey*, can be profitably reinterpreted through this Ovidian lens, and concludes that both the *Odyssey* and the *Aeneid*, poems central to traditional definitions of epic, demonstrate the impossibility of pinning down the epic man as the philosophical personification of a perfected humanity. In this essay Hardie shows the centrality of Ovid for an understanding of epic and indeed suggests that as a strong rereading of its literary precursors, Ovid's poem makes visible hidden aspects of the figurative and moral construction of earlier epics.

My essay seeks to make a contribution to the history of the allegorical epic through consideration of Ovid's *Metamorphoses,* a poem undoubtedly central to the tradition of Latin hexameter narrative, but whose status both as an epic and as an allegorical poem is problematic. Metamorphosis as a narrative device is often supposed to be inimical to the deepest concerns of the epic genre, not least because by denying death as the end of human stories it is held to destroy the moral seriousness of epic. I shall press the generic issue in two directions: first by exploring the connection between the moral allegoresis of epic and metamorphosis, and second by asking why it might be that a poem of transformations should mark so significant a point in the development of personification allegory in ancient epic. Common to both parts of my discussion will be the emergence of a tension between the allegorical drive to fix and define univocal categories, and the text's resistance to interpretative fixation. If I wanted to give these two opposing tendencies allegorical labels, I could call the first Atlantean, after the giant immobilized through petrifaction, and the second Protean, after the shape-shifter who performs a whole series of transformations in order to elude those who would pin him down.[1]

METAMORPHOSIS AND ALLEGORY: THE LINGUISTIC TURN

The linguistic turn has become perhaps the favorite strategy of modern critics of the *Metamorphoses:* Ovid is read as the poet who (re)fashions the world in his own words. Already in *Amores* 1.3 the poet's promise to give immortality through his poetic language—indeed to give existence itself— to his as yet scarcely fashioned, and pointedly unnamed, mistress is set on a par with the poetic immortality of women famous for their involvement in tales of metamorphosis (Io, Leda, Europa). The linguistic screw is given another turn if we attend to the language itself of metamorphosis, as Frederick Ahl has done, with reference mostly to the lexicon of phonetic and morphological change, by way of prolegomenon to his discussion of Ovid's use of punning techniques. For Ahl the fundamental equivocation is that between the two senses of Latin *elementa,* "(physical) elements" and "letters of the alphabet." He claims: "As the material elements shift, transforming man into animals or plants, so the elements in words are shuffled to reproduce the changes in language itself."[2] But the correspondence between the physical and the verbal may also be traced at the semantic level, of metaphor, simile, allegory, and other transferred uses of language, including translation and allusion. In Latin the lexicon of physical metamorphosis largely overlaps with the lexicon of linguistic change. *Tra(ns)latio,* "metaphor," is a verbal noun from *transfero,* which may mean "transform" (and also our "translate," for which Latin also uses *uerto,* literally "turn, change"). Cicero uses *immutatio,* "a changing," as a label to cover the Greek terms *tropos,* "trope" (literally "a turning"), and *schema,* "figure" (*Brutus* 69). Quintilian defines a figure (*figura,* literally "shape") as "arte aliqua nouata forma dicendi," "a shape of speaking altered by some art" (*Institutio Oratoria* 9.1.14). Cicero's definition of allegory as "continuae tralationes," "continuous metaphors" (*Orator* 94) might equally be translated as "successive transformations," a precise description of the *Metamorphoses.*

These lexical equivalences open up the possibility for metamorphosis to function as a narrative figuration of figurative language, as linguistic events are projected into the world "out there" as narrative fictions. The connection between metamorphosis and allegory may be envisaged as an axis between the literal and the figurative. Allegoresis (interpretative allegorization) takes a fragment of literal narrative and converts it into a figurative discourse. Thus the literal narrative of Circe's transformation of human beings into animals is converted into a tale about the figurative bestialization of the human soul through enslavement to the passions. A theory of allegory based on authorial intention will hold that originally a figure of speech has been literalized as the basis for a narrative. Paul de Man puts it thus: "From the recognition of language as trope, one is led to the telling of a tale. . . . The temporal deployment of an initial complication, of a structural knot, indicates the close . . . relationship between trope and narrative, between knot and plot. If the referent of a narrative is indeed the tropological structure of its discourse, then the narrative will be the attempt to account for this fact."[3] Just so, a tale of metamorphosis may take a figurative expression and spin from it a narrative fleshed out with persons, times, and places, converting the paradigmatic structure of metaphor into a syntagmatic chain. Many critics have pointed to Ovid's habit of generating tales of transformation out of a literalization of the figurative;[4] not so many, incidentally, have observed that this is one of the ways in which Ovid continues what had become a central feature of the Latin hexameter tradition through the structures of analogy and image deployed by Lucretius and Virgil.

This is a road open to two-way traffic: Jonathan Bate has noted recently, speaking of the bestial in Lear, that "Shakespeare converts literal Ovidian metamorphoses into metaphors."[5] This shuttling between the verbal and the physical also characterizes Ovid's dealings with similes, figurative adjustments in perception or conceptualization that often anticipate physical transformations—what Leonard Barkan has called "protometamorphoses."[6] For example, Apollo's dying boyfriend Hyacinthus is compared (in a traditional kind of simile with a specific Virgilian model) to a series of drooping flower heads; a few lines later the boy's blood is (literally) transformed into the flower that bears his name.[7] Given the loss of most of the poetry of metamorphosis prior to Ovid, in particular that of the Hellenistic period, it is difficult to say how specifically Ovidian this constant allegorical matching of shape to narrative is, but the surviving fragments of the earlier tradition hint at a fair degree of innovation, or at least systematization, on Ovid's part.[8]

ANTHROPOLOGIES HOMERIC, VIRGILIAN, AND OVIDIAN

The first regular tale of human metamorphosis in Ovid's poem is that of Lycaon (1.209–243). As the first such narrative, it invites us to accord it a paradigmatic status within the poem as a whole.[9] Here the metaphor "Man is a wolf"[10] becomes the occasion for a story about a savage man whose figurative wolflikeness finally turns him into a wolf. At the end of the tale Ovid makes very heavy use of what W. S. Anderson has labeled the "vocabulary of continuity" to ram home the underlying points of similarity between the man Lycaon and a wolf.[11] This handling of a terminal metamorphosis "fixes" the meaning of the story, "making sense" of a bizarre and "primitive" tale.

Or so it would seem. Denis Feeney has properly located Ovid's Lycaon narrative within a centuries-long tradition of defining the human with reference to the categories of god and beast that lie on either side.[12] In the Homeric epics the boundaries between the three categories are tested, but ultimately no transgression is possible. Jasper Griffin and others stress that Homer imposes a kind of censorship on the marvelous and the magical, including the motif of metamorphosis. "The Homeric world is characterized by a rigid distinction between the main categories of existence that offers little room for compromise or ambiguity."[13] The other obstinately remains the other. The Homeric anthropology emphasizes the inescapably fixed limits of human nature through a systematic set of contrasts with the not-human, on the one side the divine and on the other the bestial. And it is true that the chief examples in the *Odyssey* of a transformative power that transgresses these limits, the figures of Proteus and of Circe, are encountered by the human heroes in places on the margins of the human world.

Allegorization, especially moral allegorization, threatens this rigid classificatory system, to the extent that the gods and the animal (and inanimate) world become figures of, and thus collapse into, the category "human." Take two versions of the Circe story: in the Homeric narrative the companions of Odysseus have the heads, voice, bristles, and appearance of pigs, but "their *nous* remained fast in its place as before" (*Odyssey* 10.240). Here, despite the radical physical alteration of the companions, we are left in no doubt as to what is human and what is not. On the other hand, the moral allegorization, which extracts from the Circe story a lesson about the dehumanizing effects of the passions, inverts the Homeric narrative by replacing a tale of physical transformation and mental fixity with a tale of mental alteration within an unaltered body, and as a result the limits of the human are put in question. But in a developed system of philosophical allegorization this propensity to alteration away from the "human" is controlled by an a priori, philosophically defined conception of what humans are (or should be). That is to say that the nonhuman is still exploited as a source of figures with which to prescribe the properly human.

In Ovid the figuration of the human is not controlled by an overriding philosophical authority. Many readers have of course been tempted to find just such an authority in the Speech of Pythagoras in the last book of the *Metamorphoses,* and to see in it a ground for the interpretation of the rest of the poem. But the Pythagorean version of change simply will not fit as a model for the greater part of the mythological metamorphoses. A lack of fit, incongruity, it must be said, is the usual impression of the modern reader when confronted with ancient philosophizing allegorizations of myth, and it is tempting to see an implicit comment to this effect on the part of Ovid himself. That is, the Speech of Pythagoras presents itself as a mimicry of allegorizing commentary, a kind of explanatory appendix, but we are duped if we take this autoallegorizing seriously. The apparently authoritative speech of the philosopher Pythagoras provides no external *point d'appui* outside the poem from which finally to make sense of the poem but is itself inescapably implicated in the fictional web of the *Metamorphoses.* It succumbs to what we might now regard as a postmodernist failure of metanarrative and ends up as simply another set of stories about change.[14]

Any attempt to press Lycaon's wolf-metamorphosis into the service of a definitive statement of what humans are must confront the previous history of the race of which Lycaon is a member.[15] Lycaon is the kind of *human* that he is because he is one of the race of humans born of the blood of the Giants blasted by Jupiter (1.156–162). His attempt on the life of Jupiter is another version of the Giants' assault on Olympus; the two stories could even be thought of as allegorical retellings of each other. To become human, the Giants have already undergone a metamorphosis: "Lest no . . . memorials should remain ["ne . . . monimenta manerent"][16] of her offspring, Earth changed their blood into the shape of men" (159–160). Here the vocabulary of permanence[17] will be betrayed (in typically Ovidian fashion) by the further transformation to which the Giants' son Lycaon, himself one of those "enduring monuments," will be subject. It is becoming very difficult to say what exactly *does* constitute the human.

As we read on in the *Metamorphoses,* the external policing of the boundaries of the human becomes harder to maintain. The open-ended set of analogies between the human and the nonhuman that is constructed by the relentless series of transformations in the poem has the effect of emptying the category of the "human" of any substantial content that is not "other." Recently Ernst Schmidt has argued that the metaphorical function of metamorphosis is the key to the understanding of the *Metamorphoses,* which he describes as "the narrative aetiology of the world as a store of metaphors for mankind."[18] But this is a world where the literal meaning of humanity has become impossible to define, where "this isthmus of a middle state" has been washed over by the seas on either side, and the only enduring image for the human might be that Renaissance favorite, Proteus.[19] Schmidt is reduced to an empty essentialism that cannot proceed beyond talking about "man in his unalterable human nature."[20]

Schmidt also understands the *Metamorphoses'* focus on humanity to function as a generic marker of the work's status as epic, but an epic that represents "instead of the one epic hero, man of all times."[21] The *Odyssey's* first word, *andra,* "man," marks that poem's concern with the nature of the one man, Odysseus, who to some extent may be exemplary for all people. That man is immediately qualified in the first line of the *Odyssey* as *polutropos,* literally "of many turns."[22] The versatility of Odysseus, his ability to turn to all manner of shifts, to disguise himself physically or verbally, is of course the quality through which he successfully returns to his centered place in human society on Ithaca. Odysseus's changeability is at the service of the hero's own mastery, of himself and of others, and is not the sign of an essential instability. "The *polutropos* . . . is always master of himself and is only unstable in appearance."[23] Quite the opposite is true of the many turnings of Ovidian humans, very few of whom have any control of their own mutability.

I tentatively raise the possibility that viewed from a generic perspective, this feature of the Ovidian "epic" world may be understood as a reflex of the distance between Homeric and Virgilian anthropologies. The *Aeneid*, like the *Odyssey*, has the central agenda of defining a "man" ("arma uirumque"), a task given greater urgency by the contemporary relevance of this act of definition (what and who is Augustus, what should the Romans be?). Instead of a *polutropos* hero, we find a man forced to "tot uoluere casus," "roll around so many misfortunes" (*Aeneid* 1.9); the incongruity of an active verb applied to the passive sufferings of a hero rolled around by misfortunes was resolved by the ancient commentators through its classification as an example of hypallage.[24] The career of Aeneas in the *Aeneid* is one that begins and ends with doubts about the stable identity of others, and possibly of the hero himself, as an examination of the language of transformation at the beginning and end of Aeneas's story will demonstrate. In book 2 Aeneas is confronted with the dream-vision of a Hector strangely altered from expectation: "Alas, the look of him! How much changed from that Hector," "ei mihi, qualis erat, quantum mutatus ab illo" (2.274). At the end of the poem, after a scene of literal metamorphosis as the Fury sent down by Jupiter transforms herself into a screech owl in order to terrify Turnus, Turnus is first taunted by Aeneas with the impossibility of escape through shape-shifting (12.891–893): "Turn yourself into all shapes [uerte omnis tete in facies], summon up all your nerve and skill; pray to fly aloft on wings to the stars, or to bury yourself close in the hollow earth."[25] But if this taunt has the immediate effect of reinscribing the Virgilian narrative within the limits of reality and mortality that prevail in the Homeric poems, Turnus then undergoes a different kind of metamorphosis through diminution of powers, changing into a shadow of his former self, unrecognizable to himself. The approach of death seems to undermine his self-definition, rather than confirm it in the Homeric manner: "As he ran and came on he did not recognize himself" (903); "Our tongue is powerless, our body's familiar strength does not hold up, and not a sound or word will come" (911–912, in the dream-simile).[26] "Quantum mutatus ab illo!" Both passages are used by Ovid in tales of metamorphosis: with the description of Hector compare, for example, *Metamorphoses* 6.273: "Alas how very different was this Niobe from that Niobe of before" ("heu quantum haec Niobe Niobe distabat ab illa"), a figurative mutation, consequent on the mother's loss of her sons, that will soon be followed by the literal metamorphosis through petrifaction of the living woman. Valerius Flaccus, humorously perhaps, reuses Aeneas's anguished exclamation in the context of a narration of the story of Io in *Argonautica* 4.398: "How she looked, how much changed from the heifer that she was to begin with!" ("qualis et a prima quantum mutata iuuenca!").[27] Less humorously Virgil places the image of Io transformed into a cow on the shield of Turnus at the end of *Aeneid* 7 (789–792), a book very much under the sign of Circe, whose palace and weird animals are described right at the beginning. The "great matter" of the shield device of the transformed Io is an emblem of the dehumanization suffered already in *Aeneid* 7 by the Italians, and by Turnus in particular. If Turnus's realization near the end of book 12 that Jupiter is his enemy appears to mark his emergence from his "Circean" bestialization, Ovid spots the irony in Turnus's final loss of identity through transformation into a dream-shadow of himself when he picks up a detail of that passage in his own account of Io at *Metamorphoses* 1.647: "And, if only the words would come, she would have asked for help, and told him her name and misfortune" ("et, si modo uerba sequantur, / oret opem nomenque suum casusque loquatur").[28]

But Io's metamorphosis is one of those in which a personal, human consciousness does survive change into animal shape (see above). The *Aeneid*'s parting irony lies in the implicit contrast between the defeated enemy Turnus, sadly changed but in a sense also restored to humanity, and the conquering hero, for Aeneas's identity—and humanity—are subjected to an intensive destabilization at the end of the poem, as the violence of his emotions sways him between identifications with a fulminating Jupiter, a storm wind, an avenging Fury, and a reincarnation of the dead Pallas.[29] This scene of alienation, as has often been noted, presents the strongest contrast with the scenes of reintegration within the society of living humans that conclude the two Homeric epics. If then the world of the *Metamorphoses* is one in which it is impossible to identify and stabilize the centrally and inalienably human, can we understand this as a commentary on—even an implied allegorization of—a Virgilian anthropology?

PERSONIFICATION ALLEGORY

The *Metamorphoses* are not in fact usually accorded an important place in the history of the allegorical epic, save in one important respect: Ovid's development of personification allegory. What intrinsic relationship might there be between metamorphosis and personification? Joseph Solodow comments well on one of the connections, seeing in the univalent and abstracted nature of the personification "brilliant examples of the general striving towards clarity", which for him is the defining feature of Ovidian metamorphosis, as a making visible, plain and clear, of essences. "The figure of Hunger displays the same clarity as does Lycaon after his metamorphosis. Essence lies on the surface. Though in one it is the end of a process whereas in the other it is a given, the result is the same."[30] There is a paradox in this affinity between personification and metamorphosis, for a personification seems to represent the *unchanging* essence of some abstraction; and this paradox Solodow resolves thus: "Metamorphosis . . . is . . . a change which preserves, an alteration which maintains identity, a change of form by which content becomes represented in form." Thus for Solodow metamorphosis is to be understood as primarily a process of abstraction. The difference between metamorphosis and personification might appear to be that the abstraction involved in metamorphosis usually results in theriomorphic representation rather than anthropomorphic *personification*. Yet of the four major personifications in the *Metamorphoses*, Envy (*Invidia*, 2.760–782) and Hunger (*Fames*, 8.799–808) are persons of a distinctly dehumanized and desocialized character. Fame's (*Fama*, 12.39–63) shape and personality are left very indistinct, but she is the immediate descendant of a very inhuman Virgilian personification. Only Sleep (*Somnus*, 10.592–645) might unproblematically be described as a sleeping human being. The active personifications in his house, however, are the artificers of dreams: Morpheus, Icelos, and Phantasos, "persons" who between them are responsible for the whole gamut of mutable forms, human, animal, and inanimate, that populate the stage of the *Metamorphoses*.

But if metamorphosis considered in its aspects of abstraction and fixation tends to coincide with personification, conversely personification betrays an inherent shiftiness. The "givenness," as Solodow would have it, of a personification is in fact bound up in process. In the first place a personification may be regarded as the product of a process of metamorphosis, the changing of a linguistic abstraction into a concrete person. As Georgia Nugent puts it in her study of Prudentius's *Psychomachia*, "Personification allegory performs yet another substitution, in fact, an inversion: allegory attempts to *turn* the word back into an object, to reify it. This is a fraudulent turn, or *trope*, which is inherent in the making of allegories."[31] Personification is a particularly visible example of the deceptive and transformative power of words, the ability of words to construct a reality and impose it on the "real world." And this, as we have seen, is as fair a description as any of what is going on throughout the *Metamorphoses*.[32] Personifications may also be the *de facto* end product of that kind of allegorical interpretation whereby a person, human or divine, possessed of a highish degree of mimetic reality is transformed into a figure for a virtue or mental attribute: Athene is changed into wisdom, or *polutropos* Odysseus, the versatile and manifold human hero, is turned into the monolithic paragon of philosophical virtue.

The personification thus appears in the disguise of *im*mutability, a mask concealing the processes of metamorphosis that brings it into being. Further, when a personification is put to work in a narrative, her (or his) actions are radically transformative: the personification has the power to *change* "real" human actors into versions of herself. Ovid's Erysichthon is the type of this kind of transformation. He steps into the narrative as a stagy villain, but nevertheless an epic actor of full human status; once Hunger has got at him he is turned into a demonic eating machine, not surprisingly, since Hunger has "breathed *herself* into him" (*Metamorphoses* 8.819).[33] While it may be strictly true that "metamorphosis into an abstraction is not something that ever happens in Ovid"[34] in the way that in Spenser Malbecco is transformed into an abstraction with the *name* Gealosie, Erysichthon is well described by Harold Skulsky as a "victim . . . refined into an abstraction."[35]

The two Ovidian personifications whose direct action on human characters is narrated, Envy and Hunger, are both closely related to the Virgilian Fury, Allecto, by origin a fully mythological being, but one who has almost been sublimed into a personification. Feeney writes of her: "She is a creature who *embodies* [my emphasis] and revels in all manner of evil. . . . She need not necessarily have been so. Euripides' Lyssa is an interesting case of a divine agent of madness who remains rational, emancipated from her characteristic effect. Allecto, on the other hand, *is* her essence." After thus virtually defining Allecto as a personification of madness, Feeney goes on to note that "above all, Virgil stresses how variable and multiple she is: "tot sese uertit in ora," "She turns herself into so many shapes."[36] For Feeney this variety is the occasion for a discussion of the variety of Allecto's modes of action within the narrative. This is a perceptive move, but it obscures what I think is another important point about Allecto's multiformity and changeability, namely, the close connection with her status as a personification. Her primary mode of action is indeed to transform her victims into versions of herself.

Virgil's narratives of the approach of Allecto to her victims, most clearly in the case of her assault on Turnus, establish a transformative pattern followed by Ovid and Statius. The personification approaches the human, often initially in a disguise (another kind of transformation) that is then cast aside; she then infects or inspires her victim, the crucial point of metamorphosis, simplified by Ovid, followed by Statius, into expressions of the kind "She breathes herself into the man." The effects of the personification then find two forms of expression: first in the use of abstract nouns and verbs referring to the passion or emotion of which the personification is an abstraction, and second in a simile or similes, a "purely" linguistic kind of transformation.[37] The narrative action of the personification has the effect of triggering a hallucinatory explosion of figurative language, for in the personification resides the essence of language's power to reshape the world in its own image.

FAMA

The one Ovidian personification taken directly from the *Aeneid* is Fame, *Fama.* In the *Metamorphoses* she appears appropriately at the beginning of book 12 at the point where Ovid sets out to rework the subject matter of the Homeric epics themselves (12.39–63).[38] She is the personification of Homeric *epos* (but also the spirit presiding over Ovid's own retelling of the Homeric epics). In the *Aeneid* Fame is the most developed example of a personification allegory. She is introduced as a negative force, an evil (*malum*), a female demon spawned by an angry Mother Earth to oppose the dispensation of the masculine ruler of Olympus; yet curiously she also insists on being read as a figure for the male poet's own propagation of words.[39] As chthonic source of disruption she has strong affinities with Allecto; there is also a marked parallelism between the representation of Fama and that of the Jovian double of Allecto, the Dira whom Jupiter dispatches at the end of book 12 in order to effect a closure within the human narrative.[40] These connections form part of a wider pattern of association within the *Aeneid,* and in later Latin epic, between *fama,* female rumor-mongering, and lament, madness, and infernal demons.[41] And like Allecto, Fama is a distorter and a shape-shifter, whose twistings and perversions have the effect of transforming the human narrative. For a personification she is notably inhuman; the genealogy that makes of her a sister of the giants Coeus and Enceladus might incline us to visualize her as an anthropomorphic monster, but she is then represented as a far less humanoid *monstrum,* with a multiplicity of wings, eyes, tongues, mouths, and ears, and in her nocturnal flight and rooftop perching she turns into a kind of bird.

Fama is a linguistic construction of the linguistic slipperiness that has infected the story of Dido at this point. Jon Whitman, in his excellent discussion of Fama, observes that she appears at a "moment of moral and linguistic breakdown,"[42] immediately after Dido's attempt to impose her own reading on events: "She calls it a wedding, with this name she disguises her fault" (*Aeneid* 4.172).[43] But Fama may also be read in a larger context as a figure for the fictional powers of the epic poet himself: Fama herself is self-reflexively caught up in the chain of *fama,* "as they relate," "ut perhibent" (4.179).[44] Furthermore the whole Dido and Aeneas story, a meeting that could never have taken place, is notably a fiction of epic *fama.*

The intervention of Fama in *Aeneid* 4 is the beginning of a narrative structure, which interrupts the primary action of the Dido and Aeneas story and which continues at 198–221 with the African prince Iarbas's transmission, through prayer, of the human rumors about Dido and Aeneas up to the divine level of Jupiter, an upward motion reversed when Jupiter sends down *his* conveyor of words, Mercury, as winged messenger-god, the Jovian double of the chthonic Fama, to order Aeneas to leave Carthage. Mercury breaks his downward journey to alight on the weird mount Atlas (246–258). Elsewhere I have analyzed this sequence with reference to the trope of hyperbole (in generic terms, the "greatness" of epic).[45] I now wish to shift *my* ground and consider it in the light of the trope of allegory. And allegory, it will appear, is inseparable from metamorphosis.

Right at the beginning hyperbole and metamorphosis are united in the allegorical image of Fama's expansive power: "Small at first through timidity, but she soon raises herself into the sky" (4.176). This is a kind of metamorphosis recognized by Ovid (*Metamorphoses* 15.434, Pythagoras on the city

of Rome): "Through growth she changes her shape." Pythagoras's authority for this statement is none other than Fama herself: "Even today rumor
[*fama*] has it that a Trojan city, Rome, is rising" (431–433).[46] But quantita-
tive change, hyperbolic exaggeration, is not the only effect of Virgil's Fama.
She is also responsible for the qualitative change involved in distortion and
misrepresentation: "as persistent in fictions and distortions as she is the messenger of truth" (4.188). This echo of the Hesiodic Muses' claim "We know
how to speak many falsehoods like true things, and we know how to utter
true things, when we wish" (*Theogony* 27–28) is usually referred to the power
of the epic poet to create fictions.[47] But the "fictional/true" opposition also
structures the practice of allegory: Jesper Svenbro analyzes the interpretative practice of Theagenes, the first recorded allegorizer of Homer, in terms
of a transposition of the Hesiodic distinction between truths and lies from
the social conditions of poetic discourse to the interior of the discourse,
where it becomes the binary opposition between surface sense, the "lies",
and the deep allegorical sense, the truth.[48] Fama's account of the winter of
luxury in Carthage tells the story in another way, but *her* form of "all-egory,"
"other-saying," perverts the expected distribution of truth and falsehood.[49]
Her version of the story moralizes, with a tendency to reduce the complex
human situation to the abstractions of *luxus* and *cupido* (*Aeneid* 4.193–194);
it is like a prevalent moralizing interpretation of the Phaeacian court in the
Odyssey, on which Dido's court is modeled, as a figure for decadent luxury
and hedonism, an "Epicurean" voluptuarism.[50] One might think also of that
reductive moralization of the real-life history of Cleopatra and Antony, a clear
example of "allegorizing" to ideological ends. Iarbas's account to Jupiter of
what is going on (206ff.) repeats this "allegorical" version of "reality" but then
adds another layer of allegory when he calls Aeneas a Paris (215).[51] The Epicurean color of the moralizing interpretation of the Phaeacians seems to
tinge Iarbas's own rebuke to Jupiter at 208–210: "Do we shudder for nothing when you hurl your bolts? Are they blind, those flames in the clouds that
fill our minds with terror, and is it empty rumblings that they stir up [inania
murmura miscent]?" This materialist view of the thunderbolt would transform Jupiter and the other gods into nothing more than the "empty report,"
inanis fama (or *Fama*), the words with which Iarbas concludes his complaint
(218).[52] At this point the literal reality of the epic narrative is in danger of
drifting before the winds that lead to allegorization. The primary narrator
lays his hand on the tiller to guide us back to a very present and very epic
(and Ennian) Jupiter "the all-powerful heard," "audiit omnipotens" (4.220).[53]
    The initial expansion and subsequent upward progress of Fama thus gen-
erate a series of competing interpretations of the epic action and of the cosmic order of epic. Jupiter's authoritarian intervention, through his straight-
speaking messenger Mercury, aims at reimposing an Olympian order on the
narrative and its meanings. This is the context for the description of the

strange figure of Atlas, the man-mountain on whom Mercury alights on his downward flight. The mountain is the product of a metamorphosis, but change in the past is now memorialized in an image of eternity: mountains are proverbially the most enduring of monuments. This terminal metamorphosis contrasts with the indefinitely proliferating, Protean, metamorphoses of the giantess Fama. Atlas within the *Aeneid* is also a figure for the origins of epic, for at the end of the first book we learned that he had been the teacher of the exemplary bard Iopas (1.740–741). We might say then that the source of epic tradition has been set in stone. Moreover, this terminal metamorphosis is of the kind that does not alter the subject's previous shape: Atlas still has a head, shoulders, chin, and beard.[54] The petrified Atlas remains in some sense the same. However, as we advance through *Aeneid* 4 we will find that he may also be read allegorically, but in the manner of that kind of philosophizing allegory that attempts authoritatively to fix meaning: the picture of the ever-during Atlas foreshadows the famous simile later in book 4 that compares Aeneas unmoved in the face of Dido's pleas to an oak weather-beaten but fast-rooted on a mountaintop (4.441–446), an image of Aeneas in his ideal role as the impassive Stoic hero, unchangeable in his inner self while outside only tears are "rolled over," "mens immota manet, lacrimae uoluuntur inanes" (449).[55] This heroic role corresponds to the philosophizing abstraction of Odysseus into a figure of the wise man.[56] But, as we have seen, the events of the poem will finally demonstrate the impossibility of pinning down the epic man as the philosophical personification of a perfected humanity.

NOTES

1. For discussion of the wider implications of this tension for the history of epic, see Hardie 1993, chap. 1 ("Closure and Continuation").

2. Ahl 1985, 53; see also pp. 10, 25 (grammatical and physical senses of *forma*), 51, 182 ("SIMILitudo, like FORMa, is a grammatical as well as an artistic term in Latin").

3. de Man 1978, 23–24.

4. E.g., Haege 1976, 90–93.

5. Bate 1993, 191; see also p. 236.

6. Barkan 1986, 20–21. See Haege 1976, 85–93, for a systematic treatment of the literalization of simile and metaphor. This was also the subject of a paper presented by James C. Abbott at the 1993 meeting of the American Philological Association.

7. *Metamorphoses* 10.190–216.

8. A metaphorical approach to the earlier myths of metamorphosis is the fundamental tactic in Forbes Irving's excellent study (1990); see, for example, p. 60, on animal metamorphoses: "These stories play upon traditional ideas and metaphors about the relation between men and animals to present an imaginative and mythi-

cal expression of familiar human concerns." There is a danger that the accidents of survival may tempt an overly Ovidian exegesis of the earlier material: cf. p. 62: "The imagination Ovid shows in his treatment of the stories can often be a help in interpreting them. He will point to or bring to the surface underlying themes which *must* have been a part of the appeal of the earlier versions of the story *even if* they were never made explicit" (my emphasis). Forbes Irving refers to an early essay on the linguistic, metaphorical, and allegorical rationalization of metamorphosis by J. G. L. Mellman (*Commentatio de causis et auctoribus narrationum de mutatis formis* [Leipzig, 1786]), which I have not seen.

9. The programmatic function is noted by Solodow 1988, 175–176. The qualifications of Anderson 1989 do not affect the points I wish to make.

10. This happens to be the example used by Black (1962) to illustrate his "interaction view" of metaphor. For a semiproverbial example in Latin, see Plautus *Asinaria* 495: "A man is a wolf to a man, not a man, when he doesn't know what kind of a person he is."

11. Anderson 1963, 4–5.

12. Feeney 1991, 194–195.

13. Forbes Irving 1990, 10; for an important earlier essay, see Rahn 1953; 1954.

14. For similar reflections, see Feeney 1991, 205 (drawing on Solodow 1988, 162–168).

15. On the plurality of myths of human origin, see Bömer 1969, 70; Feeney 1991, 194.

16. The jingle "monimenta manerent" may play with a Varronian etymology of "memoria a manendo ut manimoria potest esse dicta" (*De Lingua Latina* 6.49).

17. See Solodow 1988, 186–188.

18. Schmidt 1991, 60.

19. Giamatti 1968; see pp. 437–443 on the Renaissance image of man as Proteus. Ovid uses Proteus as a figure for the infinitely versatile lover at *Ars* 1.759–762.

20. Schmidt 1991, 45. Schmidt embraces the paradox at p. 39: "Er ist unveränderlich, nicht trotz, sondern wegen der Verwandlung. Das ist nur scheinbar paradox." It will be clear that I do not agree with Haege's observation in the conclusion to his sharp discussion of the place of man in nature in the *Metamorphoses* that in Ovid "zwischen dem Wesen des Menschen und dem des Tieres klafft ein Abgrund" (Haege 1976, 191). In a number of cases (Io, Callisto, Actaeon: see Haege, pp. 109–115) Ovid does narrate a transformation of the Homeric Circe type, contrasting the continuity of the prior human consciousness within a strange animal body (see Frécaut 1985, 115–143), but these cases cannot claim a privileged place within the Ovidian anthropology.

21. Schmidt 1991, 77.

22. The specific meaning in the Homeric context has been much debated (see Heubeck et al. 1988, 69).

23. Murnaghan 1987, 10 n. 12, drawing on the classic studies in Detienne and Vernant 1978. But note that Pucci (1987, 149) attempts to deconstruct the integrity of the Odyssean hero, in terms of a "decentered polytropy," drifting into "panotropy." *Polutropos* is used only twice in the *Odyssey*, the second time at 10.330, in Circe's address, where it could be read ironically of Circe's failure to "turn" Odysseus.

24. Servius ad loc.: "*Voluere casus,* that is to say, to be rolled by misfortunes [*casibus uolui*]. And it is the figure of hypallage, which occurs whenever words are to be understood by the opposite." For a contrasting combination in Virgil of permanency and "rolling around," cf. *Georgics* 2.294–295: "*immota manet* multosque nepotes, / multa uirum uoluens durando saecula uincit" (see also note 55 below).

25. See Hardie 1992, 70, with 77 n. 16. On the relation between bird metamorphoses and the escape prayers of Greek tragedy, see Forbes Irving 1990, 106–107: e.g., Euripides *Hippolytus* 1290ff.: "Why don't you hide under the ground in shame or change your life for that of a bird to escape this misery?"

26. The Homeric model is *Iliad* 16.805–806 (Patroclus after Apollo loosens his breastplate): "Confusion seized his mind, his splendid limbs were loosed under him, and he stood there astounded"; Turnus's more complete forgetfulness of (at least his physical) self is achieved through simultaneous imitation of Lucretius 6.1213–1214 (the effects of plague): "And some were even gripped by a total obliviousness, so that they could not even recognize themselves ("atque etiam quosdam capere obliuia rerum / cunctarum, neque se possent cognoscere ut ipsi," which in turn imitates a detail in Thucydides' description of the Athenian plague (2.49.8), a biological catastrophe that entailed the collapse of personal and social identity in the city: "Others on first recovering suffered total loss of memory and did not recognize themselves and their relative"). Note the further "turns" within Turnus at *Aeneid* 914–915: "tum pectore sensus / *uertuntur* uarii."

27. The humor lies partly in the fact that *mutata* is used of a figurative change within a story of literal transformation.

28. The Io episode displays further traces of the last scenes of the *Aeneid:* Inachus repeats the lament of Juturna for Turnus (cf. *Metamorphoses* 1.661–663 with *Aeneid* 12.879–881); Io's persecution by Juno with an Erinys (1.725) is ended through the reconciliation of Jupiter and Juno, a plotline strongly reminiscent of the last half of the *Aeneid;* cf. perhaps also the bulls simile of Turnus and Aeneas at *Aeneid* 12.715–722. Another echo of Turnus's predicament is found in that of Actaeon at 3.198ff.: "fugit Autonoeius ["of the same mind", a speaking matronymic] heros / et se tam celerem cursu miratur in ipso / ut uero uultus et cornua uidit in unda, / 'me miserum!' dicturus erat: uox nulla secuta est; / ingemuit: uox illa fuit, lacrimaeque per ora / non sua fluxerunt; mens tantum pristina mansit." The Ovidian imitation sensitizes the reader to the connection between the hunted deer simile of Turnus at *Aeneid* 12.749–755) and the stag of Silvia at 7.483–502, a beast that has undergone a kind of reverse metamorphosis into an almost human creature (and which is alluded to at *Metamorphoses* 3.240).

29. See Hardie 1993, 34, 40. Note in general that the imperial ideology of the apotheosis of the dead ruler, to which Virgil subscribes as epic poet, also destroys the absolute boundary in the Homeric world picture between human hero and god; on the Ovidian handling of this boundary, see Feeney 1991, 203–205.

30. Solodow 1988, 197–198. Cf. Barkan 1986, 66 (quoted by Feeney 1991, 190): "For all its emphasis upon the blurring of clear categories, metamorphosis is as much concerned with reduction and fixity as with variability and complexity." Similar points had already been made by Albrecht (1961, 179), following Dörrie (1959).

31. Nugent 1985, 30. But Nugent's claim (p. 92) that "the first allegorical work

can be seen as a surprisingly sophisticated meditation on some of the conceptual problems which the allegorical genre itself entails" is to overlook the amount of work that has already been done by Ovid and Statius.

32. Cf. Nugent 1985, 54–55, on the deception (*fraus*) of Avaritia: "This transformation has been accomplished explicitly on the linguistic level, by a change in *naming* [my emphasis]." Cf. also Feeney 1991, 383, on the *fraus* practised by Statius's Virtus, who also puts on a disguise, in a kind of metamorphosis.

33. This trick with reflexive pronouns is an Ovidian favorite, one of the wordplays that force our attention to the duplicities of personification and other kinds of allegory: see Frécaut 1972, 32, 36.

34. Burrow 1988, 155.

35. Skulsky 1981, 35–36.

36. Feeney 1991, 163.

37. I illustrate the points from Virgil's Allecto and Turnus episode, Ovid's Hunger and Erisychthon episode, and Statius's Virtue and Menoeceus episode. For disguise, see *Aeneid* 7.415–419; *Thebais* 10.639–649; for reflexive pronouns, see *Metamorphoses* 8.819: "seque uiro inspirat"; *Thebais* 10.673: "seseque in corde reliquit"; for abstract nouns, see *Aeneid* 7.461–462: "amor ferri, scelerati insania belli, ira"; *Metamorphoses* 8.828: "ardor edendi" (semipersonified with *furit*); 845: "dira fames" (where *dira* hints at the Virgilian model for the personification of Fames in the Dira Allecto); *Thebais* 10.677: "leti . . . amorem." For similes, see *Aeneid* 7.462–466 (boiling cauldron); *Metamorphoses* 8.835–839 (insatiable sea and fire, the latter undergoing personification into a voracious "eater"); *Thebais* 10.674–675 (Menoeceus inspired by Virtue like a cypress struck by lightning; the tree is personified, a process reinforced by allusion to the Ovidian metamorphosis of the boy Cyparissus into the cypress tree: with 10.677 ["letique inuasit amorem"] cf. *Metamorphoses* 10.132 ["uelle mori statuit"]). Wofford 1992, 136–137, points to the "allegorical force" of the Virgilian Allecto, and to the "figurative density" of the narrative of her action.

38. See Zumwalt 1977.

39. Feeney 1991, 186–187. In Callimachean terms the epic poet is a Jovian thunderer (see note 40).

40. Fama is a kind of chthonic version of Jupiter's thunderbolt, borne by Earth in answer to Jupiter's blasting of her other gigantic children. In line 148, "ira . . . deorum" can be taken as either an objective genitive (her anger against the gods) or a subjective genitive (the anger of the gods, whose manifestation aroused earth to produce Fama): the grammatical ambiguity mirrors Earth's parodic doubling of Jupiter's activity. Furthermore *Aeneid* 4.175 alludes to a Lucretian description of the thunderbolt at 6.340–342; and Fama "inflames" at 4.197. Terrorist tactics are common to Jupiter (12.851–2) and Fama (4.187). Ovid comments on the association of the two at *Metamorphoses* 12.49–52 (the description of Fama): "the mutterings of a low voice, like the noise that comes from the waves of the sea, if you listen at a distance, or like the sound produced by the last rolls of thunder when Jupiter has made the black clouds rattle." This is the literary-historical background to Valerius Flaccus's statement of the hostility of Jupiter to Fama at *Argonautica* 2.117–122.

41. Fama and Furies: "illam Terra parens *ira* inritata *deorum*" (*Aeneid* 4.178) hints at the etymology of *Dira* from *dei ira*, "anger of god." At Valerius Flaccus *Argonautica*

2.115ff. Venus's use of Fama is modeled on Juno's use of Allecto: at 128 note Venus's Fury-like power to "*uertere*domos," "(over)turn households" (*Aeneid* 7.336: "odiis uersare domos"), and her adoption of a disguise (like Statius's Virtus) to approach the Lemnian women.

42. Whitman 1987, 53.

43. Whitman (1987) also puts his finger on the way in which Fama comments on a quality of metamorphosis at the heart of the *Aeneid*: "Unlike Homer's brief figure of social discord, the rhetorical flight of Virgil's "Fama" is a comment on the stylistic and conceptual, as well as emotional, dilemmas of the poem. In a world *turning inside out and outside in*, it is necessary to find some conceptual category to encompass the action" (p. 53; my emphasis); "Virgil's world is a world in radical transition, always threatening to slip into incomprehensibility"(p. 55).

44. Feeney 1991, 187.

45. Hardie 1986, 273–279.

46. Is it accidental that (purely grammatically) there is an ambiguity about the reference of *haec* in line 434, either to *Roma* or *fama*? The epic, annalistic history of Rome is notably one of boundless extent arising out of the most small-scale origins: Fama is thus a peculiarly apt figure for an epic about Rome.

47. See Feeney 1991, 248, on Ovidian Fama: "plasticity of tradition and variable nature of poetic truth." The *Theogony* is the first allegorical poem of antiquity; could "falsehoods like the truth" be understood of the procedures of personification allegory employed by Hesiod?

48. Svenbro, 1976, 133–134.

49. Virgil's own narrative, however, also licenses a reading of Fama's distortions as merely a selective retelling of the tale; for *luxus,* cf. *Aeneid* 1.637: "at domus interior regali splendida luxu"; "turpique cupidine captos" at line 194 is partly the story told at the end of 1.673–674: "quocirca *capere* ante dolis et cingere flamma / reginam meditor" (Venus addressing her son Cupido).

50. [Heraclitus] *Homeric Allegories* 79.2: "Epicurus, the Phaeacian philosopher."

51. His speech is itself caught within the *fama* that is the narrative of the *Aeneid* (204: *dicitur*), as Feeney notes (1991, 187).

52. On the convergence of Jupiter and Fama see note 40 above.

53. And by this act of hearing Jupiter inserts himself in the chain of *fama*; as mythological actors they operate on the same stage of reality (or unreality): with lines 220–221 ("[Jupiter] turned his eyes to the city of the queen," "oculosque ad moenia torsit / regia") cf. line 196 ("[Fama] turned her course to King Iarbas," "ad regem cursus detorquet Iarban."

54. For examples of "Gestaltgleichheit" in Ovidian metamorphosis, see Haege 1976, 103–106. At *Metamorphoses* 4.657ff. Atlas in fact undergoes a more thoroughgoing metamorphosis, as his beard and hair change into (*abeunt*) woods, etc. Ovid also makes Atlas undergo a change in size (see Haege, pp. 172–173: "Gross-klein"; Acis is the only other example of a change from small to big in the *Metamorphoses*) analogous to that of Fama: "tum partes altus in omnes / creuit in immensum" (660–661).

55. This line alludes to a passage in an earlier work (*Georgics* 2.294–295,quoted in note 24 above) describing an oak tree, which cries out to be taken as a figure for the permanence of the Roman state (so Kraggerud 1963, 44 n. 106). In turn "mens

immota manet" is the model for Ovid *Metamorphoses* 2.485: "mens antiqua manet" ("the mind [of the metamorphosed Callisto] remained as it was before"); I readily confess that my "metamorphic"reading of the *Aeneid* is not (and cannot now be) innocent of the Ovidian reception of the earlier text. The Ovidian imitation prompts yet further rereadings of both Virgilian passages: at *Aeneid* 4.449 "mens immota manet" could be understood of the survival of Aeneas's mind despite his figurative metamorphosis (into the tree, into Mount Atlas), and at *Georgics* 2.294 "immota manet" of the tree becomes questionable in the light of the linguistic violence inflicted on it: of *uoluens* (literally "rolling them by") R. F. Thomas comments: "The thought is bold, as 'the tree is said to *do* that which it *sees done*'" (a figure related to the hypallage in *uoluere* at *Aeneid* 1.9; see note 24 above); and on the lines 296–297 Thomas remarks: "The personification is intense, as the tree almost takes on the appearance of an Atlas":Thomas is referring to *Aeneid* 8.137, but there is an obvious connection to the Atlas of *Aeneid* 4. A pretty versatile tree!

56. Here I would correct Greene 1970, 83 and 84: "The great shaggy ice-bound figure sustaining the sky is an *exemplum* of heroic self-denial, of austere exposure to the elements for the sake of the world community. Atlas embodies the qualities which Aeneas has temporarily forgotten"; "This cloak and the idle sword, studded ostentatiously with jasper, point the contrast with Atlas' huge battered head." Greene fails to note the echo of Atlas in the "storm-tossed oak" Aeneas.

WORKS CITED

Abbott, James C.
    1993.   "The Problem of Metaphor in Ovid's *Metamorphoses*." Paper presented at the annual meeting of the American Philological Association, Washington, D.C., 29 December 1993.
Ahl, Frederick.
    1985.   *Metaformations: Soundplay and Wordplay in Ovid and Other Classical Poets*. Ithaca, N.Y.: Cornell University Press.
Albrecht, M. von.
    1961.   "Die Verwandlung bei E. T. A. Hoffmann und Ovid." *Antike und Abendland* 10: 161–180.
Anderson, W. S.
    1989.   "Lycaon: Ovid's Deceptive Paradigm in *Metamorphoses* 1." *Illinois Classical Studies* 14: 91–101.
    1963.   "Multiple Changes in the *Metamorphoses*." *Transactions of the American Philological Association*. 94:1–27.
Barkan, Leonard.
    1986.   *The Gods Made Flesh: Metamorphosis and the Pursuit of Paganism*. New Haven: Yale University Press.
Bate, Jonathan.
    1993.   *Shakespeare and Ovid*. Oxford: Clarendon Press.
Black, Max.
    1962.   *Models and Metaphors: Studies in Language and Philosophy*. Ithaca, N.Y.: Cornell University Press.

Bömer, Franz.
1969.   *P. Ovidius Naso, Metamorphosen, Buch I–III*. Heidelberg: C. Winter.
Burrow, C.
1988.   "Metamorphoses in *The Faerie Queene*." In *Ovid Renewed*, edited by Charles Martindale, 99–119. Cambridge: Cambridge University Press.
de Man, Paul.
1978.   "The Epistemology of Metaphor." *Critical Inquiry* 5.1: 13–30.
Detienne, Marcel, and Jean-Pierre Vernant.
1978.   *Cunning Intelligence in Greek Culture and Society*. Translated by Janet Lloyd. Hassocks, Sussex: Harvester Press.
Dörrie, H.
1959.   "Wandel und Dauer: Ovids *Metamorphosen* und Poseidonios' Lehre von der Substanz." *Altsprachliche Unterricht* 4:95–116.
Feeney, Denis.
1991.   *The Gods in Epic*. Oxford: Clarendon Press.
Forbes Irving, Paul M. C.
1990.   *Metamorphosis in Greek Myths*. Oxford: Clarendon Press.
Frécaut, Jean Marc.
1985.   "Un thème particulier dans les *Métamorphoses* d'Ovide." In *Journées ovidiennes de Parménie*, edited by Jean Marc Frécaut and D. Porte. Brussels: Latomus, 115–143.
1972.   *L'esprit et l'humour chez Ovide*. Grenoble: Presses Universitaires de Grenoble.
Giamatti, A. Bartlett.
1968.   "Proteus Unbound: Some Versions of the Sea God in the Renaissance." In *The Disciplines of Criticism: Essays in Literary Theory, Interpretation, and History*, edited by P. Demetz, T. Greene, and L. Nelson. New Haven: Yale University Press, 437–475.
Greene, Thomas.
1963.   *The Descent from Heaven: A Study in Epic Continuity*. New Haven: Yale University Press.
Haege, H.
1976.   *Terminologie und Typologie des Verewandlungsvorgangs in den "Metamorphosen" Ovids*. Göppingen: n.p.
Hardie, Philip R.
1993.   *The Epic Successors of Virgil*. Cambridge: Cambridge University Press.
1992.   "Augustan Poets in the Mutability of Rome." In *Roman Poetry and Propaganda in the Age of Augustus*, edited by A. Powell. London: Bristol Classical Press, 59–82.
1986.   *Virgil's "Aeneid": Cosmos and Imperium*. Oxford: Clarendon Press.
Heubeck, Alfred, Stephanie West, and J. B. Hainsworth.
1988.   *A Commentary on Homer's "Odyssey."* Oxford: Clarendon Press.
Kraggerud, E.
1963.   *Aeneisstudien*. Oslo: n.p.
Murnaghan, Sheila.
1987.   *Disguise and Recognition in the Odyssey*. Princeton: Princeton University Press.

Nugent, S. Georgia.
1985.   *Allegory and Poetics: The Structure and Imagery of Prudentius's "Psychomachia."* Studien zur klassischen Philologie 14. Frankfurt am Main.
Pucci, Pietro.
1987.   *Odysseus Polutropos: Intertextual Readings in the "Odyssey" and the "Iliad."* Ithaca, N.Y.: Cornell University Press.
Rahn, H.
1954.   "Tier und Mensch in der homerischen Auffassung der Wirklichkeit." *Paideuma* 5.7/8: 431–480.
1953.   "Tier und Mensch in der homerischen Auffassung der Wirklichkeit." *Paideuma* 5.6: 277–297.
Schmidt, E. A.
1991.   *Ovids poetische Menschenwelt: Die "Metamorphosen" als Metapher und Symphonis.* Heidelberg: n.p.
Skulsky, Harold.
1981.   *Metamorphosis: The Mind in Exile.* Cambridge, Mass.: Harvard University Press.
Solodow, Joseph B.
1988.   *The World of Ovid's "Metamorphoses."* Chapel Hill: University of North Carolina Press.
Svenbro, Jesper.
1976.   *La parole et le marbre: Aux origines de la poétique grecque.* Lund: n.p.
Whitman, Jon.
1987.   *Allegory: The Dynamics of an Ancient and Medieval Technique.* Oxford: Clarendon Press.
Wofford, Susanne L.
1992.   *The Choice of Achilles: The Ideology of Figure in the Epic.* Stanford: Stanford University Press.
Zumwalt, N.
1977.   "Fama subversa: Theme and Structure in Ovid *Metamorphoses* 12." *California Studies in Classical Antiquity* 10.

6

• • •

Tasso's Trees

Epic and Local Culture

Jane Tylus

AlthoughVirgil's *Aeneid*—one of the two literary epics addressed in this essay—is known to most students of epic, Torquato Tasso's *Jerusalem Delivered*, written in 1579, is not as familiar to modern audiences. A product of Italy's Counter-Reformation of the mid-sixteenth century, Tasso is a testimony to the contradictions of that era. His ambitious epic poem about the First Crusade of 1099 is both a nostalgic return to a period when all of Christian Europe was united against a common enemy—Islam—and a demonstrably hollow attempt to make the contemporary Church and its imperial aspirations a new vehicle for unification. By focusing on an episode common to both the *Aeneid* and *Jerusalem Delivered*, that of the "bleeding tree," Tylus demonstrates that Virgil and Tasso reveal the tensions involved in generating universal agendas from local, cultic narratives, and her reading allows us to explore a dialectic that may be as crucial for traditions of oral epic as it is for written epic.

Even as he protested the annihilation of local cultures by the totalitarian regimes that flourished during his lifetime, T. S. Eliot was defining literature as an art form that in its most ideal manifestations escaped from vulgar provincialisms to embrace a universal poetics. Virgil and Dante in particular tend to be singled out in Eliot's writings of the 1930s and 1940s as the writers who best exemplified the kind of universality that Eliot so highly privileged. That both of these writers produced epics suggests the extent to which Eliot perceived literature's traditionally "highest" genre as one that left mundane, local concerns aside for the sublimely cosmopolitan.[1] It is no surprise that in his influential essay "Virgil and the Christian World," Eliot celebrates the Trojan hero's willingness to become a "fugitive from a ruined city and an obliterated society" and embrace the *imperium Romanum* that was his to bring into being.[2] For Eliot, who saw tradition as the great impersonal force into which poets' individual talents were subsumed, Aeneas's willingness to pursue his destiny is ultimately a figure for Virgil's decision to follow *his*, as he exchanged linguistic and cultural variety for "a language of the classics" that transcends local origins to speak to audiences of all places and all times.[3]

This essay will attempt not so much to counter Eliot's provocative and influential reading as to ask how epic itself has taken part in the splintering of literature into "high" and "low," if not always with the kind of confident assurance that Eliot's critique implies. Such splintering might best be approached by way of the definition of epic we have proposed in the introduction to this volume: epic tends to focus on deeds of significance to a community. How a community is defined, however, and what qualifies as "significant" are contested issues not only among contemporary scholars, but often within epic poetry itself. The tendency of much epic to employ, both implicitly and explicitly, the figure of analogy—masterfully epitomized in written epic by the ubiquitous simile—attests to a poetic sensibility anxious to include within its domain a unified and sympathetic audience. Homer's evocative similes comparing the shipwrecked Odysseus to a hungry wolf, the incomprehensible Trojans to squawking geese flying overhead, and the sounds of battle to a rushing waterfall functioned among other things to make a distant narrative more immediate, much as the analogies between the Moors and diabolical practices made Roland's exotic enemies more terrifying to a twelfth-century Norman audience. Complex patterns of analogy can thus be said to function as an ever-widening gyre within which a particular narrative is circulated and rendered relevant and familiar to a community that may be—as Homer's audiences clearly were—at some distance from an original story.

It can even be said that many poets of epic undertake to thematize precisely this journey toward significance. As in the *Aeneid*, epic frequently involves the plight faced by a hero who chooses or is forced to leave his home. His departure into and circulation in a world that transcends his immediate community become the very conditions for his own, and by extension, the poem's significance, a topos that involves any number of works from the *Odyssey* and the *Aeneid* to *Beowulf*, the *Chanson de Roland*, and *Paradise Lost*. But the creation of such significance for a larger community that the poem seeks to define and expand through analogy may have its costs, as the hero's departure from his home and, in many cases, his failure to return often suggest on an overtly thematic level. This is particularly the case when the aspirations of the epic poet coincide with the aspirations of a specific religious or political ideology (to which Eliot was acutely sensitive). The recent work of Gregory Nagy has been crucial for many reasons, and certainly not the least is the extent to which it has tied numerous heroes of the Greek *nostoi* (the stories of return) to particular localities where they were objects of cultic worship. As Nagy elaborates, the development of Homeric epic in archaic Greece submerged and synthesized "the diverse local traditions of each major city-state into a unified Panhellenic model."[4] In this process, the timeless Olympian gods become the (new), powerful deities from whom favors must be sought and from whom they are granted, whereas "the central heroes of th[e] epic tradition [no longer] have an overtly religious dimension in the narrative."[5] Even as the hero wanders far from home to gain a reputation and a name—the *kleos* sought by Achilles and Odysseus alike—he suffers a corresponding dwindling of his demonic powers, tied as they necessarily are to a particular place.

Writing in a period when epic had recently reappeared on the European horizion, the Italian poet Torquato Tasso turned to his own two most influential models in the genre and declared that "in writing [epic] poetry, [neither Virgil nor Homer] wished to narrate particulars, like the historian, but like the philosopher, to form universals ["gli universali"], whose truth is much more stable and certain."[6] Virgil (and the collectivity of poets we call Homer) would no doubt have found this latter-day account of their poetics baffling, much less correct. And yet in pinpointing the desire to "formare gli universali," Tasso both reveals something inherent in his *own* epic agenda during the years of the Counter-Reformation in which he was writing his massive *Gerusalemme liberata* and touches on something crucial in many other epics. This is the tension involved in producing a work that would be "Panhellenic," "Roman," or in Tasso's case, "Roman Catholic": one that transcended the contingencies and limitations of immediate communities and local cults in order to fashion universal audiences and heroes with universal reputations. For Virgil and Tasso in particular, this move also involves the conscious shaping of a universal culture, that of the fledgling Roman Empire or a Catholic empire attempting to recuperate its losses after the Reformation through overseas expansion. Yet both poems become the hallmark of an elite culture no longer rooted in local landscape but divorced from, even antagonistic to, the practices of local, popular culture.

This is a divorce on which both Virgil and Tasso consciously reflect. As Eliot noted, Virgil's poem is the first epic to make its hero a "truly displaced person," a hero who has no Troy to which he can return.[7] Tasso's poem elaborates the journey of its central character, Godefroi de Buillon, from his homeland in France to a new home, Jerusalem, in the course of the First Crusade. But in so thematizing what is seen as the necessary loss of an immediate homeland, the two poems also derail the very system of analogy by which epic poets traditionally seek to make their local stories accessible and significant to a wider audience. In Virgil, as will be seen, analogy threatens to become *only* a poetic figure rather than a magically expansive system linking a local hero to universal traditions. And with Tasso, analogy becomes ultimately suspect, as the resemblances that it generates come to imperil the work's ideological distinctions between Christian and Muslim, sacred and demonic. In both cases, the building blocks used to turn a "local" story into an epic are infected, on the one hand, by their potential impotence in the face of other forces, and, on the other hand, by their daunting uncontrollability.

One result of Tasso's and Virgil's labors is the kind of high literature that can easily be read apart from its local contexts and grasped from within the canon of "Literature" itself, the touchstones, to cite Eliot once again, that supposedly compose the cultural landscape of Europe. But even as both poems articulate for their respective eras a definition of epic as elite—as over against the lies and unpolished manner of Homer's poetry, in the case of the *Aeneid,* or the vulgarities and irreverence of Ariosto's *Orlando furioso,* in the case of the *Gerusalemme liberata*—they likewise call attention to the insufficiencies of that definition. As the following pages will recount, Virgil's and Tasso's shattering of the comforting systems of analogy provokes critical reflection on the process through which high literature is fashioned and forces us to question where, pace Eliot, epic's roots in fact reside.

. . .

Virgil's fifth Eclogue, the center and perhaps central poem in the Roman poet's slender collection of bucolic verse, features two shepherds whose lament for the death of their friend Daphnis becomes a celebration of his entrance into the realm of Olympian deities. Set within a calm, rustic landscape, the song is based on a consoling system of correspondences that attest to the vital and reassuring harmony between heaven and earth that the singer Menalcas alludes to at the end and Mopsus at the beginning: "vitis ut arboribus decori est, ut vitibus uvae,/ ut gregibus tauri, segetes ut pinguibus arvis,/ tu decus omne tuis" ("As the vine gives glory to its trees, as the grape to the vines, as the bull to the herd, as the corn to rich fields, you alone give glory to your people," *Eclogue* 5.32–34]).[8] Composed of short phrases linked by the quiet repetitiveness of "ut . . . ut" ("as . . . as") and the less frequent "qualis" ("as when," the Latin word that in Virgilian epic will typically launch an extended simile), this and other passages like it assume a vision of community in which human life echoes the order and predictability of agrarian life, and divinities in turn guarantee the fertility that allows the farming year to be an orderly one. Analogy thus serves to express the intimacy between the local community of which Menalcas and Mopsus are a part and the newly established cult of Daphnis, who despite his Olympian status takes special pride in attending to his own people's needs. Having become his community's attendant spirit, Daphnis has not so much died by the end of the poem as assumed a role that will ensure the future of the rustic populace. The eclogue as a whole thus defines for its readers the creation of a local and popular cult, the purpose of which, to quote Pierre Klossowki, "is to intercede with a deity in order to avert his anger, gain his assistance, or remind him of favors granted."[9]

It is precisely this vision of centeredness and intimacy between the human and divine that other eclogues in the collection challenge—eclogues written, like the fifth, in one of the bleakest periods of Roman history, the long decade of civil wars in the 30s that were precipitated by the assassination of Julius Caesar. In this light, *Eclogue* 5 constructs against all odds a magical vision of Roman community based on simple ritual and reverence for a stable past. And not surprisingly, the other eclogues threaten to destabilize the system of correspondences and control found at the book's center. *Eclogue* 1 in particular reveals how precarious this control is as it conveys the bleak reality of Italy's current political situation. The poem stages the melancholy confrontation between two very different protagonists, the happy, elderly Tityrus, recently freed by the triumvir Octavian after long years of slavery, and the despondent Meliboeus whose lands have been taken from him by the same Octavian, who wants to reward his soldiers for their fidelity. The space of local cult that served as the link to Olympian deities in *Eclogue* 5 thereby becomes a contested space in a manner prescient for Virgil's later epic. For the fortunate Tityrus, the local *cultus* has been radically *un*productive; he had to travel to Rome after his own sacrifices to local gods had gone unanswered. He had offered many a victim, he had turned to many gods while he labored usefully in his village. Only in the great city did the new, young *deus,* Octavian, become "the first to respond" to his request for freedom. For Meliboeus, however, the land from which he is banished held for him precisely the promise and productivity Tityrus claims he was denied, and he lovingly dwells on the "fontes sacri" he must leave behind.[10]

The disjunction that Meliboeus's and Tityrus's exchange belies is most explicit in Tityrus's bitter line that it is impossible to compare his rustic village to the great city in the way that one compares great things with small: "putavi/ stultus ego huic nostrae similem," he abruptly claims (*Eclogue* 1.19– 20). The *failure* of analogy that Tityrus's line implies suggests not so much a challenge to the local vision celebrated in *Eclogue* 5 as an inevitable incommensurability between the city with its great *deus* and the village with its minor ones. And yet such incommensurability by no means prevents the "urbem, quam dicunt Romam" ("the city they call Rome") from ruling over the distant village from which Meliboeus is exiled. At the end of the dialogue between the freed slave and the departing farmer, the "local" haunts that are praised and fondly remembered by Meliboeus in the form of "familiar streams and sacred springs" are gradually overset by an *umbra.* This is no longer the nurturing beech shade with which Meliboeus opened the poem or the cavernous shade beneath which Menalcas sings in *Eclogue* 5, but the long shadows falling from mountains whose heights return us to the "height" of Rome.[11] In Meliboeus's absence, the *fontes sacri* will fall victim to the *impius miles,* or cruel soldier. Tityrus's god is not Meliboeus's: "iste deus qui sit, da, Tityre, nobis"—"Who is your god?" Meliboeus asks after Tityrus's panegyric, with a possibly pejorative emphasis on the "iste."[12] And yet he is a god who has established control over Meliboeus's former farm.

If *Eclogue* 5 presents us with an agrarian community linked both to the harmonious patterns of the seasons and human labor and to the reassuring links between human and divine, *Eclogue* 1 traces a pattern of discomfitting propriations and expropriations, as a distant cult of a Roman leader is transported to a place of *fontes sacri*. This displacement of local rural deities by the urban *deus* whose reign extends over the vast Roman Empire is developed on a much broader scale in the *Aeneid*. The precursor to the exile Aeneas, who carries his *di penates* to a land that remains for much of the poem unknown, is a Meliboeus who had likewise been exiled to "shores unknown." Yet throughout the *Aeneid* Virgil goes to great efforts to suggest that the ruler for whom he was writing—no longer called Octavian but Augustus, recently proclaimed emperor of Rome when Virgil began the *Aeneid* in 27 B.C.—greatly respected a local *cultus* that long predated the arrival of his Trojan ancestors on Italy's shores.

Book 8, Aeneas's journey to Evander's kingdom, is one such example of the supposed reverence for the local in the imperial age. After finally arriving in Italy and being blessed by an image of *pater* Tiber and a white sow, Aeneas walks through the "thick underbrush" of the Capitoline Hill, where he observes the cavern called Pan's grotto, restored by Augustus as the Lupercal at the base of the Palatine. The Capitoline itself is said to be a place whose "dread sanctity had awed the trembling rustics" (*Aeneid* 8.349).[13] Even Aeneas and Evander (and by implication, present-day Romans) "shuddered at the woods and the rock" (8.349–350). Yet Evander, the Arcadian king who befriends Aeneas upon his arrival, points out that although the local god who inhabits "this grove, this hill" is unknown, the Arcadians believe that "they have looked on Jove himself . . . as he summoned the storm clouds" (8.352–354). On the one hand, Virgil's self-conscious allusions to the Arcadians who inhabited ancient Rome return him to the rural poetics of the *Eclogues*. On the other, in the context of *Aeneid* 8 itself, it is clear that *this* Arcadia is already in the process of yielding to the superior culture of future Romans. As the poem reminds us throughout, Saturn is the original god of Latium, having arrived there as an exile himself. That Jupiter should take prominence over his exiled father, Saturn, in the farmers' uncertain minds suggests the pattern of displacement that was at work in the First Eclogue. Rural inhabitants such as Tityrus and the simple Arcadians, that is, have chosen a cosmopolitan deity over a local one.

One must look to the *real* local *cultus* of Italy—that of the Latins, who maintain their fidelity to Saturn[14] —and to Aeneas's response to them in order to discover the true dynamics of apotheosis at work in Roman ideology. When finally landing in Italy after his many wanderings, Aeneas immediately prepares to build a city, following what may be called an innocent and even naive policy of diplomatic engagement. In each place he has landed, in fact, he has imagined the possibility for a peaceful coexistence of cultures that does not preclude the mingling of the *advena* (the newcomers) and the indigenous inhabitants. Again and again after leaving Troy, Aeneas arrives with his household gods in order to duplicate and to parallel in his own fashion what

he already finds. Thus he establishes a settlement in Crete, begins to build
a city that mimics Dido's Carthage, and eventually erects a city in Latium
near the town of Latinus. But these attempts to create a space for a new community alongside a prior one are continually met with cries of sacrilege that
suggest that two local cultures cannot exist together in peace. On Thrace,
Aeneas wounds the transformed Polydorus and must flee the "cursed land";
on the island of the Harpies, his men slaughter the Harpies' cattle and must
flee; in Carthage, Aeneas's liaison with Dido leads to his hasty abandonment
of the queen and her suicide. Once in Italy, Aeneas's son wounds the cherished stag of the Latin princess and thus helps to initiate the war between
Latins and Trojans that takes up the better part of the work's second half.
All of these incidents point not to the coexistence of local cults but to the
necessary *clashing* of local cultures that are not bound beneath a single law.[15]

It is, to be sure, coexistence that Aeneas and even the gods seem to desire, a coexistence that is often implied by the analogy of marriage. But with
its *failed* narrative of a marriage between two different leaders and two different communities, the Dido story that is so central for the *Aeneid*'s first half
has obvious implications for the second half of the poem, in which Aeneas
and King Latinus alike are continuously told that they can expect a peaceful and fruitful marriage of their peoples: one that will result, for Latinus
and his Italian deities, in a blazing apotheosis. In lines recalling the fifth
Eclogue, in which Daphnis moves from his rural community to the Olympian
heights, Latinus is told that marriage to the "externi" will "exalt his name to
the stars" ("nostrum / nomen in astra ferant," *Aeneid* 7.98–99). That Faunus
is the source of the oracle suggests that Faunus himself, grandson of Saturn
and father of Latinus, will also be so venerated, and the prophecy is indica-
tive of an assumed commensurability of what would seem to be two separate,
local cultures. Yet the last action of the poem takes place near a wild olive
tree long sacred to Faunus ("forte sacer Fauno," 12.766) from which the Trojans had "shorn the sacred stem" so that they might do battle, a violation
that calls attention to a more pervasive disrespect for ancient local custom
("nullo discrimine," 770). For in truth, the local *cultus* of Italia never possesses the kind of force it is prophesied as having. Rather, it is supplanted by
an Aeneas who requires a connection to the land on which that *cultus* is based
in order to become Italy's new ruler. Only through marriage to Lavinia, the
Latin princess and thus the descendant of ancient Saturn, can Aeneas be
bonded peacefully to this land. The child of this marriage, however, young
Silvius, does not figure in the genealogical chart of the deity who is apothe-
osized in the *Aeneid,* Julius Caesar. Nor is he an ancestor of the reigning deity of Virgil's own time, Augustus (who presides in book 8 over a glorious triumph in which Egypt's "monster gods" who parade, subdued and submissive,
before him, bear a stunning resemblance to the hybrid deities of Italy of
which we as readers have just learned: the bird-man Picus, the satyrlike

Faunus). The "local" line that Silvius represents, the *cultus* that reaches back to the Italian Faunus, Picus, and Saturn himself, is merely one line, the *failed* line of Saturn's rustic progeny.[16] It is Saturn's other line, the line that expelled him from power, that of Jupiter, Venus, Aeneas, Aeneas's Trojan son Iülus, and finally Julius Caesar, that will "triumph" over the Italians' local haunts. "Hither now turn your two eyes: behold this people, your own Romans," Anchises tells Aeneas in Hades. "Here is Caesar, and all Iülus's seed, destined to pass beneath the sky's mighty vault. This, this is he, whom you so often hear promised, Augustus Caesar, son of a god, who shall again set up the Golden Age amid the fields where Saturn once reigned" (6.788–794). Saturn is mentioned, to be sure, but only in the context of the *end* of his reign: "regnata . . . Saturno quondam." Jupiter rather than Saturn has absolute authority over Italia and the promises of Faunus's apotheosis through Lavinia's marriage are revealed to be deceptive at worst; at best, misleading.

Virgil thus articulates the demonstrable *need*, if not the unequivocal desire, for a single law, for a universalizing deity who will bring coherence and order to a disorderly empire composed of various popular and local cults. It is in this light that one might glance at an episode that is surely one of the eeriest in the *Aeneid*, Aeneas's confrontation with the mangled body of Polydorus. An episode that Virgil added to the considerable legacy of Aeneas at a rather late stage of his poem,[17] this event seems to represent Virgil's belated commentary on the role of *Eclogue 5*, with its comforting correspondences between loving cultivation of the land and reverence to one's local deities. Aeneas's landing on the isle of Thrace at the beginning of book 3, his first stopping place after fleeing Troy with a group of exiles, is celebrated with a ritual of thanksgiving for having arrived at what he imagines to be a permanent haven. But the ritual he begins to celebrate as he tears boughs from overhanging trees to prepare an altar is abruptly brought to a halt when the plant bleeds and unnaturally speaks. Aeneas only then learns of the horrible murder of a Trojan comrade who fell prey to a greedy king. In an eerily disembodied voice that emanates from the very plant Aeneas has torn, Polydorus recounts that the Thracian king killed him after he carried Troy's gold to Thrace for safekeeping, and begs Aeneas to put to rest his mangled body. Thanksgiving gives way to burial, safe haven retreats before a "terra scelerata" ("cursed land," 3.60), and Aeneas journeys tirelessly, along with the patient reader, for nine more books.

The meanings of this curious exchange and its long literary aftermath have been plumbed by numerous critics, not the least of whom was Sigmund Freud.[18] Freud's psychoanalytic treatment and the many studies it has influenced have largely omitted, however, the deeply religious overtones connected to the episode and ones that demonstrate why the passage serves as a powerful example of the tensions at work in moving from the local to the "universal." As he assembles the altar on which he will make his sacrifice, Aeneas declares his wish to name the land as his own. His first task after leaving Troy is to build a city that he calls "Aeneadae" ("moenia prima loco. . . . / Aeneadasque meo nomen de nomine fingo," 3.17–18). It is shortly after this declaration that the earth recoils, spewing forth black blood, filling the hero with horror ("A cold shudder shakes my limbs, and my chilled blood freezes with terror," 29–30). Naming an alien land after himself is something Aeneas will never try to do again in the course of the poem, and his reluctance or refusal to do so is instructive. Virgil wrote his poem in an age when Aeneas was enjoying a *cultus* of his own, both in the city of Lavinium, which he purportedly founded, and among elite Roman families eager to link themselves to Augustus.[19] The incident with Polydorus abruptly silences Aeneas's cultic aspirations, and Virgil pointedly resists referring to them later when in book 7 he shows us Aeneas surveying the land that would indeed become Lavinium. But the failure of Aeneas to name a land after himself is important in a more general way, insofar as it suggests that this father of a "universal" people will never be able to make the local land of Italy his own. Thrace, of course, is not Italy, and Aeneas must leave the place where he finds Polydorus's body if he is to be the father of the future Romans. But with its clash between Aeneas's intentions and the "terra scelerata," the episode is a harbinger of the reality that Aeneas will be forced to confront throughout the poem: one in which land and genealogy are continually divorced, as apparent from the unfulfilled prophecy spoken by Anchises in the underworld that the Trojans will link their universal gods to the woodland deities of Italy's countryside.[20]

Figuratively speaking, Aeneas is always a wanderer, exiled from the *terra* he plaintively evokes in *Aeneid* 12 before his final battle with the Italian Turnus. This is the same *terra* that will groan for Turnus's death—a Turnus who dies defending his own boundaries, his *cultus* and his bride. Indeed, as Turnus falls in battle, "up spring with a groan the Rutulians all; the whole hill reechoes round about, and far and near the wooded steeps send back the sound" (12.928–929). With these lines we see the final echoes of what Virgil evokes as the once-harmonious link between a leader, his people, and the land. The embodiment of the Latin past and its popular cults, Turnus *must* die so that Aeneas and the universal Jupiter can triumph: Jupiter, Turnus declares shortly before battling with Aeneas, has always been his sworn enemy ("'Tis the gods daunt me, and the enmity of Jove," 12.895) But even though the price Turnus must pay for his defense of Italia's local religion is the ultimate one of death, the price that Aeneas must pay for universality is high as well: his alienation from the consoling systems of correspondences mapped out by *Eclogue* 5 and alluded to before Turnus's death, and his demise as a hero of local cult. Aeneas is thereby free to become the "public property" of an entire people, as Karl Galinsky has usefully suggested.[21] But this freedom also attests to the failure of local culture in the world of empire, even as Augustus was trying to reclaim a local Italian *ethos* as a basis for his own legitimacy. The *Aeneid* can thereby be said to articulate an unresolvable tension between *fontes sacri*—the culture of Meliboeus of *Eclogue* 1 and the Latins of the *Aeneid*—and an imposed family of deities and the heroes who escort them to unfamiliar soil.

As we will see, the Polydorus episode returns vividly in Tasso's *Gerusalemme liberata,* a poem indebted to the *Aeneid* and one whose central character remains like Aeneas in permanent if chosen exile. This is a character who refuses to be engaged in the episode that recapitulates Aeneas's encounter with Polydorus, one in which landscape acquires a valence unprecedented in the history of epic: the forest of canto 13 into which countless Christian knights wander only to return, haunted by the speaking plant life that mimics Polydorus. Yet this landscape is the product of cultic projections tied not to a Christian piety centered, as so much late medieval piety was, in local practices revolving around saints' images, relics, and shrines but to a demonic ritual associated with the enemy's Islam. In a strategy hardly unique to the *Gerusalemme liberata,* the iconoclastic Muslims are ironically associated with an idolatrous, cultic religion that becomes the dark double of Catholicism itself—a Catholicism invested in various expressions of popular piety. These expressions vie in turn with the universalizing principles espoused by the Tridentine Council in the years immediately following the Reformation, and by a Tasso interested in imposing on the local history of the Crusades a universalizing dimension he associated with epic. If Virgil sought to make Aeneas and his poem the "public property" of the Roman people, Tasso likewise attempts to make his own epic and its central character, Godefroi or Goffredo, the public property of a Counter-Reformation Europe anxious to establish its hegemony not only over the Muslim and Protestant worlds but over a newly discovered America as well.

As Timothy Hampton has demonstrated, the *Liberata* attempts to escape from the particularities of history—the particularities not only of the First Crusade, but of a Reformation that is never far from Tasso's poem—into the realm of universal truths.[22] A reclaimed Jerusalem long seen as the geographical and symbolic center of the universe serves appropriately as the goal of a reunified Christendom, brought together in the opposition to a common enemy, Islam. But Tasso's Christians are themselves caught up in the kind of local and pietistic worship that the Church in Tasso's era was anxious to control, and the Muslim inhabitants of Jerusalem are at times depicted as uncannily similar to Christ. If the analogies that link the local to the universal are deceptive in the *Aeneid*—Aeneas cannot lay claim to any single local landscape in the poem, and the Italians fail to raise their deities to universal status—in the *Gerusalemme* the system of correspondences on which epic significance depends is at odds with the very Catholic and, as we will see, elite Counter-Reformation ideology that Tasso articulates. In the course of fashioning a universal epic program and audience, the poem forcibly wrests itself from the practice of the *vulgo:* the rustic sentiments of Virgil's fifth Eclogue and, more immediately, the dominant Italian legacy of a communal poetic found in Dante, Ariosto, and the popular genre of hagiography. With Tasso, epic and a universalizing Catholicism are severed from their origins in local cult and the local community of a Jerusalem that the Crusaders wrest from the Muslims—only, as the poem itself prophesies, to lose Jerusalem again less than a century later when the Muslims take it back.

·   ·   ·

In their first sighting of the poem's sacred center, Tasso's Crusaders memorably link the wounding of Christ on the cross with the staining of Jerusalem itself:

> Dunque ove tu, Signor, di mille rivi
> sanguinosi il terren lasciasti asperso,
> d'amaro pianto almen duo fonti vivi
> in sì acerba memoria oggi io non verso?
>
> (3.8)[23]

> Thus where you, Lord, have left the earth stained by a thousand rivers of your blood, shall I not at least pour forth two living fonts of bitter plaint for such a harsh memory?

The implicit connection between Christ's blood and the Crusaders' tears suggests that the warriors about to liberate the holy city will symbolically cleanse the earth where Christ was crucified, purging the crimes that the present Muslim inhabitants cannot extirpate themselves. Indeed, between the third canto, where this prayer appears, and the last one, when the Crusaders finally "liberate" Jerusalem from its Muslim usurpers (*usurpatori*), the warriors fall prey to a series of errors for which they must perform often elaborate penance. It is only in the poem's final moments that they appear capable of extirpating land that Christ's enemies, new and old, have contaminated. Curiously, however, the penultimate stanza of the poem evokes not an act of cleansing but an act of bloodshed that mirrors the Crusaders' earlier allusion to Christ's bleeding body:

> corre di tenda in tenda il sangue in rivi,
> e vi macchia le prede e vi corrompe
> gli ornamenti barbarici e le pompe.
>
> (20.143)

> Blood runs in rivers from tent to tent and stains the booties there and spoils their barbaric ornaments and their pomp.

The blood that "runs in rivers" is the blood not of Jerusalem's illustrious warriors but of defenceless *fuggitivi* (fugitives) whom Goffredo, the Christians' holy captain, has pursued to their stockade and killed ("segue il corso poi de' fuggitivi./ Fuggon quegli a i ripari, ed intervallo/ da la morte trovar non ponno quivi"; "He follows the path of the fugitives. They flee to their stockades, and here they find no interval from death"). The poem ends with the victorious Goffredo approaching the sacred shrine of Christ's tomb while still dressed in his own "sanguinoso manto," his bloody mantle stained, like the "barbaric ornaments," with the fugitives' blood.

The verbal echo remarks not only on a failed ritual of purgation—the "terra" is more bloodstained than ever before—but on a haunting parallel between the pagan fugitives and Christ, pursued and victimized by powerful enemies.[24] More suggestively, it links the Muslim fugitives and Christ with the land itself, a unification that seems to elude the victorious Christians who come to Jerusalem to reclaim what is supposedly their own. Worshipping at Christ's tomb in his "bloody mantle," a tomb that was liberated not for all time but only until the Muslims reconquered Jerusalem some ninety years later, Goffredo seems paradoxically alienated from Christ and the very land he has sought to recover, covered as he is with victims' blood.[25]

On the one hand, it could be argued that Goffredo's bloodthirsty pursuit of fugitives after the battle has already been won is simply in keeping with the character he has demonstrated throughout: that of a *capitano* who is supremely directed in his goal to recapture Jerusalem and render it safe for future pilgrims. In the opening stanzas of the *Liberata*, God "looks down" at the sluggish Christian army and notes that Goffredo alone "longs to drive the wicked pagans from the holy city" ("vide Goffredo che scacciar desia/ de la santa città gli empi pagani," 1.8). This unwavering devotion motivates God to make Goffredo the captain of the army, and Goffredo does not disappoint his maker. Unlike the other Christian warriors, Goffredo is unmoved by anything "earthly" that might distract him from his task, such as the pagan sorceress Armida, who has been sent into the camp to lure away its most renowned heroes, and whose charms Goffredo steadfastly resists. And, unlike most of the other warriors, Goffredo never leaves the poem's symbolic center, never straying from the Christian camp outside Jerusalem's walls. His only ventures outside the rigid constraints he has set for himself in fact involve two visions that suggest that he has been temporarily given the ability to witness "universal" truths. In the first vision Goffredo is translated to heaven, where he learns that God will bring back his "wandering companions" (14.18); in the second the archangel Michael "to other men unseen" invites Goffredo to "see all the mighty host of Heaven assembled" about Jerusalem as the Crusaders finally prepare to take the city (18.92, 96).

It is precisely of Goffredo that Tasso seems to speak when, in an "Allegoria" he appended to his poem when it was virtually complete, he notes that "allegory . . . [which deals with] passions and opinions and manners, not merely as they are in appearance, but principally in their intrinsic essence ["essere intrinseco"] . . . [can] only be understood fully by those who comprehend the nature of things ["solo da i conoscitori della natura delle cose possono essere a pieno comprese"].[26] Taken to heaven to learn of "la natura delle cose," beneficiary of a divine vision that purges for him the "thick cloud of humanity" (18.93) by which others are hampered, Goffredo is the poem's singular example of a figure to whom it is given to know the *essere intrinseco,* and thus to appreciate what the "Allegoria" posits as the absolute divide between good and evil. Goffredo embodies a universal moral standard that is impervious to the nuances and peculiarities of local usage, and hence resistant to any similarities between the "empi pagani" he longs to drive from Jerusalem and the Christians. Whereas the other warriors will assist an admittedly false Armida who doubles as a damsel in distress, Goffredo lets it be known that he "well understands that there is no believing anyone who denies belief to God" (4.65). He thereby refuses to read into the body of the Muslim any saving grace. His unwillingness to see in that body anything other than "belve in fèro ludo/ cinte d'intorno, o 'n sanguinosa caccia" ("beasts encircled all around in fierce game or bloody chase")[27] suggests that for him, the "local" is always to be read in universal, and hence allegorical, terms: pagans are bad, Christians are good, to recall a line from the earlier crusading poem, the *Chanson de Roland.* The belief in these absolutes allows Goffredo to take Jerusalem from Muslims who, as in the *Chanson de Roland,* are simply called heathens, and to slaughter the *fuggitivi* in the poem's penultimate stanza.

But the fact that the verbal echo at poem's end creates an analogy between *Christ's* bleeding body and those of the fugitives, and the fact that the imitation is articulated in a visually evocative language common to contemporary traditions of local and popular piety that existed outside the official domain of the church, must give one pause. This is a language that was becoming increasingly suspect with the Counter-Reformation's attempts to refute charges of Catholicism's ostensible paganism, for as such was it characterized by the Reformation's most ardent spokespeople.[28] The Church's distrust of the politics of local piety was manifest in its decisions during the final meetings of the Tridentine Council in the 1560s to centralize the process through which "local" heroes became saints and to interrogate more fully those who proclaimed themselves the recipients of divine or mystical visions.[29] Moreover, an earlier incarnational theology that had informed not only popular piety but early humanism was countered by an official insistence on the ineffability of the Christian mystery. What then is Tasso's relationship to a tradition that had thrived into the sixteenth century, one grounded in a radical Franciscanism that preached the doctrine of Christ's essential imitability, and one that the Church wanted to replace with something more in keeping with a hierarchial and doctrinaire Catholicism?

This is where we may turn to the figure in the poem who is most skillful at creating analogies disturbingly reminiscent of the very traditions that Tasso's Church had begun to question: the sorcerer Ismeno. Just as the closing stanzas threaten to elide the differences between the Muslim fugitives and Christ, Ismeno, a Muslim convert, exemplifies a threatening mixture of Islamic and Christian earlier in the poem ("Questi or Macone adora, e fu cristiano,/ ma i primi riti anco lasciar non pote;/ anzi sovente in uso empio e profano/ confonde le due leggi a sé mal note"; "He now adores Mahoun [Muhammad], and he was a Christian; but still he cannot abandon his first rituals but often mingles in impious and profane use the two laws that he ill understands," 2.2). The sorcerer's most daring feat, his enchantment of the forest outside Jerusalem, typifies this mingling of laws in such a way as to paralyze the most ardent of Crusaders. In order to stop the Christians from cutting down the trees to construct huge siege towers to attack the city's high walls, this figure who confounds the "due leggi" of Islam and Christianity enchants the forest by calling up spirits from Averno. In a terrifying scene, warrior after warrior enters the *selva* to try to chop down the trees and again and again fails, overcome by the illusion (*simulacro*) that there are living bodies incarnate in the wood.

No one is more affected by the enchantment than Tancredi, whose own attachment to the Muslims is apparent in his passion for the enemy warrior Clorinda. Shortly before Ismeno enchants the forest, Tancredi unknowingly and fatally wounds Clorinda in a midnight skirmish outside the walls of the city. In a dramatic scene of revelation, Clorinda removes her helmet, Tancredi recognizes the woman he fought, and she asks to be converted to Christianity at his hands. Still in mourning when the forest becomes enchanted, Tancredi offers to go into the wood and conquer the spell that has driven away other Christian warriors (one was frightened by the eerie noises issuing from the wood, another by the fire that seemed to destroy the trees and threaten his life). When Tancredi enters the wood, the forest in contrast is utterly serene. Yet when he draws his sword and strikes a tall cypress at its center, suddenly "manda fuor sangue la recisa scorza,/ e fa la terra intorno a sé vermiglia" ("the split bark issues blood and stains the earth about it crimson," 13.41). Horrified, Tancredi nonetheless proceeds to strike the cypress again, causing the wounded tree to speak—not in the voice of Virgil's Polydorus, but of Clorinda, who accuses Tancredi of killing her a second time: "Tu dal corpo che meco e per me visse,/ felice albergo, già mi discacciasti:/ perché il misero tronco, a cui m'affisse/ il mio duro destino, anco mi guasti?" ("From the body that was with me and through me lived, happy abode, you have already cast me forth; why do you yet lay waste the wretched trunk to which my harsh lot bound me?" 13.42). Paralyzed by the encounter, Tancredi returns to Goffredo and admits ignominious defeat, even as he continues to acknowledge the similarity between tree and flesh: "Stilla sangue de' tronchi ogni ferita,/ quasi di molle carne abbian persona" ("Any wound distills blood from the trunks, as if they had an embodiment of soft flesh," 13.49).

This passage is one of Tasso's most evocative allusions to Virgil, as Polydorus returns in the forest of Ismeno, a "terra scelerata" from which Tancredi, like Aeneas, is forced to flee. And, like Virgil's eerie passage, Tasso's handling of the Polydorus episode, mediated though it is through the later epics of Lucan, Dante, and Ariosto, is deepened and enriched by an understanding of its precise cultic valences, the Christian imagery with which it is preoccupied.[30] The staining of the ground with blood recalls us not only to the preceding canto of Clorinda's death, in which her blood is said to flow like a warm stream ("caldo fiume") over her vestment (12.65) but to canto 3, where, as we have seen, the Crusaders portray for themselves in prayer the image of Christ's bleeding body. But it is not only the bleeding body of Christ that the scene in the forest threatens to evoke. The incarnational language in which the canto is cast links a Clorinda ostensibly trapped between life and death to a Christ who took on human flesh to save humankind and, in the evocative imagery of late medieval piety, enable humans to imitate him. In short, just as Christ's body will reappear in the poem's penultimate stanza as the bleeding bodies of the *fuggitivi* and thus as an ironic index of Christ's universality, so does it reappear in the thirteenth canto as the suffering Clorinda—the bleeding body trapped in a tree—reproduces Christ crucified *on* a tree.[31]

In refusing to strike the tree again, Tancredi reveals himself not only as "pius Aeneas" but as a character who privileges incarnational fictions over the ethereal, "bodiless" Clorinda he witnessed shortly after Clorinda's death in canto 12. One of Clorinda's final acts is to request baptism at Tancredi's hands as she dies, a baptism made poignant by the fact that as Clorinda (and we as readers) only belatedly discover, she was born to a Christian mother. Although she cannot speak, "she seemed to tell Tancredi, 'Heaven is opening; I depart in peace'" ("e in atto di morir lieto e vivace,/ dir parea: 'S'apre il cielo; io vado in pace,'" 12.68), and it is as a newly baptized Christian, now in heaven, that she appears to the grieving Tancredi in a dream later that night. With Tasso accentuating the language of seeming (*parere*), Clorinda "seems to dry [Tancredi's] eyes with sweet acts of pity and say that he removed [her] from those who are living in the mortal world" and made her worthy "to rise to God's bosom amid the blessed and immortal ones" (12.91–92). Tancredi awakens "consoled" and proceeds to prepare her funeral rites. But his subsequent refusal to strike the tree attests to his privileging the bleeding body over an intangible vision of a woman supposedly in heaven. The Clorinda whose blood had flowed from her breast in a "caldo fiume" in canto 12 has become the Clorinda who in canto 13 protests one more act of suffering, this time on the "misero tronco" to which she is bound by her "harsh destiny." Like Goffredo's slaughter of the Muslim fugitives, Tancredi's slaughter of Clorinda, not once, but twice, has the effect of turning her into Christ; and in many ways Tancredi's second act of violence makes that analogy even more tangible. That Tancredi hesitates, that he leaves the forest and admits to Goffredo that he is unable to "split the bark," suggests the extent to which he recognizes the power of an analogy to which Goffredo will be subsequently and purposefully blind when he pursues the *fuggitivi*.

Indeed, from Goffredo's Counter-Reformation perspective, only in a world controlled by forces from the underworld are such analogies possible at all. This is an underworld controlled by Ismeno, and one that insists on comparisons between ancient and contemporary, between local spirits incarnated in trees and universal deities incarnated in Mary's womb. And yet in the popular and hagiographical tradition from which Ismeno no less than Tancredi might be said to emerge, such analogies are ubiquitous, as one exemplary story from the late medieval *Libro dei Cinquanti Miracoli della Vergine* attests. Like so many of the accounts of miracles provoked by Mary, this story has at its heart a tale of Ovidian metamorphosis and enchantment: the staff that thieves left on top of the grave of a saintly man they had killed in the forest begins to grow roots that thrust into the dead man's mouth and leaves that are inscribed with the first words of the *Ave Maria,* "come piacque a messer Domenedio . . . e alla gloriosa vergine Maria" ("as it pleased God our Lord and the glorious virgin Mary").[32] The wonder inspired by such a supernatural event ("fuori di natura") ultimately leads to the community's sanctification of the place in the forest ("quella luogo fu avuto in grandissima riverenzia") and the establishment of a local cult of Mary.

These are the popular marvels that Ismeno imitates, Tancredi reveres, and Goffredo rejects, and one might venture that Tasso himself rejects them as well. The enchanted forest finally does get cut down by the Christians' most valiant warrior, Rinaldo, and his refusal to listen to the cries of the trees and their infernal *simulacrae*—and hence to Polydorus—is portrayed not as an act of sacrilege but as an unequivocal victory for the Christians. Like Goffredo, Rinaldo too has been chosen by God above, as we know from Goffredo's heavenly vision.[33] His conquest merely confirms what Virgil's poem likewise made clear: land is given to one by the "universal" gods, not because of any painstaking and intimate relationship with it and the customs and culture that derive from caring for it (hence the etymological links between *cultivation, culture,* and *cult* at work in the late medieval narratives recounting miracles of the virgin). Tasso's emphasis on the poet's interest in "universals" follows naturally from the poem's plot, in which epic significance can be imparted only from above—by those who know the *essere intrinseco* of things—not from below, within a world of tangible local customs and stories that devolve around the body of Christ rather than official doctrine.

With Rinaldo's victory over the enchantment, the Christians beseige the *santa città,* and Goffredo claims Christ's sepulchre as his own. If the parallelism between Christ and the *fuggitivi* just before Goffredo reaches the sepulchre does *not* unsettle, it is only because, like Goffredo, we too have come to resist the work of analogy as demonic and to see any commensurability between the local and the universal as inherently suspect. But the price of that decision is high. For one thing, in ignoring the ironic reproduction of Christ's bleeding body in the very place where he was crucified, and in thereby ignoring the poem's penultimate stanza, we ignore the analogies between two "local" religions that share common ground. Tasso himself lets us know that he is well aware of Islam's essentially iconoclastic nature at the same time that he generates a generally unconvincing view of the Muslims' diabolical practices. They are labeled "pagani" and accused of worshipping idols, "adoring" Muhammad, and consorting with demons such as Allecto, of whom it was also Juno's fate—marginalized local deity such as she is in the *Aeneid*—to call up from hell.[34] For another thing, we thereby consent to a vision not only of epic poetry and the religion it celebrates as virtually severed from their basis in a material landscape of shared stories and communities, but of Tasso's poem as severed from the epic tradition itself. Cutting down the forest both deprives its local inhabitants, the birds and the beasts, of their nests—"Lasciano al suon de l'arme, al vario grido,/ e le fère e gli augei la tana e 'l nido" ("With the sounds of arms and the varied outcry the beasts leave their lairs and the birds their nests," 3.76)—and uproots those earlier *selve* of the epic canon, Dante's, Ariosto's, and Virgil's as well, relegating them to the status of a poetics not ordained by God.[35]

One moment at the exact center of the poem marks precisely this severing of *vulgo* from elite, as the warriors gather together for Mass on the very site where Christ had experienced the Passion. The captains and clergy sit close to the altar, the common soldiers farther away, and so it falls out that the "primieri" are able to hear and see the Mass, the others able only to *see* it from afar. Turning the Last Supper, which the Mass commemorates, into a ritual that only the elite can fully experience separates the epic narrative at the heart of Tasso's Christianity into two very different stories. On the one hand, a story for and about a Goffredo who has learned to renounce not only earthly delight but, as in the heavenly journey he takes shortly after Tancredi's failure in the wood, the earth itself. On the other hand, a story for and about the *vulgo,* who are drawn to the palpable and bodily, to that which can be manifested as physical presence. Illiterate in Latin and Tasso's learned Italian, they can only see the mysteries that depend on local manifestation for fulfillment. These are precisely the bodily manifestations that Goffredo and the Counter-Reformation poem that glorifies him need to contain and critique, with the aim of ensuring that the world will no longer suffer from enchantments of any kind. In a decisively different vein from Virgil but with strikingly similar results, Tasso charts a narrative whereby epic poetry and the imperial projects to which epic attends efface their origins in local cults and local communities, thereby silencing what for Eliot would be the taint of provincialism. The result, as Tasso himself seems to have realized, given his painstaking revisions of the *Gerusalemme liberata* after it was published, was a dazzling, but finally disappointing vision of universality.

NOTES

1. See Eliot 1957, "What Is a Classic?" particularly pp. 67–70, where he discusses universality and provincialism.

2. Eliot 1957, "Virgil and the Christian World," 127.

3. For comments on local culture, see Eliot 1988, "Notes toward the Definition of Culture," 123–140.

4. Nagy 1979, 7. See also chap. 6, "Lamentation and the Hero," which closes with the distinction between the local specificity of cult—"The hero of cult must be local because it is a fundamental principle in Greek religion that his power is local"— and the timeless universality of the Panhellenic tradition and the Homeric poetry that embraces and articulates it.

5. Nagy 1979,, 116.

6. I quote from Timothy Hampton's translation of the passage from the *Apologia* (Hampton 1990, 93). Hampton's argument that Tasso fears "the ambiguities of particularity" and therefore seeks the "stability and certainty of the universal" has been an important influence on this essay; see Hampton, pp. 88–94.

7. Eliot 1957, 127.

8. All citations and translations from Virgil's *Aeneid* and *Eclogues* are taken from Fairclough 1974.

9. Klossowski 1990, 128.

10. That Virgil's sympathies may well lie with Meliboeus in the dialogue is indicated by a line relevant to the shepherds' participation in local cult. At one point, Meliboeus explicitly calls attention to the fact that the local fountains Tityrus rejected do, in fact, hold Tityrus dear; when Tityrus was "absent" in Rome, Meliboeus claims, the very trees and sacred fountains called for him ("Tityrus hinc aberat. ipsae te, Tityre, pinus, / ipsi te fontes, ipsa haec arbusta vocabant," 38–39).

11. "et iam summa procul villarum culmina fumant/ maioresque cadunt altis de montibus umbrae" ("Even now the house-tops yonder are smoking and longer shadows fall from the mountain-heights," 82–83).

12. I owe this insight to Laura McClure, of the Classics Department at the University of Wisconsin.

13. "iam tum religio pavidos terrebat agrestis/ dira loci, iam tum silvam saxumque tremebant" (8.349–350). Might we not note in the reference to the *pavidos agrestis* and the dual emphasis on their terror some condescension on Virgil's part when speaking of those rustics who allow themselves to become so frightened by a mysterious landscape?

14. Book 8 is more ironic than I have indicated; the supposedly local religion of

the Capitoline Hill turns out, through the vehicle of the Arcadians themselves, to have been a Greek importation.

15. Perhaps one of the most telling lines in *Aeneid* 4, when Aeneas is building a city in Carthage, is that which for many critics makes Dido a dissembling woman desperate for marriage with Aeneas. After the two have begun their affair, Dido refers to their relationship as a "marriage" ("coniugium vocat; hoc praetexit nomine culpam," "She calls it marriage; with that word she covers her fault," 4.172). But in a city such as Carthage, which worships Juno as its preeminent deity, the ritual that Juno effects around the cave in which Aeneas and Dido first make love enacts for Dido the *equivalent* of a marriage rite. For Aeneas, it does not. In this clash, one culture is necessarily silenced ("Urbs antiqua *fuit*. . . Karthago"—"There *was* an ancient city called Carthage," we learn at the opening of the *Aeneid* [1.11–12]), and the other necessarily privileged.

16. For suggestive interpretations of the Italian deification of hybrid figures who supposedly led their people from savagery to civilization, see Brelich 1976.

17. See Williams 1989, 215.

18. More specifically, Freud saw in Tasso's version of Virgil's text a manifestation of the universal compulsion to repeat. See Freud 1961, 16,, where Freud suggests that Tancredi's wounding of Clorinda for a second time in the enchanted forest is "the most moving poetic picture" of "the compulsion to repeat." For two recent readings of the poem that draw on Freud's insights, see Ferguson 1982 and Bellamy 1994.

19. See Galinsky 1969, 141–190, and Momigliano 1987, 272–274.

20. See Susanne Wofford's observation that Virgil uses "Roman place names as tropes to legitimize Aeneas's claims to the Italian land retrospectively" (1992, 180). Wofford also calls attention to the actual *distance* of Aeneas and the Trojans from the land; and it is the sacrifice of Palinurus that "indicates the cost not only of creating such an aetiology for the land . . . but also of a certain type of poetic figuration itself—the cost to poet and hero of possessing the land as a poetic or a political conquest" (p. 181).

21. Galinsky 1969, 190.

22. See Hampton 1990, 89: Hampton quotes from the *Apologia* ("The poet will have brought the truth and particularity of history to verisimilitude and universality, which is proper to his art") and comments: "As epic poetry becomes poetry, 'considering' things in their universality, historical particularity loses its significance. As events and characters are placed into the unity of a plot they lose their essentially historical character and become poetic—that is, in the parlance of both Tasso and Aristotle, philosophical." Quint 1983 also discusses Tasso's avoidance of historical particularity in the *Gerusalemme liberata,* although in the context of Tasso's reliance on Platonism rather than on Aristotle. Quint 1993 is a more persuasive reading of Tasso's construction of a "universal" epic, as Quint elaborates Tasso's only partially successful suppression of the sectarian and nationalistic boundaries that divided late sixteenth-century Europe.

23. Tasso 1982 (the edition of Fredi Chiappelli). English translations of the *Liberata* are taken from Tasso 1987 (Ralph Nash's translation); I have made minor revisions throughout.

24. There are admittedly several other moments in the *Liberata* when it is Chris-

tian blood that "flows" in a manner reminiscent of Christ's. When the warrior Sveno is killed in the desert en route to Jerusalem, his blood becomes a river ("di sangue un rio," 8.19). Somewhat more problematically, in a passage I will address below, when Clorinda is wounded by Tancredi—a Clorinda who is still, technically, a Muslim, although within several lines she will be baptized by Tancredi himself—her blood is also said to flow like a river.

   25. The *Conquistata* will make this paradox less likely—the poem ends not with bleeding bodies, but with a lengthy procession and pomp that rivals the "ornamenti barbarici e pompe" stained by the pagans' flowing blood. In fact, in the *Conquistata*, nature itself crowns Goffredo's victory as he enters the holy city: "E' giá tranquillo il mar, sereno il vento,/ l'aria piú chiara assai ch'ella non suole;/ tanto col vincitore il ciel s'allegra,/ e la natura, dianzi afflitta ed egra" ("The sea is calm, the wind serene, the air more pure than it is wont to be; thus sky and nature alike, once so ill and afflicted, rejoice with the conqueror," 24.132). The fugitives on whom the penultimate stanza of the *Liberata* had dwelled are relegated to a verse tucked into the middle of the last canto. In lines so altered as to be unrecognizable, they are compared to "belve in fèro ludo/ cinte d'intorno, o 'n sanguinosa caccia" ("wild animals surrounded in fierce struggle, or in bloody hunt," 24.118). Any equation that might have been made between Christ's bleeding body and the *fuggitivi* can no longer be imagined. Citations are from Tasso 1934 (Bonfigli's edition of the *Gerusalemme conquistata*); translations are my own.

   26. The "Allegoria del Poema" can be found in Tasso 1875, 1: 301 (Guasti's edition of Tasso's prose works); the translation is from Tasso 1987, 469 (Nash's translation). As Tasso scholars have noted, the "Allegoria" has a singularly complicated relationship to the poem itself; Tasso's letters from the period suggest that it was largely a creation to appease the Roman inquisitor, Silvio Antoniani, who needed to approve the text before it could be published. See, among others, Murrin 1980, 121–128, and Derla 1978. Rhu 1993 provides a translation of the "Allegoria," as well as a splendid introduction to the young Tasso's theoretical works.

   27. The phrase is from the later *Conquistata*, 24.118.

   28. Berger 1988 offers a lively discussion of an animism that Protestants such as Spenser associated with Catholicism; see p. 78 in particular: "The Catholic abuses suggested in the early cantos [of Book I of *The Faerie Queene*] are traced back and reduced to an archaic pagan sensibility which projects anthropomorphic idols as if it never received the Word. The historical failure represented as the Church of the Middle Ages is seen as a betrayal of the original Gospel experience and as a regression to the inherent tendency of the *silva vanus*, the Flesh, to resist enlightenment." Berger's comments are particularly suggestive as regards the enchanted forest in the *Liberata*. More generally, see Eire 1986.

   29. On the effects of Tridentine doctrine on popular culture in Italy, see Niccoli 1987.

   30. There is an interesting parallel with the *Inferno*, in which Dante's miserable suicide, Piero della Vigna, parodies his own would-be crucifixion: he is trapped like Tasso's Clorinda in a "body or tomb, I know not which to say" (13.43). But Tasso's episode of the bleeding trunk is complicated in ways that Dante's is not. As we know from the formidable announcement posted at the gate of hell, Inferno is God's hand-

iwork, and the fact that hell's inhabitants parody the holiest mysteries of Christianity does not subvert those mysteries but attests to their universality: even in hell, even among pagans, one is forced to acknowledge the truth of Christ's birth, death, and resurrection, and Dante's sinners do so without realizing to what they are attesting. The forest within which Clorinda speaks is the result of horrible charms, "too awful to say," of the Muslim sorcerer who was born a Christian, and unlike the pilgrim Dante, Tancredi has no Virgilian guide to assist him.

31. Barberi-Squarotti 1993, 249, observes rightly that Tancredi can't convince himself that Clorinda is simply a diabolical apparition: "è, anzí, una verità che va oltre il fatto e la vicenda.". The observation is an important one, for it suggests that Tancredi insists on seeing the tree as a material realm inhabited by a transcendent being—and thus as a vehicle for incarnation.

32. See the third selection from *I Miracoli della Vergine,* entitled "D'uno che vendé ciò che egli aveva e dièllo a' poveri" (Of one that sold all he had and gave it to the poor), in de Luca 1977, 4: 730–732.

33. Ugone tells Goffredo: "If high Providence elected you as the chief captain of the venture, he also destined that [Rinaldo] must be the sovereign executor of your commands" (14.13).

34. From the very start of the poem, Tasso depicts Clorinda as adverse to Ismeno's patently un-Islamic practices. In canto 2, the sorcerer is condemned not by the narrator for his confounding of "due leggi," but by Clorinda, when she chastises Jerusalem's king, Aladino, for letting Ismeno persuade him to remove an image of Mary from the Christians' temple and place it in the mosque instead, "so that it will be a fated protection for these gates" (2.6). Clorinda angrily insists that the wizard has little reverence for Muslim law ("Fu de le nostre leggi irriverenza/ quell'opra far che persuase il mago"), and she blames Ismeno for trying to "contaminate" Islam "con nova / religion" (2.50–51) that believes in the power and efficacy of images. Such an episode shows that Tasso was well aware of some of the central practices of Islam; it also suggests that the demonization of Islam in the text proceeds not from ignorance but from ideology.

35. My thanks to Paul Bucklin, whose senior thesis on Tasso suggestively discusses ways in which the *Gerusalemme liberata* makes Tasso's predecessors, Dante included, suspicious heretics in light of the "true" Counter-Reformation faith.

WORKS CITED

Barberi-Squarotti, Giorgio.
 1993.   *Il sogno e l'epica.* Turin: Genesi.
Bellamy, Elizabeth J.
 1994.   "From Virgil to Tasso: The Epic Topos as an Uncanny Return." In *Desire in the Renaissance: Psychoanalysis and Literature,* edited by Valeria Finucci and Regina Schwartz, 207–232. Princeton: Princeton University Press.
Berger, Harry, Jr.
 1988.   *Revisionary Play: Studies in the Spenserian Dynamics.* Berkeley: University of California Press.

Brelich, Angelo.
1976.   *Tre variazioni romane sul tema delle origini*. Rome: Anteneo.
de Luca, Don Giuseppe, ed.
1977.   *Scrittori di religione del trecento*. 4 vols. Turin: Einaudi.
Derla, Luigi.
1978.   "Sull'allegoria della *Gerusalemme liberata*." *Italianistica* 7: 473–488.
Eire, Carlos.
1986.   *War against the Idols*. Cambridge: Cambridge University Press.
Eliot, T. S.
1988.   *Christianity and Culture*. New York: Harcourt, Brace & Co.
1957.   *On Poetry and Poets*. London: Faber and Faber.
Ferguson, Margaret.
1982.   *Trials of Desire*. New Haven: Yale University Press.
Freud, Sigmund.
1961.   *Beyond the Pleasure Principle*. Translated and edited by James Strachey.
             New York: Norton.
Galinsky, Karl.
1969.   *Aeneas, Sicily, and Rome*. Princeton: Princeton University Press.
Hampton, Timothy.
1990.   *Writing from History*. Ithaca, N.Y.: Cornell University Press.
Klossowki, Pierre.
1990.   *Diana at Her Bath/ The Women of Rome*. Translated by Stephen Sartarelli
             and Sophie Hawkes. Boston: Eriadnos Press.
Momigliano, Arnaldo.
1987.   *On Pagans, Jews, and Christians*. Middletown, Conn.: Wesleyan Uni-
             versity Press.
Murrin, Michael.
1980.   *The Allegorical Epic: Essays in Its Rise and Decline*. Chicago: University
             of Chicago Press.
Nagy, Gregory.
1979.   *Best of the Achaeans*. Baltimore: Johns Hopkins University Press.
Niccoli, Ottavia.
1987.   *Profeti e popolo nell'Italia del Rinascimento*. Rome: Laterza.
Quint, David.
1993.   *Epic and Empire*. Chicago: University of Chicago Press.
1983.   *Origin and Originality: Versions of the Source*. New Haven: Yale University Press.
Rhu, Lawrence.
1993.   *The Genesis of Tasso's Narrative Theory: English Translations of the Early
             Poetics and a Comparative Study of Their Significance*. Detroit: Wayne State
             University Press.
Tasso, Torquato.
1987.   *Jerusalem Delivered*. Translated by Ralph Nash. Detroit: Wayne State Uni-
             versity Press.
1982.   *Gerusalemme liberata*. Edited by Fredi Chiappelli. Milan: Rusconi.
1934.   *Gerusalemme conquistata*. Edited by Luigi Bonfigli. Bari: Laterza.
1875.   *Le prose diverse di Torquato Tasso*. Edited by Cesare Guasti. 2 vols. Flo-
             rence: Le Monnier.

Virgil
    1974.   *Virgil.* With an English translation by H. Ruston Fairclough. 2 vols.
               Rev. ed. Cambridge: Harvard University Press.
Williams, Gordon.
    1989.   *Technique and Idea in the "Aeneid."* New Haven: Yale University Press.
Wofford, Susanne.
    1992.   *The Choice of Achilles: The Ideology of Figure in the Epic.* Stanford: Stan-
               ford University Press.

7

•　•　•

Appropriating the Epic

Gender, Caste, and Regional
Identity in Middle India

Joyce Burkhalter Flueckiger

Indian epic includes not only the well-known *Mahābhārata* and *Rāmāyana*—
narratives dating from antiquity that have survived for centuries—but also a
myriad of other traditional stories in verse that vary in their themes and social
meanings from community to community. In the central Indian region of
Chhattisgarh, the Candaini epic vividly draws on the local folklore repertoire;
it is an oral tradition performed—like other contemporary Indian epic—in
discrete episodes that figure in the larger narrative known to the audience.
The narrative, a distinctly nonheroic tale that challenges conventional notions
of epic, relates a love story and features a female heroine. Joyce Flueckiger argues that it derives much of its cultural and political meaning from its strong
identification with the region and thus stands as perhaps the most resonant
expression of what might be called Chhattisgarhi folklore, constantly viewed
by the community as its "own" epic.[1]

In the first essay of this volume,[2] Gregory Nagy suggests that a particular genre
can be identified as epic only by placing it in relationship to other genres
performed within a particular folklore community. Accordingly, features of
narrative, poetic composition, and heroic characters and themes that have
typically characterized the analytic category of epic would not in and of themselves be enough to give definition to "epic."[3] Such is true in India, where
there are numerous folk narrative traditions that are long, sung, and heroic
but that do not hold the significance of "epic" for the communities in which
they are performed. What distinguishes "epic" from these narratives is the
nature of the relationship epic narratives have with the communities in which
they are performed: "Epics stand apart from other 'songs' and 'stories' in
the extent and intensity of a folklore community's identification with them;
. . . the oral epic is the most geographically wide-spread form that still preserves a community's identity."[4]

Thus narratives that serve as "epic" in one region, in which performers

This essay appeared in Joyce Burkhalter Flueckiger, *Gender and Genre in the Folklore of Middle
America,* copyright © 1996 by Cornell University. Used by permission of Cornell University Press.

and audiences self-consciously identify the narrative as "theirs," may be performed in another region without the level of necessary self-identification to be categorized as "epic." For example, the Dhola-Maru epic tradition of northern and western India is also performed in the central Indian region of Chhattisgarh, the area of study for this essay, and yet it is known here specifically as a Rajasthani (western Indian province and cultural region) story, representing a somewhat exoticized "other," exemplified by the hero flying away on a desert camel not native to Chhattisgarh. The northern and central Indian martial epic of Alha is also performed in Chhattisgarh but is associated with specific historical kingdoms outside the region and is perceived to be someone else's history. Likewise, although the pan-Indian *Rāmāyana* epic tradition is arguably the most significant religious narrative in the plains of Chhattisgarh, its singers and audiences call it a Hindi, rather than Chhattisgarhi, story (*kathā*). The hero and heroine, Ram and Sita, are divine royalty and, in dramatic performances of the tradition, are dressed in generic north Indian royal costuming rather than Chhattisgarhi dress and jewelry that would identify them by region and caste. Placed in the context of these long, sung, heroic narratives available in the repertoire of Chhattisgarhi regional performance genres, the epic of Candaini stands apart in the extent to which it has been appropriated by various communities within the region as "their own." This essay examines the ways in which this process of appropriation has identified and given identity to the folklore region of Chhattisgarh.

GEOGRAPHIC AND SOCIAL BOUNDARIES OF THE EPIC

Performance of the Candaini narrative is not limited to Chhattisgarh; its performance spreads across geographic and linguistic borders, from Chhattisgarh to the Gangetic plains of northern India, in the province of Uttar Pradesh (or U.P.). The tradition is called Candaini in Chhattisgarh and Canaini or Loriki (from the names of its hero and heroine) in U.P. Candaini differs from many Indian epic traditions in that it is not associated with a particular caste or regional historical events, nor is it associated with a religious cult. Thus it can and has been appropriated by a spectrum of communities as "theirs" in a way in which many other narrative traditions cannot be.

While folklorists may identify the narrative traditions in these two regions as "the same" because of their shared characters, constant plot elements, and shared motifs, it is important to point out that the wide geographic mapping of Candaini is a reality to those folklorists and not to the epic's performers and audiences. They know and understand the tradition as rooted in geographically circumscribed performance and social contexts, as being identified with—"belonging to"—specific communities, in this case, a cowherding caste in U.P. and the broader regional folklore community in Chhattisgarh. None of the singers whom I met on the plains of Chhattisgarh knew the "same" story was sung in U.P. When I mentioned this to one of the epic singers, he exclaimed: "Do you mean they really sing *our Chhattisgarhi* Candaini way up there?"

When I went to Chhattisgarh to begin my dissertation fieldwork in 1980, one of my first "strategies" was to elicit from villagers a core repertoire of folklore genres that they considered to be "Chhattisgarhi," unique to or characterizing that linguistically and historically defined region. I would ask something like "What do you celebrate here in Chhattisgarh, what do you sing?" A core repertoire gradually emerged from the varied responses. Its genres did not exhaust their performance repertoire but included those traditions whose performance the inhabitants themselves perceived to be identified with and give identity to the region. The epic traditions of Candaini and Pandvani (a regionalized variant of the pan-Indian *Mahābhārata* tradition) were always on this list.

The longer I was in Chhattisgarh and as I became more knowledgeable about its various performance traditions, and thus not perceived to be quite such an unknowing outsider, indigenous commentary began to break down the nature of the social communities with which performance traditions were identified, by caste, age, and gender. Candaini and Pandvani most always retained their *regional* identification, however; the community with which they are primarily identified is more inclusive, having a wider geographical and social spread, than that of any other genre from the core repertoire. Candaini was repeatedly identified as "a Chhattisgarhi story," "our story."

The social boundaries of the performance communities (and note I have shifted to plural here) associated with the Candaini epic tradition in Chhattisgarh have shifted rather dramatically in the last twenty to twenty-five years; so it is important to look carefully at what it means for an epic to be "ours," asking who is the "we" that is being represented. Further, at what level is identification being made, textually, performatively, or both? I suggest that increasing mass media and literacy in Chhattisgarh in recent years have affected both the performances that identify and the identity of the "we."

THE EPIC STORY

Epic narratives exist both as oral and performance traditions, a distinction Laurie Sears and I made in *Boundaries of the Text* between a general knowledge of the "whole story" (a summary) that many in the folklore community would be able to relate and the epic as it is performed in a marked, *artistic* enactment of that oral tradition.[5] The *performed* epic in India is sung in episodes,[6] with the assumption that audience members frame the performance both within the larger epic story (oral tradition) as well as within the folklore repertoire of which it is a part. Thus while scholars have spent considerable energy recording epic stories "from beginning to end," counting the number of hours and pages required to do so, this is not how the epic is received by indigenous audiences. Further, there are certain episodes of the epic that are more frequently performed than others; and there may be episodes that exist only in the oral tradition, and not in performance at all.

What follows is a narrative summary of primarily the Chhattisgarhi epic variant, drawn from the oral tradition (summaries that were told to me) and performances I attended. I have noted some of the major differences between this and the U.P. variant of the epic, and more of the substantive differences between the two variants will become apparent in the analyses that follow. In Chhattisgarh, Candaini is the story of the hero Lorik and heroine Candaini, both from the Raut cowherding caste. The hero and heroine are each married to other partners, but Candaini leaves her husband when she learns he has been cursed by the goddess to be impotent for twelve years. On her way back to her maternal village, Candaini is accosted in the jungle by the untouchable Bathua. She cleverly escapes his evil intentions, but he chases after her and terrorizes the inhabitants and cattle of the village. In desperation, the villagers ask the hero Lorik to rescue them; ultimately he defeats Bathua through nonmartial (and, I might add, rather unheroic) means. During this contest, Candaini first lays eyes on him, falls in love, and proceeds to seduce him. After some delays, primarily due to Lorik's hesitancy and cowardice in decision making, the hero leaves his wife Manjari, and he and Candaini elope together to Hardi Garh.

In Chhattisgarh, Candaini performances center upon and elaborate various adventures from this elopement journey (*uṛhāī*, literally, "flight"). In fact, when I asked villagers what the story was about, most responses began with some variant of "It is the story of the elopement of Lorik and Candaini." Eventually, Lorik receives word that his brothers have all died in battle, and their wealth and cattle have been dissipated throughout the Chhattisgarhi countryside, leaving his mother and wife destitute. Lorik returns home with Candaini to avenge his family's honor. He succeeds in reclaiming his cattle, through battle in the U.P. variant and by wandering the countryside as a mendicant, collecting his cattle, in Chhattisgarh. When the task is completed, he takes up the position of head of the surviving extended family, including his first wife. But, it is said, Lorik did not take pride in his success. In U.P. versions, he finds that his former physical prowess and strength have dissipated, and he kills himself. In Chhattisgarh, sad and dissatisfied after his return, Lorik one day mysteriously wanders off into the countryside, never to be seen again.

In the Chhattisgarhi village of Garh Rivan (home of Lorik in the epic and a present-day village near the cattle bazaar town of Arang in Raipur District), one performer sang the epic's closing episode as that of a lovers' argument. As the couple was sitting in a boat in the middle of the village tank (or pond), the argument got so vehement that the boat overturned. Candaini swam to the bank and took refuge in a goddess temple. The goddess was so angered at Candaini's sudden and inauspicious intrusion that she beheaded our heroine, only to regret her action later and restore the head. In a village goddess temple on the banks of the tank of Garh Rivan, there are today two images (one beheaded and the other whole) of the heroine Candaini, which keep the goddess company. The heroine is not called a goddess, but simply honored as "our *rāutīn*," or cowherdress. Lorik, it is said, was never seen after this episode and is presumed to be still wandering in the Chhattisgarhi countryside.

The narrative as performed in both Chhattisgarh and northern India is not a religious epic, nor are its performances an integral part of any particular ritual or festival, although it is often performed at two festivals that have themselves been "imported" into the Chhattisgarhi ritual calendar, *gaṇeś caturthī* and *durgā pūjā*, perhaps as a way of localizing them. Villagers say the epic is sung primarily for "entertainment" (*manorañjan*): nonprofessional performers may sing for small groups of friends and neighbors, and professionals may perform at annual village fairs or provide entertainment during long winter evenings. These nonritual performance contexts do not, however, diminish the significance of the epic for the communities in which it is performed. In U.P., while the characters are not deified, they are they held up as models to be emulated, of "who we would like to be." In Chhattisgarh, by contrast, they are "who we are," in larger-than-life proportions.

THE U.P. VARIANT AS CASTE EPIC

To understand the differences in the performatively identified communities of the Gangetic plains of U. P. and Chhattisgarh, it will be useful for us now to take a closer look at both narrative and performative variation in these two areas. My analysis of the U.P. epic variant is based on two published versions of the epic collected and transcribed by S. M. Pandey in the 1970s, one in the dialect of Awadhi and the other in Bhojpuri, as well as upon personal communication with Pandey in the early 1980s.[7] I will call this U.P. variant the Loriki/Canaini tradition, taken from Pandey's titles. The Chhattisgarhi data is drawn from my own fieldwork (1980 through 1993, intermittently) and Verrier Elwin's translation of a partial version.[8]

Uttar Pradesh is in the heartland of orthodox Brahminic Hinduism, while Chhattisgarh lies on its periphery. Chhattisgarh's cultural and religious traditions are influenced by the high percentage of tribal groups that have now been integrated into the Hindu caste system. These include folk performance and festival genres, social and marriage patterns, and women's dress, tattoos, and jewelry. Of particular interest to us in our examination of the epic is the relatively higher status of women in Chhattisgarh compared to women in U.P. This may be partially explained by tribal influences, but also influential is the fact that the rice-growing economy of central India requires a higher proportion of female labor participation than does the wheat-growing economy of the north. Thus women in Chhattisgarh are not considered to be quite the economic liability that they are in U.P.[9]

In both performance areas, U.P. and Chhattisgarh, the epic tradition seems to have originated with the local cowherding castes—Ahirs in U.P. and Rauts in Chhattisgarh. In U.P., where Ahir males continue to be both primary performers and audience members, however, the tradition has remained more closely identified with that caste. Pandey cites two Awadhi proverbs in U.P. that clearly identify Canaini with the Ahir caste:

> However clever an Ahir be
> Nothing but Canaini singeth he.

> However many times an Ahir may read the Puranas
> He will not sing anything but Canaini.[10]

Certain clans of Ahirs in U.P. identify with the epic more than just performatively; they look to the epic as the history of their caste. Gwal Ahir singers of the contemporary folk-song genre called *virhā* believe the Loriki-Canaini to be the oldest extant record of their caste group. Although most of them admit to not knowing the epic well, they claim that many of their songs and narratives are based upon it, and many social and religious traditions unique to the caste derived from it.[11]

The differences between caste-epic identification in U.P. and Chhattisgarh can be partially attributed to the differences in each caste's self-perception, status, organization, and ideology. The Ahirs of U.P. have traditionally viewed themselves as a local warrior caste and continue to promote that image of themselves. As certain Ahirs gained in political and economic power in the late nineteenth century, they joined forces in an effort to raise their caste status by appropriating customs (such as donning the sacred thread) and ideologies of the *kṣatriya varṇa* caste category (a process the Indian anthropologist Srinivas has called "sanskritization").[12] Another way to confirm their warrior status was to try to associate themselves with the Yadav cowherding caste of the divine cowherder Krishna, calling themselves Yadavs instead of Ahirs. Ahir intelligentsia "rewrote" certain historical documents to prove this connection[13] and formed a national Yadav organization that continues to coordinate and promote the mobility drive of the caste. Integral to this movement are retellings of caste history that reflect its martial character; the epic is an important channel for some of these retellings. Hence the cowherder Lorik is portrayed as a warrior first, whose primary role is to defend the honor of the caste, often through a defense of the honor of its women. Consequently, epic battles rather than the elopement become the central episodes of the narrative, and the elopement is consciously underplayed. Elopement and the freedom of individual choice it implies threaten caste endogamy and the strict maintenance of caste boundaries necessary in the effort to raise status. Further, the implicit freedom of elopement contradicts the social control of women articulated elsewhere in the U.P. variant of the epic.[14]

Further, the male hero Lorik is the central character of the U.P. variants, rather than the heroine Candaini, as is the case in Chhattisgarh. The northern tradition is, in sum, a male, martial epic tradition that has been appropriated to promote a particular image of the Ahir caste.[15] A common saying in eastern U.P. asserts: "If Loriki is recited for one month, somewhere there will be a battle."[16] The martial ethos of the epic is perhaps most dramatically visualized in a bazaar pamphlet titled (in Hindi) *Lorikāyan: The Battle of Hardīgarh* (interestingly, this episode is the only one that has been published in this popular format).[17] Its cover pictures Lorik as the classical indian warrior, standing on a battlefield, holding up a broken chariot wheel, with bodies and weapons strewn across the field and arrows flying through the air.

THE CHHATTISGARHI VARIANT AS REGIONAL EPIC

Older Chhattisgarhi informants told me in 1980 that in Chhattisgarh, too, Candaini singers used to be primarily from the cowherding Raut caste. Its multicaste audiences and the seemingly easy adaptation of the epic to innovative performance styles available to performers from a wide spectrum of castes suggest, however, that it was never "caste-owned" in the sense that it is in U.P. A possible explanation for differences in the caste-epic relationship are the respective castes' self-image.

One fifty-year-old Raut male gave the following account of the dispersion of the caste. In "former days" all the Rauts of the area used to go to Garh Rivan (the home of Lorik in the epic and the present-day village mentioned above) to celebrate the Raut festival of *mātar*.[18] Then one year, King Kadra, of a basket-weaving caste, battled against the Rauts. Many Rauts were killed, and the survivors scattered from Garh Rivan and settled "here and there." Since that time, according to the informant, Rauts have no longer gathered at Garh Rivan to celebrate *mātar*, but rather celebrate it in their own villages. We cannot know from such an account whether or not the caste was, in fact, ever a cohesive martial or administrative power. Their perception, however, is that they were once stronger and more unified than they are now.

In the more recent past, Chhattisgarhi Rauts have traditionally seen themselves as "village servants," who herd and milk the village cattle, rather than as warriors who protect caste honor and boundaries.[19] Lorik, as a Chhattisgarhi Raut, is not portrayed as the U.P. martial hero brandishing a sword, riding on a horse, but primarily as a lover whose only weapon is his herding staff and who travels on foot. Further reflecting a Chhattisgarhi ethos in which women have more mobility and arguably higher status than their sisters in the Gangetic plains, the *heroine* is the primary initiator of action in Chhattisgarhi performances; it is frequently *she* who protects and saves Lorik rather than the other way around. Thus, although the singing of the epic may have been first associated with the cowherding caste of its singers, the tradition as it has been documented in the last fifteen to twenty years does not suggest a strong caste identity.[20]

Part of what gives the epic tradition its regional identification in Chhattisgarh is its performance contexts and the broad social base of its audiences and performers today. Two basic performance styles of Candaini have developed in Chhattisgarh. Both styles are most commonly called simply Candaini, but when the styles *are* distinguished, the first is called Candaini *gīt* or song, and the second *nācā*, or dance-drama. As mentioned earlier, traditionally, Candaini *gīt* singers were male members of the Raut caste who sang the epic both professionally and nonprofessionally to primarily male audiences, but with women sitting on the sidelines. Rauts sang without musical accompaniment; but essential to their performance was a companion (*rāgī* or *saṅgvārī*) who joined in the last words of every line and served as a respondent. Today, it is difficult to find Rauts who still sing in the *gīt* style without instrumental accompaniment. The only such singer I knew died in 1988, and none of his sons were interested in learning or continuing his father's tradition. As one informant observed, "How can this [that is, style with no musical accompaniment] compete with video halls?" The repetitious response by the *rāgī*, however, is still one of the primary characterizing features of both instrumentally accompanied *gīt* and *nācā* Candaini performance styles.

The dates and circumstances in which members of the Satnami caste took up the *gīt* style of Candaini performance are undocumented and vague in caste and regional memory. Yet when I was looking for epic performances in the 1980s, I was frequently told that I would find Candaini only in those areas with large numbers of Satnamis. The Satnamis are a sect that converted in the 1800s from the outcaste Camar, a leather-working caste, but whose conversion did not raise their status from that of the lowest caste groups. It is probable that when *they* began to sing Candaini professionally, it began to attract more diverse audiences and to take on its current regional identification. The Satnamis added musical accompaniment to the *gīt* performance style, including, minimally, harmonium and *tabla*; but, as mentioned above, they have retained the combination of lead singer and one or more "companions," whose response lines end with *mor* or *tor*.[21]

Because I have little comparative data to use from "purely" Raut performances, it is difficult to know exactly how the narrative may have shifted when the Satnamis began to sing the epic professionally, particularly in its portrayal of the "villain" character, the Camar Bathua who tries to accost Candaini in the jungle. In one Satnami performance, however, Lorik meets Bathua again after their initial confrontation in the heroine's maternal village. Bathua reappears as the bodyguard of a foreign king whom Lorik has offended (by chopping off the nose of one of his subjects), so the king sends Bathua to punish him. This time their confrontation *is* martial, and Lorik is unable to defeat the untouchable physically. He is pinned to the ground, and Candaini has to beg Bathua for mercy. The Camar gives in but says Lorik must tie him up so that the king will think he has been defeated, not compassionate. Lorik eventually wins the kingdom through both battle and trickery and names it after the untouchable Bathua. When I later discussed this episode with several non-Satnami villagers, they told me that Satnamis have tended to glorify the character of Bathua and that a Raut singer would never have included such an episode, glorifying the heroism of the Camar.

The second Candaini performance style, called *nācā* (literally, "dance"), includes song and dance, spoken conversations between characters, and narration in the *gīt*, responsive style.[22] According to *nācā* performers, the *nācā* is said to have developed in the early 1970s in response to the strong influence of the increasingly popular Hindi cinema, an essential element of which is also song and dance. A *nācā* troupe consists of up to eight or ten performers, some of whom are actors and others musicians. An important feature of the *nācā* is the inclusion of costuming and minimal props. The hero Lorik carries a herding staff and wears traditional Raut festival dress, decorated with peacock feathers and cowrie shells; male performers put on saris and typical Chhattisgarhi jewelry to act out the female roles. The musicians sit at the side of the stage and accompany the songs of the actors or provide their own sung narration in the Candaini *gīt* style. Candaini is only one of many narratives performed in the *nācā* style, but *nācā* troupes that specialize in Candaini do so to the exclusion of other narratives. Although this style has grown in popularity, it is expensive to patronize. When sufficient funds for the *nācā* cannot be raised, or if troupe members are singing nonprofessionally, the *gīt* style, without dance, can still be heard.[23]

The performance context of the *nācā* is important in establishing the epic's regional character. Troupes are usually multicaste, heavily represented by Satnamis, but also by other middle-level castes, including Rauts. One performance troupe I met consisted of ten members from six different castes. Troupes are hired by village/neighborhood councils for annual village fairs or festivals or as independent entertainment events. Occasionally, a family will sponsor a performance to celebrate the birth of a son or a wedding. *Nācā* audiences, too, represent the caste spectrum of a particular village or urban neighborhood, male and female. *Nācās* are performed in public space such as a village or town square or main street, accessible to everyone. Persons from surrounding villages frequently walk several miles to attend *nācās* in neighboring villages, and audiences may reach as many as 200 participants.

The enthusiastic and responsive participation of women in the primary audience of the Candaini *nācā* stands in sharp contrast to the all-male audiences and performance contexts of the U.P. variants of the epic. In 1980 when I asked female audience members if *women* ever sang Candaini in Chhattisgarh, they all answered negatively. I did hear segments of the epic narrative and reference to its characters in other female performance genres, which they did *not*, however, identify as "Candaini" because of the performance context and singing style. "To sing Candaini" means to sing in a public context and, more specifically, to incorporate at some level the responsive singing style of the Candaini *rāgī*, with his end-line words of *tor* or *mor*. What these women were singing was identified by context as a harvest-dance song, not by content as Candaini.

In recent years, there have been a handful of individual female performers who *have* performed professionally the *gīt* style of Candaini, accompanied by male *rāgīs* and musicians. They are usually self-taught and have gained meteoric popularity because of their unusual position as professional, public *female* performers. Several audience members told me: "Who *wouldn't* go to hear a woman? There's more entertainment in that!" One such female performer is Suraj Bai, who, in 1987, was hailed in a local English-language newspaper as "the melody queen." She had represented Chhattisgarh at national and state folk festivals and had performed on nationwide television and radio; yet, the newspaper article bemoaned, she still worked as a daily-wage laborer. Over the last five years in Chhattisgarh, the epic tradition of Pandvani is experiencing a similar rise in popularity, primarily attributable to the fact that the tradition is being performed by two professional female singers, Tijan Bai and Ritu Varma, who have gained notoriety through their performances on television and radio. Both women have traveled extensively around India and even as far as Paris and New York for festivals of India.

Although Candaini female performers are still unusual, the worldview expressed by both female and male performers of the Chhattisgarhi epic is a female-centered one.[24] The heroine Candaini is the dominant character in the pair of lovers and the initiator of most of the epic action. She and other women are not portrayed as property to be exchanged and protected (as they are frequently depicted in the U.P. variants); rather, they are resourceful and take initiative, relying not on the ritual power of their chastity, as women frequently do in dominant-discourse narratives, but upon their own intuitive common sense.

Candaini's dominant role in the Chhattisgarhi epic first becomes evident when she makes the decision to leave her husband when their relationship is not fulfilling to her. Then it is she, rather than Lorik, who initiates their relationship; she sees him in the competition with her assailant Bathua and sets about to seduce him. In one version, she asks her brother to build a swing for her next to the path that Lorik uses every day to get to his wrestling grounds. As Lorik passes by, Candaini asks him to swing her. When he declines, she curses him. This so angers him that he violently swings her, causing her to fall off the swing and giving him the opportunity to catch her.[25]

The next time they meet, Candaini suggests a joking sexual relationship with Lorik by calling him her *devar* (younger brother-in-law), with whom such a relationship is permissible. Having grown up in the same village, they would normally call each other brother and sister, precluding a sexual relationship; changing the terms of address is often one of the first indications of a change in the nature of a relationship in Chhattisgarhi rural life and oral traditions. Finally, Candaini openly invites Lorik to visit her during the night, telling him how to get past various guards that stand at the entrance to her palace. As their relationship develops, it is also she who suggests and pushes for the elopement to Hardi Garh.

Candaini's resourcefulness and courage are illustrated by numerous examples from Chhattisgarhi episodes of the epic. In one performance, when the couple is eloping and their way is blocked by a flooded river, Candaini, not Lorik, figures out how to cross. She first procures a small boat from the ferryman stationed at the crossing. Lorik accuses her of negotiation of more than transportation with the ferryman, however, and in jealousy splits the boat and its owner in two with his sword. He then goes into the jungle and cuts down some green wood to build a raft, which, of course, immediately sinks. It is Candaini who knows it must be built with dry bamboo, tied together with lengths of a forest vine. When the ferryman's wife comes to bring him his breakfast and sees him dead, she immediately suspects the eloping couple of murder and creates a magical mouse to hide in their raft.

Halfway across the river, the stowaway mouse bites through the ropes holding together the raft. Candaini manages to reach the far shore, but Lorik does not know how to swim and starts to drown. The heroine unties her braid, jumps in, and saves him, presumably by pulling him ashore with her hair.[26] Candaini's ingenuity and physical strength in this episode stands in sharp contrast to a similar scene in the U.P. variant in which Lorik's wife calls upon the power of her chastity (her faithfulness to her husband, *sat*) to cause the waters of a river to part.

A female worldview is again reflected in a wonderful episode of the eloping couple's journey through a kingdom of all women. Candaini sends Lorik into the town to buy them some betel leaf (*pān*). He is tricked by the *pān*-seller to follow her home, where she "keeps her best *pān*" (to feed *pān* to a member of the opposite sex in Chhattisgarhi folklore is often to initiate a sexual relationship, or may be used as a metaphor for intercourse itself). Once the *pān*-seller has trapped Lorik in her house, she threatens to beat him with a bamboo pole and stuff his skin with straw, poke his eyes out with a needle, and, finally, brand him with a hot crowbar unless he promises to marry her. After each threat, he gives in, only to recant a few minutes later. Finally, Candaini comes looking for her partner and meets the *pān*-seller in the bazaar. The *pān*-seller begs the epic heroine to help her with a man who refuses to marry her. Candaini discovers a sari-clad Lorik in the woman's courtyard, having been so disguised so as to hide his male identity in the all-female kingdom. Once his identity is made known, the two women agree to play a round of dice to determine who will win him as husband. Note that although this is a reversal of the gender roles in Sanskritic, male dicing games, which are played to win a woman in marriage or as a sexual partner, the motif of women dicing over the fate of men is found in other Chhattisgarhi folk narratives. Candaini triumphs in her dice game with the *pān*-seller and frees Lorik from his captivity. One can hardly imagine the martial hero of the U.P. variants of the epic permitting the *pān*-seller's physical humiliations to be forced upon him or to be dependent upon rescue by a woman in a women's world.

Even in several episodes in which Lorik takes the primary role in a confrontation, it is still a woman who tells him how he can win, and the means are rarely traditional "heroic" ones. The first such confrontation is between Lorik and the Camar Bathua. Candaini's mother says the only man who can successfully confront Bathua is the "sporting hero Lorik."[27] Lorik's wife, Manjari, however, warns him that he will not be able to defeat the Camar in a normal wrestling competition. She suggests that the confrontation be one in which the men are buried up to their waists in separate pits by the other man's wife. The man who can first get out of his pit and beat the other man will be the winner. Lorik agrees to this. When the women are burying each other's husbands, Manjari begins to throw gold coins on the ground. This so distracts the Camar's wife that she only loosely packs the dirt around Lorik and then runs to pick up the coins. Meanwhile, Manjari has time to bury Bathua firmly. When the time comes for the men to try to get out of their pits, Bathua is stuck. Lorik jumps right out and soundly defeats the Camar.

Candaini's beauty and a male's desire for her are the source of several major conflicts in the Chhattisgarhi variant, and in these situations she is physically threatened and needs physical protection like the women in the U.P. versions. As we have seen above, however, if Lorik is left to his own strength and resources, he may or may not be able to provide Candaini with the necessary protection. Judging by her resourcefulness in other situations, one senses that if she had no male to protect her physically, Candaini would come up with alternative solutions. Furthermore, when her chastity *is* protected by Lorik, only her personal honor is at stake. The personal honor of a Chhattisgarhi Raut woman does not necessarily extend to the honor of her family and caste. One of the main episodes in the U.P. variant making this connection between the three levels of honor—the story of Lorik saving Manjari from having to marry a king outside the Ahir caste—is not present at all in the reported and performed versions I have seen in Chhattisgarh. The other U.P. episode making this association explicit is Lorik's defeat of Bathua, which saves the honor of Candaini and the Ahir caste. In Chhattisgarhi versions, Candaini's mother, in asking Lorik for help, is not as concerned with honor as with physical safety: Bathua is terrorizing the entire village, so that everyone is afraid to go out of their homes, and the cattle are dying from lack of fodder and water.[28]

As the role of women increases in importance in the Chhattisgarh variant, we have seen that the character of the hero also shifts. He is no longer the ideal protector and warrior. When he does engage in battle, he usually employs nonmartial, often unheroic, means to win; when the battle is honest, he battles without the aid of large armies, elephants, or other military paraphernalia, which support him in U.P. versions. He is a simple cowherder whose weapons are his own physical strength and herding staff. In this epic variant that centers around elopement love, the hero's status as warrior is less important than that as lover.

An important way Lorik's lover role is highlighted in Chhattisgarh is through the elaboration of the character of Bawan Bir, Candaini's impotent first husband. His impotence and passivity give emphasis to Lorik's sexual prowess and virility. One *nācā* performance portrayed Bawan as a buffoon who is always wiping his nose with his fingers and licking the snot off of them. During the twelve years of his impotence, he wanders the forest as a *sādhu* (religious ascetic) but is easily frightened by any strange noise and welcomes Canda's company when she comes to the forest to try to persuade him to give up his asceticism. Both Satnami and Raut versions agree that Bawan Bir's impotence is the result of a curse cast upon him by the goddess Parvati. A Satnami version of the curse incident recounts that Bawan used to tease the Raut girls who picked up cow dung in the jungle every day. One day, Parvati took the form of one of these girls, and Bawan began to tease her. She revealed her true form to him and cursed him with impotence for his audacity. The Raut version says that one day Bawan Bir left a leaf cup of milk sitting on the ground, from which he had drunk. Shiva, in the form of a snake, came up to the cup and drank out of it. Subsequently, he began to acquire the rather obnoxious personality of Bawan Bir, quarreling with and scolding his wife, Parvati. When Parvati realized why this personality transformation had occurred, she cursed Bawan with impotence.

Bawan Bir is also impotent in the U.P. epic variant; the fact, however, is given little elaboration in the performances reported by Pandey. In the Awadhi version, we learn of the impotence in a single line. The performer tells his audience that Bawan is a eunuch with no hair on his body, but he gives no reason for the condition, although the audience knows the reason is a curse from Durga. Another story circulates in Ballia, U.P., that Bawan encircled his large penis around a Shiva *liṅga*, a phallic representation of Shiva, and that the god cursed him with impotence for trying to compete with him.[29] Whatever the reason, Bawan's impotence is overshadowed in the

U.P. versions by his martial nature. He, too, is a powerful warrior when he battles and defeats Lorik's older brother and confiscates all of their family wealth and cattle, and again in the battle in which Lorik regains this wealth at the end of the epic.

APPROPRIATING THE PERFORMATIVE "EXTERIOR" OF THE TRADITION

As varying social groups have appropriated the epic within its traditional performance range from U.P. to Chhattisgarh, both the textual content, "interior," and performative "exterior" of the tradition have responded to and reinforced the identities of these groups. While the epic in U.P. has served to represent the caste both to itself and to other castes in the region, in the Ahirs' effort to consolidate and raise their caste status, in Chhattisgarh, traditionally, it has been self-reflexive, mirroring the region to itself, contributing to a Chhattisgarhi self-awareness of difference, particularly, for example, regarding the status of women and marriage customs.

To say that the region has "appropriated" the epic in the Chhattisgarhi contexts described above is, perhaps, to give unwarranted self-conscious agency to a relatively loose social body.[30] In the last ten to fifteen years, however, "appropriation" *is* the word to describe the emergence of "new" performance contexts and audiences for Candaini, both within and outside of Chhattisgarh. The tradition has been self-consciously crafted and packaged for both Indian and international audiences as representative of the *region* (not a particular caste, class, or gender). This appropriation coincides with increased availability of mass media technologies and communications (television and radio), as well as the academic and popularized interest in "ethnicity" that has developed in India over the last decade (as evidenced, for example, in international festivals of India and modified "ethnic dress" as high fashion among the upper middle class of urban India).

Radio, television, and the cassette industry have provided significant new contexts for folklore performance, including the epic. Akashvani (All India Radio) has both local (Chhattisgarhi) and national (Hindi) programming, with regularly scheduled folklore programs as a part of both. Such programming expands the social boundaries of groups to whom many performance genres are traditionally available; songs that women used to sing among themselves while transplanting rice or in the privacy of their courtyards are now blared over speakers from tea stalls and bus stands in urban neighborhoods and village main streets. Although prior to its appearance on media channels, the epic was spoken of as being "Chhattisgarhi," its performance on radio and television has solidified the epic's geographic regional identity, drawing its boundaries more literally than "live" epic performances, since such programming is limited to specified districts but also has become uniformly available throughout those districts, even in those villages and neighborhoods in which the epic has never been performed.

In 1985 when I was trying to trace down various performance traditions in the burgeoning town of Dhamtari, I was frequently asked why I didn't simply turn on the radio on Wednesday afternoons for Akashvani's Chhattisgarhi folklore programming, from which I could simply tape the "best singers" directly from the radio, without all the complications of live performance. Both radio and television performances are taped in rather sterile recording rooms, with specific time frames (much abbreviated from any live performance), without a live audience with whom to interact and jointly craft the performance. Further, these performances are taped under the direction of radio-station personnel who often have certain aesthetic criteria that they feel "typify" the particular genre in question, although most of them are not "native" to the region. These criteria include less repetition, more instrumentation, and particular voice quality and stage presence of singers. When I articulated some of these differences between a half-hour radio performance of a Candaini episode and its elaboration during a four-hour, late-night epic performance in a village square, adding that there was little *manoranjan* (literally, "entertainment," but with the implication of emotional satisfaction) hearing it over the radio, these same informants generally wholeheartedly agreed, although they often felt somewhat differently about television performances. In the mass media, the epic is taken out of its traditional performance contexts and recontextualized in a setting in which it "represents" on an external performative level through style and instrumentation, but in which its interior is frozen, unresponsive, generic.

Radio and television programming has affected the careers of particular singers who are chosen and promoted by the staff. This has been the case especially for the female epic performers referred to above. Once heard repeatedly on local radio or television, they are then invited to statewide folklore singing competitions and folklore festivals in major urban centers, such as New Delhi, Bombay, Calcutta, and even London, to "represent" Chhattisgarh. As individual singers themselves become famous, the genres associated with them become more popular as well, both within and outside of the region.

Representative of the growing "academic" interest in Chhattisgarhi folklore by members of an urban, educated class, who have not traditionally participated in epic performance as singers or audience, is the playwright/director Habib Tanvir, a Muslim born in Chhattisgarh's heartland, now living in New Delhi. His troupe, Naya Theatre (New Theatre), consists of a majority of actors and actresses drawn from Chhattisgarh's villages, nonliterate "traditional" dancers and performers. Along with his interest in experimental theatrical forms, an overriding concern of Tanvir's is to promote the appreciation and preservation of Chhattisgarhi folk performance traditions.

To this end, he has held numerous folklore workshops in Chhattisgarh itself for performers of these traditions. The aim of these workshops is for performers to share with each other their repertoires and for Tanvir himself to document them, often then integrating their themes and forms into his "new theatre." In a 1985 interview, while in Calcutta staging his play *Charan Das Chor,* Tanvir explained this task as follows:

> I had to work in two ways. I had to purify their forms and themes to make them more authentic and contemporary. I found that the folk form was getting spoiled and diluted by the combined influence of urbanization, mass media, and low-grade Hindi films. The first part of my job was to weed out the falsities and purify the form. Not for the sake of purity, but because the folk form is both beautiful and a powerful medium for a message.[31]

For one of his Chhattisgarhi folklore workshops, held in the late 1970s, Tanvir called together the "best" Candaini singers he had met in his tours of the region. Singers from a range of castes shared their stylistic and thematic repertoires. One of these singers was the Satnami Devlal; he was also one of several workshop participants chosen to go to Delhi to work with Tanvir for several more weeks. According to Devlal, Tanvir stressed to the singers the importance of keeping their tradition alive, and that one of the ways to do this was to keep the *entire* narrative in performance, singing it "from the beginning," when the hero and heroine were children and so on, rather than focusing so exclusively on the elopement episode.

I attended (and was the primary patron of) one of Devlal's Candaini performances that resulted in what I have called a "failed performance," with most of the approximately 200-member audience walking away within the first hour of the performance. I have analyzed the reasons for this elsewhere,[32] but one important reason cited by audience members was that he was singing "stories we don't know," from this reconstructed larger repertoire of epic episodes. What they expected and wanted to hear was some variation of the elopement narrative. Devlal was also experimenting with form. He framed the performance as if it would be a *nācā,* a form influenced by the corrupting "low-grade Hindi films" to which Tanvir referred, but did not wear the expected costuming, did not perform the expected "song and dance"; so that another major complaint of the dissatisfied audience was that "he should have worn a *sari.*"

Literate and nonliterate residents of Chhattisgarh alike have voiced, over the years during which I have returned to Chhattisgarh since 1980, a certain unease about Tanvir's appropriation of Chhattisgarhi folklore for display outside the region. Even as he is attempting to promote an appreciation of the region and its performance genres, many inhabitants feel that the process serves no benefit to Chhattisgarh itself. Several residents of the town in which Devlal performed, who have known him since his childhood and over the years in which he developed his epic-singing skills, complained that when Tanvir chose particular singers such as him, they often forgot the Chhattisgarhi roots from which they had come, were no longer satisfied to sing in "traditional" contexts, demanded too much money, and were no longer responsive to their audiences.

Drawing on a workshop held for Candaini performers, Tanvir later wrote a script based on the epic to be performed by his Naya Theatre troupe, called *Son Sāgar,* the name of one of Lorik's beloved cattle. I was able to sit in on one of the rehearsals of this play in 1985. The actors and actresses of the troupe are Chhattisgarhi, as is the language of the play; it opens with a traditional *vandanā* (invocation to the goddess Sarasvati) and is framed and interspersed with lines sung in the traditional *gīt* style. But, performed on a modern stage, outside of traditional performance contexts, it is not Chhattisgarhi Candaini, at least as it is understood by the folklore regional community. Although, according to Tanvir, there is room for improvisation, the lines are relatively fixed, memorized, and unable to be responsive to particular contexts and audiences—and if even if they were, the performance contexts would not be Chhattisgarhi.

In newly emerging performance contexts such as radio, television, and the modern stage, the epic has become decontextualized, so that it can be performed anywhere. In a sense, the audiences are not "live"; they are dispersed, unknown, and unseen. Further, the Chhattisgarhi dialect of the sung "text" is itself often not understood fully, if at all, by newly emerging Hindi or English-speaking audiences. What characterizes the epic for these audiences is its performative *exterior,* the unique singing and instrumental styles of epic performance, which themselves become relatively frozen, or at least enough so that they are recognizable as "Chhattisgarhi." In these contexts, the epic tradition has become an artifact, frozen in time and space, held up for admiration and nostalgia; thus though perhaps unresponsive to what may be perceived to be more traditional shifting performative and social contexts "on the ground," so to speak, it is responsive in a very different way to newly emerging middle-class audiences.

The Candaini living epic tradition has shown a tenacious ability to adapt to shifting and emergent performance contexts: to take up the cause of a caste trying to raise its status in U.P., and in Chhattisgarh to integrate non-Raut singers into the circle of its performers and instrumentation and the *nācā* song and dance into its performance style as it competes with Hindi cinema and video halls. Over the last decade, however, while performers continue to be drawn from low-caste groups, the performance contexts of the Chhattisgarhi epic have bifurcated. The first are those live performances in traditional, late-night, open-air village squares in which primarily lower-class/caste audiences continue to interact with and help to shape the interior "text" of the tradition. It remains to be seen how flexible this interior can be in its interaction with a rapidly changing social world, how long or in what ways its performances can compete with video halls, movie theaters, and television, and who the singers and performers will be in the next generation. The second context is physically distanced from its audiences, on stage or over the airwaves, audiences that now include an increasingly educated middle class. For these audiences, the epic's narrative interior no longer reflects "who we are," but its performative exterior may remind them nostalgically of "who we were."

NOTES

1. A version of this essay appears in Flueckiger 1996, where the Candaini epic is contextualized within the broader regional repertoire of Chhattisgarh; it is a substantially revised version of an essay that appears in *Oral Epics in India* (Blackburn et. al, 1989).

2. See Chapter 1, "Epic as Genre."

3. See, for example, Oinas 1972; Chadwick and Zhirmunsky 1969; Johnson 1980.

4. Blackburn and Flueckiger 1989, 6.

5. Flueckiger and Sears 1991, 6; Bauman 1977, 3.

6. Blackburn and Flueckiger 1989, 11.

7. The Awadhi variant was recorded in Allahabad District, U.P., and published as *The Hindi Oral Epic Loriki* (1979); the Bhojpuri variant was recorded in Benaras, U.P., and published as *The Hindi Oral Epic Canaini* (1982).

8. Elwin 1946, 338–370; episodes of Elwin's version are surprisingly similar to the episodes I heard in performance, even though they were documented forty years earlier.

9. Miller 1981, 71; Flueckiger 1996, 8–9.

10. Pandey 1979, 17.

11. Coccari 1984.

12. Mandelbaum 1972, 444.

13. One such volume is Khedkar 1959.

14. See Flueckiger 1996 for an expanded discussion of the epic episodes that illustrate the martial and caste emphases of the U.P. variant.

15. I add the characterization "male," since women are not part of its primary audiences and may listen to its performance only when it is held in a setting that allows them to "overhear" from behind a curtain or wall. According to Pandey (personal communication), Ahir women may know the general outline of the narrative but have not incorporated its characters and plot into their own female performance genres.

16. Pandey, oral communication, June 1982. I heard a similar saying in Chhattisgarh regarding the *Mahābhārata* (except argument was substituted for battle) in an explanation for why *Rāmāyana* performances were more common—a wonderful indigenous articulation of the creative power of performance.

17. Many oral epics in India are published in these bazaar pamphlet forms; the Chhattisgarhi Candaini, however, has not yet been so published. This particular U.P.

publication and its cover illustration seem to be patterned after the popular pamphlets of another martial epic performed in U.P., the Alha Kand, whose episodes are also named after its numerous battles.

18. See Babb 1975, 36–37, for a description of *mātar* as celebrated in the Chhattisgarhi plains.

19. This image is changing, however. During my last trip to Chhattisgarh in the summer of 1993, I heard many complaints from village landlords that Rauts were no longer willing to "serve" the village, that they were choosing to commute to the city for work instead. It has left many landowners desperate for "servants" (*naukar*), and many are being imported from the neighboring province of Orissa, where there is high unemployment and hence a willingness to relocate for work. It is doubtful that the Rauts will reappropriate the epic now to promote this newly emerging identity, since they have already abandoned the epic as performers, although they still participate as audience members of the Chhattisgarhi regional folklore community.

20. Rauts do have other narrative performance traditions whose musical accompaniment—five– to six–foot bamboo flutes—give the genre its name, *bās gīt;* and *bās gīt* remains specifically associated with the caste, although it is listed in the core Chhattisgarhi folk repertoire referred to earlier.

21. One informant told me that the primary difference between the Candaini and Pandvani epic traditions was the characteristic line ending of *mor* and *tor* of Candaini and *bhaiyā* or *bhaige* (literally, "brother") of Pandvani.

22. Many *nācā* performers are able, therefore, to perform in the *gīt* style and may do so for their own entertainment.

23. See Flueckiger 1988 for a description of one performer who experimented with combining elements of *gīt* and *nācā* in a public performance for which there were not sufficient funds to hire an entire *nācā* troupe.

24. See Narayana Rao (forthcoming) for a discussion of the Sanskrit classification of low castes and women within a single category.

25. Elwin 1946, 349.

26. Loose hair in Chhattisgarh has sexual connotations unless framed in ritual contexts of mourning or goddess possession.

27. Elwin 1946, 345.

28. Ibid.

29. Pandey, personal communication, June 1982.

30. There are genres other than epic that *have* been appropriated by folklore groups and communities within the region, however, in a self-conscious way. For example, in 1985 one village headman talked specifically about the role he thought folk festivals could play in establishing a sense of village identity and improving morale. He told me he had introduced the festival of *gaurā* to his village several years ago, one of the performance genres consistently mentioned in the repertoire list of "what we in Chhattisgarh celebrate." He had asked several daughters-in-law who came from villages in which *gaurā* was traditionally celebrated if they would be willing to introduce the festival to their village of marriage. He thought this particular festival would be appropriate because of the numerous folklore groups it could involve and the large public procession to the village tank that ends the festival. After several years of its performance in his village, the headman seemed satisfied with its results.

31. Bose and Bhattacharjee 1984.
32. Flueckiger 1988.

WORKS CITED

Babb, Lawrence.
1975.   *The Divine Hierarchy: Popular Hinduism in Central India.* New York: Columbia University Press.
Bauman, Richard.
1977.   *Verbal Art as Performance.* Rowley, Mass.: Newbury House.
Blackburn, Stuart, and Joyce Burkhalter Flueckiger.
1989.   Introduction to *Oral Epics in India,* edited by S. Blackburn, P. Claus, J. Flueckiger, and S. Wadley, 1–11. Berkeley: University of California Press.
Blackburn, S., P. Claus, J. Flueckiger, and S. Wadley, eds.
1989.   *Oral Epics in India.* Berkeley: University of California Press.
Bose, Nandini, and Pradipta Bhattacharjee.
1984.   "Folk Theatre: Neither Exclusive nor Esoteric." *The Sunday Statesman,* April 22.
Chadwick, Nora Kershaw, and Victor Zhirmunsky.
1969.   *The Oral Epics of Central Asia.* Cambridge: Cambridge University Press.
Coccari, Diane.
1984.   "The *Bir Babas* of Banaras: An Analysis of a Guardian Deity in North Indian Folk Hinduism." Ph.D. dissertation, University of Wisconsin.
Elwin, Verrier.
1946.   *Folksongs of Chhattisgarh.* Madras: Oxford University Press.
Flueckiger, Joyce Burkhalter.
1996.   *Gender and Genre in the Folklore of Middle India.* Ithaca, N.Y.: Cornell University Press.
1989.   "Caste and Regional Variants of an Epic Tradition." In *Oral Epics in India,* edited by S. Blackburn, P. Claus, J. Flueckiger, and S. Wadley, 33–54. Berkeley: University of California Press.
1988.   "'He Should Have Worn a Sari': A Failed Performance of a Chhattisgarhi Oral Epic." *The Drama Review* T117: 159–169.
Flueckiger, Joyce Burkhalter, and Laurie J. Sears, eds.
1991.   Introduction to *Boundaries of the Text: Epic Performances in South and Southeast Asia,* 1–16. Ann Arbor: Center for South and Southeast Asian Studies, University of Michigan.
Johnson, John William.
1980.   "Yes Virginia, There is an Epic in Africa." *Research in African Literatures* 11: 308–326.
Khedkar, V. K.
1959.   *The Divine Heritage of the Yadavas.* India: n.p.
Mandelbaum, David G.
1972.   "Cultural Adaptations and Models for Mobility." In *Society in India:*

Change and Continuity, 2: 442–467. Berkeley: University of California Press.

Miller, Barbara D.
1981.   *The Endangered Sex: Neglect of Female Children in Rural North India.* Ithaca, N.Y.: Cornell University Press.

Narayana Rao, V.
Forth-   "What is Folklore in India? "In *South Asian Folklore: An Encyclopedia,*
coming.   edited by Peter J. Claus and Margaret Mills. New York: Garland Publishing.

Oinas, Felix.
1972.   "Folk Epic." In *Folklore and Folklife,* edited by Richard Dorson, 99–115. Chicago: University of Chicago Press.

Pandey, S. M.
1982.   *The Oral Epic Canaini.* Allahabad: Sahitya Bhawan Pvt.
1979.   *The Oral Epic Loriki.* Allahabad: Sahitya Bhawan Pvt.

The Boundaries of Epic Performance

8

• • •

Problematic Performances

Overlapping Genres
and Levels of Participation
in Arabic Oral Epic-Singing

Dwight F. Reynolds

Dwight Reynolds focuses on the Egyptian oral epic of *Sīrat Banī Hilāl*, which relates the heroic exploits and westward migration of the Bedouin Arabic Bani Hilal tribe during the tenth and eleventh centuries and belongs to an age-old narrative cycle that includes both poetic and prose genres. Though the epic circulated widely for centuries, the twentieth-century tradition has survived more narrowly. It is still performed in northern Egypt, however, where it is perpetuated by hereditary, professional singers whose spirited and multifarious renditions resonate deeply within the community. Reynolds suggests that this tradition derives much of its strength and appeal from the artistry of these oral poets, who skillfully manipulate generic and performance boundaries, constantly generating and sustaining levels of dynamic interplay between themselves and their audiences.

One of the central ideas of performance studies is that performance is a distinct, identifiable type of human communication that in turn allows for or even requires special types of interpretation. Key to this idea is the understanding that performances are bounded or framed behaviors that are marked for the purpose of recognition.[1] The implication is thus that within the context of performance events at least two types of communicative behavior will be found: "performance" and "nonperformance." By expanding our theoretical focus, however, from the internal analysis of a single genre of performance, such as oral epic-singing, to the larger domain of entire performance events, we encounter problematic areas where genres appear to "overlap" or "interpenetrate," where the "breakthrough" into and out of performance occurs over and over again, or where different "levels" of performance seem to be present all at the same time.[2] These phenomena directly challenge any simple definition of performance as an object of study.

In focusing upon this central idea of complex performances, I hope to suggest a line of thought that might lead us to examine the problem of complex units, such as whole performance events, composed either of multiple genres or multiple movements into and out of performance such that the problem of boundaries and their interpretation arises, and further, to speculate on the ramifications of such problematic boundaries for performance studies.

Thus in this essay I would like to examine this metaphorical conceptualization of boundaries, frames, margins, and edges within the question of where performance and nonperformance do (or do not) meet in the northern Egyptian Arabic oral epic tradition of *Sīrat Banī Hilāl* (The epic of the Bani Hilal Bedouin tribe). Specifically, what I want to offer here is a portrait of a performance tradition as a whole, rather than the analysis of the style of a specific singer or the close analysis of an individual performance event. In other words, I am making the claim that just as individual singers can be observed to deploy a certain standard repertory of techniques of composition and interactions in their performances, we can also trace the rough parameters of an entire regional tradition through the observation of many performances in order to provide an image of the typical, recurring elements in the larger tradition. I hope that this broader portrait may provide both the material and impetus for comparative analysis with other epic traditions around the world.

In brief, I will examine three types of problematic boundaries here. By problematic I mean aspects of this northern Egyptian oral epic performance tradition that appear to challenge our commonly received notions of the "boundedness" of epic as a textual genre and as a performance genre. These three types are: (1) the boundary between the epic itself and the auxiliary genres of song with which it is most commonly performed; (2) narrative strategies within the epic that transgress or bring into question the boundaries of the epic story world; and finally, (3) audience interaction and participation in the epic performance event that create "overlapping performances."

THE *SĪRAT BANĪ HILĀL* TRADITION

The gist of the story of *Sīrat Banī Hilāl* is historical: the Bani Hilal Bedouin tribe did indeed exist, and they did indeed embark upon a major migration from their homeland in the Arabian peninsula, across Egypt and Libya, and into Tunisia and Algeria. The Bani Hilal then controlled much of the hinterlands of North Africa for more than a century. These events took place between the tenth and eleventh centuries and form the core narrative of the epic tradition. Later, in the mid-twelfth century, the tribal confederation suffered a series of military defeats at the hands of an eastward-expanding Moroccan dynasty, after which the tribe ceased to exist as a political and social entity. Interestingly enough, though it appears that historically the Bani Hilal were destroyed by outside forces (that is, the Moroccan Almohad dynasty), in the folk epic tradition the tribe defeats itself.

Wracked by a series of internecine conflicts, the various clans go to war against one another until the tribe is annihilated, providing an even more tragic close to the tribe's history.

In all probability it is the disappearance of the tribe itself that has allowed its history to become appropriated as a pan-Arab epic tradition. If the tribe had survived, it is quite probable that the exploits of the Hilali heroes would have remained a tribal history restricted to poets of the Bani Hilal tribe. Instead, the tales of the Hilali migration, their battles and conquests, their romances, their winning of brides, and so forth have been woven into a narrative of extraordinary length that has been documented in Arabic oral tradition in virtually every corner of the Arab world, from Morocco in the west to the Sultanate of Oman in the east. We possess historical evidence documenting the performance of this poetic tradition from the fourteenth century onward; in addition, a rather impressive manuscript tradition emerges from the eighteenth century onward, and a tradition of cheap chapbook publications dates from the late nineteenth and early twentieth centuries. Finally, in the late twentieth century, we have a number of audio and video recordings of live performances from several different regions.[3]

A primary characteristic of this tradition, however, is that it exists in many different types of performance. In some areas it is narrated as a prose tale cycle, in some areas in prose embellished with brief passages in verse, in some areas as chante-fable, where the narration of events is in spoken prose, and the speeches of the heroes are in sung or cantillated poetry, and finally, in some regions the entire story (with the exception of brief introductory passages) is performed in sung, rhymed verse to the accompaniment of one or more musical instruments. It is this latter mode of performance that I will address here. This sung, versified mode of performance was much more widespread in previous centuries, but in the latter half of the twentieth century it is found in only two main regions: northern and southern Egypt.

I will focus specifically on the northern Egyptian performance tradition as performed by the hereditary, professional epic-singers of the Nile Delta region. By *hereditary* and *professional* I mean that the occupation is almost always inherited by descent and that this is the sole livelihood of these performers. These epic-singers constitute a defined social group within northern Egyptian rural society and are understood to be one of the several groups commonly referred to as Gypsies [*Ghajar*]. This group in particular, however, the Ḥalaba, are associated with two occupations: blacksmithing/tinkering and epic-singing. Over a number of years I have studied a single village that is home to fourteen households of professional epic-singers. These fourteen households are, in addition, related by blood and/or marriage to another seventeen households of epic-singers scattered across northern Egypt. This population almost certainly constitutes the entire extant body of hereditary epic-singers in northern Egypt.

With the full understanding that there can be no such thing as a complete version of the epic, in order to communicate some sense of the proportions of this tradition, I can cite three versions of the epic that I recorded from three different poets in the village, each of which can be said to cover the general narrative scope of the tradition as it exists in this region. One version was thirty-four hours long, approximately 5,500 verses (and a verse here is an end-rhymed unit 24 to 30 syllables long—in contrast, for example, to the southern Egyptian quatrain style of performance in which a verse is 8 to 12 syllables long). A second version is fifty-three hours long—that is, approximately 12,000 verses. And a third rendition had reached seventy hours in length when we had to abandon the effort due to the poet's health, and represented approximately two-thirds of his repertory. A rough estimate based upon the poet's listing of the episodes he had yet to sing would place his version at well over a hundred hours in length. Incidentally, when these "full-version" recordings (field experiments I purposefully conducted to explore the narrative breadth of the tradition) are contrasted with recordings I made of naturally occurring performances, the poet who sang the thirty-four hour version beginning to end typically takes nearly twice that time to sing each episode when performing for an enthusiastic audience.

As for the topic of problematic boundaries of performance, the first area I will explore is that of the interaction between the epic as genre and the auxiliary genres with which it is typically performed. Different performance situations in the village of al-Bakātūsh draw different types of audiences and create rather differently structured events. Until the very recent past, *Sīrat Banī Hilāl* was typically performed at weddings, saints' festivals, in coffeehouses, at circumcision ceremonies, at harvest festivals, or in a private evening gathering, that is, a *sahra* or a *lēla*. This latter is currently by far the most common epic-singing event. During my various stays in the village in 1983, 1986-1987, and 1988, I was able to attend well over a hundred such gatherings and was able to record seventy-six full performances and fragments of an additional twenty. It is from this specific type of event that I draw most of the following examples.

AUXILIARY GENRES: *MADĪḤ, MAWWĀL,* AND *SĪRA*

The *sahra* as a performance context for epic-singing in al-Bakātūsh is defined by the *sahra*'s patron or host, who will have negotiated with a poet to perform that evening. When the poet arrives, a round of tea and cigarettes will probably be offered before the performance is set in motion. When the poet deems fit, he begins by readying his instrument, putting rosin on the bow and on the *rabāb*'s two strings, and finally tuning the instrument and testing it briefly against his voice. After first pronouncing the *basmalah* ("In the name of God, the All-Merciful, the Compassionate"), he plays a brief musical introduction. This instrumental interlude serves to alert guests who may still be waiting outside that the performance is about to begin. The first genre sung is a song of praise to the prophet Muhammad (*madīḥ* or *madḥ al-nabī*). This may be accomplished in a few short verses by citing some of the Prophet's best known attributes (his compassion, his beauty, etc.), by allusion to well-known tales from the Prophet's life (he who ransomed the gazelle. . . , he to whom the camel spoke . . .), or by the poet's choosing to recount one or more such tales at length. Unlike the monorhymed odes of the epic, these songs of praise are constructed in quatrains, usually rhymed *abab/cdcd/efef*. . .

This opening praise song to the prophet Muhammad unifies the audience and casts them immediately into an interactive mode through its repeated references by name to the prophet Muhammad, to which listeners respond with one of the nearly obligatory traditional blessings, "May God Bless and Preserve him [ṣallā llāhu ʿalayhi wa-sallam]" or "Upon him Be God's Blessings and Peace [ʿalayhi al-ṣalāt wa-l-salām]."

In most performances of epic-singing in al-Bakātūsh, the praise song to the prophet Muhammad will be following directly by a *mawwāl*, a short lyric poem of five, seven, or occasionally nine verses that is performed in a rhythmically free and often very melismatic style in which a single syllable may be lengthened and sung over several notes. During the *mawwāl* there is a marked shift in presentation style and in the role played by audience members. Here the focus is the quality of the singer's voice, his ability to ornament the melodic patterns, and rather than responding phrase by phrase, the audience typically waits until the end of the brief song and responds to the entire text as a whole with approbation or criticism. The themes of the *mawwāl* are also quite distinct from the earlier praise of the Prophet, for this is a song form that focuses on the trials and tribulations of everyday life. Its texts are often couched as advice to the listeners in a proverbial rhetoric using stock images of Egyptian folklore. The forces of Fate are addressed directly as Time, Destiny, the Nights, or the World; the lion functions as a symbol of the ruler, the mosquito as the interloper or sycophant, the camel as the stalwart man, the doctor as an image of the Beloved, since she or he alone can cure the disease from which the Lover suffers. But the *mawwāl* is a complaint addressed in the end to one's fellow human beings and not to God; it is not a plea for intercession, but rather a plea for understanding.

Mawwāl (Shaykh Biyalī Abū Fahmī, 2/11/87; rhyme pattern aabaa)

1. iṣ-ṣabr ʿuqbuh farag li-llī nshaghil bāluh

Patience-its result is release for him whose mind is occupied
   (with cares and troubles),

2. aḥsan min illī yifaḍfaḍ yiḥuṭṭ il-fikr fī bāluh

(Which is) better than he who grumbles
and fills his mind with thoughts.

3. mā fīsh aḥsan min illī yiṣbur

There is nothing better than he who is patient

4. li-ḥikam iz-zaman wi-awānuh

(and endures) the judgments of Fate and his Era;

5. min ḥusn ʿaql il-gadʿ biyi ʿdil aḥmāluh

From the good sense of the stalwart fellow he is able
to balance his loads (in life)!

This aphoristic mode of thought is of course reminiscent of many different epic-singing traditions, such as the proverbial mode used in Mandé hunter songs or the brief aphorisms used by Muslim singers in Yugoslavia or even the improvised *terme* songs of Central Asia traditions.[4] In all of these traditions, the proverbial or aphoristic song occurs at the point of transition into the more heroic epic genre. In the case of the Arabic tradition, it promotes a fundamental shift away from the *ideal* as represented in the life of the prophet Muhammad toward the level of *identification* with the characters in the epic who display at one and the same time both superhuman characteristics and all-too-human weaknesses and failings.

Finally, the poet directs us into the epic world, but in order to do so he moves carefully through a complex series of steps that are repeated whenever he commences the epic or returns to the epic after an interruption. The poet begins with a brief scene-setting that informs the listeners where he is in the overall story. If this is the very beginning of a *sahra,* he will include the phrase "The narrator of these words said [qāl ar-rāwī]" or "The author of these words said [qāl mu ʿallif ik-kalām]." The following brief prose introduction is narrated in an ordinary, though occasionally rhythmic, voice. While narrating, he begins to ornament the prose with rhymes [Arabic *sajʿ*], which occur at progressively regular intervals. Then a character within the epic must be emotionally moved to speak—that is, the situation a character is in must produce such fear, joy, or sadness, for example, that he or she is compelled to rise and compose a poem that addresses the situation. When the character begins to recite the poem, the poet moves into full song. It is this movement into an "authoritative speech-act" that brings us into the world of epic speech. Once we have arrived in that world, many different voices can be deployed, including that of third-person narrator, but the movement from speech to song, from the outer world to the world of epic verse is always accomplished by the shift into an authoritative first-person utterance.[5] I have elsewhere analyzed this process in much closer detail as a series of very intricate shifts of voice, melody, and poetic form.[6] The basic steps, however, are as follows:

instrumental music —> rhymed prose —> emotional crisis —> sung epic verse

When entering this world of authoritative heroic speech—that is, the epic verse itself—the performing poet briefly reiterates all of the framing devices of the *sahra* performance. He stops and performs a short musical interlude. Then the opening verses of the poem will be in praise of the Prophet (a miniature *madīḥ*). The poet then calls upon the audience to listen to the words of the epic character in a verbalized quotation marker parallel to the opening formula "The narrator said" and usually describes the character as being in emotional turmoil:

Quotation Marker (Shaykh Ṭāhā Abū Zayd, 6/1/87)

O listeners to these words, wish God's blessings on the Prophet,
Ṭāhā, fortunate is he who visits him [i.e., on pilgrimage].[7]

The emir Barakāt said-and his heart was in pain;
The fire of his heart in his soul did sear him.

When the epic character actually begins to sing, he or she sings either a full *mawwāl* or several lines of aphoristic poetry in the style of the *mawwāl* but in the form of epic verse:

Aphoristic Verses (Shaykh Ṭāhā Abū Zayd, 6/1/87)
Said King Faḍl from what had befallen him:
"It is a wretched world, and Fate is a tyrant!

Ah! From the world and the reversals of all that happens in it,
In my opinion Fate spins in circles.

After the good things of the world and the cup of sweetness,
There is no escape from drinking also from the cup of bitterness.

Each stage of the evening performance to that point is thus reproduced in miniature as a frame for the "language of heroes" (to borrow a phrase from Richard Martin):[8] instrumental introduction/praise of the prophet Muhammad/quotation marker/aphoristic verse/narrative material. This frame is repeated each time the poet begins to sing, even after brief interruptions, providing a constant mirroring between the performance of the living epic-singer and the performances of the heroes of the epic.

In the following short example, Khaḍra the Noble (mother of the hero Abū Zayd) has had her livestock stolen by a marauding band claiming to be collecting a "tax" from her. The dialogue between Khaḍra and the head of the raiding party has been recounted succinctly in prose, and the poet now leads us back into epic verse with Khaḍra's lament:

Transition into Epic Verse (Shaykh Ṭāhā Abū Zayd, 6/2/87)

Spoken:

"So Khaḍra wept in anguish; she could not have wept harder. See now what Khaḍra will say, and we shall now cause the listeners all to hear it. He who loves the Prophet wishes God's blessings upon him!

[Audience: May God Bless and Preserve him!]

[Musical Interlude]

Sung:

My first words are in praise of the Chosen One, the Hashemite [Muhammad],
We have no intercession [with God] save him.

Said Khaḍra when Fate leaned upon her,
"By the life of my Lord [God], there is no god but He.

The Creator of creation . . . Ah! . . . and He knows their reckoning,
In His power He knows, yes, all matters indeed.

I shall complain of my sufferings to [King] Faḍl, yes, the hero,
Under whose protection these long years I have remained.

If he is able to defend my rights,
I shall stay the coming years here with him.

[But] if he is not able to defend my rights,
I shall go seek a people who defend their refuge seekers!

Where shall I go? Whence am I coming?
My lowly state pains me; woe is he whose strength has been crushed by Fate."

In terms of frames and boundaries, the *sahra* performance as conducted in northern Egypt thus challenges our ideas of where the beginning of the epic lies. The poets themselves answer that the epic begins after the formula "The narrator said." Yet the intense replication of the musical interlude, the praise song to the prophet Muhammad, the verbalized quotation marker, and the aphoristic rhetoric of the *mawwāl* sequence within the epic to frame the speech of heroes suggest that the "auxiliary" genres are in fact critical parts of the epic itself. Richard Martin, who has studied the speech-acts of characters within the *Iliad* in such rich detail, has also pondered the framing of the *Iliad* as a whole in order to ask, "What speech-act does the poem make?"[9] My response to Martin's observations and question, in part, is that despite the highly significant relationship between the *madīḥ*, the *mawwāl*, and the *sīra*, which I have summarized here, when asked to provide a translation or summary of the epic, I instinctively find myself beginning simply with the *sīra*, that is, the "epic" itself, and discarding the accompanying genres, perhaps unwittingly repeating a decision possibly taken by the scribe of the *Iliad* long ago. In northern Egyptian performances of the Hilali epic, the speech-act of the poem is indeed parallel to the speech-acts of the heroes within the poem. Thus without the constant dynamic of the interaction between the frame of the larger epic-singing event and the frames of the heroes' performances within the epic, a highly significant part of the epic tradition as a whole would indeed be lost. In addition, as I have explored in some detail in other publications, this constant equation of the speech of poets and the speech of heroes is part of a larger social dynamic involving the proper roles of poets and heroes that places the epic at the very center of symbolic conflict within the context of the village.[10]

NARRATIVE STRATEGIES

The second set of observations I would like to make concerns narrative moves within the epic performance. The first example is of a process found in many traditions—that is, the process of glossing the text in a series of asides or excursive remarks that overtly depart from the narrative and are openly addressed to the audience. In the following example, a poet comments to his listeners about the rank and respect accorded to the poets of old (with obvious reference to the contrasting status of poets in modern village society):

Shaykh Biyalī Abū Fahmī, 2/14/87

Spoken Narrative

So [King Ḥasan of the Banī Hilāl] said to him, "O poet Jamīl." He answered him, "Yes, O father of ʿAlī [=Ḥasan]."

He said to him, "You have journeyed among many peoples, among the great ones of the noble Arabs—has anyone given you gifts and treated you as generously as have I and my Arabs?"

Poet's Excursus

Now the poet was of great politesse [Arabic *adūb*, emphatic form of "polite"]. The poet was of great politesse, for every poet who picks up the *rabāb* is of great politesse. Why? Because he sits with good people. Because a poet never possesses bad manners. He travels with his *rabāb*. . . . I do not laud poets merely because I am a poet! [laughter from audience]. . . . It is because the histories tell us so! The poet was of great politesse. Were he not of great politesse, he would never pick up the *rabāb* and sit with good people. How could he be a poet of kings and Arabs and be impolite? He was of great politesse. And the audience, as well, when they listened to a poet, they were the pinnacle of respectfulness.

There is another less obvious but equally effective means of moving back and forth through the boundaries of the story world: a poet may make a request or an observation concerning his host or audience by manipulating a character within the epic. If an audience member falls asleep, for example, the poet may cause a hero within the story to fall asleep, and begin singing in a softer and softer voice. Knowledgeable listeners will immediately begin looking about to see who is going to be the butt of the poet's joke. The poet sings more and more softly, and then another character arrives at the scene to shout "Wake up!" The shout usually rouses the unsuspecting napper and provokes a round of laughter among the other listeners. Or, when seeking a glass of water, the poet may cause the hero to ride out into the desert, and then describe in great detail the sun and the heat and how the hero's throat is getting scratchy and sore: "Yes, the sun is beating down and the heat is intense, . . . his sword is so hot he cannot touch it, . . . and the sweat is pouring off his stallion. . . . He is getting thirsty . . . oh so thirsty." [In fact, when this paper was first presented, Margaret Beissinger, who was sitting in the front row, leapt up to pour the speaker a glass of water. Reynolds responded, "Well, it is clear that not all boundaries are problematic, since certain rhetorical devices function quite well cross-culturally!" Ed.]

A particularly fascinating use of blurred boundaries occurs in this epic tradition when heroes within the epic are portrayed as also being epic poets in their own right, and we are then treated to the description of a performance of praise songs to the prophet Muhammad or bits of epic poetry as sung by a hero within the epic. The result is thus a complete reduplication of performance event, host, poet, audience, and song. And it is exactly at this moment that northern Egyptian epic-singers often choose to express their social or political commentary about life in the village. The hero in the epic who is singing as a poet may criticize his patron or his audience, and of course should any offense be taken by our host or listeners, the performing poet denies any intent on his part and distances himself from the offending words as part of the epic—after all, it was the hero Abū Zayd who sang them![11] In these three short examples—a poet's aside to his audience in an attempt to strengthen his own social position by reference to the epic story world, waking a sleeping listener or asking for a glass of water by manipulating the story line, and burying social commentary inside a performance within a performance—we can see in miniature the powerful dialogue that exists between the worlds inside and outside the epic as mediated by the poet who has primary control of the boundaries between them.

AUDIENCE PARTICIPATION

Audience members listening to a performance of *Sīrat Banī Hilāl* in northern Egypt, as in many traditions, may take a very active role in shaping the performance by critiquing or encouraging the poet, by requesting particular scenes, or by pointing out that a particular detail has been overlooked. But in this tradition, audience members may also find themselves suddenly part of the actual stuff of the performance, rather than in the somewhat exterior role of supporters, encouragers, or critics. This may occur in one of several different ways. First, as we have seen, the poet may direct commentary or observation toward an audience member by manipulating the plot or characters of the epic as demonstrated above. In addition, there is a genre of performance that is often performed along with the epic in which audience members themselves are the material used by the poet. This genre is called *ḥitat baladī*, which can be loosely translated as "bits of local color," and consists primarily of a comic routine in which the poet attempts to weave the names of his listeners, their characteristics, references to families, friends, land, and so on, into a loose narrative recounted in rhyme. This genre also constitutes a form of social Russian roulette, since one never knows whether one is going to be mentioned in a positive or negative fashion, complimented or made the butt of a joke. In this sense the situation is similar to attending performances in certain comedy clubs in the United States, where the performer is likely to abandon pre-prepared material and make jokes with or at audience members at any moment. This is a performance drawn directly from the performance context.

But there is still another means by which audience members become part of the very fabric of the performance. During tea breaks and other interruptions, listeners often engage in discussions of the epic and its characters; this in turn often leads to discussion of events external to the epic that are parallel or relevant to the discussion. For example, the motif of a hero in the epic sleeping at prodigious length (the *Heldenschlaffe* of European folktales) one evening provoked a long series of first-person narratives recounted by listeners. One man told of a time when he had been returning in the evening from a trip outside the village and was so tired that he fell asleep on his donkey. When he finally arrived home in the middle of the night he simply continued to sleep on his mount at the door of the house till the following morning when his wife finally discovered him, still sound asleep! Another listener jumped into the discussion with the tale of how he had one time had a similar experience but had actually fallen off his donkey on the way home and remained asleep, his donkey standing by peacefully all night long, and had awoken in the morning alone, in the middle of a strange field, lying alongside the path!

The final story in this series was told by two listeners who had served in the army together and had received leave to go home for one of the holidays. They caught the train with several friends from the same village and, since they were stationed many hours from home, eventually all fell asleep, only to wake up in the middle of the night in the next province having traveled quite a distance past the village in the other direction. But when they piled off the train in confusion at two in the morning in a strange city, who should they find standing in front of the station (through God's mercy!) but a man from their own village with his taxicab who had just delivered someone to the station and was now planning on heading home to the village for the holiday, too. Everyone arrived safely and in time for the feast!

When we finally returned to the epic, the poet took his cue from his listener's tales and wove references to their stories into his narration of the epic. In this tradition, this process of weaving elements from the epic into discussions that then provoke performances by audience members of first-person narratives, proverbs, folktales, and other conversational genres is quite common, as is the poet's response of making reference to, or even citing, these audience performances in subsequent portions of his rendition of *Sīrat Banī Hilāl.* The thread linking different elements of the performance event as a whole often runs through an entire series of different genres performed by a series of different performers.

CONCLUSION

In our first set of examples we saw that the auxiliary genres commonly performed with epic in this northern Egyptian performance tradition provide a highly significant frame not only for the epic as genre but for the performances that occur within the epic itself. These frames or cues are essentially formal devices and are only partially rooted in narrative developments. By contrast, the second set of examples we examined were ones in which the poets manipulate narrative elements so as to affect or comment upon situations outside the narrative story world. They constitute narrative strategies much as Kenneth Burke conceived or, strategies that purposefully appear to blur any possible divisions between the inner and outer world of the performance.[12]   And finally, we have seen examples of how chains of performances can be sparked, creating interactions in which the role of performer constantly shifts, and a dialogue of performances exists alongside the more usual dialogue of comments, criticisms, and compliments.

From these examples I conclude that the clarity and rigidity with which performance boundaries and genre boundaries are maintained, or the lack thereof, are qualities specific to individual traditions and must therefore be carefully observed, documented, and compared along with other more commonly recognized characteristics of performance, text, and context. It seems clear that some traditions may in fact draw a great deal of their strength and potency from forcefully maintaining strict boundaries of genre or performance. I think it also clear that this particular oral epic tradition, *Sīrat Banī Hilāl* as performed in northern Egypt, thrives on the dynamic interplay between the creation of performance boundaries and the willful obscuring and even violation of those boundaries. Here then is an example of an oral epic that draws a portion of its popularity and vitality from the constant negotiation of its margins by playing with the space in which performance and non-performance meet. There is surely a spectrum of possibilities of which this is but one, thus this closing question: Where do the other epics of the world lie on this same spectrum?

NOTES

1. See, for example, Briggs 1988, Bauman 1977, and Hymes 1971. For an earlier and broader statement, see Goffman 1974, particularly chap. 10, "Breaking Frame."
2. See Hymes 1981, "Breakthrough into Performance" and "Breakthrough into Performance Revisited."
3. For an overview of these materials, see Reynolds 1989.
4. See Bird 1972; Lord 1974; Reichl 1992.
5. The authoritative role of the first-person utterance has been an enduring feature of Arabic literature from the earliest periods onward, particularly in genres that are close to, or imitate, oral traditions. See Reynolds 1991.
6. Reynolds 1995, chap. 5, "The Interplay of Genres."
7. Ṭāhā is an epithet of the prophet Muhammad formed from the two Arabic letters *Ṭā* and *Hā*.
8. See Martin 1989.
9. Ibid., 237.
10. Reynolds 1995, chap. 3, "Poets Inside and Outside the Epic."
11. A remarkable incident from southern Egypt in which a poet was not able to disclaim an offending verse is analyzed in detail in Slyomovics 1987.
12. See Burke 1931.

WORKS CITED

Bauman, Richard.
    1977.   *Verbal Art as Performance*. Prospect Heights, Ill.: Waveland Press.
Bird, Charles.
    1972.   "Heroic Songs of the Mande Hunters." In *African Folklore*, edited by Richard Dorson, 275–293. Bloomington: Indiana University Press.
Briggs, Charles.
    1988.   *Competence in Performance: The Creativity of Tradition in Mexicano Verbal Art*. Philadelphia: University of Pennsylvania Press.
Burke, Kenneth.
    1931.   *Counter-Statement*. New York: Harcourt Brace.
Goffman, Erving.
    1974.   *Frame Analysis: An Essay on the Organization of Experience*. Cambridge, Mass.: Harvard University Press.

Hymes, Dell.

1981.   *"In Vain I Tried to Tell You"*: *Essays in Native American Ethopoetics.* Philadelphia: University of Pennsylvania Press.

1971.   "The Contribution of Folklore to Sociolinguistic Research." *Journal of American Folklore* 84: 42–50.

Lord, Albert B., trans.

1974.   *Serbo-Croatian Heroic Songs Collected by Milman Parry.* Vol 3, *The Wedding of Smailagič Meho.* Cambridge, Mass.: Harvard University Press.

Martin, Richard P.

1989.   *The Language of Heroes: Speech and Performance in the "Iliad."* Ithaca: Cornell University Press.

Reichl, Karl.

1992.   *Turkic Oral Epic Poetry: Traditions, Forms, Poetic Structure.* New York: Garland Publishing.

Reynolds, Dwight Fletcher.

1995.   *Heroic Poets, Poetic Heroes: The Ethnography of Performance in an Arabic Oral Tradition.* Ithaca, N.Y.: Cornell University Press.

1991.   "Orality and Veracity: The Construction of Voice in Early Arabic Literature." Paper presented at the meeting of the Middle East Studies Association, Washington, D.C., 23 November.

1989.   "*Sīrat Banī Hilāl:* Introduction and Notes to an Arab Oral Epic Tradition." *Oral Tradition: Special Issue on Arabic Oral Traditions* 4 (1–2): 80–100.

Slyomovics, Susan.

1987.   *The Merchant of Art: An Egyptian Hilali Oral Epic Poet in Performance.* Berkeley: University of California Press.

9

• • •

Worshiping Epic Villains

A Kaurava Cult in the Central Himalayas[1]

William S. Sax

It is perhaps no surprise that India's ancient epic *Mahābhārata* continues to thrive in the Central Himalayas of North India as a form of ritual drama. More astonishing is the fact that in one remote valley the villains of *Mahābhārata* are major cult figures, and subjects of religious veneration. In this essay, William Sax describes that cult and analyzes current processes of social change that are rapidly transforming it.

In the Central Himalayas of North India, India's great epic *Mahābhārata* lives on. Indeed, it is the greatest single source of folklore in this predominantly Hindu region,[2] constantly invoked to explain everything from the nature of south Indian cross-cousin marriage to the origin of warts. While the vast majority of local persons identify with the heroes of the epic, there is one valley, high and isolated, in which the villains rather than the protagonists of the story are worshiped as divine kings. The situation, however, is complex and ambiguous: as the valley is integrated ever more closely into the contemporary world, its epic traditions are transformed. In what follows, I hope to show how *Mahābhārata* lives on, and also how it changes in response to wider social processes. But before doing so, I must say something about the epic itself.

Mahābhārata is the longest epic poem in the world, more than eight times the length of the *Iliad* and the *Odyssey* combined, a veritable encyclopedia of Indian culture.[3] In one of its recensions, it boasts: "Whatever is here may be found elsewhere; what is not here cannot be found anywhere else" (*"yadihāsti tadanyatra, yannehāsti na tatkvacit"*). The central narrative of *Mahābhārata* involves a dynastic rivalry between two sets of cousins, the five Pandava brothers versus the hundred Kaurava brothers. The Pandavas are the protagonists, sons of gods, born in order to rescue Earth from her oppression by demons who have taken birth in other royal lineages. Their social father, Pandu, was cursed to die if he made love to a woman, and so the five are actually half-brothers, begotten on Pandu's wife Kunti by various deities. There is also a sixth half-brother named Karna, born before Kunti was married. Soon after birth, she set him adrift in a river, and later he was found and raised by a lower-caste couple, so that neither he nor his five half-brothers know they are related. The irony of the situation only increases when Karna becomes a firm ally of Duryodhana, eldest of the Kauravas. Karna is one of the two "villains" who is worshiped in western Garhwal; Duryodhana is the other.

Although the Kauravas' father Dhritarashtra was eldest, his blindness made him ineligible to rule, and so the throne went to his younger brother Pandu. The two sets of cousins grew up in an atmosphere of rivalry, which intensified after Pandu died and the administration of the kingdom was taken over by the Kauravas' blind father Dhritarashtra. For a time the kingdom was divided in two, but when the Pandavas performed an elaborate royal sacrifice to lay claim to universal lordship, Duryodhana felt threatened, and he responded by inviting the Pandavas to a dice match in which the eldest brother, Yudhisthira, lost everything: his wealth, his kingdom, himself and his brothers, and finally their common wife Draupadi. Duryodhana ordered his vicious brother Duhshasana to drag her into the assembly hall and strip her naked. But this proved to be impossible because in answer to her prayer, Krishna provided Draupadi with an endless sari. Enraged by the Kauravas' cruelty, Bhima, the second Pandava brother, vowed that he would take revenge by drinking Duhshasana's blood and breaking Duryodhana's thigh.

The blind king Dhritarashtra restored to the Pandavas their weapons and their freedom, but in a subsequent gambling match Yudhisthira again lost everything, and they were exiled for thirteen years. They spent their final year in exile without being recognized, and therefore, by the terms of the wager, Duryodhana should have restored half the kingdom to them. But this he refused to do, and his intransigence led to the great *Mahābhārata* war. It lasted for eighteen days—a vast holocaust, a bloody sacrifice that consumed the earth's great kings and champions, including Karna (dishonorably slain by Arjuna at the urging of Krishna, while attempting to free his mired chariot) and Duryodhana (also treacherously slain at Krishna's urging, by Bhima who violated the rules of fair play by breaking Duryodhana's thigh in a club fight and thus fulfilling his vow). This great slaughter brought to a close the third age of the world and ushered in *kaliyuga*, the final and most decadent age, in which we now live.

Both the Kaurvas and the Pandavas belonged to the Bharata lineage, from which the word *Mahābhārata* is conventionally said to be derived, namely, "the great *mahā* [story of the] Bhāratas." But according to both popular and learned etymologies, the proper derivation is "the Great (*mahā*) War (*bhārata*)," and the eighteen-day battle is undeniably the central event in the epic. This should come as no surprise since *Mahābhārata*, like India's other great epic, *Rāmāyaṇa*, was originally composed and performed for the warrior class of Kshatriyas in ancient India, and thus reflects their central values and concerns.[4] *Mahābhārata* is in fact a kind of extended meditation on the moral dilemmas arising from the fact that war is both terrible and necessary. On the one hand, it is wrong to slay anyone, especially one's friends and kin, as Arjuna explains to Krishna immediately before the great battle (their dialogue is famous as the *Bhagavadgītā*). It is also wrong to gain victory through deception and trickery, but this is precisely what the Pandavas did at Krishna's urging, a fact that has generated much debate and discussion amongst Hindus. On the other hand, Earth must be defended against evil, and this responsibility lies squarely with the warrior class, men like the Pandavas, whose *dharma* or code for conduct may include violence. *Mahābhārata* can of course be interpreted in many ways: many scholars in India and elsewhere have tried to discern a historical kernel beneath the sprawling epic, while some currently influential interpretations see it as a vast, transformed sacrifice,[5] or as the first and greatest example of devotional Hinduism.[6] But in a general sense—especially in its contemporary representations in comic books, films, television, and performance genres— *Mahābhārata* remains a powerful Indian metaphor for the struggle between good and evil.

MAHĀBHĀRATA IN GARHWAL

Traveling in India, one is continually struck by the many ways in which both *Rāmāyaṇa* and *Mahābhārata* are popularly invoked. This boulder is said to have been placed by Bhima; that cave is said to have been a resting place for Rama and Lakshmana, heroes of the *Rāmāyaṇa*, as they searched the forest for the kidnapped Sita; here is the site where Arjuna the Pandava performed asceticism in order to gain his magical weapons; there is the place where Rama left his footprint in the rock. Through such localizations, the epics are made immediate on both the local and the national scale: many of India's holiest places derive their importance from their association with the epics. Rama, Lakshmana, and Sita spent the first and most idyllic part of their forest exile in a place called Chitrakut, which is today identified as a pilgrimage place in the North Indian state of Madhya Pradesh. Before attacking his enemy Ravana's island fortress of Lanka, Rama prayed to the god Shiva, and the place where he did so is known today as Rameshvaram, one of the most important Hindu pilgrimage places in the world. Rama's supposed birthplace of Ayodhya is not only a famous pilgrimage place but also a politically contested site.[7]

Places throughout peninsular India are mentioned in the *Mahābhārata*, but the main action of the story takes place in the north, roughly between present-day Delhi and the Himalayan foothills. It is widely believed that Indraprastha, the capital of the Pandavas, was located on the present site of Delhi's Old Fort, while Kurukshetra, scene of the *Mahābhārata*'s climactic battle, is still a famous place of pilgrimage. But nowhere does *Mahābhārata* have such tremendous social and religious importance as in the former Himalayan kingdom of Garhwal, in the Himalayan districts of the state of Uttar Pradesh, where it is invoked to account for the origins, not only of social customs and features of the landscape, but also of the local people, who consider themselves descendants of the Pandavas. Sanskrit versions of the epic mention Badarinath, the foremost local pilgrimage place, and one that was intimately associated with the kings of Garhwal.[8] Garhwalis believe that the Pandavas were born at the local temple town of Pandukeshvara below Badarinath, that the attempted assassination of the Pandavas by burning them in the palace made of lac took place at Lakha Mandal in the Yamuna River valley, that the kingdom of Virat where the Pandavas spent their final year of exile was in the Jaunsar region of Garhwal, and that the Pandavas made their final ascent to heaven through the Garhwal Himalayas.

The major vehicle by which Garhwalis express and explore their understandings of *Mahābhārata* is *pāṇḍav līlā*, a local tradition of ritual performance. The word *pāṇḍav* refers of course to the five Pandava brothers, but what about *līlā*? The word means "play" in both the nominal and verbal senses of the English word.[9] In the first place it means free, spontaneous play, like the play of a child, and this concept is, in effect, the Hindu answer to certain theological problems. If god is self-fulfilled and complete, then what could motivate him (or her or it) to create the world? In some strands of Hindu philosophy this question is answered in terms of *līlā*, so that God's creative activity is likened to the playfulness of a child. The term is also used in this sense to address questions of theodicy, so that when confronted with death and suffering, Hindus are more apt to say "It is God's *līlā*" than "It is God's will."

But *līlā* also means "play" in the sense of drama and theater. A *līlā* is a play about religious themes, so that *pāṇḍav līlā* is the "play of/about the Pandavas." At this point, the reader might suppose that *pāṇḍav līlā* is a kind of folk drama, but it is more precisely described as a "ritual drama." It is a ritual because, like religious ceremonies but unlike secular theater, it is believed to be efficacious; that is, it is performed for specific ends, such as helping the crops grow, keeping disease and misfortune at bay, and promoting health and well-being by pleasing the gods, who are physically present upon the stage. During performances the five Pandava brothers, their common wife Draupadi, and other gods and goddesses enter the bodies of the men and women playing their parts. There is no "fourth wall" here: participants are constantly slipping back and forth between the roles of spectator, bard, character, and dancer, and as character or dancer they are normally considered to be the incarnations of those epic characters whom they represent. Such divine incarnation is frequent in Hinduism, where there is no ontological gulf separating humans and gods.[10]

In performing *pāṇḍav līlā*, Garhwali society collectively represents itself to itself by means of a public ritual performance. But this representation clearly favors the Rajputs, who identify themselves as members of the class of Kshatriyas or warriors. Performances of *pāṇḍav līlā* make implicit claims about who and what these Rajputs are.[11] There are several reasons for saying this, the most important having to do with blood and ancestry. Most local Rajputs claim to be descended from the Pandavas, and thus *pāṇḍav līlā* is understood as a form of ancestor worship. Such an understanding is also revealed by the generic term for *pāṇḍav līlā* in western Garhwal: *sarāddh*, from Sanskrit *śrāddha*, the annual rite of ancestor worship that is obligatory for all Hindus. Rajputs are thus doubly linked to the Pandavas: not only do they perform a metaphorical *śrāddha* for them by sponsoring a *pāṇḍav līlā* performance, but in addition a central part of that *līlā* involves a dramatic search by the Pandavas for the necessary materials to perform a *śrāddha* for their dead father, king Pandu.

Pāṇḍav līlā is also self-definitional for Garhwalis because Garhwal is prominently mentioned in Sanskrit versions of the epic, lending plausibility to the local belief that much of the story happened there. After all, the Indian literary tradition refers to the *Mahābhārata* as "history" (*itihāsa*), as opposed to the more purely literary "poetry" (*kāvya*) exemplified by India's other great "epic," the *Rāmāyaṇa*.

A third reason that *pāṇḍav līlā* is self-referential has to do with the importance of the weapons that are carried by the dancers: a scythe for Draupadi, a staff for Yudhisthira, clubs for Bhima and his son Babarik, bows and arrows for Arjuna and his son Nagarjuna, a scythe for Nakula, and a slate for Sahadeva. The iron arrowheads of Arjuna and Nagarjuna are clearly the most powerful objects in a performance.[12] They must be held in the right and not in the unclean left hand. They must never be allowed to touch the ground lest their "power" or "energy" (*śakti*) escape. Large penalties (usually a goat or its cash equivalent) are levied on those who accidentally drop them, and women, low-caste people, and those in a state of pollution are not allowed to handle them. In Jakh village in 1991 my assistant Dabar Singh and I were invited to dance, then later told that I would have to do so with a headless shaft. We politely declined. In the next *līlā* we attended, in Kaphalori village, I was allowed to dance with an "empowered" shaft complete with arrowhead. I found the experience exhilarating.[13] At the beginning of a *pāṇḍav līlā*, the old weapons that were used by the fathers of the present generation in the previous *pāṇḍav līlā*, perhaps twenty or thirty years ago, are taken down from a secret and honored place (often under the eaves of a house) where they have been kept free from pollution and negative influences. They are placed on the altar in the dancing square, and kept there for the remainder of the performance. Meanwhile a new set of weapons is fashioned—sometimes on the spot by the local blacksmith—and used in the current performance. After the *līlā* is over, these new weapons are placed under the eaves, and the old weapons of the previous generation are ritually disposed of at some holy place, often a water source. In this way the Rajputs' martial energy—the *kṣatra* of the Kshatriyas—is embodied in the weapons of the *pāṇḍav līlā* and passed from generation to generation.

Finally, *pāṇḍav līlā* may be considered a form of self-representation, because of the kinds of episodes that are selected for dramatic representation. Because of *Mahābhārata*'s great length, some principles of selection must be employed in choosing these, and martial episodes are clearly favored. This is in keeping with Garhwali Rajputs' self-image as warriors, an image that was strengthened when they were defined by the British as one of the "martial races" of India and were actively recruited for the colonial army. Even today, military service is a highly prestigious career, sought after by many local youths. The theme of martial prowess runs right through *pāṇḍav līlā*, and the fight to the death between Arjuna and his son Nagarjuna is of particular importance. East of the Alakananda River, this event is represented far more often than any other. Not only is it sung of by bards and enacted by possessed players, but it is danced literally hundreds of times over the course of a nine-day *līlā*. Every night, each surrounding village is given the opportunity for its two best dancers to display their skill, which they do by dancing the Arjuna-Nagarjuna dance. This lasts until the wee hours of the night, with anywhere from fifteen to thirty pairs of dancers performing the same episode. In terms of sheer quantity, this father-son battle is represented more than any other episode. But it is also enacted (in a less complex fashion) in the Mandakini River basin and in the far west in the Tons River basin, making it one of the few features that is common to *pāṇḍav līlā*s throughout Garhwal. The details of the episode are much too complex to be recited here;[14] suffice it to say that one of its messages seems to be that a Kshatriya must always accept a challenge, even when it comes from a kinsman, a brother or even a father. To refuse a challenge is to lose one's most precious possession—one's honor—and so the fight between father and son once again points to war's dual nature, its necessity as well as its tragedy.

It should be clear by now that for the people of Garhwal, *Mahābhārata* is much more than just a book. This seems an obvious enough statement, but I find that it needs to be made—repeatedly—to my academic friends and colleagues. As members of a bibliocentric profession, many us have bound copies of *Mahābhārata* on our shelves, and it is only natural for us to think of it as a book. But it would be well to remember that even the critical edition of *Mahābhārata* is only one version among many; that the story has been translated into many languages of many nations; that it traveled throughout Asia as far as Vietnam and Indonesia;[15] that to begin with it was not a book at all, but rather an oral epic; and that the problems associated with establishing a critical edition proved intractable. Over thirty years ago the editor of the critical edition wrote that the "essential fact in *Mahābhārata* textual criticism is that the *Mahābhārata* is not and never was a fixed rigid text, but is fluctuating epic tradition. . . . To put it in other words, the *Mahābhārata* is the whole of the epic tradition: the entire Critical Apparatus."[16] There are many *Mahābhārata*s, not just one, and that is why I refer to "*Mahābhārata*" and not to "the *Mahābhārata*." I want to insist that books are just one part of this tradition; that they have no ontological or epistemological precedence; that *Mahābhārata* is not only a book but also a political model, a bedtime story, a tradition of dance, a dramatic spectacle, and much more. In Garhwal, it is an ancestral tale, one that is periodically enacted as a form of ancestor worship, and one that provides a basic—probably *the* basic—paradigm for what it is to be a Rajput.

A CULT OF THE KAURAVAS IN WESTERN GARHWAL

In the far west of Garhwal, near the Himachal Pradesh border, is the Tons River basin, an area that has long been associated with unorthodox social and religious customs such as bride-price, intercaste marriage, and especially fraternal polyandry of the sort exemplified by the marriage between Drau-padi and the five Pandava brothers. When my village friends in district Chamoli, in the eastern part of Garhwal, heard that I was planning to travel to this area, they did their best to dissuade me. I was warned that men did not return from the valleys of the Rupin and Supin rivers (tributaries of the Tons): the women there enslaved them, turning them into goats or frogs by day, and back into men at night "for their pleasure." Rumors of poison cults abound: the women of the area are said to worship supernatural beings who demand one human sacrifice per year. A friend of mine, a traditional healer, went so far as to empower some salt with special magical spells, telling me that if any local woman were to offer me food, I should sprinkle this salt on it, and if it turned blood red, then I shouldn't eat it. A retired government officer said that several decades ago when he toured through the area, when-ever he was offered food by the local people it would first be tasted by a pre-pubescent girl, in order to demonstrate that it was not poisoned.

I had long been aware of rumors of a Kaurava cult in this region,[17] but had dismissed them as fantasies. I reasoned that because some of the cus-toms of the area were very unusual, people in other parts of Garhwal assumed that the entire culture was inverted and strange, and this was why Garhwalis elsewhere were so willing to believe the most outlandish tales about the lo-cal people. The idea that there might actually be a group of people who wor-shipped the Kauravas struck me the way it strikes most most Hindus—as ut-terly implausible.

But I was wrong. Soon after arriving in the area for the first time in the winter of 1991, I was directed to the large and imposing temple of Raja Karan ("King Karna"), the presiding deity of Singtur, a traditional land division or *paṭṭī* whose social and religious life centers on the god. Karna's main temple is in Dyora village, but there are others scattered throughout Singtur, including a temple of his putative son Vikhasan.[18] Raja Karan is regarded by the population of Singtur as their king: he is served by numerous lineages of priests, musicians, carpenters, and watchmen; he is often called upon to settle local disputes, which he does through his oracle (*mālī*); he is the subject of a rich devotional folklore; and like other kings he travels frequently, sometimes in royal processions to the villages under his rule, sometimes to drive away other gods encroaching on his domains, and sometimes as a pilgrim to local sacred places.

In many respects, Raja Karan and his priests are social and religious reformers. For example, they are fierce prohibitionists, opposed to drinking in general and especially on religious occasions. They are opposed to animal sacrifice within the temple compound, even though it is practiced in other nearby temples, and they seek to reform local marriage customs. Despite the stereotypes noted earlier, polyandry is not generally practiced in Singtur or the neighboring areas.[19] However, the prevalent form of marriage, by bride-price, is still unorthodox, and Raja Karan's priests refuse to accept money in exchange for their daughters.[20] The reason, they say, is that Raja Karan was famed for his generosity (one of their most popular epithets for him is *dānī rājā* or "the giving king"), and so they, like him, are keen to give their daughters as a pure gift. In doing so, they conform to the normative type of marriage among North Indian Hindus, the *kanyādāna* or "gift of a virgin." In these and other respects they self-consciously distinguish themselves from Duryodhana and his subjects higher up the valley, where such reforms are only just beginning. How appropriate that Raja Karan's divine kingdom should lie midway between the more conventional cult of the Pandavas in the lower end of the valley and the cult of Duryodhana in the high mountains. The tragic figure of Karna, unknown brother of the Pandavas and devoted ally of the Kauravas, still mediates between the two sides, just as he did in the epic.

The people of Singtur assured me that there were indeed several temples of Duryodhana higher up the valley, the chief ones being located in the villages of Jakhol and Osla. Some of them also told me that there was a Duhshasana temple nearby.[21] They said that the oracle of Duryodhana, whenever he was possessed, had to lean on a crutch for support, since Duryodhana's thighs were broken in his final combat with Bhima.[22] I was told that Duryodhana used to go on royal tours throughout the region, and that wherever he halted, the people of that village were obliged to offer their finest animals, grain, milk, and butter to the god and his priests. So frightened were they of his curse that they would do so without demur. The people of Singtur asssured me that they had suffered a great deal at the hands of Duryodhana and his minions. For years their high-altitude herdsmen were forced to offer the finest of their flocks as annual tribute, until one year five brothers defeated Duryodhana's followers, even though they were vastly outnumbered, thereby ending the custom.[23] When I asked why it was that Duryodhana and Karna were now rivals when once they had been allies, people usually answered that the quarrel was not between the gods, but between their human devotees.

Why would anyone wish to worship the Kauravas? Duryodhana and his brothers are symbols of evil, of *adharma*, and Karna is a tragic figure strongly associated with death and defeat. Duryodhana makes only the briefest appearance in *pāṇḍav līlā*s elsewhere in Garhwal, and Karna is considered as so inauspicious that people in that area do not even read the *karṇaparva* or "Book of Karna" from the *Mahābhārata* without first performing a goat sacrifice: they believe that if they do so, catastrophe will strike.

The short answer is that people do not worship Duryodhana because he is evil, but rather because he is powerful. Specifically, he is thought to have the power to bring rain or to withhold it, something that is obviously of crucial importance to local farmers. There are other reasons too for worshipping the Kauravas, and these are really no different from the reasons people elsewhere in Garhwal give for worshipping the Pandavas: in both cases they have to do with people's ideas about who they are, and how they became that way. The belligerence of the Kauravas, their eagerness to do battle, fit in well with local Rajputs' images of themselves as courageous and warlike. People sometimes say that Duryodhayana did not really die, but rather fled to the Tons Basin after he was injured in the *Mahābhārata* war. It has been claimed that people from this area fought on the side of the Kauravas, and that the present inhabitants are their descendants[24]—in other words, that Duryodhana is king of his subjects in the Rupin and Supin valleys, just as he was king of their ancestors. In worshipping him they are remaining loyal to their ancestral traditions; to do otherwise would be dishonorable.

Neither the kings of Garhwal nor the British ever had much authority in this area, and its people were notoriously "turbulent and refractory,"[25] a reputation that persists to the present day. Political and religious authority is vested in deities like Duryodhana and King Karna, who are regarded as divine kings. Gods in this region have for a long time been among the most prominent political actors, and the boundaries of their domains are the subjects of continual and lively dispute.[26] Devotion to the ancestral god is, therefore, a kind of protonationalism, in which loyalty to one's lineage, caste, and region are all mutually reinforced in the cult of the deity. To its neighbors, Duryodhana's domain might look like an "evil empire," but to those within it, loyalty to the cult is an appropriate and honorable attitude.

So perhaps my earlier skepticism was wrong, and this exotic Himalayan valley harbored an equally exotic religious cult, in which the most notorious villains of Hindu mythology were adored by the local population. This was, after all, explicitly stated by Garhwali scholars and journalists, and by people living in the area. There have always been those who insist that only indigenous interpretations are valid, so perhaps this interpretation, clearly indigenous, was correct. The problem, of course, is that there is always more than one interpretation: "natives" have different points of view just as anthropologists do, and neither perspective is monolithic. This was implied by my friends in Singtur, who told me that in the upper valleys, the old ways were dying. Villages outside of Duryodhana's core territory were reluctant to invite him to visit, and so his annual tours were growing fewer, his domain shrinking, his influence diminishing. Inspired by Raja Karan's example, people were beginning to question the old ways, and now there were two factions in Duryodhana's main village, divided over animal sacrifice and the use of intoxicants. Young men had returned with university degrees from as far away as Delhi, and Duryodhana's followers were beginning to claim that he was actually Someshvara, a form of the great Hindu god Shiva. But I was told that despite these changes, there could be no doubt that that the god worshipped in the upper valleys was Duryodhana.

I pondered this information while trying to arrange a visit to the god's chief cult center, in the village of Jakhol. This was not easy to do, as it was winter and the mountain trails were buried in snow and often impassable. One evening I was explaining my interest in Duryodhana to a fellow patron of the tiny inn where I took my meals, when a small group of men sitting next to us fell silent. One of them angrily called out: "Who says our god is Duryodhana? His name is Someshvara!" I realized that my opportunity had arrived. The situation was very delicate, so I asked the man, Kula Singh from Jakhol village, to come outside with me where we would not be overheard. I apologized to him for causing offense, and said that I was only repeating what I had been told by the local people. Perhaps he would be willing to take me to Jakhol and show me the truth. He said that he would indeed be willing to take me there, but not now—it was midwinter, and the paths were too dangerous. But if I would come for the god's spring festival, I could stay with him, and he would help me with my research.

Later that spring I spent several days in Kula Singh's house, observing and participating in the god's festival, and three years later, in 1994, I returned again. During these two trips I discovered that, just as my friends had said, there were two factions in Jakhol. The "traditionalists" supported old customs such as demanding sheep and goats as tribute and sacrificing them in front of the deity, while the reformers regarded this as a form of theft inappropriate for a religious institution. There was also a dispute over the way in which the god makes his appearance during festivals. Traditionally, he is carried outside on a "chariot," actually a kind of palanquin, made of freshly cut pine saplings, and the young men of the village have great fun leaping on the saplings, jumping up and down on them and trying to break them. (The practice hearkens back to an incident in the god's biography when, according to local folk songs, he had been forgotten by everyone except a group of children, who began a festival in which his image was worshipped in childish ways.) The reformers felt that this custom demeaned the deity by showing him disrespect; moreover, people were allowed to wear shoes when they approached the "chariot," and it was quite possible for low-caste persons to pollute the deity by coming in contact with him during the melee. Raja Karan's temple had abolished similar customs, animals were no longer sacrificed in front of the god, and when he left the inner sanctum he was placed on a tiger skin, symbol of royalty, rather than on a wooden palanquin. Reformers in Jakhol wished to follow suit, and to that end they convinced the rival faction to take the god on a pilgrimage to the famous nearby temple of Kedarnath. They felt that after completing such a virtuous act, he would certainly adopt a vegetarian diet and be more circumspect about ritual pollution. Sometimes the rivalry between these two factions from the same village got rather nasty. During my visit for the spring festival in 1991, there was an altercation between the reformers and the traditionalists, and that evening the reformers sought me out and earnestly requested that I bring my camera the next day. They were certain that their rivals were going to shoot them, and they wanted me to document the massacre for posterity.

But despite the depth of feeling on these issues, the fact remains that both sides are committed, at least publicly, to the view that the god is Someshvara and not Duryodhana. In my two visits to Jakhol I have recorded several of the god's songs, including his "history" as sung by temple musicians; spoken at length with two of his priests; recorded a number of brief, quasi-historical songs from lay villagers; and conducted a lengthy interview with Sundar Singh, who, as both village elder and chief administrative officer of the deity, probably knows more about Someshvar and his history than any other person. Everyone I talked to in Jakhol—priests, Rajputs, and musicians—was unanimous that the god was not Duryodhana. The most common argument in support of this position was based on iconography: the image was held to be that of Shiva, with the river Ganges emerging from his head, a half-moon in his hair, a garland of serpents on his throat, and earrings, though this was impossible to confirm, as outsiders (including local officials) are not allowed to view the image. Others claimed that the traditional form of worship was of the sort that is directed only to Shiva. Probably the most articulate spokesperson for this point of view was Sundar Singh, who told me in 1994 that the reason the old men used to call the god "Duryodhana" is that in their day no one had taught them any better. But, he said, when educated persons began coming from outside and looked closely at the image, they realized that it was not Duryodhana. I have also been told that it is not the main image that is called Duryodhana, but rather a smaller image that is visible on the upper part of the palanquin when the god emerges during his festivals. According to this story, the image was made by a famous blacksmith named Bisar Katha, from across the border in Himachal Pradesh. He made this second image in order to add to the splendor of the main one, but when he made a third image, the local people saw that it was a replica of the first, and they went to kill him. With his dying breath he said: "I served you, and yet you're killing me, just like the Kauravas and the Pandavas, so I name this image Duryodhana."[27] Although some of these denials are inconsistent or demonstrably inaccurate, nevertheless the god's subjects agreed that he was Someshvara and not Duryodhana.

Yet it still seemed to me (and to Raja Karan's subjects from Singtur) that the temple up the valley belonged to Duryodhana. Perhaps I accepted the Singtur people's version because they were my friends. Maybe I believed them because my anthropological fascination with cultural difference encouraged me to see a Duryodhana cult that wasn't really there. In the welter of inconsistent and mutually exclusive interpretations, one thing that emerged quite clearly was that each interpretation was related to some specific interest, not least my own. But self-interest often requires self-deception: just because there are multiple perspectives on some issue does not mean that they are all equally true. In the end, I persisted in believing that there was a Duryodhana cult because of the evidence. There is, for example, the matter of the god's songs. In 1991, one of the village musicians had referred to the deity both as Duryodhana and as Someshvara,[28] but by 1994 all references to Duryodhana had disappeared from his song. Similarly, while attending a *pāṇḍav līlā* in Singtur in 1991, I recorded some folk songs from two men from Jakhol in which they referred to the god both as Duryodhana and as Someshvara. In informal conversation in Jakhol, many people called the god "Duryodhana," which the reformers found rather embarrassing. One of the god's priests admitted to me that they used to worship the god as Duryodhana, and only recently began worshiping him as Shiva. Along the top of the exterior walls of the temple in Jakhol are a number of carvings, prominent among which is one of two men facing each other, each flanked by their supporters: underneath are carved the names "Duryodhana" and "Arjuna."

But the most persuasive evidence of all was provided by the god himself. Surely his testimony is authoritative, since villagers in the upper valleys respect and fear him as their ruler. In 1994, he returned from a brief tour to some nearby villages and was ritually welcomed home to Jakhol, at which time he possessed his oracle, as is customary. It was the beginning of winter, and there had been a prolonged dry spell, but as we stood in the flagstone square before the temple, dark storm clouds whirled around us, and we were briefly pelted with hail, while the slopes above the village were blanketed with fresh snow. The god's speech exemplifies many of the issues already discussed, such as the tension between the two village factions, the god as a divine king, and the difficulties that arise when ancestral traditions undergo change and transformation:

Oracle: Education (*sīkhī*) is happening! I will accept whatever you do and say. Keep your old traditions, keep them! But times are changing, and I'll change with them.

Sundar Singh: We are only children. Our ancestors' ancestor—Dhangkato and the others—came with you, but when they challenged you, you destroyed them. We will do as you say.

Oracle: It would be best for you to unite with the others.

Sundar Singh: I also want this. But things happen.

Oracle: You should unite, yes, but the two sides are always quarreling; you won't listen to each other. This new generation has also dishonored me. Everyone has his own opinion.

Sundar Singh: We are not acting for ourselves; we do whatever you tell us. Please protect my family.

Oracle: I'll protect all my subjects (*janatā*), not just your family. Everyone knows how my rituals are conducted, and they should act accordingly. They say that even the musicians have their freedom, but we'll see how free they are!

Sundar Singh: Musicians, messengers, watchmen, priests, subjects—if we are separate from you, then where is our place? We follow you.

Oracle: Stay within your limits, follow my orders, and all will be well. Maintain your dignity (*maryādā*); don't slip from your old traditions. Let the others slip instead.

Sundar Singh: You have the power and the virtue (*guṇ*), not us. The rain has fallen.

Oracle: Yes. I'll take care of the rain.

Sundar Singh: Let the domain (*mulk*) be united.

Oracle: Wait four days, then see. I'll provide rain; don't worry.

During this speech, the oracle supported himself by leaning on what looked rather like a long metal sword with an unusually short handle. Was it not the crutch about which I had already been told, required by Duryodhana because his thighs had been dishonorably broken by Bhima in combat? His speech was punctuated by frequent interjections—"Ak! Ak!"—was this not, as one man from Singtur suggested when he heard my tape recording, an expression of pain from his broken thighs? After the possession was over, the oracle leaped up to a standing position, obviously relieved that the trance was complete—was he also relieved of Duryodhana's pain?

CONCLUSIONS

Who is the god worshipped in the upper valleys of the Tons River basin? It seems likely that formerly he was widely recognized as Duryodhana, but nowadays his identity is less certain. Perhaps, by the time this essay is published, he will have completely metamorphosed into Someshvara. Duryodhana's followers are clearly aware that other Hindus regard them as perverse and backward because they worship a notorious villain; therefore they are in the process of "reinventing" their deity. That this process should now be gathering momentum is hardly surprising, given the fact that these formerly isolated valleys are being integrated with the rest of India with unprecedented speed. A generation ago, there were no roads into the area, few visitors from outside, and virtually no public education. Today the transportation network is burgeoning,[29] domestic and international tourism is rapidly expanding, and government or private schools are found everywhere. One local youth obtained a law degree in Delhi several years ago and returned to become a very influential proponent of the view that the god is Someshvara and not Duryodhana.

The problem with trying to determine, once and for all, such an abstract matter as the identity of a god is that it is a matter of beliefs and meanings, which are notoriously unstable. The god means different things to different people—and even to the same people—in different contexts. Moreover, collective ideas about his identity change over time. There are relatively stable periods when such ideas are fairly consistent, as seems now to be the case in the cult of Raja Karan, and there are times of rapid change, as seems now to be the case in the cult of Someshvara. To assume that the god has a permanent, stable personality is as mistaken as assuming that a person has one. Cultural representations of gods, like representations of selves, are neither monolithic nor unchanging, but rather are related to the ever-changing contexts of culture and history.

NOTES

1. Special thanks to Rajmohan Singh Rangad and his family for sharing their home in Gaichwan village with me in 1993–1994. Thanks also to Terry Austrin, Jacob Neusner, Jane Simpson, and Alf Hiltebeitel for their comments on a previous draft. The research upon which this essay is based was made possible by a grant from the University of Canterbury.

2. Chandola, 1977, 18.

3. The critical edition (nineteen volumes) was edited by V. S. Sukthankar (1933–1966). The only complete English translation is that of K. M. Ganguli, first published by P. C. Roy in 1883–1896 and recently reissued (1981–1982). J. A. B. van Buitenen translated two volumes before his death, and a team of scholars is carrying on with what will certainly become the standard English translation (1973–). The most useful condensed English translation is still that of C. V. Narasimhan (1965).

4. Pollock 1986, 15.

5. Hiltebeitel 1976, 1988.

6. Biardeau 1976, 1978.

7. An invaluable study relating Hindu pilgrimage places to the *Mahābhārata* is Bhardwaj 1973. Other useful overviews of Hindu pilgrimage include Bharati 1970, Eck 1981, and Morinis 1984. Among a plethora of recent studies of Ayodhya and its continuing religio-political importance are Embree 1990 and van der Veer 1987.

8. Galey 1986.

9. For the concept of *līlā*, see Haberman 1988; Hein 1972, 1987; and especially Sax 1994.

10. Egnor 1980; Fuller 1992; Sax 1991b; Waghorne and Cutler 1985.

11. Blackburn and Flueckiger (1989) have also argued that in India, epics are defined in terms of "the extent and intensity of a folklore community's identification with them; they help to shape a community's self-identity" (p. 6); and that "most important, oral epics in India have that special ability to tell a community's own story and thus help create and maintain that community's self-identity" (p. 11). Flueckiger's essay in this volume also shows how a folk epic changes along with the characteristics of its community.

12. The arrowheads are not always used. Since they must receive blood sacrifice, they are not used in villages where such sacrifice is prohibited. In addition, they are not common in western Garhwal.

13. After receiving the bow and arrow from a dancer representing the Pandavas' guru Drona, one holds both of them above one's head, looks up, and spins around while shaking them. Several small bells are attached to the bow, so that the sound of their jingling mixes with the pounding of the drums. There in the firelit square, under the bemused gaze of several hundred villagers, I had the distinct feeling that it was not I who was spinning the weapons around, but *they* were twirling *me*.

14. See Sax 1997.

15. Desai 1970.

16. Sukthankar 1933, cii.

17. Nautiyal 1971, 133–134; Sharma 1977, 79; Thukral 1987, 41.

18. This character is not found in the Pune edition of the epic. There is, however, a figure named Vikarna, one of the ninety-nine younger brothers of Duryodhana, who speaks up on Draupadi's behalf during her humiliation in the assembly. Possibly Vikhasan has some relation to him.

19. Polyandry is found in the Jaunsar and Jaunpur regions, a few hours' journey away. See Majumdar 1963.

20. For discussions of bride-price in general, see Tambiah 1973; for bride-price in the Central Himalayas, see Fanger 1987; Sax 1991a.

21. According to one of the god's priests in Jakhol, there are a total of fourteen temples dedicated to the god in the immediate vicinity. I have been unable to confirm reports of a Duhshasana temple.

22. There is a Duryodhana temple in Kerala with a priest who, when possessed by Duryodhana, dances on one leg for several hours (Tarabout 1986, 223, 483; cited in Hiltebeitel 1991, 178). I thank Alf Hiltebeitel for this reference.

23. This "mini-*Mahābhārata*" is the subject of a long folk song that I have transcribed and translated into standard Hindi with the help of Bhuli Das of Dyora village and hope to publish soon.

24. Nautiyal (1971, 133–134) cites the *Mahābhārata* to this effect, but I am unable to verify his claim.

25. Saklani 1987, 44, 174ff.

26. Ibbetson and MacLagan 1919; Raha 1979; Rosser 1955; Sax 1991a; Sutherland 1988.

27. Duryodhana is said to be a partial incarnation of the demon Kali or "discord."

28. *jai ho, durijodhan mahārāj, dāsī durijodhan falāne dās jakhol, devatā kā, someśvar devatā kā dāsī, jai ho devatā somesor, teri māyā.*

29. In 1991 I had to walk over ten kilometers and cross a major river to reach Jakhol from Sankari. In 1994, I took the twice-daily taxi service.

WORKS CITED

Bharati, Agehananda.
1970.   "Pilgrimage Sites and Indian Civilization." In *Chapters in Indian Civilization*, edited by Joe Elder, 1: 83–126. Dubuque: Kendall-Hunt.
Bhardwaj, Surinder Mohan.
1973.   *Hindu Places of Pilgrimage in India : A Study in Cultural Geography.* Berkeley : University of California Press.
Biardeau, Madeleine.
1978.   "Études de mythologie hindoue: 5. *Bhakti* et *avatāra.*" *Bulletin de l'École Française d'Extrême Orient* 65: 111–263.
1976.   "Études de mythologie hindoue: 4. *Bhakti* et *avatāra.*" *Bulletin de l'École Française d'Extrême Orient* 63: 87–237.
Blackburn, Stuart H., and Joyce B. Flueckiger.
1989.   "Introduction" to *Oral Epics in India*, edited by Stuart H. Blackburn, Peter J. Claus, Joyce B. Flueckiger, and Susan S. Wadley, 1–11. Berkeley: University of California Press.
Chandola, Anoop.
1977.   *Folk Drumming in the Himalayas: A Linguistic Approach to Music.* New York: AMS Press.
Desai, Santosh N.
1970.   "*Ramayana*—An Instrument of Historical Contact and Cultural Transmission between India and Asia." *Journal of Asian Studies* 30 (1): 5–20.
Eck, Diana.
1981.   "India's Tīrthas: 'Crossings' in Sacred Geography." *History of Religions* 20 (4): 323–344.
Egnor, Margaret.
1980.   "On the Meaning of akti to Women in Tamil Nadu." In *The Powers of Tamil Women*, edited by Susan S. Wadley, 1–34. Syracuse: Maxwell School of Citizenship and Public Affairs.
Embree, Ainslie Thomas.
1990.   *Utopias in Conflict: Religion and Nationalism in Modern India.* Berkeley: University of California Press.
Fanger, Alan C.
1987.   "Brideprice, Dowry, and Diverted Bridewealth among the Rajputs of Kumaon." In *The Himalayan Heritage*, edited by Manis Kumar Raha, 139–153. Delhi: Gian Publishing House.
Fuller, Christopher J.
1992.   *The Camphor Flame: Popular Hinduism and Society in India.* Princeton: Princeton University Press.

Galey, Jean-Claude.
1986.   "Totalité et hierarchie dans les sanctuaires royaux du Tehri-Garhwal."
         Purusartha 10: 55–95.
Ganguli, K. M.
1981–1982.   *The Mahābhārata of Krishna-Dwaipayana Vyasa.* 4th ed. 12 vols. Origi-
             nally published by P. C. Roy (Calcutta, 1883–1896).
Haberman, David L.
1988.   *Acting as a Way of Salvation: A Study of Rāgānuga Bhakti Sādhana.* New
         York: Oxford University Press.
Hein, Norvin.
1987.   "Lila." In *The Encyclopedia of Religion*, 8: 550–554. New York: Macmillan.
1972.   *The Miracle Plays of Mathura.* New Haven: Yale University Press.
Hiltebeitel, Alf.
1991.   *The Cult of Draupadi.* Vol. 2, *On Hindu Ritual and the Goddess.* Chicago:
         University of Chicago Press.
1988.   *The Cult of Draupadi.* Vol. 1, *Mythologies: From Gingee to Kurukṣetra.*
         Chicago: University of Chicago Press.
1976.   *The Ritual of Battle: Krishna in the Mahābhārata.* Symbol, Myth and
         Ritual Series, edited by Victor Turner. Ithaca, N.Y.: Cornell University
         Press.
Ibbetson, Denzil, and Edward MacLagan.
1919.   *A Glossary of the Tribes and Castes of the Punjab and Northwest Frontier
         Province.* Lahore: Government Printing, Punjab.
Majumdar, D. N.
1963.   *Himalayan Polyandry: Structure Functioning and Culture Change: A Case-
         Study of Jaunsar Bawar.* New York: Asia Publishing House.
Morinis, E. Alan.
1984.   *Pilgrimage in the Hindu Tradition: A Case Study of West Bengal.* Delhi: Ox-
         ford University Press.
Narasimhan, Chakravarthi V.
1965.   *The Mahābhārata: An English Version Based on Selected Verses.* New York:
         Columbia University Press.
Nautiyal, Shivanand.
1971.   *Gaḍhvāl ke lokanṛtya gīt* (Folkdance songs of Garhwal). Prayag: Hindi
         [1902 *śāka*]. Sahitya Sammelan.
Pollock, Sheldon I.
1986.   *The Rāmāyaṇa of Vālmīki: An Epic of Ancient India.* Vol. 2, *Ayodhyākāṇḍa.*
         Introduction, translation, and annotation by Sheldon I. Pollock.
         Edited by Robert P. Goldman. Princeton: Princeton University
         Press.
Raha, Manis Kumar.
1979.   "Stratification and Religion in a Himalayan Society." In *Himalayan An-
         thropology*, edited by James F. Fisher. The Hague and Paris: Mouton.
Rosser, Colin.
1955.   "A 'Hermit' Village in Kulu." In *India's Villages*, edited by M. N. Srini-
         vas. Bombay: Asia Publishing House.

Saklani, Atul.
  1987.   *The History of a Himalayan Princely State: Change, Conflicts, and Awak-ening.* Delhi: Durga Publications.
Sax, William S.
  1997.   "Fathers, Sons, and Rhinoceroses: Masculinity and Violence in the Pandav Lila." *Journal of the American Oriental Society* 117 (1): 278–294.
  1994a.   *The Gods at Play: Līlā in South Asia.* New York: Oxford University Press.
  1994b.   "Who's Who in the Pandav Lila?" In *The Gods at Play: Līlā in South Asia.* New York: Oxford University Press.
  1991a.   *Mountain Goddess: Gender and Politics in a Himalayan Pilgrimage.* New York: Oxford University Press.
  1991b.   "Ritual and Performance in the Pandavalila of Uttarakhand." *In Essays on the "Mahābhārata,"* edited by Arvind Sharma, 274–295. Leiden: E. J. Brill.
Sharma, Man Mohan.
  1977.   *Through the Valley of Gods: Travels in the Central Himalayas.* New Delhi: Vision.
Sukthankar, Vishnu S.
  1933–1966. *The Mahābhārata. 19* vols. Poona: Bhandarkar Oriental Research Institute.
Sutherland, Peter.
  1988.   "The Travelling Deities of the Western Himalaya." Unpublished manuscript.
Tambiah, Stanley J.
  1973.   "Dowry and Bridewealth and the Property Rights of Women in South Asia." In *Bridewealth and Dowry,* edited by Stanley J. Tambiah and Jack Goody, 59–169. Cambridge Papers in Social Anthropology, no. 7. Cambridge: Cambridge University Press.
Tarabout, Gilles.
  1986.   *Sacrifier et donner à voir en pays Malabar.* Paris: École Française d'Extrême Orient.
Thukral, Gurmeet, and Elizabeth Thukral.
  1987.   *Garhwal Himalaya.* New Delhi: Frank Bros & Co.
van Buitenen, J. A. B.
  1973–.   *The Mahābhārata.* Chicago: University of Chicago Press.
van der Veer, Peter.
  1987.   "'God Must be Liberated!' A Hindu Liberation Movement in Ayodhya." *Modern Asian Studies* 21.2: 283–301.
Waghorne, Joanne Punzo, and Norman Cutler, eds.
  1985.   *Gods of Flesh, Gods of Stone: The Embodiment of Divinity in India.* Chambersburg, Pa.: Anima.

SECTION FOUR

. . .

Epic and Lament

• • •

10

The Natural Tears of Epic

Thomas M. Greene

In his magisterial study of epic, *The Descent from Heaven*, written over thirty years ago, Thomas Greene provided us with a rich way of reading the canonical epic tradition by focusing on scenes with messengers bearing news from the gods. His essay in this volume commands a similar sweep of epic texts in its attention to what Greene calls "the epic *telos* of tears." Moving from the oldest extant epic, the Babylonian *Gilgamesh*, to Milton's *Paradise Lost*, Greene traces the literary epic's profound engagement with grief and tragic ritual, thereby arguing for the capacity of the written epic to create a community of shared mourners.

The adventurous scholar who attempts in our day to say something fresh about that class of texts conventionally called epic is condemned to deal with a certain burden of suspicion. This suspicion will reasonably arise even if the scholar limits him- or herself, as I have been asked to do, to canonized texts of the European tradition. It isn't really clear that all those various poems can legitimately be huddled under a single generic umbrella. It isn't clear that the scholar's generalizations can survive all the inevitable exceptions that fail to prove but rather subvert them. It isn't clear what credence is due to a reader who fails to command all the relevant original languages—and few of us do command them all, least of all myself. Confronted with this formidable and justified burden of suspicion, one can proceed only humbly and pragmatically, moving with caution through the available texts and facts in the hope that some useful patterns will emerge.

One starting place for thinking about Homeric epic is the malicious little dialogue of Plato, the *Ion*. Socrates' interlocutor in that work is a fatuous rhapsode, quick to boast of his Homeric recitations and impervious to his companion's irony. But despite its irony, the dialogue can serve as a useful source for conventional attitudes toward Homeric performance. With Socrates' encouragement, Ion dwells upon his own emotional involvement in the poetry he recites, his ecstasy of intense feeling, above all on the tears he sheds as he chants Homeric verse. Socrates goes on to ask Ion if he is aware that he produces similar effects upon the spectators.

> Yes, indeed [is the reply], I know it very well. As I look down at them from the stage above, I see them, every time, weeping, casting terrible glances, stricken

with amazement at the deeds recounted. In fact, I have to give them very close attention, for if I set them weeping, I myself shall laugh when I get my money, but if they laugh, it is I who have to weep at losing it. (*Ion* 525c–e)[1]

Tears, it appears, are the best criteria of the rhapsode's success; tears are actually the goal of his performance. It would be easy to dismiss as insignificant this exposure of Ion's artistic calculations if Plato didn't return to the same theme in a much more important and famous passage, the attack on allegedly antisocial poetry in book 10 of the *Republic*. Here again Plato links Homeric poetry with the pleasurable shedding of tears and in this case with tragedy.

> I think you know that the very best of us, when we hear Homer or some other of the makers of tragedy imitating one of the heroes who is in grief, and is delivering a long tirade in his lamentations or chanting and beating his breast, feel pleasure, and abandon ourselves and accompany the representation with sympathy and eagerness, and we praise as an excellent poet the one who most strongly affects us in this way. (*Republic* 10.605c–d)

This passage asserts what was already implicit in the *Ion*, the fact that the sharing of grief was perceived in the fourth century as the characteristic response to the most privileged poetry. The rhapsode Ion's pride in his power of eliciting tears does correspond to the objective judgment of his sober critic.

Plato of course was writing four centuries after Homer and cannot necessarily instruct us about the responses of archaic audiences to poetic recitations. But at least one distinguished scholar, John Herington, thinks there was little difference.[2] It may be worth noting at any rate that the proper response to heroic poetry becomes an issue almost at the outset of the *Odyssey*, when the bard Phemios's song of *nostoi*, "that bitter song, the Homecoming of the Achaians," is interrupted by Penelope in tears, commanding him to choose another subject. Penelope's grief stems from her own personal loss. But Telemachos's response seems to underscore the inevitable convergence of pain and song. "You must nerve yourself and try to listen," he tells her, as others listen to stories of suffering.[3] Penelope's tears here at the beginning anticipate her husband's tears when later in the poem he listens to another bard. But the scene which for our purposes is decisive is the reunion of husband and wife in book 23, that scene that the Alexandrian critics already described as the *telos* of the poem's narrative. Whether or not the remainder of the poem is authentically Homeric, Sheila Murnaghan has rightly called this scene "the definitive conclusion to the *Odyssey*'s plot."[4] The dramatic power of the reunion lies in its mingling of joy with the bitterness of loss, so that the mutual tears stem from the inextricability of love and pain.

> Now from his breast into his eyes the ache
> of longing mounted, and he wept at last,
> his dear wife, clear and faithful, in his arms. . . .
> The rose Dawn might have found them weeping still

had not the grey-eyed Athena slowed the night
when night was most profound, under the Ocean
of the East.

(Odyssey 23.259–262; 271–273)

That mutual release culminates and resolves the long story of the couple's privation. It responds to our first encounter with Odysseus, weeping alone on Calypso's island. The narrative of the hero is bracketed by tears, as indeed it is punctuated with more tears as Odysseus leaves Circe's shore for Hades, as he first glimpses his mother Antikleia, as he listens to Demodokos, as—once returned to Ithaka—he fails to recognize it, and as he is reunited with Telemachos. All those moments anticipate the final moment of poignant reunion, as does the incessant grief of Penelope throughout the poem and still other lachrymose scenes such as the episode at Menelaos's palace where the host, his wife Helen, their guest Telemachos, and even his companion Antilochos, all break down in sobbing and can only be restored by Helen's magical potion, so powerful that it inhibits weeping for an entire day.

The corresponding scene in the *Iliad* contrives a far more improbable mutuality, when the old king of Troy is led by Hermes to the tent of his son's killer. The supreme, shattering force of that confrontation lies in the blessed release of tears accorded Priam and Achilles together, a mutuality of grief so intense that it overrides the presence of the corpse of Hector.

So [Priam] spoke, and stirred in the other a passion of grieving
for his own father. He took the old man's hand and pushed him
gently away, and the two remembered, as Priam sat huddled
at the feet of Achilleus and wept close for manslaughtering Hektor
And Achilleus wept now for his own father, now again
for Patroklos. The sound of their mourning moved in the house. Then
when great Achilleus had taken full satisfaction in sorrow
and the passion for it had gone from his mind and body, thereafter
he rose from his chair, and took the old man by the hand, and set him
on his feet again, in pity for the grey head and the grey beard.

(Iliad 24.507–516)[5]

It is hard to believe that the original audiences of the *Iliad* did not respond to this moment as fourth-century audiences apparently did. Achilles himself, Gregory Nagy has argued, has already become "the very essence of grief" within the poem.[6] The release in tears in that magnificent scene becomes ultimately a scene of mourning for all the unnumbered dead of the poem and the war, the almost unbearable toll of the fallen that the narrative pitilessly records. That scene of unspeakable private grief is then followed by the public grief of Hektor's funeral, where each lament of the three principal women mourners is followed by the formulaic phrase "So she spoke in tears." In the calculating sentimentality of the rhapsode Ion, tears may have been the pragmatic *telos* of the recitation, but in the severe and noble pathos of the two Homeric poems themselves, tears can properly be said to constitute the authentic narrative *telos*.

This is important because, as I now want to argue, the resolution of tears that ends both Homeric poems ends *most* of the European poems that we commonly describe as epics. Most of them conclude quite literally in tears, and those few that fail to do so tend to center on a pivotal scene of mourning. The only difficulty in making this argument is that the pattern is so common as to risk tedium in the enumeration. A brief overview will have to suffice.

Beowulf, like the *Iliad,* ends with a funeral for its eponymous hero, or rather with a double funeral. After the deep pathos of the hero's sacrificial death, his body is ritually burned, and the sound of weeping, writes the poet, mingles with the roar of the rising fire. The ashes are then buried in a barrow about which twelve warriors ride; their lamentation concludes the poem. In the *Chanson de Roland,* the grief for the betrayed rear guard when the main body of the army discovers its loss is itself epic in scope. Twenty thousand faint with sorrow; not a single knight fails to shed tears piteously. In the very closing lines, an angel appears to the battle-weary Charlemagne to send him off according to God's will on another expedition. "'God,' cries Charlemagne, 'how wretched is my life!' His eyes shed tears, and he tugs his white beard"(4001–4002).[7] That is the end of the poem, as the one supreme loss described earlier is assimilated into a lifetime of painful service. As for the *Nibelungenlied,* its final pages are damp with universal tears for the massive bloodletting it records, and as it happens, *its* last sentence is also devoted to the same theme: "Christian and heathen, wife, man, and maid, were seen weeping and mourning for their friends."[8] In the twelfth-century Russian epic *Igor's Raid,* the narration of the raid itself is overshadowed by the mourning that follows it, mourning that affects not only widows and survivors but even the bereaved landscape.

> The grass droops with condolements
> and the tree with sorrow
> bends to the ground. . . .
> The Russian women
> have started to weep. . . .
> anguish spread flowing over the Russian land.
> (299–342)[9]

I will pass over the flood of tears shed in the Iranian *Sháhnáma* when the hero Rustam discovers too late that he has wounded unwittingly and fatally his son Suhráb.[10] But I hope that these cumulative examples will suggest that the primary epic as a genre is not so much concerned with heroic achievement in itself as with the affective cost of achievement. What the poem works toward, what it leaves us with, is that acute personal recognition of pain, often the restorative sharing of pain, which it presents as the inescapable burden of action.

One might well ask why this should be the case, why so many communal poems in so many separate cultures should move toward this particular dramatic culmination. This is a mystery not easily penetrated, but perhaps a kind of clarification begins to emerge from these lines from the *Iliad* already quoted above:

> When great Achilleus had taken full satisfaction in sorrow
> and the passion for it had gone from his mind and body, thereafter
> he rose from his chair, and took the old man by the hand.

These lines do not indicate that Achilles' sorrow has been dissipated; they do not remove the burden of loss accumulated over the poem as a whole. They state rather that the passion of sorrow has been dispelled, meaning presumably that profound restless disquiet that has harassed and tormented Achilles since the death of Patroklos. Achilles has taken satisfaction in sorrow through the act of weeping, as presumably has Priam, and this satisfaction, this catharsis of passion, allows the one man to take the other by the hand. That peculiar satisfaction that does not repress loss but somehow finds it acceptable flowers in the aftermath of participatory mourning, and this satisfaction, this quiescence in tragedy, is a reconciliation that we as audience can share. If, as I've suggested, our grief in this scene resolves our shock from the unnumbered dead of the poem, we still feel the weight of that toll, but our passion also has yielded to somber quietude. We are left with a recognizable response to pain that we share with Achilles and Priam and those who mourn in the other poems I've quoted. Typically, epic grief is shared by two or more characters who are then joined by the audience. That shared stillness within tremendous ruin is what heroic poetry brings to us and brings us to, and the hard acquisition of that stillness derives from a ritual that many cultures have independently produced. It is of course a tragic ritual, and to recognize this is to understand better Plato's reference to "Homer or some other of the tragic composers," or his reference to Homer elsewhere in the *Republic* as "the most poetic and first of the tragic poets (*Republic* 10.607a), or again Aristotle's assertion that "[Homer's] *Margites* . . . stands in the same relation to our comedies as the *Iliad* and *Odyssey* to our tragedies" (*Poetics* 1448b–1449a).[11]

The conclusion in tears, the epic *telos* of tears, is already found in the oldest extant poem that has earned the name of epic, the Old Babylonian *Gilgamesh*, although in its case the climactic grief is solitary rather than shared. The hero Gilgamesh has become obsessed with his own mortality and has undertaken a long voyage to visit a certain Utanapishtim in quest of enduring life. His host first discourages his hopes but is finally persuaded to give him a magic plant whose name is "The Old Man Becomes a Young Man," a plant "by which a man can attain his survival." But Gilgamesh carelessly allows a snake to rob him of the plant.

> At that point Gilgamesh sat down, weeping,
> his tears streaming over the side of his nose.[12]

A few lines later the poem comes to an end, leaving Gilgamesh with the tears of his mortality.

The tears provoked by the loss of a magical herb in this ur-epic seem to me paradigmatic. The pain of epic might be said to stem from a repudiation of that crude magic that is here stolen. The magic of the folktale, the magic of the spell, are designed to protect human beings from the kind of pain that epic confronts. It is true that remnants of magical power, for good or for evil, do survive in much heroic poetry, but when it matters most, they fail to mitigate the pain of existence, the pain that concludes and focuses the poem. Thus the wound from the boar inflicted on the young Odysseus can be healed with incantations, but incantations are powerless to bring the hero home from Troy. Just as Odysseus has to be bound to the mast to ignore the bewitching song of the Sirens, so the genre itself has to surrender that enchanting possibility of heart's ease. The Sirens sing: "Argos' old soldiery / On Troy beach teeming, / Charmed out of time we see" (*Odyssey* 12.241–243). Epic, we might say, refuses to be charmed out of time in that crude fashion the Sirens evoke. If it depends on a kind of enchantment, as it sometimes seems to claim, its power is of a finer temper than the Sirens evoke or the herb of Utanapishtim embodies.

Fortunately we do possess a body of legendary poetry that suggests what the primary epic might have been without the renunciation of magical solace. The collection of narrative poems gathered in the Finnish *Kalevala* represents a world that does depend quite explicitly on magic; in fact a large proportion of the text consists of spells. This circumstance affects, not surprisingly, the status of tears. In poem 41 of the *Kalevala*, the poet-seer Väinämöinen sings so sweetly that all of his auditors weep, as he himself weeps at the wonderful sound he produces. These are not the tears of existential pain but of aesthetic delight, and by the close of poem 41 they are in fact aestheticized. The singer wants his tears returned to him, and with his hermetic power he commands a goldeneye bird to collect them for him. And the bird obeys, returning the tears, which are now transformed into pearls.[13] These magical tears are marvelous jewels, brilliant to the eye, proof against erosion, innocent of suffering. Like the Sirens' songs, they are "charmed out of time." This aestheticization of the tears produced not by experience but by song—a song whose content we never learn— can usefully set off the severe resignation of epic tears that are irrecoverable, unbeautiful, subject to time. Epic grief refuses the facile comfort of the spell or the sorcerer or the magical herb in order to effect that difficult ritual of reconciliation that refuses to repress.[14]

Joseph Russo and Bennett Simon, writing on the oral epic tradition, suggest that "recitation sets up a kind of common 'field' in which poet, audience, and the characters within the poems are all defined, with some blurring of the boundaries that normally separate the three."[15] In that common field, the grief of the poet, the character, and the hearer seem to blend in a form of communion, and where the performer can be distinguished from the poet, his grief also joins in a necessary continuum. This continuum is metaphorized by Socrates in the *Ion* as a series of rings magnetized by a lodestone, beginning with the Muse, passing through poet and performer, and ending with the spectator (533d–e, 535e–536b). He might have added the ring belonging to the character, the Priam or Charlemagne or Gilgamesh. In the common field of performance, in the series of magnetized rings, the grief of the poet merges with the performer's, and the character's, and the audience's. Truly to listen to the epic is to enter that space where the conventional distinctions break down, Jean-Pierre Vernant's "au delà" of Mnemosyne, where the participation of past and present produces a hallowed communion between the two.

This communion, I submit, is most accessible through the sharing of tears. Tears break down most effectively those boundaries that epic presencing erodes. The sharing of tears provides a contact with a hero more intense than the wonder at his accomplishments; it levels the planes of human excellence, and it invites the intimacy of a simple shared humanity. This intimacy is thematized at least once in the *Odyssey*, when Odysseus in Hades tries to embrace his mother Antikleia but discovers that her body has no substance.

Now this embittered all the pain I bore,
and I cried in the darkness:
"O my mother,
will you not stay, be still, here in my arms,
may we not, in this place of Death, as well,
hold one another, touch with love, and taste
salt tears' relief, the twinge of welling tears?"
(11.234–239)

The failure of the son to embrace his mother involves, apparently, an inability to weep with her. The "relief" of salt tears, anticipating the tearful release later with Penelope, seems indistinguishable from touching the other person. Touching with love and the welling of tears form a single experience. We would not distort greatly, I think, the experience of the Homeric poems, and more broadly of heroic narrative, if we allegorized this conflation of touching and weeping to describe the participation in heroic sorrow that is the goal of epic. The audience touches the actors of the poem and is touched by them through the medium of the performer who is himself touched in two senses. Eumaeus the swineherd compares Odysseus the raconteur to "a minstrel taught by heaven to touch the hearts of men" (17.680–681). We have every reason to believe that the hearts of a minstrel's audience were indeed profoundly affected. It is appropriate that the moment of supreme feeling, the moment of communion, should coincide, in Greece as elsewhere, with the contagion of grieving at the culmination of each narrative. It is this encounter of present and past in a common reality that distinguishes the primary epic from other narratives with lachrymose endings—*Madame Bovary*, for instance.

But for those of us who seek to understand the workings of the archaic imagination, we of course are obliged to reconceive the status of the heroic past in somewhat different terms. For us, that past is not a fragment of reality already immutable and perennial. It is rather a constructed reality that may or may not contain a grain of history, as the battle of Roncesvalles contains a minor attack on Charlemagne's rear guard by Basque Christians. The reality invented by a communal imagination, from our perspective, is a projection upon a dim past whose blankness is intolerable, whose stretches of vacuity leave a people without a common identity and must be filled in by myth. Primary epic solaces that unbearable insufficiency of the available past so that a people can know where it has come from, whom it has come from, and thus who it is. The epic bard draws upon a stock of legends and amplifies them with fresh detail. But in order for the communion of grief to occur, this construct projected upon the dark backward and abysm of time has to contain in itself that intuition of vulnerability and loss that can make a communion in sorrow conceivable. The heroic past as we perceive it is not an absolute given; it betrays the contingency of the imaginary shaped to allow a ritual of reconciliation. The projected past is arranged to invite that embrace of the living with the supposed dead, who, unlike Antikleia, are now made substantial. The narrative leading up to this intuitive embrace has to guarantee the nobility of the accessible past; it has to ensure that the pathos of the close will not prove cheaply sentimental. All preliterate societies project myths against the terror of historical ignorance; heroic poetry is produced by those societies whose projected myths prove themselves available for a particular kind of communion. A spiritual circuit is closed that involves both projection and assimilation, the progressive fabrication of a myth that is then rendered present through the magic of heightened language and is absorbed, as Eumaeus says, in the hearts of men.

In the passage from primary to secondary epic, that circle of projection and assimilation will continue to operate, but not without certain interferences. In the poetry of a literate society, the story retold no longer stems from the past but from a past among others, a past whose historical validity is always open to question. The poem functions to recall the heroic story but

also to ensure that the story keeps its distance along a chronological continuum familiar to the reader. The story to be projected, in order to permit
an assimilation, no longer fills a historical void; it is obliged rather to clear
away a past cluttered with history. The ritual of shared grief no longer springs
spontaneously from a hallowed act of memory, but from the creative energy
of a given authorial imagination. There are other interferences. One lies in
the privacy of the act of reading, which now replaces the communal reception of a performance. Another interference lies in shifting ethical codes
that may condemn the very act of weeping as demoralizing. And in a Christian poem, weeping characteristically is an expression of remorse for an individual sinful past that is not necessarily the reader's past. In view of these
interferences, the surprising feature of latter-day epics is their continuity in
grief with their generic forebears.

In European cultural history, the pivotal text that alters permanently the
epic circle of projection and participation is the *Aeneid*. No one can deny
its suffusion with *lacrymae rerum*, but the status of grief in Virgil is attended
with profound ambivalence. In fact Aeneas's very usage of the over-familiar
phrase in book 1 is exposed immediately to the poet's irony. Almost everyone,
it seems, weeps at some point in the *Aeneid*, but the reader is not infrequently
left uncertain how to respond. Venus weeps; Creusa weeps; Andromache
weeps; Ascanius weeps; Evander weeps; Juno weeps; *Sinon* weeps; the hero
repeatedly and unstintingly weeps. Most famously, Dido weeps, and so
poignantly that Saint Augustine was compelled like countless other readers
to imitate her. But the tears of Dido lead to suicidal neurosis, and the line
between noble sorrow and demoralizing self-pity is progressively blurred as
her story nears its terrible end. The *Aeneid* does move closer to authentic
tears in book 11, in Aeneas's elegiac valedictory over the body of Pallas and
later Evander's passionate lamentation. But book 12 swings back to a harsher
polarization, which assigns the stigma of weeping to a series of hysterical
females—Amata, Juturna, even Lavinia, and finally all the women of Lau-
rentum wailing over their dead queen. Aeneas in the last book remains coldly
dry-eyed, and the text, never more ambivalent, invites us with one of its voices
to admire his self-control. Often the sharing of grief that the text invites seems
to remain in an ethical limbo.

One familiar moment can be taken to encapsulate the force of tears in the
Aeneid. Aeneas in the underworld sees Dido, or thinks he sees her, so wispy
and clouded is her presence. Is she really there? He cries out to her anyway,
weeping, protesting his reluctance to leave her at Carthage and begging her
now to linger. With these protests, continues the text, he tries to soothe the
burning spirit staring him down in fury, and summons tears—"lacrimas
ciebat." Both Fitzgerald and Mandelbaum translate this phrase to say that
Aeneas wept. But Virgil has already told us that. The verb *ciere* means "to stir,"
"to arouse," "to summon." Isn't it Dido's tears he wants to elicit, responding

to his own? We can't be sure, and one might take that undecidability to allegorize the poem's own ambivalence, full of tears but making ambiguous appeals to its audience.[16] Here at any rate is a moment of grief the modern reader can share, compounded of incipient regret, stirrings of guilt, love that is almost sincere, vague intuitions of loss, inextricable feelings of shadowy inadequacy voiced into the dim shadows around the speaker. Does she really hear him, if she's there? Does he succeed in stirring her tears? Or is he only summoning deliberately more of his own? Is he telling the full truth? "Quem fugis?" he asks; "Who is it you're fleeing?"—a radical question that might be read as putting his own selfhood in doubt. In this moment of supreme anguish and supreme indeterminacy, many modern readers will be able to participate.

Expressions of grief in the secondary epic of the later Middle Ages and the Renaissance would furnish in themselves matter for a monograph, and in the space available I can recall only a few scenes that a monograph on the subject would have to consider. It would need to recall the titanic howling of Orlando in Ariosto's *Orlando furioso,* the scene that is located precisely halfway through the poem and from which it rightly takes its title. Orlando's berserk rage at the loss of Angelica is the mightiest and most fearful thing in that long poem; it transforms him into a murderous madman; nothing available to Ariosto can contain it, except a fanciful whimsy, which is transparently fictitious. That frenzy of suffering tends to be more muted in one of the darkest of Renaissance epics, Spenser's *Faerie Queene,* although it too contains moments of bitter tears. But even more significant than those moments is the repeated blunting of Spenser's heroic narratives by his characteristic pullback in book after book from accomplishment and affirmation, making the ostensibly successful story into a fable of regret. The Red Crosse Knight may be united to Una, but he is soon obliged to leave her, "The which he shortly did, and Una left to mourne." That deadening line ends the narrative of book 1, as the whole poem ends with a piercing cry for a culminating Sabbaoth that never comes.

In Spenser's poem as in other Christian epics, the communion of the reader with the fictive character no longer crosses so much a stretch of time but rather the gap between the particular guilty experience of the one and the other. The poet's principal task in these instances is to effect a presencing of the more or less invented character that specifies his or her guilt, but not so narrowly that the reader is unable to share sympathetically that remorse that the Christian epic takes as its *telos.* Thus Spenser's reader, not a resident of Faeryland, must be able to respond to the torture of Red Crosse by Penance, Remorse, and Repentance at the House of Holiness, where "his torment often was so great, / That like a Lyon he would cry and rore, / And rend his flesh" (1.10.28). The Christian poet projects a myth of redemption not on the darkness of the past but on the darkness of the errant human soul in order that the reader can complete the projective circle with an assimilation of purgative pain.

The supreme example of that circle in Western literature is found in cantos 30 and 31 of Dante's *Purgatorio*, after Dante the pilgrim is faced with the beloved and accusing eyes of Beatrice. He turns instinctively to Virgil for support, only to discover that his guide has disappeared, after which, he writes, not all the earthly paradise could "keep my dew-washed cheeks from turning dark again with tears"(30.53–54).[17] But this loss is only the beginning of Dante's ordeal, his own personal crisis in the poem, as he hears the reproving voice of the woman watching him reproachfully.

> "Dante, because Virgil leaves you, do not weep yet, do not
> weep yet, for you must weep for another sword."
>
> (30.55–57)

The other sword is judgment for his life of sin after the death of his lady. The threefold repetition of the verb *piangere* (to weep) anticipates the pilgrim's conduct during the pitiless inquisition that follows, drawing tears so copious that he is briefly rendered incapable of speech. The moment of their anguished release is evoked by a simile of exceptional periphrastic elaboration, a simile that compares the rigidity of the sinner's heart to the snows of the Appenines, packed and congealed, until finally "the ice that was bound tight around my heart became breath and water, and with anguish poured from my breast through my mouth and eyes"(30.97–99). The scene between the accuser and accused is at once the most intimate of the poem, the most private exposure of his personal history, and at the same time a reenactment of the sacrament of penance, which requires those tears of contrition that are shed as well as the verbal confession of misconduct that the tears almost choke into silence. But after the snow has melted, after the hardened heart has publicly melted, then in effect the story of Dante's purgation is over. He is allowed to cross the stream of Lethe, which washes away the memories of evil action, and then the stream of Eunoe, which restores the memories of good. In all the remainder of the poem, Dante will witness much and learn much, but his own personal odyssey is over. Beatrice makes it clear that the journey through hell and purgatory has been necessary to melt the ice of his hardened conscience. Its melting was the true *telos* of the pilgrimage of the first two canticles.

The simile of the melting mountain snow will recur in the closing pages of Tasso's *Gerusalemme liberata*, a rich example of dialectical imitation, in the lachrymose reunion of the Christian knight Rinaldo and his former lover, the former enchantress Armida. The pagan armies have been defeated; Jerusalem has been won; Armida the infidel is contemplating suicide near the battlefield when the approach of Rinaldo causes her to faint. His tears revive her; his promises of devotion and service restore her, and like mountain snows melted by the sun, she also weeps and surrenders her future to him. His tears, comments David Quint, signal "a new mutuality in their love," replacing the overheated narcissism that had earlier passed for passion.[18] The mutuality is reinforced by the mingling of tears, tokens of compassion, tenderness, and joy. Specifically, Armida's tears signal the repudiation of enchantment as Rinaldo's signal the sacrifice of heroic self-will. This scene, which really ends Tasso's narrative, recaptures that austerity of the post-magical, that surrender to common humanity, which we have already found in the stark endings of the older epics. In that surrender punctuated with weeping, Tasso's poem like so many others finds its goal.

We can finish this quick overview by recalling the close of the plot of *Paradise Lost*. The crisis of the marriage between Adam and Eve, which is also a crisis in the future of humanity, is resolved at the end of book 10. Once they have fallen, they don't know who they are or where they are; they don't know what the future contains, if there will be any future; they don't know what their marriage will be, poisoned as it is by mutual rancor. Adam in a soliloquy searches for answers fruitlessly but ends, as he says, only in an "abyss of fears and horrors" (10.842–844). It is Eve who takes the first step toward redemption by asking her husband's forgiveness, as he then accords it and asks for hers. Together they grope their way as a couple through the remainder of the book toward what, in Milton's view, is the only right solution.

> they forthwith to the place
> Repairing where he [God] judg'd them prostrate fell
> Before him reverent, and both confessed
> Humbly thir faults, and pardon begd, with tears
> Watering the ground, and with thir sighs the Air
> Frequenting.
>
> (10.1098–1103)

With this ritual of contrition, a ritual not without its heroism, a future becomes possible for the marriage and for all of us.

The next two books will be devoted to that severe future, until husband and wife, fully instructed, are led out of the garden into a world of struggle and hope.

> They looking back, all th' Eastern side beheld
> Of Paradise, so late thir happie seat. . . .
> Some natural tears they dropd, but wip'd them soon;
> The World was all before them, where to choose
> Thir place of rest, and Providence thir guide.
>
> (12.641–642, 645–647)

In the Judeo-Christian history of fallen humanity, this marks a beginning, but in the history of epic poetry, we can read this passage retrospectively as a kind of end point. There would be later narrative works of epic resonance, many marvelous works, but the specific mingling of credible human achievement with the perception of terrible cost would, after Milton, become more difficult to bring off. Its availability in *Paradise Lost* is already in doubt. Later, the projective circle of epic would encounter the interference of Enlightenment rationality. Milton's guilty couple wipe away their tears as a gesture of Christian hope, despite its severe constraints, but for Milton's posterity, that hope would become less constrained, and tears would be relegated to the bourgeois *larmoyant*. The ritual of reconciliation would become progressively rare or else conventionally facile. As Adam and Eve wipe their faces, they are wiping away something precious, the vestiges of a tradition; the chain of Plato's rings has slackened and dissolved.

NOTES

1. Quotations from Plato are from Edith Hamilton and Huntington Cairns, eds., *The Collected Dialogues of Plato* (New York: Pantheon, 1961). In this edition, the *Ion* is translated by Lane Cooper, the *Republic* by Paul Shorey, and the *Theaetetus* by F. M. Cornford.

2. Herington (1985) supports this argument by the observation that "one has only to recite Homer aloud, before a real or imagined throng of people, to reexperience the emotions described by Ion" (p. 13). It is true that we have relatively little information concerning the response of Greek theater audiences to the performances of tragedies, but one early indication is suggestive. Herodotus records an instance in which the tragedy performed produced so many tears that its author was punished: "The Athenians . . . showed themselves beyond measure afflicted at the fall of Miletus, in many ways expressing their sympathy, and especially by their treatment of Phrynichus, for when this poet brought out upon the stage his drama, *The Capture of Miletus*, the whole theatre burst into tears, and the people sentenced him to pay a fine of a thousand drachmas, for recalling to them their own misfortunes. They likewise made a law, that no one should ever again exhibit that piece" (Herodotus 6.21; trans. G. Rawlinson [New York: Modern Library, 1942]).

3. *Odyssey* 1.353; trans. R. Fitzgerald (New York: Vintage, 1990).

4. Murnaghan 1987, 180.

5. Trans. R. Lattimore (Chicago: University of Chicago Press, 1961).

6. Nagy 1979, 77–78.

7. My translation.

8. Trans. M. Armour (New York: Dutton, Everyman's Library, 1934).

9. Trans. V. Nabokov (New York: Random House, 1960).

10. See *Sháhnáma of Firdausi*, pt. 3, secs. 23–25; I refer to the translation of A. G. Warner and E. Warner (London: Kegan Paul, Trench, Tribner and Co., 1906).

11. Plato and Aristotle make analogous remarks elsewhere. Plato states at *Theaetetus* 152e that all agree on "the supreme masters in each of the two kinds of poetry: Epicharmus in comedy, Homer in tragedy." Aristotle writes in *Rhetoric* 1403b: "It was long before [the proper method of delivery] found a way into the arts of tragic drama and epic recitations: at first poets acted their tragedies them-

selves." For these quotations from Plato and Aristotle, I am indebted to Herington 1985, 213–214.

12. Trans. M. G. Kovacs (Stanford: Stanford University Press, 1989), pp. 106–107. For the meaning of the name Gilgamesh, see page xxvii in the introduction to Kovacs's translation.

13. I refer to the translation of F. P. Magoun, Jr. (Cambridge, Mass.: Harvard University Press, 1963), pp. 278–279.

14. It is true that Hesiod placed stress on the power of poetry to bring "forgetfulness of evils and a rest from cares" (*Theogony* 55; see also lines 98–103). But this description has to be interpreted in the light of the pain and discord contained in Hesiod's own poetry.

15. Russo and Simon 1968, 492.

16. My attention was first drawn to the suggestive ambiguity of this line by Marion Wells.

17. Trans. C. Singleton (Princeton: Princeton University Press, 1973).

18. Quint 1983, 115.

WORKS CITED

Herington, John.
    1985.   *Poetry into Drama: Early Tragedy and the Greek Poetic Tradition.* Berkeley:
                 University of California Press.
Murnaghan, Sheila.
    1987.   *Disguise and Recognition in the "Odyssey."* Princeton: Princeton University Press.
Nagy, Gregory.
    1979.   *The Best of the Achaeans: Concepts of the Hero in Archaic Greek Poetry.* Baltimore: Johns Hopkins University Press.
Quint, David.
    1983.   *Origin and Originality in Renaissance Literature: Versions of the Source.* New Haven: Yale University Press.
Russo, Joseph, and Bennett Simon.
    1968.   "Homeric Psychology and the Oral Epic Tradition." *Journal of the History of Ideas* 29: 492.
Vernant, Jean-Pierre.
    1988.   *Mythe et pensée chez les Grecs: Études de psychologie historique.* Paris: Éditions la Découverte.

11

The Poetics of Loss in Greek Epic

Sheila Murnaghan

Study of lament has begun to be a major part of the feminist reinterpretation
of epic, including both textual study and anthropological accounts of female
lament in modern Greece. Sheila Murnaghan draws on this scholarship to trace
a continuum from male lament, which turns the speaker back toward an
affirmation of kleos and epic purposes, to female lament, which ignores the
death-defying fame that epic provides as compensation for heroic loss. Murnaghan's essay makes an important contribution to debates about just how subversive lament can be in epic. In spite of the ways that female lament can seem
to disrupt or challenge the heroic code, Murnaghan argues that epic cannot
do without lament, since lament not only begins the process of generating
praise from grief but also presents the body of the enslaved and mournful widow
as inspiration for the creation of the husband's unending fame. Murnaghan's
interpretation leads us to form a more polyvocal and performative—and less
monumental—theory of epic than more traditional readings would, one in
which the poem's celebration of martial and heroic values coexists with the
challenges to those values raised by lament.

The classical epic exhibits a complicated, ambiguous, and sometimes trou-
bled relationship to the genre of lamentation. The lament is at once constitutive of epic and antithetical to it, one of epic's probable sources and a
subversive element within epic that can work against what epic is trying to
achieve. Lamentation thus has an important role to play in current attempts
to rethink the nature of epic, to challenge a vision of epic that can be summed
up in the term "monumental." This vision, which is embodied both in critical accounts of the epic and in the claims various epics make for themselves
(and which this brief summary inevitably caricatures), presents epic as a massive, univocal, and celebratory form of high art.

As a genre of poetry performed on a particular social occasion and having an important function within a major and pervasive social ritual, lament helps us to find the connections between epic and more occasional,
more popular poetic forms; it allows us to trace epic's dependence on the
"speech genres" of ordinary communal life[1] and to appreciate epic's more
dialogic, polyvocal dimensions. For written products of oral traditions such
as the Homeric epics, focusing on the poem's connections to lament helps
us to recognize works like the *Iliad* and the *Odyssey* as originally themselves

forms of performed and performative speech embedded in specific social occasions.

As a genre of which the chief practitioners are women, lamentation also has an important role to play in feminist reappraisals of epic. The laments incorporated into the larger structures of epic may bear traces of authentic women's voices and offer women's perspectives on actions that are carried out primarily by men and primarily to promote male interests. For the Homeric epics, these projects are furthered by an ongoing, living tradition of women's laments in rural modern Greece, which have been collected and studied by anthropologists such as Anna Caraveli-Chaves, Loring Danforth and Nadia Seremetakis. The connection between these contemporary laments and those preserved in ancient Greek literary sources was established in Margaret Alexiou's groundbreaking work *The Ritual Lament in Greek Tradition* and has been further analyzed by Gail Holst-Warhaft in her recent study *Dangerous Voices: Women's Laments and Greek Literature.* Through modern Greek women's laments, the Homeric epics can be placed in a poetic tradition that is performed, nonliterary, tied to ritual, female-authored, and remote from the supposed mainstream of Western European high culture: a tradition very different from the Homer-Virgil-Dante-Milton sequence on which comparative studies of the epic often focus.

Finally, the content of lamentation gives it an equivocal relationship to epic. As a grieving response to the loss of an individual, lamentation is an urgent expression of that person's value, and so is a form of praise. Lament is thus prototypical of epic as a genre that confers praise—*kleos* in Homeric epic—on the actions of heroes, and more particularly on the actions of dead heroes, who have earned their right to be praised through the manner of their deaths. Thus laments, along with panegyrics delivered to living leaders, lie at the source of many traditions of heroic poetry. But, unlike panegyric, lament is praise inspired by the speaker's sorrow and regret at the subject's loss. As C. M. Bowra puts it, "Lament is born from grief for the dead, and though praise is naturally combined with it, grief has the chief place."[2]

Lamentation threatens to undermine the *kleos*-conferring function of epic because it stresses the suffering caused by heroic death rather than the glory won by it; lamentation calls into question the glorification of death sponsored by martial societies and the epics that celebrate them. The anti-epic dimension of lament is explored in this volume for Roman epic by Elaine Fantham. In the drama of epic's realization of its generic identity, the female-dominated subgenre of lament plays a role analogous to that of epic's female characters in its heroes' realizations of their goals: originary yet marginal, indispensable yet subversive. And this is also the role of the locality Greece in the drama of epic's achievement of its place at the heart of the Western European tradition.

Although no actual women's laments survive from ancient Greece, their power can still be measured in the legal and literary responses they called forth. Women's laments were felt to be sufficiently threatening to society, whether as spurs to violent revenge or as challenges to the value of dying for the state, that they were officially restricted through legislation, most famously that enacted by Solon in Athens in the sixth century B.C.E.[3] In addition, their functions were appropriated for the classical city by two state-sponsored literary genres. In one, the *epitaphios logos,* or public funeral oration, designed to glorify death in battle for the city and minimize its cost in individual suffering, women's laments are submerged in a new official, male-centered discourse.[4] But in the other, tragedy, women's laments are represented as part of a complex but controlled exploration of the social order and the threats that it faces, especially from the intense personal attachments expressed in lamentation.[5]

Like tragedy, the Homeric epics confront lamentation by representing it, incorporating laments into the larger structures of their plots. This is particularly the case in the *Iliad,* where the final third of the poem is centered on the consequential and much-lamented deaths of Patroclus and Hector. The discussion that follows will focus on how the Homeric epics depict their own relationship to lamentation, particularly as a transitional event that inhabits the border between experience and song. Because laments transcend the distinction between speech and act—in that a song of lament can equate itself with the activity of mourning the dead—lamentation plays a key role in the Homeric epics' remarkably thorough canvassing of the process of epic commemoration, from the moment of heroic death to its eventual glorification in everlasting song.

A sense that lament both is and is not to be equated with epic and with *kleos*-conferring poetry in general is conveniently expressed within Homeric poetry by a lexical distinction. The epics include two different terms for lamentation: *thrēnos* and *goos.* The *thrēnos* is the commissioned work of professional outsiders, "composed and performed at the funeral by non-kinsmen." The *goos* is a less formal composition, improvised in response to the grief of the occasion and always sung—or wailed—by the dead man's relations or close friends.[6] The *thrēnos* clearly represents the kind of formal, enduring artwork that the *Iliad* and the *Odyssey* see their events as turning into, even though the term is used only once in each epic.

Although rare, those references to *thrēnos* are significant, involving the commemoration in death of the *Iliad*'s two chief heroes, Hector and Achilles. One occurs in the account of Hector's funeral at the end of *Iliad* 24, where we are told that professional singers were the *exarchous thrēnōn,* "leaders of thrēnoi" (*Iliad* 24.721). This mention of *thrēnoi* is followed by three speeches labeled *gooi* delivered by Hector's female relatives Andromache, Hecuba, and Helen. The other mention of *thrēnoi* comes in the last book of the *Odyssey,* where we learn that the Muses themselves *thrēneon,* "sang thrēnoi" (*Odyssey* 24.61) at the funeral of Achilles. The connection between these *thrēnoi* sung at Achilles' funeral and enduring *kleos* in poetry as compensation for heroic death is made explicit by the later lyric poet Pindar in a key passage in one of his odes: "Nor did songs desert him when he died,/ but the maidens of Helicon stood around his pyre and his tomb/ and poured forth a *thrēnos* full of fame [*thrēnon poluphamon*]./ For it seemed just to the gods/ that a great man—even though dead—be endowed with the songs of goddesses" (*Isthmian* 8.62–66). And *thrēnos* was the technical term for a genre of lyric poetry that continued the traditions of archaic epic—and may well also have predated epic and contributed to its development.

Although the *thrēnoi* mentioned in the *Iliad* thus fulfill the purpose Homeric epics claim for themselves and are evoked at strategically important moments of summing up in the plots of the two poems, they are not themselves actually represented. Rather, the narratives of the *Iliad* and the *Odyssey*—their accounts of the events that they are converting into *kleos*—contain many references to the more informal, personal, performative, and transient form of the *goos*, and a number of *gooi* are actually quoted within the *Iliad*. The most structurally prominent are the three laments at Hector's funeral mentioned above, but these are preceded by Thetis's proleptic *goos* for Achilles and Achilles' lament for Patroclus in book 18 (*Iliad* 18.52–64, 324–342); by two laments delivered by Briseis and Achilles over the body of Patroclus in book 19 (*Iliad* 19.287–300, 315–337); by the spontaneous laments of Hecuba and Andromache when they learn of Hector's death in book 22 (*Iliad* 22.431–436, 477–514); and by Achilles' further lament for Patroclus during his funeral in book 23 (*Iliad* 23.19–23). In addition, much of the speech of women in the Homeric epics, although not formally marked off as lament, is closely related to the *goos* in language and theme.

As the epics thematize the creation of *kleos* out of the lived experience of heroic society, their many internal depictions of *goos* occupy an intermediate status between that experience and its reflection in song. This intermediate status can be seen in the way in which laments affect their audiences, evoking a markedly personal response in each listener. Far from drawing their listeners' attention to the glorious achievements of their subjects, these laments inspire them to think of their own sorrows, fragmenting their audiences into isolated and private mourners. This is especially clear in the responses of the women, both Achaean women and Trojan captives, who hear Briseis's lament for Patroclus: "Thus she spoke, grieving, and the women groaned in response, / with Patroclus as their excuse [*Patroklon prophasin*] but each for her own troubles" (*Iliad* 19.301–302; cf. 19.338–339, 24.509–512).

These private, unarticulated experiences of grief stand at one end of a spectrum of possible responses to song presented in the Homeric epics. Next to them one might put Telemachus's weeping in book 4 of the *Odyssey* when he hears Menelaus and Helen tell stories about the Trojan War. Telemachus's weeping is to be compared to Odysseus's in book 8 of the *Odyssey*, triggered by an actual performance of songs from the Trojan cycle by a professional bard. Odysseus's weeping is pointedly juxtaposed to the different response of the Phaeacians, which presumably most nearly reflects the response that epic expects for itself: in contrast to that of the women around the body of Patroclus, the response of the Phaeacians is communal (and one function of song dramatized in that episode is its capacity to promote social cohesion), detached from the experiences involved, and at the same time attentive to them. For audiences like the Phaeacians, epic song promotes forgetfulness of one's own personal concerns. Like the performers of praiseworthy acts, the listeners who allow that praise to be realized cannot properly perform their function if they are distracted by grief.[7]

As brief embedded narratives, the laments in the Homeric epics hint at a broader range of experiences than those that are selected to form the subjects of epic song, telling stories that are peripheral to the main plots of the larger epics or pointedly excluded from those plots. The memories evoked in laments are often of private moments, out of the arena of public, heroic action, such as the words of encouragement Briseis remembers hearing from Patroclus when her husband and brothers had all been killed (*Iliad* 19.295–299) or Hector's interventions on Helen's behalf amid the behind-the-scenes reproaches uttered in the Trojan court (*Iliad* 24.768–775). Unlike epic itself, which claims to provide an accurate record of past events,[8] the lament is, in part, a fictional genre, in that its speakers dwell on fantasies, hoped-for events that now can never take place: for example, the deathbed parting of Hector and Andromache, in which, as she regretfully imagines it, he would have stretched out his hands to her and would have spoken a special *pukinon epos*, a "wise word," that she could always have remembered in her grief (*Iliad* 24.744).

Between them, as they mourn Patroclus, Briseis and Achilles tell what is in effect a version of the story that the *Iliad* itself cannot tell, the impossible alternative to the *Iliad*'s plot, Achilles' return to Phthia, a version in which Patroclus acts as Achilles' surrogate. Briseis evokes Achilles' marriage to her, which Patroclus was to have brought about: "You said that you would make me the wedded wife/ of Achilles, and would lead me in ships/ to Phthia, and would celebrate the marriage feast among the Myrmidons" (*Iliad* 19.297–299). Achilles imagines Patroclus filling in for him as father to Neoptolemus, introducing Neoptolemus to his patrimony: "Before this my heart in my chest had hopes/ that I alone would die far from horse-pasturing Argos,/ here in Troy, and you would go back to Phthia,/ so that you might bring back my son from Scyros/ in a swift, dark ship, and you might show him everything:/ my possessions, my slaves, and my great, high-roofed house" (*Iliad* 19.328–333).

Spoken largely by women, laments are the medium by which a female perspective on epic action makes its way into these male-centered texts.[9] Like the modern Greek women's laments that descend from them (or from their real-life models), these public opportunities become testaments of what it is like to be a woman in a world focused on male interests and values. "Tears become ideas," to borrow a phrase from the anthropologist Stephen Feld, and the unsettling experience of loss generates a description of the social structure as seen by its most vulnerable members. Extending the status of mourning as an imitation of death, lamenting women provide accounts— verbal imitations—of the social death they experience when they lose the men through whom they are defined. Thus Andromache's laments for Hector stress her future as a captive, recalling her speech to him in book 6 where this prospect is linked to her total dependence: "Hector, for you are my father and my revered mother,/ and my brother, and you are my flourishing husband" (*Iliad* 6.429–430).

For Briseis, who has a similar history, Patroclus's death is a *kakon ek kakou,* "evil following on evil" (*Iliad* 19.290), one of a string of misfortunes consisting of the deaths of the men through whom she has known her place in the world: first her husband, then her brothers, now Patroclus, whom she was counting on to attach her to Achilles and resituate her in Phthia. With Patroclus's death, Briseis has been derailed on her widow's journey from the care of her husband back to her original family and on to a new husband. The link between lamentation and the social dislocations to which women are subject is made clear in a speech of Penelope's to the disguised Odysseus in *Odyssey* 19. There she describes her unresolved relationships to Odysseus (who is absent but not certainly dead) and to Telemachus (who is in transition from being a reason to stay in Odysseus's house to being a reason to leave it) as the causes of her constant mourning—she grieves and laments while going about her daily tasks—and of her similarity to the nightingale, whose song is a perpetual expression of female lamentation (*Odyssey* 19.509–553).[10]

Particularly interesting in this respect is Helen in her lament for Hector in *Iliad* 24, since she, like Briseis, represents a complicated variant on the wife who has lost her husband and is herself lost without him. Helen in Troy has clearly been a displaced person, whose sense of self-worth is no longer adequately expressed in her relationship to her nominal husband Paris and who is surrounded by blame from the other Trojans. It appears she has been attempting to repair her status, and her sense of her own value, by forming a link to the more admirable Hector. This effort is reflected in her seductive attempt to get him to sit down and stay when he visits her and Paris in book 6, where she also voices her regret at having followed Paris to Troy in the first place (*Iliad* 6.344–358). In book 24 she mourns Hector as a kind of champion who protected her position among the Trojans. She addresses him as "by far the dearest of all my brothers-in-law" and describes how "I never heard an evil or rude word from you,/ but if someone else in the halls should speak one,/ one of my husband's brothers or sisters or brothers' wives,/ or my mother-in-law (my father-in-law was gentle always),/ you would check that person, advising against it" (*Iliad* 24.768–771). Like other speech forms embedded in the Homeric epics, lament is an agonistic genre, and mourning can be a competitive event.[11] Helen's jibe at the previous speaker, Hecuba, brings to light a normally hidden world of competition among women, centered on the validating attention of men.

Critics have noted that the laments delivered at Hector's funeral recall the speeches of the same three women earlier in the poem, and especially during the episode in book 6 when he encounters all three of them during his return to Troy. As noted above, Andromache in both places dwells on her future as Hector's widow, and Helen couples regret at her past behavior with an attempt to establish a tie to Hector. Hecuba's lament focuses on the favor shown to Hector by the gods, especially as expressed in the miraculous preservation of his body, and this recalls her maternal concern for his physical needs, as expressed in her attempt to get him to drink wine in book 6 and her pointing to her once-nourishing breast as she tries to keep him from facing Achilles in book 22.

This thematic repetition can be read as a formal device, a way of providing closure by making these laments sum up each speaker's previous role. But it can also be understood as an index of how fully women's speech is in general identified with the genre of lamentation, so that the themes of laments naturally show up in speech that is not marked as such. Penelope's metalament in *Odyssey* 19 makes it clear that lamentation is her perpetual mode, and it is striking how much of other women's speech in the epics shares the themes of formal laments. In this respect, epic resembles tragedy, the form that has been characterized as an appropriation and reworking of women's laments, in that women become speakers there primarily when something has gone wrong, and so their proper language is that of complaint.

For example, when in the story of Meleager told by Phoenix in *Iliad* 9, Cleopatra, Meleager's wife, succeeds where all others have failed in inducing Meleager to fight, her intervention is described in terms that suggest a lament.[12] We are told that she *lisset' oduromenē,* "implored him grieving," and the content of her speech is a compressed version of one of the topoi of formal lament, the sufferings of a fallen city: "She told him all/ the troubles that come to people whose city is captured./ They kill the men; fire reduces the city to dust,/ and strangers lead away the children and the long-robed women" (*Iliad* 9.591–594). Cleopatra's identity as a mourner is underscored by her alternative name, Alcyone, which she gets from her mother, who like the halcyon, another bird who represents perpetual lamentation, constantly mourns her rape by Apollo.

Similarly, Richard Martin has pointed out that two speeches by women in the *Iliad* that are labeled with the term *muthos,* which designates speech that is also a significant form of social performance, are both effectively laments.[13]

One is Helen's response to Priam's request for an identification of Agamemnon during the scene on the wall in book 3 (*Iliad* 3.171–180). Helen's *muthos* begins with a statement designed to cement the relationship to Priam she later celebrates in her lament for Hector: "You are revered by me, dear father-in-law, and admired." It evokes the lost home and family she has left behind and includes a wish to have died rather than to have acted as she did: since she did not die, she is in a constant state of grief, *to kai klaiousa tetēka*, "therefore I am wasted away with weeping." Like Penelope, who often expresses her sense of loss by voicing doubt about whether her life with Odysseus really happened, Helen concludes by identifying Agamemnon as her brother-in-law "if this ever was." The second *muthos* uttered by a woman in the *Iliad* is spoken (or rather "wailed," *kōkusen*) by Hecuba to Priam as he departs for the Achaean camp to ransom Hector's body (*Iliad* 24.200–216) and expresses grief both for her dead son and for her husband, who she feels sure will never return.

While lamentation is the main mode of female speech, it is not exclusive to women. Throughout the Homeric epics men are portrayed as uttering *gooi* and draw on the topoi of lamentation in their other speeches. This is particularly the case with Achilles, who is the only male character whose *goos* is actually quoted in Homer, and who stands out for his preeminence in all the speech genres of heroic life.[14] Achilles' use of lamentation is not, however, to be understood simply as a sign of his verbal competence; it is also a mark of the unusual, marginalized position he adopts in his project of winning *kleos* by staying out of battle rather than entering it. Achilles' alienation from male Achaean society leads him into a closer association with lamentation, which is registered in a variety of ways: his close tie to his mother Thetis, a figure especially identified with lamentation; his vision of himself in his speech to the embassy in book 9 as a mother bird, the archetypal figure of lamentation, as we have seen (*Iliad* 9.323–327); and most overtly in his actual laments, especially the one in book 19, which follows on and echoes the speech of Briseis, who is not only a woman but also a slave.[15]

Not only is Achilles' role as a speaker of laments atypical, but it is also limited by his ongoing allegiance to his identity as a warrior. This is clear from his earliest responses to Patroclus's death, in the exchanges he has with Thetis at the beginning of book 18. Achilles' situation at that point dramatizes one of the central and most enduring themes of lamentation, the contrast between the living speaker and the dead person.[16] This is underscored at the beginning of the book when, just before he learns of Patroclus's death, Achilles recalls the prophetic words of Thetis, who told him that the best of the Myrmidons would die *eti zōontos emeio*, "while I was still living" (*Iliad* 18.10). In many mythic dramatizations of grief the mourner's survival is treated as more than a matter of chance, as he or she is portrayed as actually responsible for the death of the person who is mourned. A common version of this is the figure of the murderous mother, most memorably represented by Procne, the woman who becomes the nightingale, whose unending lamentation both expresses her loss of her son Itys and represents her punishment for killing him.[17]

Achilles' story also represents the mourner as responsible for the death he mourns, and Achilles voices a painful sense of that responsibility:

> nor was I at all for Patroclus the light of salvation,
> nor for my other companions, of whom many were broken
>   by splendid Hector,
> but I sat by the ships, a useless burden on the earth.
>
> (*Iliad* 18.102–104)

In the case of the male warrior, his responsibility demands not a state of perpetual lamentation, but the transformation of grief into action. With Achilles, the mourner's characteristic wish to die is modified into a resolution to avenge his loss:

> Now there will be even for you endless grief
> for your dead child, whom you will not receive again
> returning home, since my spirit does not urge me
> to live or to go among men, unless first Hector,
> struck by my spear, is destroyed in his spirit
> and pays back his despoiling of Patroclus, son of Menoetius.
>
> (*Iliad* 18.88–93)

By prefacing his resolve with the grief it will cause for Thetis, Achilles acknowledges that the vengeful action that assuages his mournful wish to die will also itself lead to his death. The difference, of course, is that his death in battle will also bring him *kleos,* as his words later in the same speech make clear:

> Now let me gain good glory [*kleos esthlon*],
> and make some one of the long-robed Trojan
>   and Dardanian women,
> wiping tears with both hands
> from her tender cheeks, groan bitterly,
> so that they may know how long I stayed away from the war.
> Don't hold me back from the battle, much as you love me.
>   You will not dissuade me.
>
> (*Iliad* 18.121–126)

This speech also shows how Achilles' entwined aims of alleviating his pain and increasing his glory involve transferring his suffering to someone else, in this case a Trojan woman. The mourning of the Trojan woman is both requital for the death of Patroclus and a sign of Achilles' power; furthermore, her grief inspires awareness of Achilles' greatness in the particular form in which he has been demonstrating it throughout the *Iliad:* the Trojans' lack of suffering during his absence from battle.

When Achilles introduces his resolve to fight Hector by telling Thetis she will have to grieve, he registers the way a warrior's glory brings suffering to his friends and relatives as well as to his enemy; this is particularly marked in the case of parents, whose grief for their slain sons responds to a misfortune beyond what is natural or expected. It is hardly surprising, then, that the hero's mother is often portrayed as trying to dissuade him from action, as Achilles anticipates that Thetis will at the end of the speech just quoted. This female impulse to block heroic action is linked to the predominantly female activity of mourning in the lamentlike *muthos* of Hecuba in book 24, mentioned above. There Hecuba explicitly proposes to Priam that, rather than him going off to approach Achilles, he and she should sit apart in the palace and weep for Hector (*nun de klaiōmen aneuthen/ hēmenoi en megarō, Iliad* 24.208–209—although she does go on to add that she wishes she could take revenge on Achilles by sinking her teeth into his liver).

In keeping with Achilles' role as a preeminent warrior, whose function is to turn grief into action, he becomes at the end of his story an advocate of keeping lamentation in its place. In his meeting with Priam in book 24, once he and Priam have experienced their parallel mourning—he for his father and Patroclus, Priam for Hector—the desire for *goos* leaves Achilles' mind and body, and he makes Priam stop mourning too, telling him: *ou gar tis prēxis peletai krueroio gooio,* "There is no practical use to chilling lamentation" (*Iliad* 24.524). This determination marks Achilles' return, however brief, to the world of the male fighting force, for whom lamentation is a transient experience that merely punctuates recurrent action in battle.

The same tension between lamentation and heroic action is found in the meeting of Hector and Andromache in *Iliad* 6. In this episode of transitory connection between husband and wife, Hector, in effect, responds to Andromache by adopting her language. Hector draws on the conventions of female lamentation to express sympathy for Andromache's position, but he also recasts them so as to incorporate an emphasis on achieved *kleos* that is absent or muted in women's own laments. In a characteristically female attempt to restrain a hero's devotion to combat, Andromache asks Hector to return to the city wall and fight more defensively, basing her appeal on her past and future status as a mourner. She evokes her past losses of parents and brothers and urges him to pity her "so that you do not make your child an orphan and your wife a widow" (*Iliad* 6.432). The power of her appeal can be seen in Hector's sympathetic response, in which he echoes her proleptic grief and expands on her one-line account of her future. He speaks of his certainty that Troy will one day fall and says that no one's suffering— not his mother's and father's nor that of his many brothers—horrifies him as much as the thought of hers "when some one of the bronze-wearing

Achaeans/ leads you off weeping, having taken away your day of freedom"
(*Iliad* 6.454–455).

Hector's use of the "ascending scale of affection"[18] to identify Andromache
as the one for whom he grieves most links this speech to more formal laments,
in which that motif is common as a way of asserting the intensity of the
speaker's pain. Thus Achilles, in his lament for Patroclus in book 19, pro-
claims, "I could not suffer anything worse,/ even if I were to learn of the death
of my father" (*Iliad* 19.321–322); and Priam responds to the news of Hector's
death by thinking of Achilles, who has killed so many of his sons, "for none
of whom, much as I grieve, do I mourn so much/ as for one, for whom sharp
grief will carry me down to Hades:/ Hector" (*Iliad* 22.424–426).[19]

Hector follows this expression of concern with an even more detailed vision of Andromache's future humiliation as she is forced, suffering and
against her will, to weave and draw water for her captors. But he then shifts
gears to import into this vision an account of his own future *kleos*, for which
Andromache will serve as a carrier. Turning his attention away from her pain,
he imagines what she will signify to someone looking at her, and actually
quotes that imaginary onlooker's words of praise for him:

> And someone might say, looking at you shedding tears,
> "This is the wife of Hector, who was the best at fighting
> of the horse-taming Trojans, when they fought around Ilion."
>
> (*Iliad* 6.459–461)

Even while grieving for Andromache, Hector is concerned with his future
reputation, fantasizing about the figure he will cut in the eyes of a detached
spectator at a later time, when what is best remembered is who was the best
fighter and when the fighting around Troy has become a memory from the
past. He briefly reconceives Andromache's captivity in a foreign land, not as
a hardship, but as a means for transmitting his fame to a distant place and
a different time. Thus this vision links the content of lament (the theme of
the captive woman) to lament's possible function of promoting praise. The
intrusion of this bit of proto-*kleos* here shows the inevitable limits of Hector's
engagement with the language and perspective of lamentation. And, in any
case, Hector's quasi lament itself comes already prefaced by his explanation
of why he cannot honor his feelings of grief:

> My spirit does not command me [to fight defensively]
>   since I have been trained to be excellent always
> and to fight among the foremost Trojans,
> winning *kleos* for my father and for myself.
>
> (*Iliad* 6.444–446)

It has been suggested that Hector's projection of his own future *kleos* here
is typical of him in particular, part of a pattern in the *Iliad* of characterizing

Hector as "a man already living in the poetic tradition that is to overtake him."[20] A similar quotation of future praise occurs in his next speech, his prayer to Zeus for his son Astyanax. There Hector's imagination fixes on the successful transmission of glory from father to son, which makes heroic achievement complete:

> Zeus and the other gods, grant that this one,
> my child, be, even as I am, outstanding among the Trojans,
> and great in force, and may he rule over Ilium.
> And may someone one day say, "This one is greater
>   than his father,"
> as he returns from battle. And may he bear bloody spoils,
> having killed an enemy man, and may he delight the heart
>   of his mother.
>
> (*Iliad* 6.476–481)

Shortly afterwards, in book 7, there is also a passage in which Hector imagines the tomb of a man whom he has slain as inspiring a eulogy similar to that evoked by Andromache,: "This is the tomb of a man who died long ago,/ whom once shining Hector killed as he was excelling" (*Iliad* 7.89–90). The similarity of these passages points up how Hector's speech to Andromache assigns to his beloved wife a role that is typically that of a defeated enemy and thus supports the vision of heroic warfare as ultimately self-defeating expressed by Andromache when she opens her appeal to Hector with the words "Your force will destroy you" (*Iliad* 6.407). Indeed, Andromache performs in Hector's fantasy a function much like that of the unnamed Trojan woman whose mourning Achilles envisions as a mark of his success in avenging Patroclus. Since that woman is, in the event, Andromache herself, the *Iliad* reveals that Andromache's suffering actually benefits both of the mortal enemies Hector and Achilles: both win glory by causing her grief.

Although Hector's fantasy of Astyanax's future glory also incorporates Andromache as an enthusiastic observer of her son's achievements, Andromache's own laments for Hector share none of his interest in his future fame.[21] In general, the concern of lamenting women for their own sufferings means that they have no use for what concerns a warrior most: the disembodied reputation that outlives the services through which it is earned.[22] Their stress on the discontinuity created by death leads them to underrate the sense of unbroken tradition on which the notion of heroic immortality through *kleos* rests. This can be seen in the lament of Hecuba when she first learns of Hector's death:

> Child, I am wretched. Why should I live, suffering
>   as I am bitter sorrows,
> since you are dead? You who were for me night and day
> a boast [*euchōlē*] throughout the town, and a benefit

to all the Trojan men and women in the city, who revered
you like a god. For you were for them a great glory [*kudos*]
while you were alive. But now death and fate have come upon you.

(Iliad 22.431–436)

Hecuba here speaks of Hector's fame as it was when he was alive, using
terms—*euchōlē*, "boast," and *kudos*, "glory"—that are closely related to *kleos*,
the term for eternal fame as realized in epic song, but connote the more
provisional, time-bound character of a living person's reputation.[23] Her language actually attributes Hector's fame to herself and to the Trojans, reflecting the way in which such fame is shared between the living hero and his
beneficiaries, who at once confer that fame by honoring him and partake
of it. Here the widespread tendency of lamenters to dwell on the contrast
between past and present[24] becomes an assault on the continuity of fame,
which is what the Homeric warrior values above all else (as Hector's apol-
ogy to Andromache, quoted above, makes clear). The praise contained in
Hecuba's lament is undercut by the way she presents Hector's glory as tied
to his living presence. In the context of Homeric poetry, then, women's
laments are subversive, not just because they dwell on the negative consequences of heroic action, but because they ignore the death-defying *kleos* that
provides a positive compensation for heroic sacrifice and constitutes a major function of epic itself.

Andromache's two laments for Hector focus on her widowhood wholly as
a state of humiliation and pain and include a very different vision of
Astyanax's future from that in Hector's prayer. In the first of them, she describes how Hector's physical death will lead to social death for his son. She
predicts that Astyanax will be dispossessed of his ancestral lands, and gives
a detailed account of the life of an orphan, whose father's death makes him
panaphēlika, "entirely cut off from his contemporaries" *(Iliad* 22.490). Included in this account is a quoted taunt that counters and inverts the quoted
praise in Hector's prayer. As the orphaned child begs for food at a noble
banquet,

a child with both parents living shoves him away from the feast,
striking him with his hands and taunting him with reproaches,
"Go away, you! Your father is not feasting with us."

(Iliad 22.496–498)

Andromache sees Hector's death as disrupting the communication of
glory between father and son in both directions. As she puts it, "Neither can
you be for him,/ Hector, a benefit, since you have died, nor he for you" *(Iliad* 22.485–486). Instead, it brings to fulfillment the opposite, a bitter heritage of misfortune transmitted to Andromache from her father and shared
by her with Hector. This community of suffering is stressed in Andromache's
language: Hector's death proves that she and Hector "were both born to a

single fate" (*Iliad* 22.477–478); she describes her father as raising her *dus-moros ainomoron*, "he ill-fated, me bitter-fated" (*Iliad* 22.481), and herself and Hector as having produced Astyanax *su t'egō te dusammoroi*, "you and I ill-fated both" (*Iliad* 22.485). Andromache here resembles Briseis, for whom Patroclus's death belongs to an endless chain of misfortunes that was briefly suspended while he lived, a vision that is similarly conveyed through verbal repetition in Briseis's lament: *hos moi dechetai kakon ek kakou aiei*, "how evil following on evil comes over me always" (*Iliad* 19.290). Patroclus's death both activates and extends Briseis's previous misfortunes, the death of her husband and the destruction of her city, which Patroclus, while alive, had prevented her from mourning (*Iliad* 19.295–297).

In her second lament, delivered at Hector's funeral, Andromache again stresses Astyanax's ruined future and this time draws a direct connection between the battlefield achievements on which Hector prides himself and the suffering that await her and Astyanax. Addressing Astyanax, Andromache envisions two terrible futures for him:

And you, my child, either you will
follow me and there you will perform unworthy labors,
toiling for an ungentle man [*pro anaktos ameilichou*],
    or some one of the Achaeans
will hurl you, taking you by the hand, from the tower,
    to a grievous death [*lugron olethron*],
enraged because Hector killed his brother,
or his father or his son, since indeed many Achaeans
bit the vast earth at the hands of Hector.
Your father was not gentle [*ou gar meilichos*]
    in grievous combat [*en dai lugrē*].
                                        (*Iliad* 24.732–739)

Hector's success in combat is intimately tied to both versions of Astyanax's future, both the murder that would be an avenging imitation of Hector's own actions and enslavement to an oppressive master, with whom Hector is identified by the echo of *ameilichou*, "ungentle" in *ou gar meilichos* "not gentle." Similarly, the grievous combat in which Hector participated is linked by the adjective *lugrē* to the grievous death, the *lugron olethron*, of Astyanax and— a few lines later—to the grievous sufferings, the *algea lugra*, of Andromache herself (*Iliad* 24.742).

In the line that immediately follows this passage, Andromache identifies Hector's lack of gentleness as the reason that he is lamented:

Therefore [*tō*] the people mourn him in the city,
and you have imposed unbearable lamentation and grief
    upon your parents,
Hector, and to me especially you have left grievous sufferings.
                                        (*Iliad* 24.740–742)

This suggestive *tō*, "therefore," links the praise implicit in lamentation to the brutality essential to combat.

As she gives voice to her role as the bearer of Hector's *kleos*, Andromache's words fill in what Hector's gloss over when he imagines her enslaved and mournful figure as the inspiration for a detached assessment of his excellence as a warrior. Making a connection that recalls Achilles' declaration in book 18 that he will reestablish himself as a warrior by making a Trojan woman mourn, Andromache insists that the creation of *kleos* begins with grief for the hero's friends and enemies alike. In doing so, she gives an implicit analysis of why heroic epic cannot do without lamentation, the genre in which "grief has the chief place," even though laments often seem to subvert epic's purposes or at least to distract us from epic's central claims. Before it can be converted into pleasant, care-dispelling song, a hero's achievement is measured in the suffering that it causes, in the grief that it inspires.[25]

NOTES

1. For this approach, see Martin 1989, 44.

2. Bowra 1952, 10.

3. On this legislation, see Alexiou 1974, 14–23; Holst-Warhaft 1992, 114–119.

4. On the *epitaphios logos* as representing a deliberate rejection of the lament, see Loraux 1986, 42–50.

5. Holst-Warhaft (1992, 127–170) interprets tragedy as an appropriation and denigration of women's laments. Foley (1992) paints a more ambiguous picture, arguing that tragedy registers both the danger of lament and the authenticity of the issues it raises.

6. Alexiou 1974, 11–14.

7. On grief (*penthos*) as antithetical to *kleos* and on the audience's noninvolvement in the story as an essential element in the realization of *kleos*, see Nagy 1979, 95–100.

8. For this aspect of Homeric poetics, see Ford 1992.

9. On the laments of the *Iliad* as occasions when women emerge as commentators on the events of the poem, see Easterling 1991.

10. On this speech, see further Murnaghan 1992, 262–263. On the widespread association of birdsong with mourning, see Alexiou 1974, 97; and Feld 1982.

11. For mourning as the occasion of similar competition among women in modern Inner Mani, see Seremetakis 1991, 89–92, and pp. 130–144 for a case in which a woman makes use of lament to disclaim rather than to claim a relationship with a dead man (she has been engaged to him but wants to remain free for another marriage). For non-Greek depictions of women competing as mourners, see Ovid *Amores* 3.9.53–56; Holst-Warhaft 1992, 7.

12. As Nagy (1979, 111) points out.

13. Martin 1989, 87–88.

14. See Martin 1989, esp. 222–223, for this characterization of Achilles. Martin places Achilles' affinity for lament within the context of his deployment of the larger

heroic speech genre of recollection, classifying lament as a version of recollection (pp. 131, 144–145). Although Martin is surely right that lament's connection to future fame also allies it with other commemorative genres (see p. 86), the classification of lament as simply a form of recollection overlooks the range of its themes, which include fantasy and speculation about the future as well as memories of the past, and obscures the degree to which a man who laments is using a mode of speech that is primarily feminine and antiheroic.

15. For a detailed reading of the relationship between Achilles' and Briseis's laments that stresses Achilles' marginalization, see Pucci 1993.

16. Alexiou 1974, 171–175.

17. Loraux 1990, esp. 77–100. On the relationship between that figure and the lamenting mothers of Homeric poetry, such as Hecuba, Thetis, and Penelope, see Murnaghan 1992.

18. For the expression, see Kakridis 1949, 18–27, and, for its application to this episode, pp. 49–53. Kakridis identifies the motif as a link between this episode and the story of Meleager, the narrative in which a wife successfully uses the language of lament to persuade her husband to fight to defend her (although there as an alternative to not fighting at all rather than, as in Hector's case, fighting too aggressively).

19. See also *Iliad* 24.748, 762.

20. Martin 1989, 136–137.

21. Andromache seems no more concerned with Hector's *kleos* as a source of reflected glory for herself than as a compensation to him for his loss of life. She herself expresses no interest that would be met by the consideration raised by G. S. Kirk (1990, 222) in his attempt to soften the element of exploitation in Hector's words at 6.460–461: "His reaction to Andromakhe's imagined fate might seem strangely self-centered; that would be typically heroic, but Hektor knows she will be remembered mainly through himself." In general, Homeric women in their laments represent themselves as losing the kind of status conferred by fame, stressing the annihilating displacement suffered by women whose male defenders are gone. Cf. Penelope in the *Odyssey*, who twice explicitly declares that her *kleos* has been compromised by Odysseus's absence (*Odyssey* 18.251–255, 19.124–128). Cf. also *Iliad* 22.431–436, discussed below.

22. As Holst-Warhaft (1992, 112–113) points out, none of the three women who lament at Hector's funeral praises him as a hero in battle.

23. On the distinction between *kleos* as the term for fame that transcends mortality and its near doublets, *kudos* and *euchos*, which is equivalent to *euchōlē*, see Muellner 1976, 82, 110.

24. Alexiou 1974, 165–171.

25. Sultan (1991) gives a suggestive account of modern Greek Akritic song as a genre in which, similarly, women's interests are opposed to male heroic action and yet women's voices are essential to the process of making heroic glory immortal.

WORKS CITED

Alexiou, Margaret.
    1974.   *The Ritual Lament in Greek Tradition.* Cambridge: Cambridge University Press.

Bowra, C. M.

1952.   *Heroic Poetry.* London: Macmillan.

Caraveli-Chaves, Anna.

1980.   "Bridge between Worlds: The Greek Women's Lament as Communicative Event." *Journal of American Folklore* 93: 129–157.

Danforth, Loring.

1982.   *The Death Rituals of Rural Greece.* Princeton: Princeton University Press.

Easterling, P. E.

1991.   "Men's *kleos* and Women's *goos:* Female Voices in the *Iliad.*" *Journal of Modern Greek Studies* 9: 145–151.

Feld, Steven.

1982.   *Sound and Sentiment: Birds, Weeping, Poetics, and Song in Kaluli Expression.* Philadelphia: University of Pennsylvania Press.

Foley, Helene.

1992.   "The Politics of Tragic Lamentation." In *Tragedy, Comedy, and the Polis,* edited by Alan H. Sommerstein, Stephen Halliwell, Jeffrey Henderson, and Bernhard Zimmermann, 101–143. Bari: Levante Editori.

Ford, Andrew.

1992.   *Homer: The Poetry of the Past.* Ithaca, N.Y.:Cornell University Press.

Holst-Warhaft, Gail.

1992.   *Dangerous Voices: Women's Laments and Greek Literature.* London and New York: Routledge.

Kakridis, Johannes Th.

1949.   *Homeric Researches.* Lund: C. W. K. Gleerup.

Kirk, G. S.

1990.   *The "Iliad": A Commentary.* Vol. 2, *Books 5–8.* Cambridge: Cambridge University Press.

Loraux, Nicole.

1990.   *Les mères en deuil.* Paris: Seuil.

1986.   *The Invention of Athens.* Translated by Alan Sheridan. Cambridge, Mass.: Harvard University Press.

Martin, Richard P.

1989.   *The Language of Heroes: Speech and Performance in the "Iliad."* Ithaca, N.Y.: Cornell University Press.

Muellner, Leonard Charles.

1976.   *The Meaning of Homeric EUCHOMAI through Its Formulas.* Innsbruck: Institut für Sprachwissenschaft der Universität Innsbruck.

Murnaghan, Sheila.

1992.   "Maternity and Mortality in Homeric Poetry." *Classical Antiquity* 11: 244–264.

Nagy, Gregory.

1979.   *The Best of the Achaeans: Concepts of the Hero in Archaic Greek Poetry.* Baltimore: Johns Hopkins University Press.

Pucci, Pietro.

1993.   "Antiphonal Lament between Achilles and Briseis." *Colby Quarterly* 29: 258–272.

Seremetakis, C. Nadia.
   1991.   *The Last Word: Women, Death, and Divination in Inner Mani.* Chicago: University of Chicago Press.
Sultan, Nancy.
   1991.   "Women in 'Akritic' Song: The Hero's 'Other' Voice." *Journal of Modern Greek Studies* 9: 153–170.

12

• • •

The Role of Lament in the Growth and Eclipse of Roman Epic

Elaine Fantham

This essay focuses on an element of epic perhaps more often associated with tragedy: the lament, a necessary response to epic death, that reconciles the readers as well as the participants to great loss. Elaine Fantham develops for the Roman epic a theory of the function of public and private lament, reinterpreting in a Roman context the meanings of rituals of lamentation and grief that have been explored until recently more often in Greek than in Roman literature. She considers not only Virgil's *Aeneid*, but the earliest Roman epic, Ennius's *Annales* (finished before 169 B.C.E., though it exists today only in fragments), Lucan's *De Bello Civili* (an epic on the civil war completed between A.D. 62 and 65, when Lucan was forced to commit suicide after his involvement in a plot against Nero's life was discovered), and Statius's *Thebaid*, published in A.D. 91/2—epics that are much less well-known than Virgil's poem—and traces the use made by epic of both public and private lament. Fantham argues that only in the late and somber *Thebaid* of Statius does lament become a countermovement equal in force to the deaths that are its occasion, itself serving as occasion and stimulus to further conflict that only divine intervention can resolve. Although she points out how often in Roman epic the language of lament is given to male figures and made to be part of an heroic response to loss, Fantham also reveals how in Virgil, and especially in Statius, private lament can become a "dangerous voice" that challenges the heroic ideology. Lament in Statius's poem is thus seen as outweighing heroic action, as the epic suffocates in a world too conscious of the negative motivation of deeds of "valor" (*virtus*).

Lament is preeminently the women's contribution to celebrating the life and death of a man or a community. Sympathy and even pride in this women's theme are reflected in the number of distinguished women scholars who have studied the social role of lament in Greek civilization: see Nicole Loraux's *Mères en deuil*, Helene Foley's "Politics of Tragic Lamentation," and the work of Margaret Alexiou on ritual lament in ancient and modern Greece, which helped me to understand the background to lament in Senecan tragedy.[1] Alexiou's pioneer work has been followed by the social studies of Loring Danforth and Gail Holst-Warhaft on the nexus between lament and vengeance in Greek communities. It might well seem that the public and private aspects of Greek lament considered in these studies leaves no scope for either Roman society or its literature to offer more than variations. Certainly many aspects of ancient lament are common to both societies, and the cultural preeminence of Homer has ensured that aspects of the great laments of the *Iliad* are reproduced in Roman literature and developed by each successive composer of Roman epic.

Epic is by no means the only poetic genre at Rome to incorporate references to and examples of lament, but although the laments of Senecan tragedy, for example, stay close to the Greek tradition, there are several ways in which Roman epic modifies and innovates. From the genre of history, and perhaps also from tragedy,[2] Roman epic introduces the public collective lament as a narrative movement, providing closure or renewed resolution. Secondly lament in post-Virgilian epic appropriates from the *miseratio* or *conquestio*[3] of forensic rhetoric the role of generating resentment (*invidia*) against the adversary. This effect approaches but perhaps stops short of the Greek coupling of lament and revenge: given the formal, urban nature of Roman life and literature, we do not have instances of spontaneous familial laments without a larger political dimension. Finally, as I hope to show, lament, already a prominent narrative marker in Virgil's *Aeneid,* develops a self-conscious, reiterated, structural role in the gendered antiphony of male heroic death and female lament of Statius's *Thebaid.* Because of the many leaders and as many combats and deaths, Statius's great war epic is dominated and shaped by its recurrent laments. For this reason I will give far more attention to this late narrative than to the better known *Aeneid,* whose superiority Statius himself will honor precisely in the context of his final, authorial lament.

ENNIUS AND LUCAN: NATIONAL EPIC AND PUBLIC ACTS OF LAMENTATION

Despite Roman epic's immense respect for the Homeric model, Rome's first self-styled poet, Ennius, created for the opening book of his national historical epic a new kind of lament, the mourning of the people deprived of their leader. Only fragments of Ennius' *Annales* survive, but one of their greatest and most memorable scenes, designed to match the great scene of Rome's ritual founding by Romulus, is the narrative of Romulus's mysterious disappearance and the people's grief for their lost leader until they are told that he will return to them as a god:

> For some long while longing possessed their hearts until they cried out,
> "O Romulus, godlike Romulus, how great a protector the gods begat for us in
> you. O father, O begetter, O blood descended from the gods! You brought us
> forth into the realms of light."[4] (Ennius frag. lxi, ed. Skutsch)

Communal public lament, given by the married women of Rome to Lucius Brutus, their country's first liberator from the Etruscan monarchy,[5] is also used in Lucan's epic of civil war, *De Bello Civili,* to anticipate the catastrophe of Pompey's death. For Lucan, Pompey, the failed defender of the free state of Rome, serves as a counterpart of those who created that state: here explicitly Lucius Brutus, but implicitly the city founder Romulus, and elsewhere Virgil's Aeneas himself. Lucan derives much of the emotional intensity in his epic from systematic anticipation of its tragic events: thus the poet foreshadows in book 7 the future public mourning for Pompey before we, the readers, live through the humiliating and treacherous scene of the great general's assassination by Egyptian conspirators. At the grim dawn on the day of Pompey's defeat at Pharsalus, Lucan marks his approaching death by describing the spontaneous laments not only of married women but of men, old men and boys.[6]

Indeed, for Lucan public mourning is so powerful a symbol that he marks the outbreak of civil war in his second book with all the symptoms of official and unofficial mourning. As if some national hero were dead, there is a public decree suspending business,[7] Rome's magistrates put off their ceremonial clothing, and the women spontaneously crowd to the temples with anticipatory lament, lament designed, we are told, to generate resentment (*invidia*) toward the gods. It is natural to compare this with the ominous anticipatory grief of Andromache for Hector in *Iliad* 6, but Lucan himself does not make this point. Instead he compares the women's public prostration and wailing and tearing of face and hair to the private grief of a family dazed by a sudden death, where the mother is suspended between old fear and new grief.[8] The poet conjures up this public lament and its private analogy not to censure such female mourning as disruptive, but to use its desperation, as Livy did the lamenting widows after the defeat of Cannae,[9] to force upon the reader a full awareness of the death of liberty foreshadowed by this war. In this opening phase of Lucan's political epic the men do not lament but depart to join the opposing forces with grim resolve. Even Cato, the one man presented throughout this narrative as a model of right decision, mourns lost public liberty as if it were the greatest of private losses, grieving over the body of the Republic "like a father left childless by the death of his sons" (*De Bello Civili* 2.297–304). But he too will reconcile himself to serving in a conflict where the only integrity is on the side of the loser.

VIRGIL'S *AENEID:* LAMENT FOR MEN AND CITIES

Lament for a leader, and lament for a doomed city, may converge and coincide. From Ennius it was the lament for a leader that survived in the imagination of later Romans: in Lucan, writing after Virgil, we have seen the deliberate assimilation by comparison of lament for the city and the individual.

In the *Aeneid* scenes of lamentation for fallen cities mark the course of war's destruction and articulate Aeneas's progress, starting with the fall of his city, Troy. The first book presents to Aeneas (and to the reader) the Il-iadic scenes depicted on Juno's temple at Carthage, including the women's supplication in *Iliad* 6, just before the death of Hector that brings on the end of Troy. In the next book Aeneas's retrospective narrative of his city's capture reveals the meaning of this scene of supplication, going beyond Homer's narrative to describe the wailing that fills the palace of Priam as women embrace the doorposts and await their capture.[10] Again Virgil ends his fourth book with the same shock and laments of women's wailing that follow the news of Dido's death. His language represents their grief for their dead queen and leader as mourning for the city itself. They wail as if Carthage itself were captured and crashing about their heads in flames.[11] From Troy to Carthage to Latium, Aeneas's course will be marked by laments until like another Dido, Queen Amata, wife of Latinus, brings on her own death, and the women of yet another city, including Aeneas's intended bride, fill the air with their cries.

> As soon as the unhappy Latin women
> have heard of this affliction, first Lavinia
> rages; she tears at her bright hair and cheeks
> of rose, then all the crowd around her raves;
> the wailing fills the palace's wide halls.
> The sad report goes out across the city.
> Now hearts sink down, Latinus in torn garments,
> dazed by his wife's fate and his city's ruin
> defiles his aged hairs with filthy dust.
>
> (*Aeneid* 12.604–611, trans. Mandelbaum)

Here too Virgil has created symmetry with the tale of Troy: for the women that we now hear wailing were seen offering their supplications to the god-dess in the preceding book (11.478–481). Now Latinus is brought to defile-ment in the dust, like Priam, and like Hector, but not by the sword of a bru-tal Greek. This is the self-defilement of ritual grief at his wife's death and the attendant fall of the city.

These are scenes of communal lament. But in the second half of Virgil's epic, with its narrative of war in Latium, more than one private lament is ar-ticulated. In book 7 there is grief for both animal and human death, but no formal or direct speech of lament. This will come when the climate of vio-lence mounts, and we follow the exploits and deaths of fully characterized heroes. The first of these laments, perhaps the most resonant with modern sensibilities, is the terrible outcry of the young warrior Euryalus's mother, on which Susan Wiltshire has written perceptively in her study of the ten-sion between public duty and personal feeling in the *Aeneid*.[12] This woman is not even named; she is *his* mother (*Aeneid* 9.216f.), and Virgil introduces her obliquely, through the words of her son's lover, and his own last request to his prince as he volunteers for their dangerous mission. We learn that this woman alone of the Trojan mothers has followed her son into the warfare of Latium, when she could have stayed with other women and old people in the peaceful Sicilian settlement (*Aeneid* 9.284–286). The young prince promises that he will treat Euryalus's mother like his own mother, Creusa— the wife Aeneas lost in his flight from Troy—and if Euryalus should perish, will give to her his prizes, in gratitude for such a son.

The son *does* perish, and his head is paraded before the Trojan encampment on a spear point. And his mother, at the news, rushes to the walls, mindless of the presence of men and danger, and fills the sky with her laments— not just the ritual wailing already mentioned, but *questibus* (9.480), a word that denotes both lament and protest or complaint.[13] These are the protests of a survivor for whom life no longer has meaning. Childless, homeless, and driven by her natural grief that she cannot even bury her son, she cries out imploring the Rutuli who possess his body to kill her, unless perhaps Jupiter will pity her by enabling her to die. This is indeed a "dangerous voice," to borrow from Holst-Warhaft's title, but not as a generator of vengeance. Rather this mother's lament is dangerous to Trojan morale, and the fighting men are unmanned and brought to weeping, until the woman is unceremoniously bundled out of sight and into the hut where she belongs.[14]

In contrast to this painful indignity, the *Aeneid* has still to transmit the unrepressed laments of two immortal women and one man. Men of course did not perform ritual lament at Rome; in any formal ceremony their role would be that of walking silently in procession in hierarchically determined clothing, their identities transformed by wearing the death masks of their distinguished ancestors. Only the next of kin would be set apart to pronounce a formal eulogy or *laudatio* before the public and to light the pyre under the body at the place of cremation. At least some funerals hired professional women mourners, *praeficae*, to sing dirges, and one striking funeral relief from Amiternum shows all this—the bier, the procession, and the professional women mourners, but also the wife, now widow, with her arms raised in lament, flanked by her two children.

Yet the closest analogy to this mother's lament is the lament of another bereaved parent, Evander. Virgil has already reported the full funeral honors and brief farewell given by Aeneas over the body of young Pallas (*Aeneid* 11.96–98) before the boy's corpse is escorted back to his city and his father Evander. In his anguish the old man utters a speech almost identical in its opening movement to that of Euryalus's mother, longing for his own death (*Aeneid* 11.152–161), but it moves ahead from backward-looking grief to the need for vengeance on Turnus. Rather than delay the Trojans from renewing the action, Evander thinks as a commander and addresses his chosen successor, sending a last message or challenge to Aeneas: it is his duty to father and son to take Turnus's life (*Aeneid* 11.162–181). So too the nymph

Opis sent by Diana to protect Camilla moves from grief at her fated death to promise and implement vengeance (*Aeneid* 11.841–849). In contrast, Turnus's sister Juturna repeats the Iliadic pattern, anticipating her brother's fate as Andromache foresees the death of Hector, abandoning hope before the event.[15] Of all the laments in the *Aeneid* this alone must precede its occasion, because the epic by design ends *at* Turnus's death, denying the traditional reconciliatory closure of burial and mourning. But these laments by immortals cannot affect the mortal participants: they go unheard except by Virgil's audience—and his successor poets.

Virgil's too literal-minded imitator Silius Italicus understands the poetic challenge of lament. As he approaches the dreadful defeat of Trasimene he even transfers to lament the Homeric technique for enhancing a hero's feats in battle, addressing his muses to ask what god will provide his poem with laments worthy of such noble deeds.[16] But pious men felt that deaths *needed* lament, not necessarily a formal speech of lamentation but a sense of lamentation performed. This is why there is such a sense of completion withheld in the *Aeneid*. We, Virgil's readers, hear the immortal Juturna's fearful outcry at her enforced survival, but any potential consolation from human honor or sympathy for Turnus's fate is cut off beyond our knowledge.

STATIUS' *THEBAID* AND THE THEMATIZATION OF LAMENT

Although Virgil raises lament above the status of an epic topos by his use of lamentation to mark the end of each failed community—Troy, Carthage, Latinus's city—it is only with Papinius Statius, the last of the Flavian epicists, that lamentation becomes a regular or required component of the rhythm and structure of epic.[17] Statius, who had received a Greek education in rhetoric and poetics from his father and was himself a professional poet, also composed extensive poems of lament for his patrons and on his own behalf.[18] Taking up some of the implications of John Henderson's study "Statius' *Thebaid:* Form Pre-made,"[19] I would like to illustrate how Statius's narrative exploits the rhetoric of lament as reaction to the action of combat and death. Henderson has made his readers fully aware of the prominence of lament and in the Latin version of his diagrammatic analysis enumerates its many forms in the epic.[20] This is brought out in his equation: "Thebes *is* a mother's lament . . . Ino: Ide: Eurydice: Jocasta: Ismenis: Atalanta . . . the clawed cheeks/ sockets of Menoeceus' mother . . . in her lament *after* Aen.9.'s Euryalus' mother."[21] Looking forward to the epic's final book, concerned primarily with the women's quest for fulfillment in lamentation, Henderson comments that Statius leaves the reader on "this one last New Mourning, with the women of Argos and Thebes to find their very own lament, since the epic cannot find breath more."[22] Yet since he interprets this epic as a poem governed by deferral, Henderson concentrates on the delaying of combat, death, and lament, rather than analyzing Statius's careful and progressive construction of his narrative around the continuing alternation and causal reciprocity of grief and killing.

Structurally the poet of the "Seven against Thebes" certainly faced problems of deferral—the postponement of warfare to the last six of the twelve books, a legacy of both the Theban myth and the post-Virgilian tradition and the mythically determined denial and withholding of burial until the poem's last phase. He also had to meet the need for variation entailed by the reiterated deaths of the Argive leaders—six in all, the last the doubly-significant death of the adoptive Theban-Argive, the exiled brother Polynices—and a balancing array of Theban heroes.

Yet despite the enforced postponement of lament and burial for the Argive leaders, scenes of lament in the *Thebaid* match scenes of death in frequency and scale, in book 3, book 5, and every one of the last four books. The first miniature of future warfare occurs in book 2 when Tydeus as Argive envoy kills the Thebans sent to ambush him but spares one man, Maeon, to carry his message of defiance to the tyrant Eteocles. In the countermovement of book 3 Maeon expresses his shame at survival and hatred of Eteocles in the public act of suicide. Here Statius offers both his own authorial praise for Maeon and a scene of Theban lamentation for his lost comrades, as a tragedian might reinforce the message of a monologue with a confirmatory chorus.

Such praises as Statius addresses to Maeon ("But you fine spirit, fine in death, shall never—your due reward—suffer oblivion. / . . . What strain of mine, blest seer whom heaven loves,/ what eulogy can add renown to match / your prowess")[23] are not, of course, lament but its complement, eulogy or blessing,[24] and the dozen authorial lines of praise and farewell to the dead man are eclipsed by what follows—the journey of the Theban bereaved to the site of ambush, and the single violent outbreak (*fragor*) of their unanimous mourning and fury at the sight of their dead kinsmen

Now from the city wives death-pale and children
And ailing parents poured by broad highways
Or pathless wastes in piteous rivalry,
All rushing to their tears, and thousands more
For solace' sake throng too, and some were hot
to see the one man's deeds, that might's travails.
The road was loud with wailing and the fields
Rechoed cries of grief. Yet when they reached
Those infamous rocks, that ghastly wood, as though
None had bewailed before, no storm of tears
Had streamed, as from a single throat there rose
A cry of utter anguish. When they saw
The bloody carnage, frenzy fired them all,

GRIEF flaming fierce, with bloody raiment rent
stands there and beats his breast and leads along
The wives and mothers.

            (*Thebaid* 3.114–126, trans. Melville)

I quote this first instance of the recurring laments of the epic in extenso to
bring out Statius's counterpoint of "deeds" (= killing) and lament. I have
capitalized GRIEF (*luctus*), to draw attention to what is still for Latin epic an
innovation—the personification of sorrow, standing like a chorus leader and
urging on the human lamentation. This, the first personification of grief to
stalk among the living in Roman epic, marks the significance that grief and
mourning will claim in the rest of the poem.[25] Next, Statius particularizes:
Ide, her fertility enhanced as mother of twin sons, searches the scene of the
ambush and "wails over every corpse."[26] Yet Ide's speech, when she finds her
sons dead in each other's arms, stands for but still does not exhaust the
lament of them all. Instead their bereavement finds its own epic model as
an old father, Aletes, recalls a domestic myth of Theban suffering inflicted
from above—the myth of Niobe whose children were killed in revenge by
Apollo and Diana. One new detail is significant in his retelling of the myth:
the Theban funeral processions for Niobe's children poured out of the gates
"and mothers beat their breasts in hate of heaven," (*invidiam planxere deis, The-*
baid 3.197). In this final phase Aletes turns to open denunciation of their
undeserved losses caused by the guilt of a cruel king.[27]

   Statius makes only too clear the use to which this mourning is put, to inspire anger and threaten punishment upon the head of Eteocles. But this,
like Maeon's curse on Eteocles, is the male response to grief: both Greek
and Roman political rhetoric knew how to exploit anger at the casualties of
war against their own commanders, as the Athenians did when they paraded
crowds of mourners for dead "kinsmen" to reproach the commanders in the
naval battle of Arginusae, and as Antonius turned the Roman jury against
Servilius Caepio for the casualties of his defeat at Arausio.[28]

   Revenge is the companion of lament even in the neutral world of Ne-
mea, where the accidental death of the child Opheltes is mourned by the
immediate outcry of his nurse Hypsipyle (*Thebaid* 5.608–635). The full out-
pouring of her lament makes possible a different emotional response from
that of his parents—the restrained grief of the child's father (5.653–655)
is contrasted with his mother's unwomanly demand for vengeance upon
the distracted Hypsipyle (5.656–660). The child's solemn funeral celebration and games fill book 6, rounding off the epic's first, supposedly peaceful half.

   In contrast the second half of the poem is constructed around a pattern
of major deaths; only the Theban casualties receive formal lament, but each
book will see one or even two of the Argive leaders meet death. Dying on

the battlefield, the adoptive Argive Tydeus earns a spontaneous outcry of loss and shame at his own responsibility and survival from his blood brother Polynices (*Thebaid* 9.49–72): this death has a sequel when two young heroes attempt to retrieve Tydeus's body from under Theban guard and themselves die heroically, receiving from the poet a blessing and eulogy modeled on Virgil's salute to the young heroes Nisus and Euryalus.

In fact the ninth book is articulated by three laments for three of the four focal deaths. Beside Polynices' outcry at the loss of Tydeus the laments for the young Theban Crenaeus and Argive ally Parthenopaeus are distinguished not so much by their grief, as by their context and relation to the death. Statius offsets the lament of Crenaeus's immortal mother, the river nymph, for her son killed swimming in his grandfather's waters, (9.356, 376–403), with the forebodings, prayer, and lament of the nymph Atalanta when she discovers that her mortal son Parthenopaeus has left for the war against her will (9.608–635). The book comes to an end with his dying words to his distant mother.[29] Two premature victims fall on opposing sides in this one book, and the ordering of their death and its recognition in lament before and after the fact play chiastic variations on the expected sequence.

The same sequence of death, lament, and urge to revenge that we saw after the ambush in book 3 controls the last three books of the poem, but now the links are extended and reconnected in a crossing of causalities. The self-sacrifice of the Theban Menoeceus in obedience to the oracle that requires his death to save the city receives a traditional, perhaps typically uncomprehending woman's lament from his mother: "You, my cruel son,/ You rushed ahead, you doomed your wretched mother!" (*Thebaid* 10.802–823). Blind to his higher patriotic purpose, this unnamed successor of Euryalus's mother illustrates otherpsychological features in the depiction of grieving or aggrieved women in Roman epic and historical tradition—the tendency to think in terms of amour propre, and envy and blame of other women. When Opheltes' mother calls up vengeance against his nurse Hypsipyle it arises from Hypsipyle's direct responsibility for the child's death, but the lament of Menoeceus's mother is personalized in a different way—it is distorted by anger against her sister-in-law Jocasta, whose womb conceived both the offending Oedipus and their sons:

> Was it to be a scapegoat for fierce Thebes,
> A creature doomed, I reared you, glorious boy,
> Like some mean low-down mother?What vile sin
> Have I committed? What gods hate me so?
> I have not shamed incestuous progeny
> by monstrous intercourse, nor has my womb
> Born grandsons to my son in wickedness.
> It matters not! Jocasta keeps her sons
> And sees them kings. Shall I then expiate

The war so cruelly . . . that Oedipus' two sons
May take turns on the throne?
        (*Thebaid* 10.793–801, trans. Melville)

This self-centered resentment and reproach against divine injustice actually precedes the apostrophe to her dead son, further contaminated by
her obsessive disavowal of any part in Menoeceus's heredity of warrior zeal,
which she blames on his paternal inheritance.[30] In this mother's long speech
there is more of anger than grief, more of protest than lament, and "the ill-
starred woman's words would still have flowed,/ Filling the place with protests" (10.814–85) if servants had not confined her, again like Euryalus's
mother, in demented isolation, to grieve as if she were some savage tigress.

In fact Statius's interpretation of the myth puts a new face upon Menoeceus's act of self-sacrifice for Thebes. In Statius it is the uncomprehending
response, falling short of true lament, by both Menoeceus's parents that
nullifies the sacrifice. The triumph of self over sorrow, of anger over grief,
is more marked still in Menoeceus's father, Creon: his pain smolders longer
and is more terrible. Indeed, Creon's anger will overwhelm not only his grief
but his respect for divine law. But first Statius must carry through the deadly
duel of the fratricides and the perverted mourning of their father Oedipus,
whose curse had created their mutual loathing. Oedipus's grief leads him
to lay angry hands upon himself, while Creon, now king, is further crazed
by power and the curse that comes with the throne of Thebes, submerging
any grief for his son in an almost universal hatred. Taking on the impiety
and cruelty of the tyrant Eteocles, he repeats the tyrant's prohibition of all
burial rites for the Argive dead (11.657–664).

Burial and lament now replace power over Thebes as the new object of
human conflict. Statius opens book 12, like book 11 of the *Aeneid,* with the
collective burial by all the Thebans of their unnamed casualties.[31] The les-
ser conflict between rival Theban kinsmen competing to bury the same un-
identifiable corpses (*Thebaid* 12. 33–34) foreshadows the greater conflict between Creon's prohibition of burial and the determination of Antigone and
other mourners to find and bury the bodies of their beloved and his
enemies—but here too there will be conflict and competition between the
bereaved.

The poet needs these straightforward Theban funerals to serve as foil to
Creon's lament for Menoeceus, when he reappears, conducting his son's
grandiose funeral rites. This speech—a perverted version of Virgil's Evander lament—is the last of the male laments in the *Thebaid.* Creon seems to
start well, bewailing Menoeceus's death yet acknowledging the exalted divine status his heroism has won. But his mind has been perverted by his inheritance of the cursed throne of Thebes: first he tries to assuage the bitterness of new kingship without his son as heir by setting the scepter and

diadem of Thebes upon Menoeceus's corpse (*Thebaid* 12.88–92). His grief has turned sour. Even the scepter and diadem are set there to spite the shade of Eteocles, and grief yields to anger in the movement we have seen before, to anger and to Creon's oath sworn by his dead son to punish anyone who attempts to give burial to the Argive dead (*Thebaid* 12.94–104). Statius marks the enormity of Creon's frenzy by the unprecedented division of the lament into two speeches and by the reactions of the bystanders. Such is the king's angry fury of grief that servants have to drag him away, as if he were some woman out of control.

Thus the burial of the Argive leaders remains as the last focus of conflict. Before the achievement of this burial under Athenian protection, and the moral resolution of the epic, the private sorrows of the house of Oedipus reach their emotional resolution. Polynices' corpse receives not one but two laments, as a Theban and an Argive, first from his Argive wife, who has scoured the battlefield by night to find his corpse (*Thebaid* 12.322–346), then from both wife and sister, alternating their dirges as they "shared the tale of Thebes' and Argos' tragedy" ("mutuaque exorsae Thebas Argosque renarrant," *Thebaid* 12.390). These laments create a *mise-en-abîme*, a reliving of the whole epic, or rather a rival version of the epic Statius has just told, seen through women's eyes and in women's terms. But in this context lament becomes a kind of weird triumph. It is not just the quest for pathos that has led Statius to give such prominence to its formal utterance: indeed, he casts aside any hint of pathos when the Argive mothers and widows achieve access to their dead. For them lament is fulfillment. "Their laments rejoice [*gaudent lamenta*]," Statius says, "and their renewed tears are jubilant [*novaeque exultant lacrimae*]," as their mourning, homing on its physical object, leads them to the beloved bodies (*Thebaid* 12.793–795). No wonder that Statius substitutes his own voice for that of these triumphant mourners to bring his poem to a close:

> Though Heaven should swell my voice a hundredfold
> to free my heart, my strains could never match
> those funerals of kings and commoners,
> those lamentations shared.
> (*Thebaid* 12.797–800, trans. Melville)[32]

F. M. Ahl has drawn on the affinity between Statius's reiterated lament for his young warrior Parthenopaeus[33] and his poem of lament for his adopted son, to stress a compassionate if pessimistic message that runs through the epic. As Ahl points out, "Innocence, beauty and life itself must almost inevitably be destroyed"—but the epic narrative itself is there to "prevent the inevitability."[34]

This compensatory hope seems to me both more positive and more sentimental than the outcome of Statius's killing fields. Just as these recurring speeches of mourning by the poet and his personages are a measure of the dead heroes' worth, so their iteration drives home Statius's message that this worth has been misused, and the grief is greater than the glory. There *is* no glory in this war. These heroes have died for nothing. There is no new liberty, no heroic code of values, to celebrate: there is only a tale of destruction willed by the gods as punishment for humankind. This war, like Lucan's, is a civil war, the negation of constructive, colonizing, or even defensive male achievement, and Statius's poem goes a long way to becoming the negation of epic. Although Statius has fundamentally the same message as Lucan, damning civil war as unheroic, antiepic, he differs from Lucan in his intensive use of lament as an instrument of condemnation, a verdict on human greed, cruelty, and folly. Lament has triumphed over heroics and put them to shame. Small wonder that the *Thebaid* had no Roman successor.[35]

NOTES

1. Alexiou 1971. See the discussion of the *kommos* (antiphonal lament) in Fantham 1982, 219–231.

2. Scholars have noted the possible influence of the Greek tragic chorus on the unattributed speeches of communal lament or protest in Roman epic from Ennius to Lucan and Statius.

3. Both terms denote the advocate's final emotional address, but while *miseratio* properly denotes the appeal to pity for his client, and *conquestio* the provocation of anger against the adversary, or a third party, these two functions often overlap.

4. Frag. lxi, ed. Skutsch: "O Romule Romule Die/ qualem te patriae custodem di genuerunt!/ O pater, O genitor, O sanguen dis oriundum!/ Tu produxisti nos intra luminis oras."

5. Livy 2.7.5 records that the married women mourned Brutus for a whole year because he had been so keen an avenger of woman's violated honor (the rape of Lucretia).

6. Lucan *De Bello Civili* 7.37–39. The laments are described as unbidden (virtually forbidden) because Caesar will be in absolute power over Rome.

7. *Iustitium:* Lucan *De Bello Civili* 2.18. On precedents for this decree, see Fantham 1992, 83.

8. See Lucan *De Bello Civili* 2.21–28 (comparison), 29–36 (behavior of lamenting women).

9. Livy 22.55.3–8: the women's laments for their war dead were so disturbing that by public decree they were confined to their homes and forbidden to make further public outcry.

10. "The vaulted walls echo with the wail and woe of women: the matrons wander, clutching at the doors/ embracing them, imprinting kisses" ("penitusque cavae plangoribus aedes / femineis ululant; ferit aurea sidera clamor. / tum pavidae tectis matres ingentibus errant/ amplexaeque tenent postis atque oscula figunt," *Aeneid* 2.487f., trans. Mandelbaum).

11. "The lamentations, keening, shrieks of women/ sound through the house, heavens echo mighty wailings" ("lamentis gemituque et femineo ululatu/ tecta fremunt, resonat magnis plangoribus aether," *Aeneid* 4.666–667, trans. Mandelbaum).

12. Wiltshire 1989, esp. 52–53 (in chap. 2, "Grieving Mothers and the Cost of Attachment").

13. "Wretched she runs out, and with a woman's wailing, tearing her hair, . . . she fills heaven with her cries" ("femineo ululatu/ scissa comam . . . caelum dehinc questibus implet," *Aeneid* 9.477–480, trans. Mandelbaum). This is followed by fifteen lines of her lament in direct speech.

14. Hardie (1993, 49) comments: "Euryalus' mother is in fact entirely selfish in her desire for death"; but he acknowledges the influence of both Euryalus's own demand to die instead of his friend and his mother's demand for death on the Virgin's Lament in Renaissance Christian epics.

15. On Juturna's lament, see Barchiesi 1978.

16. "Quis deus, O Musae, paribus tot funera verbis/ evolvat? tantisque umbris in carmine digna/ quis lamenta ferat?" *Punica* 5.420–422.

17. Until recently there was little secondary literature on the *Thebaid* in English (or indeed other languages). Readers should consult Vessey 1973, which has a full bibliography of previous work; see also Ahl et al. 1986 and most recently Hardie 1993.

18. Besides the *consolationes* for the bereavements of Statius's friends, *Silvae* 2.6 and 3.3, see Statius's *Epikedeia* (Laments) for the wife of Abascantus, for his own father, and for his adopted child, *Silvae* 5.1, 3, and 5.

19. I quote from Henderson 1991, his first and more complex paper.

20. Omitted in his English diagram: see Henderson 1991, 31. The Latin equivalence of lament is represented by eight forms: *ei mihi, heu, gem-, plang-, quer-, lament-, fle-, dol-/ O.* Three (*ei mihi, heu, O!*) are cries of grief; the others are roots of descriptive nouns and verbs.

21. Henderson 1991, 78 n. 191.

22. Ibid. 60.

23. *Thebaid* 3.98–99, 102–103, trans. Melville. A. D. Melville's translation of the *Thebaid*, the first since J. H. Mozley's rather inaccurate Loeb version, may strike the American reader as too archaic, and so convey a more artificial impression of Statius's diction than his admittedly heightened epic language.

24. *Makarismos,* the blessing invoked on the honored dead (such as Virgil's blessing on Nisus and Euryalus in *Aeneid* 9), is only a specialized form of the Greek collective *epitaphios logos,* for those who died in battle or the Roman *laudatio,* enumerating a man's virtues and achievements at his funeral.

25. Virgil is more sparing of personification but includes Grief with Avenging Cares (*Luctus et Ultrices . . . Curae*) among the phantasms that crowd the entrance to the underworld in *Aeneid* 6.274. As we shall see below, grief and vengeance are clearly and repeatedly associated in Statius.

26. Like the heroine of Sergei Eisenstein's *Alexander Nevsky,* but in that optimistic epic the heroine finds both her brother and fiancé alive.

27. The progressive articulation of response to sorrow /death between women's mourning (for the past) and men's call to revenge (for the future) echoes the contrast noted above between Euryalus's mother and Evander, or even between Lucan's

matrons and warriors in book 2. On the Maeon episode and the role of Aletes, see also Ahl et al. 1986, 2830–2831 n. 19.

28. On the provocation of resentment against the Athenian generals, see Xenophon *Hellenica* 1.7.8; against the defeated Servilius Caepio, see Cicero *De Oratore* 2.201.

29. See further note 31 below.

30. Menoeceus is in fact singled out for this sacrificial death because he is the youngest descendant of the serpent-born, earth-begotten warriors who peopled Cadmus's city of Thebes. See further Vessey 1971.

31. Grief and weeping are stressed here too; cf. *Thebaid* 12.26, 32, and the *miserabile certamen* of 33–34, disputing claims over the dead.

32. Contrast Hardie 1993, 48: "The epic ends not with triumph but with lament, or rather with the *praeteritio* of lament, a programme to inspire another epic (808 *novus furor*), to balance the programme at 1.33–45 for the epic we have already read." It will be clear that I see lament itself as a triumph—of a new kind.

33. Just before Parthenopaeus's death the goddess Diana, unable to prevent it, had addressed the boy: "You delight in the battles so bewailed" ("ululataque proelia gaudes," *Thebaid* 9.724). Statius's application of *ululare*, the vocabulary of lament, to battle is new and almost programmatic. Diana's next words ("happy, and dying only for your mother,""felix et miserae tantum moriture parenti," *Thebaid* 9.725) thematically polarize male delight in battle and parental lament. But at the end that "only" is corrected by Statius's own celebration of the mother's grief for "her son,/ Her son who kept his grace though blood was gone,/ Her son for whom two armies grieved as one"(*Thebaid* 12.806–807, trans. Melville).

34. See Ahl 1986, 2905.

35. I would like to express my warm thanks to Randall Ganiban for his valuable insights and suggestions, which have enriched and improved the written revision of this essay.

WORKS CITED

Ahl, F. M.

1986.   "Statius' *Thebaid:* A Reconsideration." In *Aufstieg und Niedergang der Römischen Welt,* edited by H. Temporini and W. Haase, 2.32.5: 2803–2912. Berlin and New York: De Gruyter.

Alexiou, Margaret.

1971.   *The Ritual Lament in Greek Tradition.* Cambridge: Cambridge University Press.

Barchiesi, A.

1978.   "Il lamento di Giuturna." *Materiali e discussioni* 1: 99–121.

Danforth, Loring.

1982.   *Death Rituals of Rural Greece.* Princeton: Princeton University Press.

Foley, Helene.

1991.   "The Politics of Tragic Lamentation." In *Tragedy, Comedy, and the Polis,* edited by A. H. Sommerstein, S. Halliwell, J. Henderson, and B Zimmermann, 101–143. Bari: Levante Editori.

Hardie, Philip.
1993.   *The Epic Successors of Virgil; Studies in the Dynamics of a Tradition.* Cambridge: Cambridge University Press.
Henderson, John.
1992.   "Statius' *Thebaid:* Form Remade." In *Roman Epic,* edited by A. J. Boyle, 162–191. London: Routledge. New revised version in *Fighting for Rome* (Cambridge: Cambridge University Press, 1998), 212–254 (text greatly modified).
1991.   "Statius' *Thebaid:* Form Pre-made." *Proceedings of the Cambridge Philological Society* 37: 30–79.
Holst-Warhaft, Gail.
1992.   *Dangerous Voices: Women's Lament and Greek Literature.* London: Routledge.
Lucan.
1992.   *De Bello Civili. Book 2.* Edited by *Elaine Fantham.* Cambridge: Cambridge University Press.
Seneca.
1982.   *Troades.* Edited by *Elaine Fantham.* Princeton: Princeton University Press.
Statius.
1992.   *Thebaid.* Translated by A. D. Melville. Introduction and notes by D. W. T. Vessey. Oxford: Clarendon Press.
Vessey, David.
1973.   *Statius and the "Thebaid."* Cambridge: Cambridge University Press.
1971.   "The Death of Menoeceus." *Classical Philology* 66: 236–243.
Virgil.
1981.   *The Aeneid of Virgil. A Verse Translation by Allen Mandelbaum.* New York: Bantam.
Wiltshire, Susan.
1989.   *Public and Private in Vergil's "Aeneid."* Amherst: University of Massachusetts Press.

Epic and Pedagogy

13
• • •

Epics and the Politics of the Origin Tale

Virgil, Ovid, Spenser, and Native American Aetiology

Susanne L. Wofford

This essay resituates study of the epic by comparing the use of origin myths in epic to the origin tale as a distinct genre, including examples from Ovid, from Joel Chandler Harris's retelling of African and Indian stories of origin, and from two Labrador Indian aetiologies. Susanne Wofford argues that epic stands against aetiology and origin tale as genres that contrast in form and purpose. Although stories of origin often naturalize violent change at the foundation of a society or nation, they also expose that violence, representing the beginnings of custom, ritual, or elements of landscape in forced impositions on a different original form. Epic, in contrast, although it appears to search for causes, in practice usually occludes them and evades especially the kinds of revelations the aetiology or origin story presents. Wofford's essay suggests that study of the traditional Western epic can be expanded and illuminated by contextualizing epic with the lived oral traditions represented in indigenous origin tales and heroic narratives and poems, and argues for teaching the European epic in a broad American context.

The question of whether and how to teach the classic epic poetry of the West has become an urgent one in universities in the United States, especially as debates about the value of the literary canon have moved to center stage in recent years. Decades ago, though, in the postwar period, when Great Books programs were established at schools like the University of Chicago (under the leadership of Mortimer Adler) and Columbia University (where a two-year general humanities requirement still is a major feature of every student's undergraduate education), the question had already been posed as a challenge to the emergence of the modern, department-based U.S. college or university. In arguing about whether to include more literature from other cultures or more works written by women or more examples of works representing the minority literatures of the United States in college requirements, most universities seem to have posed the debate as a choice: either we teach the traditional canon or we shrink the number of classic works and "open up" the canon to include other material. In this essay, I hope to suggest, briefly and in a summary way, a different, perhaps more American or more New World context for teaching the ancient and Renaissance epic: the oral literature and traditions of Native Americans. In addition, I look at origin tales written down by Joel Chandler Harris, which may have roots in American Indian as well as African storytelling traditions, and more briefly at an origin tale by Kipling. These texts, I will argue, provide a very different context within which to view the epic stories, and help to remind the student of those aspects of early epic, often submerged in the literature class, that connect it to contemporary performances of oral heroic narrative and storytelling in the late twentieth century. The reader will find in the appendix to this essay two Native American origin tales to which I will refer, and in my brief bibliography, notes on where to find more examples of similar tales. This essay is less explicitly about pedagogical method—what exactly to do and say when teaching epic this way—than it is about the value of this very different context for teaching and interpreting epic.

A cautionary note must be briefly appended about the use of Native American materials. Scholars, critics, and students must use Indian stories and legends carefully, with an awareness of the extent to which whatever is written and published may be distant from the oral original. Many Indian stories are not available in printed form, because they can be told only at a certain time or only by a certain person or because to print them would be to lend special authority to one or another version of the tales or because they are used in sacred ritual or because the teller is not literate. That said, the many strong Indian traditions in this country of heroic song, heroic legend, and origin tale remain largely unknown to most non-Indian college students. To study ancient epic and ancient aetiologies in conjunction with twentieth-century oral traditions of heroic and mythic narrative can make the Western epic central to a new and broader understanding of the American literary heritage.[1]

THE RABBIT AND THE MUSE

Musa, mihi causas memora, quo numine laeso
quidve dolens regina deum tot volvere casus
insignem pietate virum, tot adire labores
impulerit. tantaene animis caelestibus irae?

(*Aeneid* 1.8–11)

Tell me the causes now, O Muse, how galled
In her divine pride, and how sore at heart
From her old wound, the queen of gods compelled him—
A man apart, devoted to his mission—
To undergo so many perilous days
And enter on so many trials. Can anger
Black as this prey on the minds of heaven?

(1.13–19)

The *Aeneid* begins with the question of cause, and later epic poets have followed in Virgil's footsteps, claiming that the poetic form they have chosen will provide reasons and explanations for suffering, action, and motive, not to mention the presence of death or evil.[2] The cause or origin the poet needs help to know in Virgil's case is a transcendental one, and one that sums up a range of related questions: Can such anger fill the gods? If so, why? Do the gods exist as anthropomorphized beings that can feel anger? What is the relation of the divine and human spheres, and is the relation between them one of cause? These are questions that, as the story goes on, Virgil's narrator seems less and less certain his poem can answer.

The opening of the *Aeneid* gives three stories to account for Juno's anger. This displacement to another narrative level—here, a displacement to myth—suggests that the origin itself is narrative or mythic, or at least, that that is what we can know about it ("Who has known his own engendering?" asks Telemachos in the opening of the *Odyssey* [1.216],[3] before he goes to hear story after story about his father). Moreover, neither the poet nor the readers are likely to feel that the question of cause has been answered by these three mythic narratives. In posing the question of cause at the beginning, Virgil may be calling forth again the Lucretian echoes of *Georgic 2*: "felix qui potuit rerum cognoscere causas" ("Happy is the one who could know the causes of things," *Georgics* 2.490). Lucretius's assertion that to know "the first beginnings of things" (*De Rerum Natura* 1.55) is to overcome fear of death through philosophical understanding of the nature of the universe is clearly the subtext of this passage in the *Georgics*. But in the *Aeneid,* this knowledge of causes proves elusive, shadowy. The epic poet asks for inspiration to find the cause—to know the origin and provide the story that arises from it—but he can never fully achieve this task. I have argued elsewhere that this cause cannot be known partly because of the circularity of figure and narrative in the poem—do Juno and Allecto *cause* Amata's fury or represent it?[4] If they cause it, do they merely move the question of cause to another level, in a regress of narratives present on other occasions when epic poets seek causes?[5] When the poet does attempt to represent cause, the included aetiology usually disrupts, complicates, or exposes the costs of the narrative construction of value that makes the epic a national poem.

Epics, then, seek to represent cause and to tell a story of origins, and an important subset of epic also seeks to make that story into a national history, providing a surrogate memory for the nation. But when we look closely at the effort to represent origin in epic, we encounter either out-and-out evasion or the sort of narrative regression mentioned above—both moments in which the epic displays anxiety about the very project it has undertaken. The structure of epic, especially in regard to its efforts to narrate origin, contrasts with and cannot easily be made to incorporate the origin tale or aetiology. Dividing the two, as I will do provisionally in this essay, is a heuristic device, since the epic clearly includes versions of origin tales from the start, and part of the interest of the form comes from the moments of intersection—places where the origin tale is embedded in epic, often places of special figurative and allegorical density that expose the risks of representing that which itself may need to be hidden. These risks include the danger of demystifying a sacred origin by making it publicly available, and the threat that revealing violence, crime, or sexual transgression at the origin will deprive the society of its founding authority.

There is a long tradition, represented most recently in the work of David Quint and Elizabeth Bellamy, that sees epic as linear and teleological, a narration that encodes the ontological opposite of the wanderings of romance.[6] Looking at some of the roles of aetiologies within epic will show, however, that epic may not be able to trace the narrative line from origin to goal and may be much less linear and much more circling than critics have allowed.[7] Just as many epics seem not to reach their desired endings (the *Iliad,* the *Aeneid, The Faerie Queene*), so many also betray uneasiness about incorporated stories of origin, the grounds on which the epic is itself established. If the epic as a genre is linear, then, it often tells a linear story without real beginning or ending—beginning *in medias res* and ending also *ex mediis rebus.*

Aetiologies can be told for the origins of certain customs or rituals—as in some of Callimachus's *Aitia.* The epic games in book 5 of the *Aeneid,* for instance, function as fictional aetiologies both for the Roman families whose names are mentioned and for the display of horsemanship at the end for the *lusus Troiae,* a pageant or ceremony revised by Julius Caesar and established under Augustus as a regular institution.[8] They also can be told to explain the presence of a certain name or of the elements of the landscape—a tree, a particular flower. Examples of aetiologies in the *Aeneid* include the naming of several important landmarks, such as the Punta di Palinuro in southern Italy, the Punta di Miseno in the Cumae area, and (not to leave out Aeneas's nursemaid) Caieta, as well as aetiologies for Augustan custom. Examples in Ovid include the stories of the naming and creation of the laurel tree (Daphne: *Metamorphoses,* book 1) and of other trees—the weeping willow (Cyparissus: book 10), the weeping myrrh (Myrrha: book 10)—, of the origins of various flowers (Narcissus: book 3; Hyacinth: book 10), birds (Procne and Philomela: nightingale and swallow, book 6), and springs (Byblis: book 9; the poisoned pool in the story of Salmacis and Hermaphrodite: book 4).[9] All of these tales involve the description of how the poem's landscape came into being, and they pose the question of how that landscape should be interpreted.[10]

One encounters very similar story types in indigenous tales from many cultures around the world. I have chosen two Labrador Indian tales that show interesting similarities to aetiologies in the Western classical tradition: "The First Loon" and "The Origin of Robins" (retold by Lawrence Millman) (see appendix). I cannot do justice here to the complex local, political, or ideological roles that these tales may play in their individual cultures, but in teaching these works it would be important to develop a fuller understanding of their cultural context and the conditions in which they are performed or related. Here I propose a formal analysis that will allow, I hope, some legitimate comparison.

Tales of origin, in contrast to epic, have a different but recognizable narrative form and set of consequences. A brief look at several tales with which many readers will be familiar—Joel Chandler Harris's rendition of the story of how Brer Rabbit lost his fine bushy tail, and Kipling's "How the Elephant Got His Trunk"—will help to identify characteristic traits of the origin tale. In the case of Brer Rabbit, the tale that results is like the rabbit's tail itself— short, indeed short enough to be included here in full:

> "One day Brer Rabbit wuz gwine down de road shakin' his long bushy tail, w'en who should he strike up wid but ole Brer Fox gwine amblin' long wid a big string er fish! W'en dey pass de time er day wid wunner nudder, Brer Rabbit, he open up de confab, he did, an he ax Brer Fox whar he git dat nice string er fish, en Brer Fox, he up'n 'spon' dat he katch um, en Brer Rabbit, he say whar'bouts, en Brer Fox, he say down at de babtizin' creek, en Brer Rabbit he ax how, kaze in dem days dey wuz monstus fon' er minners, en Brer Fox, he sot down on a log, he did, en he up'n tell Brer Rabbit dat all he gotter do fer ter git er big mess er minners is ter go ter de creek atter sundown, en drap his tail in de water en set dar twel day-light, en den draw up a whole armful er fishes, en dem w'at he don't want, he kin fling back. Right dar's whar Brer Rabbit drap his watermillion, kaze he tuck'n sot out dat night en went a fishin'. De wedder wuz sorter cole, en Brer Rabbit, he got 'im a bottle er dram en put out fer de creek, en w'en he git dar he pick out a good place, en he sorter squot down, he did, en let his tail hang in de water. He sot dar, en he sot dar, en he drunk his dram, en he think he gwineter freeze, but bimeby day come, en dar he wuz. He make a pull, en he feel like he comin' in two, en he fetch nudder jerk, en lo en beholes, whar wuz his tail?"
>
> There was a long pause.
>
> "Did it come off, Uncle Remus?" asked the little boy, presently.
>
> "She did dat!" replied the old man with unction. "She did dat, and dat w'at make all deze yer bob-tail rabbits w'at you see hoppin' en skaddlin' thoo de woods."
>
> "Are they all that way just because the old Rabbit lost his tail in the creek?" asked the little boy.
>
> "Dat's it, honey," replied the old man. "Dat's w'at dey tells me. Look like dey er bleedzd ter take atter der pa."

(pp. 125–126)

One of the features of this tale, besides the disjunction between the voices of the white child and the African slave, is that it tells of a transformation that cannot be reversed. While some of the stories Harris records in *Uncle Remus* seem to encode an allegory of how a clever individual can outwit an oppressor whose claim to control is based simply on superior power ("Born and bred in de briar patch, Brer Fox, born and bred"), this one suggests that

Brer Fox's trick has permanently altered the shape of things—"Are they all that way just because the old Rabbit lost his tail in the creek?"—and, more-over, that that permanent change is connected to a kind of patriarchal de-scent—"Look like dey er bleedzd ter take atter der pa"—a statement qualified only by "Dat's w'at dey tells me," which leaves the source of the oral tradition unidentified—who are "they"? In most such tales of origin, we are asked to consider what kinds of truth claims are being made: here the "truth" is a fictional one—neither Uncle Remus nor Joel Chandler Harris nor the reader thinks that there ever really was a rabbit who said these things, and yet the tale tells something that is felt to be "true" metaphorically or fictionally. Un-cle Remus obscures this problem by his allusion to his authority in telling the tale—"Dat's w'at dey tells me."[11] He is an oral narrator whose claim to knowledge is a chain of storytellers that fictionally reaches back to the be-ginning—he, too, we might say, takes after his pa. This question of the fictive truth claims made by origin tales will return shortly, as we look at fictions that claim a religious or pseudoreligious authority. For now, it suffices to high-light the unidirectional metamorphosis: the change cannot be undone.

Most of these tales—including the Ovidian ones—represent an excessive violence, often exemplified in or combined with an account of forbidden sexuality or desire—brother-sister incest, father-daughter incest, rape, self-love to the point of self-destruction—followed by a catastrophic and irre-versible metamorphosis that produces the element of landscape or being in question.[12] The metamorphosis marks the ending of the tale, a clear closure that defines also the cause or reason for the change. Indeed, the metamor-phosis itself could be said to be a figure of closure, an event that resolves seemingly irresolvable tensions or oppositions in the narrative. The meta-morphoses sometimes involve a death (as in "The First Loon"), which, by the symbolic economy of the genre, seems to be the cost of an all-powerful intervention, sometimes by the gods, sometimes by an otherwise unidentified source of narrative power. Sometimes, also, these stories share the odd fea-ture that their endings seem relatively unimportant compared to the route taken to arrive at the point of conclusion.

One way to read these stories of origin, then, is to consider to what extent they are narratives about the naturalization of force or violence—to what ex-tent they are stories in which a sudden, revolutionary, and instantaneous act of force is made to seem a natural event. The fact that the endings are irre-versible emphasizes how the tales make such catastrophic acts of force seem to produce the natural world as we know it, everything appearing "just the way things are," incapable of further change. Kipling's "The Elephant's Child" and the aetiology of Brer Rabbit's tail discussed above are both stories set in the frame of a colonial project, a colonial occupation or enslaving that marks one culture's violent acquisition of another. In this setting, the view that these catastrophic metamorphoses have simply produced "nature"—indeed an improved nature, since in the case of the Kipling tale the elephant can use its long trunk to spank its irritating relatives—might seem to symbolize or reduplicate the colonial project itself, in which a violent acquisition and ostensible transformation of the colonized can be made to seem both irreversible (just the way things are) and morally superior. Obviously these tales are not all identical, and Brer Rabbit is not clearly improved by the shortening of his tail—in fact, the transformation of the big bushy tale is told as a tale of loss. Also, in neither of these two cases does a divine power intervene to authorize the metamorphosis: wit itself, enforcing its stratagems aggressively, determines the definitive shape of the rabbit's tail. But the fantasy of irreversibility serves the cultural and ideological function of establishing and legitimizing "the way things are" in a society (slavery, colonization) or in a story, and of making the desire to change such things correspondingly fantastical and unnatural.[13]

OVID

Ovid's account of Apollo's desire for Daphne, the first of the amatory tales in the *Metamorphoses*, carries a similar resonance.[14] The natural world here seems at first glance a world of tranquillity, a place of escape from the violence of history enacted in the plot of desire. The source of the power to become a tree is associated with Daphne's connection through her father to the waters and the local setting itself: "Help, father help!" she cries, as Apollo's breath touches her shoulders and her trembling hair. "If mystic power/Dwells in your waters, change me and destroy/My baleful beauty that has pleased too well" (*Metamorphoses* 1.545–547; p. 17). Peneus, her father, is, like most of the local deities in Ovid, both the river in Thessaly of this name and its god. His "mystic power," then, is fictionally that of a god, but figuratively that of the river and locality itself. This interpretation perhaps illuminates the poetic logic in the transformation of his daughter into an element of this setting, as well as establishes the limits of her escape. The locality here resists the force of Apollo and transforms Daphne, though it does not answer her prayer and destroy her beauty. Daphne loses her speed in her metamorphosis but gains a luster, a glamorous beauty (*nitor*):

> Scarce had she made her prayer when through her limbs
> A dragging languor spread, her tender bosom
> Was wrapped in thin smooth bark, her slender arms
> Were changed to branches and her hair to leaves;
> Her feet but now so swift were anchored fast
> In numb stiff roots, her face and head became
> The crown of a green tree; all that remained
> Of Daphne was her shining loveliness [remanet nitor unus in illa].
>
> (*Metamorphoses* 1.548–552; p. 17)

The loss here—of her nymph form, of her speed, of her sinuous movement—
is matched and compensated for aesthetically by the evocation of the beautiful tree and tranquil landscape.[15] As a nymph, Daphne might be said to
represent literally what should be her figurative relation to the local setting:
she should serve as the spirit of the waters and the trees, and before her transformation she had loved to roam the woods. Now, however, she has become
literally anchored in the setting. As with most characters whose wishes are
fulfilled, too, her wish to remain a virgin is granted in a more literal way than
she could have expected, yet even so Apollo embraces her and appropriates
her symbolic power for himself. If Apollo is read in part as a figure for Augustan imperial power, this tale depicts, as does that of Juturna at the end
of the *Aeneid*, the local landscape resisting the national drive of epic.[16]

At first, then, the metamorphosis seems to represent a real escape from the
violence of political or historical struggle, even if at the cost of the loss of subjectivity. But Apollo is not deterred: he seizes the laurel and succeeds in a near
rape; the tree recoils from his kisses but cannot get away, because it is rooted.
After embracing and kissing the bark, Apollo takes the leaves of the laurel as
his symbol—"My lyre, my locks, my quiver you shall wreathe"—and promises
to set the laurel tree on either side of Augustus's palace gates. He concludes:

> "My brow is ever young, my locks unshorn;
> So keep your leaves' proud glory ever green."
> Thus spoke the god; the laurel in assent
> Inclined her new made branches and bent down,
> Or seemed to bend, her head, her leafy crown.
>
> (*Metamorphoses* 1.564–567; p. 18)

The *aetion* ends with her apparent acquiescence to his appropriation of her
form and its meaning. We must stress the appearance of agreement here,
though, because Ovid does: we are not to know Daphne's true thoughts
here, but at least her recoil and horror have disappeared. The world of imperial triumph, like that of erotic desire (or hatred of love), is a world of
turmoil and movement, but Daphne has joined the landscape—the nod-
ding head of the leafy crown of the tree momentarily evokes the image of
the beautiful grove in which the action takes place—and taken on a different
kind of figurative life. On the other hand, Ovid leaves open the possibility
that Apollo simply does not recognize her resistance to his use of her, since
now she is a tree.[17]

This story might at first be read as a tale of the origin of poetry, hinted at
with the mention of Apollo's lyre. As a god skilled in prophecy and music,
Apollo is closely associated with poetry, a quality that explains how the laurel wreath comes to be the poet's symbol. Certainly this second-level aetiology of the story of Daphne as an account of the origin of poetry has deter-

mined much of the symbolics of later European poetry, exemplified best, perhaps, in Petrarch's appropriation of the "laurel" as the figure simultaneously for his poetry and his beloved. If so, it suggests that poetic power and control come at great cost—that the natural materials of the poet resist his desire and cannot be made to fit his needs without "a dragging languor" (*torpor gravis, Metamorphoses* 1.548—"a down-dragging numbness" in the Loeb) that roots them and makes them tractable. To support this reading, Ovid's method of detailing the stages of metamorphosis might be read as a literalizing of the method of metaphor: a natural simile would work by claiming that a character is like a tree, while a metaphor says that a given character is a tree. The loss of the distance maintained in the simile is rewritten here as a violent imposition of will. The implicit set of analogies that are submerged in the metaphor but that nonetheless give it its efficacy are recounted in eery detail (arms are like branches, and so on). The fact that the laurel will be ever green—the final stage of the aetiology—is itself determined by Apollo through analogy to himself: the leaves of the laurel are always green so that the analogy between God and tree can be maintained, so that the leaves will retain the mark of the divine, so that we remember that they have been appropriated as Apollo's symbol.

The exposure of the poet's figurative method as itself depending on a kind of force, and on the subjection and near rape of a female figure, fits also with a more explicitly political reading of the aetiology.[18] Ovid's story concludes with what seems to be flattery of Augustus. E. J. Kenney notes that "the laurel was prominent in the cult of Apollo, and here is the god himself giving pride of place to its associations with Augustus."[19] The story itself becomes momentarily transformed into the aetiology of Augustus's association with the laurel. The account of resistance and violent transformation is wrenched briefly but conclusively into a tribute to imperial power, where the transformation of resistance into natural landscape does seem to naturalize that power—to suggest that this is, irreversibly, how the world is. Even nature, in this understanding of the story, exists to celebrate Augustus, and the landscape that had served as protection against the violences of the political world itself becomes an ideological symbol, where its tranquility and beauty serve to hide, not deflect, the violence in the narrative.

That this is also one aetiology for poetry only seems to identify poetic metamorphic power with the political power of Augustus. One must qualify this last claim, however, both because Ovid has extensively detailed that violence and because he reminds us of the tale of resistance and escape in the moment of doubt he recaptures in the ending of the tale: "factis modo laurea ramis,/adnuit utque caput visa est agitasse cacumen," "The laurel in assent/ Inclines her new-made branches and bent down,/ Or seemed to bend, her head, her leafy crown" (1.566–567; p. 18). Ovid's wit also hints here that there is no reason to interpret the bending of the crown of a tree as a suppressed language. He acknowledges implicitly here that the narrator has lost his capacity to guess at her motives and opinions. Perhaps she has escaped more completely from being a known object of poetic narration than we or Apollo could have guessed.

The moments of narrative excess in the story—the chase, Apollo's desire, his caressing of the bark of the tree as it recoils, for instance—are in fact some of the most memorable. Such excess—what one might call the Ovidian grotesque—is so frequent in Ovid's aetiologies that one must include them within any theory of how to read these tales. His account of the rape and mutilation of Philomela can serve as an example in which the violence and grotesquerie prevent, or at least complicate enormously, the kind of political reading proposed above. Here is Ovid's account of Philomela's tongue flapping on the ground:

> radix micat ultima linguae,
> Ipsa iacet terraeque tremens inmurmurat atrae,
> Utque salire solet mutilatae cauda colubrae,
> Palpitat et moriens dominae vestigia quaerit.
> (*Metamorphoses* 6.557–560)

> The tongue lay on the dark soil muttering
> And wriggling, as the tail cut off by a snake
> Wriggles, and, as it died, it tried to reach
> Its mistress' feet.
>
> (p. 138)

The terrible humor of this account along with the recurring violent acts in the rest of the story (including the murder and dismemberment of Procne's child) make it difficult to read the tale primarily through an ideological lens, since they vividly present and dwell upon images quite extraneous to the ideological purpose or historical plot. At about the halfway point in the story, we seem again to be immersed in an account of how art emerges from violence—this time visual art, since once her tongue is cut off, Philomela weaves a tapestry to depict the rape. But the revenge of Philomela and Procne complicates the picture: more clearly than in the case of Daphne, if for a very different reason, the female victim resists becoming part of this aetiology. Once the murder of the child and the banquet have occurred, the reader's sense of horror is complete. The transformations that end the story, then, provide an escape for the reader as well as for the characters from the violences that have erupted everywhere—violence perpetrated on them, but also discovered within them. The swallow and the nightingale—Ovid wittily avoids saying who was who, since the scholarly tradition had been mixed— sail off to forest and to roof, while Tereus too becomes a bird (*volucrem*) with a long fantastic bill—a hoopoe. Nature in the form of these three birds becomes an escape for all three from the narrative of desire, rape, and revenge, yet it is a nature marked forever by this narrative. This is not a setting infused with tranquillity and beauty: the transformation produces a mourning landscape that continually points to the crime and grief that it hides.[20]

The transformation also calls attention to the role of art in the tale, in that it literalizes one of Ovid's metaphors:

> He wept and wailed and called himself his son's
> Disastrous tomb, then with his naked sword
> Pursued Pandion's daughters. As they flee,
> You'd think they float on wings. Yes, sure enough,
> They float on wings! One daughter seeks the woods;
> One rises to the roof, and even now
> The marks of murder rise upon a breast
> And feathers carry still the stamp of blood.
> And he, grief-spurred, swift-swooping for revenge,
> Is changed into a bird that bears a crest,
> With, for a sword, a long fantastic bill—
> A hoopoe, every inch a fighter still.
>
> (*Metamorphoses* 6.665–674; p. 142)

The play on words whereby the metaphor becomes literal is explicit in the Latin: "Corpora Cecropidum pennis pendere putares:/ Pendebant pennis" (6.667–668). The chiastic order emphasizes the wit but also the closure of the story: as so often in Ovid, what might have been a metaphor or an expressive gesture becomes physical. As William Anderson points out in his commentary, the two sisters have not escaped their crime against Itys, nor has Tereus escaped his grief or his desire for revenge. As birds, "the sisters continue to recall the crimes they have committed and suffered. . . . They are eternally marked with the blood of their crime. . . . The cruel vengeance which dominated and warped the minds of Procne and her sister has now become the one passion of [Tereus]."[21] The human characteristics of the hoopoe (the crest looks like a crest on a helmet, the beak replaces the spear— *pro cuspide*) reinforces the sense that Tereus cannot escape his warrior identity and the violence it led him to. By stressing his own artistic power to effect this metamorphosis, Ovid calls attention to the power of art to rework violence into something that at least accuses the evildoer if it cannot transform or deflect that violence utterly. And he differentiates his art from Philomela's more retributive craft, whose rough tapestry with words worked in was used to spur Procne to revenge. Ovid's metaphorical transformation— they are like birds, they *are* birds—creates not revenge but three creatures that symbolize and mark a nature inescapably symbolizing crime and passion, what later poets in a different tradition might recognize as fallen nature. Ovid also seems to be differentiating his tale from earlier versions of the story, since he so explicitly avoids suggesting any divine intervention in the moment of the transformation.

In this case, then, the origin story can serve to resist the tendency to represent its founding act of violence as natural and can expose, rather than hide, the violence at the origin of the creature or setting. Such a landscape, polluted, poisoned or disfigured by desire or power, is surprisingly common in Ovid. Examples of the landscapes, landmarks, trees, and other creatures that retain always the marks of crime, grief, or excessive passion include Niobe weeping forever as a rock face; Byblis, whose unsatisfied lust for her twin brother makes her first a writer, then a wanderer, searching for her brother, until, as she lies weeping on the ground, the nymphs turn her into a spring, which still weeps and keeps her name; and Myrrha, whose consummation of an incestuous love for her father sends her into exile where she becomes a tree. Myrrha, as penitent, asked to be transformed: though the tree seems to weep, she eagerly seeks the transformation. She "buried her face and forehead even in the bark" while the tree oozed myrrh, her tears, and groans in labor as her child burst the bark in childbirth. Ovid tells us that *she* has forgotten her former feeling, but the weeping continues still, transposed into the landscape:

> Quae quamquam amisit veteres cum corpore sensus,
> Flet tamen, et tepidae manant ex arbore guttae.
>
> (*Metamorphoses* 10.499–500)

> Though with her body she had forfeited
> Her former feelings, still she weeps and down
> The tree the warm drops ooze.
>
> (p. 241)

Indeed, trees often seem to become or provide an ominous setting. Tereus rejoiced on the boat as he brought Philomela to his home, and Ovid tells us that "the brute could hardly wait to seize his joys" (*Metamorphoses* 6.514–515; p. 137). But he does wait, until he can drag her off to a cabin in the woods, "silvis obscura vetustis," "hidden away among dark ancient trees" (6.520–522). We already know what deeds are appropriate for these ancient woods, the woods where one of the sisters will remain once she takes her bird form.

In Myrrha's case, finally, the tree stands as memorial both to the taboo-breaking heroine and her desires, and to the force used in the policing of that taboo. Rather than hiding or aestheticizing that violence—or justifying it through a sacrificial economy—these tales tell the story of a different origin. If read as marking an origin in crime, illegitimate passion, or horror, Ovid's *Metamorphoses* can simultaneously illustrate the dangers for the epic of exposing these origins.

TWO LABRADOR ORIGIN TALES

"The First Loon," a Labrador Indian origin tale, can be usefully compared to many of Ovid's aetiologies, especially the tales of Philomela and of Myrrha.[22] Like them, it is a tale that involves the breaking of a sexual taboo (this time against incest) and a transformation that both provides the characters with an escape and presents a lamenting bird whose song reminds listeners of the story. The tale seems told to answer the question, "Why do loons sing in such a mournful way?" and like the Ovidian aetiologies, it suggests that behind every natural form or shape or element there is a narrative. Reading the landscape, then, is reading these suppressed stories of metamorphosis. The violence in "The First Loon" occurs not in the transgression itself, which is much enjoyed by both parties, but in the policing efforts of the brothers, who stand in for the larger social group (following the orders of the *mistapeo*) in insisting on "healthiness." The moment of transformation, not detailed as in Ovid,[23] seems to hide or disguise the murder of the brother, which was the original plan: "The best way to get rid of this shame, they figured, was to get rid of the boy himself." The murder is displaced by the brother's escape into song, which is literalized as his transformation into a bird: if he can sing a hole into the ice, then he must become a singer. Singing had already been his way of identifying himself to his lover-sister: "But wherever he hid, near or far, he'd only need to sing and his sister would hear him." Now he has literally become the distant singer heard over the ice and in the north woods, the loon. Moreover, like Daphne and especially like Myrrha, the incestuous brother here seems to wish upon himself a form of self-destruction: to leap into a hole in the ice is to risk death, so that the bird form that emerges seems to contain both these suppressed deaths—the murder planned by the brothers, and the near suicide of the baby's father.

The violent policing of social norms marks the limit where transformation is necessary in order for the tale not simply to end in murder. But one is struck by the extent to which the story sides not with the efforts to prohibit incest but with the creative happiness of the lovers—not with "health" as a social category but with "health" as a physical reality ("To her, the baby looked as healthy as any she'd ever seen"). The tale also emphasizes aesthetic value in the girl's praise of the baby's "loveliness": loveliness is marred by the murder of the child, aesthetics by violence, but the tale's own status as an aesthetic form that contains both transgression and violence points to another "loveliness" that persists, *like* and *in* the cry of the loon, as the story ends. This loveliness persists, then, in the tale's odd allegiance to the two lovers and their baby, and its creative force lives on in the loon, a creature that is both produced by and serves as a figure for the father's grief. And like the figure of the loon, the story itself is marked by suppressed grief, as it registers the irreversible change in its ending—"his sweetheart would never come to him again." Within that grief there hides a less openly admitted sense of sorrow: that this original epoch when incest could occur with pleasure and without awareness of transgression is also irreversibly closed off, its distance from the present marked by the presence of the loon.[24]

"The First Loon," then, seems initially to provide authority for the establishment of an incest taboo, for in the story the very forms of nature (or at least one of them) are shown to arise in the moment that the human sphere is marked off by this distinction. At the same time, however, it both reveals the violence needed to enforce the taboo and develops a subterranean fantasy of a world without such prohibition, a world shown as both creative, "lovely," and associated with the story itself. Here too the origin tale can be read doubly: it naturalizes the human taboo—suggesting that it marks "things as they are" in nature (loons do exist) and culture (the society continues to prohibit incest and to claim the right to decide what is "healthy")— but it also marks the origin of this social structure in transgression and violence, admitting in a more underhanded way the artificial and potentially destructive result of the taboo.

A similar doubleness exists in another Labrador tale, "The Origin of Robins."[25] Here again the threat of incest provokes a violent response, violence that mysteriously transforms its victim into a figure with metamorphic powers. The parricide, which is felt to be a justified response to the father's repeated abusive acts—the abandonment of the child, the burning of the wife—apparently does not save the mother, although, as in "The First Loon," death becomes metamorphosis here when the son "[takes] pity on her, saying that she didn't have to be a human being any more." As Daphne turns to her father to escape an overly aggressive suitor, so this woman turns to her son to escape the aggression of her husband. In each case, the metamorphosis is presented as a form of escape at first, and here there is no qualification of that escape at the end of the tale. The woman chooses to become a bird; the analogy of her burned, reddened breast produces the robin: "And all at once the old woman was flying up into the sky, with red feathers on her breast where she's been burned. That's how robins came into the world." Like "The First Loon," this tale exposes the violence of the enforcement of the incest taboo, though it does so under the rubric of jealousy and the danger of the fantasy of incest. The coloring of the robin reveals the human capacity to act on violent fantasy, and more indirectly the costs of imposing the incest taboo (since we never know for certain whether incest has occurred or not—and the tale seems to present fatherly jealousy of the mother-son tie as a fantasy of incest).

The two ways I have suggested of reading origin tales point, then, to two possible and opposed results of such narratives. First, to identify an origin would seem to be to claim an authority, especially cultural authority. Origin explains, gives cause for, customs, rituals, and exclusions and claims a relation to specific settings; it even identifies birds and animals as belonging to that nation's self-understanding. As the later English student of rhetoric George Puttenham put it in 1586, "etiology" is the figure of "tell cause," which one does to gain credit—to make oneself more believable and authoritative.[26] Presumably, the convention of narrating a national history in epic arises in part from an analogous desire to claim authority for the writer and for the respective literature. Most epics tell the origin of a nation or narrate a crucial early event that defines a given culture. But—and this is the second point—once that origin is narrated, and the aetiology is no longer mystified into a form of secret knowledge held by an elite, then the violence that often precedes and causes the metamorphosis is also exposed. The possibility that the origin will be demystified once it is represented, and the consequent likelihood that a counternarrative will be generated that tells a very different version of national or cultural origin, both suggest how risky extensive use of such aetiologies can be.

ORIGIN IN EPIC

One measure of the risk of incorporating aetiology in epic is the extent to which it disrupts the otherwise rather carefully maintained double narration, according to which the actions of the gods are given as explanations for events but kept separate from them. One early example occurs in the *Odyssey*, where the bard sings of Odysseus's homecoming and then tells his listeners about the cost to the Phaeacians of having aided him. Poseidon wishes not only to impale the ship that the Phaeacians use to transport Odysseus home and to end its voyage but to end all ocean-crossing with passengers—essentially cutting the Phaeacians off from all Mediterranean trade. Zeus restricts Poseidon, however, and permits him only to hurt the ship:

> "Let her be turned to stone—
> an island like a ship, just off the bay.
> Mortals may gape at that for generations!
> But throw no mountain round the sea port city."
> When he heard this, Poseidon, god of earthquake,
> departed for Skheria, where the Phaiakians
> are bòrn and dwell. Their ocean-going ship
> he saw already near, heading for harbor;
> so up behind her he swam, the island-shaker,
> and struck her into stone, rooted in stone, at one
> blow of his palm, then took to the open sea.
>   (*Odyssey* 13.156–164; Fitzgerald, p. 234)

The Phaeacians are punished for conveying the sleeping Odysseus home. They pay the price that he perhaps ought, symbolically, to pay: the epic requires harsh labor and valiant effort for success, not tranquil sleep that takes place during a magical voyage. After this event, the Phaeacians decide to cease offering free passage to those wayfarers stranded on their beaches. If Skheria is a place somewhere in between ordinary mortality (Ithaca) and immortality (Elysium), the poem tells us that passage from that world to the ordinary world symbolized by rocky Ithaca stopped after Odysseus's homecoming: he will be the last voyager to carry mythic wealth home, to transport (as in a metaphor) the riches of this idyllic setting into the rough and far-from-ideal setting of his homeland. The tale is an aetiology, then, for something the epic is not very interested in—the island off the bay of Phaeacia, a place the poem never visits again. But the poem is interested in the break between the mythic adventures of Odysseus in books 9–12 and the largely realistic books of his return. While certain immortal powers are lent him at times by Athena (as when he is beautified and rejuvenated—which occurs once in Phaeacia and again at the end of the story in Ithaca, in a rare repeated simile),[27] Odysseus returns to an island where all seasons do not occur simultaneously, where the land is poor not abundant, the gardens cultivated with hard labor and poverty. The "hard pastoral" (as Franz Boas and Arthur O. Lovejoy would put it) of his visit with Eumaeus only serves to mark out all the more emphatically how far this is from Phaeacia, a place that seems all too much like the Ogygia he spent seven years leaving. The aetiology then is in a way an aetiology for epic itself: it is the origin tale that identifies the conditions that define the rest of the poem, the conditions that define the constraints on human will and achievement that make heroism possible, the conditions that Odysseus has sought for ten years in order to reestablish his heroic selfhood.

The fact that this is an origin tale tends to get lost in the reading of the *Odyssey* because the "tale" is seven books long—the adventures on Skheria beginning as Odysseus crawls up on the beach at the end of book 5. The aetiology of the boat-island also describes a change that is irreversible, a change that confirms the power of the gods, both because it is the physical marker of the negotiation between Zeus and Poseidon and because it marks in its larger consequences the extent of Poseidon's power. The sea will not be tamed; the anger will not abate until long after the poem's end (as Zeus prophesies in book 1); and the cost of a smooth homeward journey is the conclusion of an heroic epoch. The episode also exposes some of the narrative strain that occurs when an outrightly magical power is needed to make the epic reach its desired end. The story of Odysseus's homecoming can be read as a metaphorical account of his excellence—his *aretē*—the extraordinary heroism that allowed him to brave the sea and bring back its riches, but it also hints that without this mythical or semimythical aid, Odysseus might never have made it home and might, in fact, have become far more like the wandering adventurer he pretends to be than like the heroic figure he presents on Phaeacia. The poem wants him to be both, and it is in the moment of his passage to Ithaca that one image is to be laid over the second: his extended conversation with Athena—rare in epic—and his careful packing away of the Phaeacian gold in the Ithacan caves mark the complex doubleness that this poem demands of its hero-beggar.

A comparable example from the *Aeneid,* the death of Palinurus and the naming of the Point of Palinurus after him, similarly reveals this discomfort of epic at a moment of magical intervention. Like Odysseus, Aeneas is propelled toward his destination by a magical power that makes the fleet run smoothly. This power is divine indirectly—Neptune has promised Venus that he will allow the fleet to arrive, but the cost he exacts is "one life given for many" ("unum pro multis dabitur caput," *Aeneid* 5.815; Fitzgerald, p. 154). Aeneas is required to take the helm eventually—after we have been told that "the fleet ran safely on its course"; he is not allowed simply to sleep the whole way, as Odysseus was. But he mistakenly thinks that Palinurus had failed to be sufficiently on guard, while the poem tells us that Palinurus has been selected as the sacrificial victim, the one who pays the price for the taming of the sea, and indirectly for the epic need to use supernatural means to bring its hero home. The Homeric detail of the ship being turned into stone is matched here in the moment when Palinurus nearly saves himself: as Palinurus reaches Italy and pulls himself onto the beach, "savages/Attacked me as I clutched at a clifftop,/Weighted down by my wet clothes. Poor fools,/They took me for a prize and ran me through" (*Aeneid* 6.358–361; Fitzgerald, p. 172). His grasp on the cliff edge gives that spot its name: he is not turned to stone, but as he touches the cliff he marks the landscape. Here too the epic dodges the full implications of the aetiology: a sacrifice of a human being is necessary for Aeneas to reach Italy's shores, a sacrifice that is domesticated by being transformed into an aetiology for a local custom and place-name. The Sibyl assuages Palinurus's pain, saying:

> Neighboring folk
> In cities up and down the coast will be
> Induced by portents to appease your bones,
> Building a tomb and making offerings there
> On a cape forever named for Palinurus.
> (*Aeneid* 6.377–381; Fitzgerald, p. 173)

This irreversible narrative marking of the Italian landscape threatens to expose a political structure underlying Aeneas's conquest of Italy: deaths will be required for his victory, but they will be made to seem less devastating by being incorporated into the Roman future as the name of a locality.

An even greater threat to the piety supposedly celebrated in the poem comes during one of the few efforts Virgil makes to represent origin directly: Aeneas's account of the fall of Troy in book 2. Simply narrating the city's fall—identifying the original traumatic event—does not really identify the cause, since cause can always be pushed back one step farther: the episode implicitly asks the question, What caused the fall of Troy? When during Aeneas's speech the poem does momentarily reveal a kind of immediate cause, the effect seems to be devastating. This occurs when Venus, trying to convince Aeneas to save himself, draws aside the cloud that had veiled Aeneas's sight and invites him to see the gods directly as they tear Troy down:

> Look: where you see high masonry thrown down
> Stone torn from stone, with billowing smoke and dust,
> Neptune is shaking from their beds the walls
> That his great trident pried up, undermining,
> Toppling the whole city down. . . . .
> Dread shapes come to view—mighty powers
> Divine, warring against Troy
> [apparent dirae facies inimicaque Troiae
> numina magna deum].
>
> (*Aeneid* 2.608–624)

Here a violent act of force brings about irreversible destruction. Although Aeneas's words don't confirm that he sees exactly what Venus says he should see,[28] he does have a vision here that dire divine forces are the cause of Troy's destruction. The difficulty with this revelation of origin is precisely its horror: even Neptune is working to tear down his own city (hence the irony of his epithet).

The horror of this scene deeply influences Aeneas: "Then truly it seemed to me that all Troy fell in flames" (*Aeneid* 2.624–625). Venus has told him that it is not Paris or the hated face of Helen that is to blame, but the gods, the relentless gods: "divum inclementia, divum" (*Aeneid* 2.602). But to claim that it is the gods at fault is to present the opening for a critique of the poem's ideology—and from Aeneas's point of view to recognize the faulty logic of the civilization he has tried to defend.[29] Perhaps this provides a different perspective from which we can view Aeneas's determination to bring his *household* gods with him, as he must feel abandoned by much of the Olympic pantheon. Moreover, the notion that the gods can be blamed for human suffering and loss has been criticized by Zeus himself from early in the epic tradition (in the beginning of the *Odyssey,* for example). In any case, examples like this of revealed origin are rare in the epic, perhaps because such moments are sources of enormous trauma for the hero and of ideological disruption for the poem.

In *Epic and Empire* David Quint has written of two kinds of returning to origins, one of which he, following Freud, sees as an unhealthy repetition of origins—the repetition compulsion exemplified in the simulacra of Troy in book 3. The other kind he sees as a more successful "working through" of the past, one that truly allows a making new to follow.[30] Quint sees this more successful return to the past as occurring in the second six books of the *Aeneid*, during the war in Italy—a successful, but nonetheless very violent form of "working through." If the interpretation presented here is correct, however, then the "repetition compulsion" represented in the little Troy of book 3 and in other efforts to return to Troy should be read as an effort not to return to the past but to avoid the story of origins—to blind us, or the narrator, to the real origin, to the lessons that the revelation of the cause of Troy's fall had forced on Aeneas. These repeated returns to the past in simulacrum represent a rejection of the origin tale and a desire to forget what the origin tale knows. The anxiety about what narratives of origin may reveal is written into the poem by the desire the Trojans and the poem have to recreate Troy. As Bellamy has suggested, the poem is haunted by and yet evades Troy and the Trojan past, as perhaps it is also by the Roman Republic and the Republican past.

Epic, then, might be said to be a genre that mystifies rather than reveals origins, and that demonstrates the reasons *not* to expose the cause. This resistance to the origin tale in the epic helps to show why Virgil distinguishes the writer of epic from the happy man of *Georgics* 2 who knows causes. Although the *Aeneid* includes many Lucretian allusions and analyses, and although aspects of the poem allow for a fuller Lucretian reading (as Philip Hardie has argued), the poem more often resists knowledge of causes than seeks it, and in doing so, it is more easily aligned with national and imperial ideology. Those moments in the epic when origins are narrated can, in contrast, sometimes be moments when a submerged counternarrative is allowed to surface.

SPENSER AND SOURCE

As epic narratives often remind us, *their* origin is in other texts or other poems, the pun on "source" (fountain, spring, the original) serving to link the moment of inspiration with the turn back to literary tradition. Spenser uses this pun directly in Book 4 of *The Faerie Queene* when he refers to Chaucer (whose unfinished tale he is now completing) as the "well of English undefiled" (4.2.32).[31] In Spenser's poem, many of the sources—many of the fountains and springs—are defiled, and the cause for this is twofold: first, according to the fiction, they are polluted or given special "vertue"—Spenser provides a fictional aetiology for a given spring that explains, just as any narrative of origins will, how the spring came to be as it is; but secondly, he implies that they are polluted because Ovid polluted them. Ovid's aetiologies are the source of the spring Redcrosse and Duessa dally by in 1.7.7; and an imitative Ovidian narrative explaining the nymph's failure to pursue the "chace" is itself embedded in the text to point to this origin. The cause is thus doubly displaced, for it is fictionally the nymph's laziness, but it is also the fact of narrative itself—in this case, the preceding narrative of Ovid. The spring of special "vertue" in the beginning of book 2 even more explicitly echoes Ovid, especially his accounts of the pursuit of Daphne and the transformation of Niobe. The reader is made to wonder, then, whether the original stain is really that of fallen human nature or simply the corrupting and transgressive literary tradition represented by Ovid that has passed on to our new author springs and sources that were already defiled.[32]

Of course, in any oral tradition, the source of a tale is the tradition itself—but in Virgil, and more insistently in Spenser, the emphasis on repetition of a source text is so self-conscious that it limits the degree of explanation of cause or origin that any such aetiology can have. Spenser theorizes this pattern of repetition when he names an Ovidian narrative as the *cause* of a given emblem, personification, or element of landscape. He thus allegorizes the effacing of origin in epic. Similarly, while Virgil's narrative is still ostensibly claiming to represent national origins (as well as to appropriate the localized origins of individual places and geographic names), Spenser is clearer about the need to evade direct representation of origin. Consider the lack of representation of the origin or conclusion of the knight's quests (no imagined originary scene in the Faery Queen's court; no return to court); Arthur's lack of knowledge of his origins (knowledge that he never gains in the poem); and the related topic of the importance attached to foundlings in the poem (babies with no explained origin or family). Along with these thematic examples, one might point to the nearly obsessive allegorization in *The Faerie Queene* of the inversion of cause and effect in narrative.[33] The poem is passionately divided about whether origin or cause can ever be represented as something stable, an inevitable problem in a poem where every external event can be a figure for an internal event. In any case, *The Faerie Queene* seems surprisingly clear about the impossibility of representing cause or origin, except as another story or another figure or emblem.

To take one example, in the story of the baby with the bloody hands in the opening of book 2, Spenser tells us the unwashable blood is a "sacred Symbole" (2.2.10)—this blood is the mark of his origin on the baby and is usually read as an allegory for original sin, the Christian version of the polluted origin that defiles all. To contrast this image of origin as and in sin—something marked, fated, and irreversible—however, Spenser offers us the baby held by the bear in book 6, which Calepine gives to Sir Bruin and Matilde (6.6.29). This baby also is wrenched from violence, but given no history, no marking, no shaping. This treatment of origin as absolute and inexplicable rupture ironically leads to a more hopeful future, where, among other things, this child won't have to be a "sacred [yet polluted] Symbole." The bear baby also disappears at this moment from the poem as if no narrative is now possible about him.

Spenser differs strikingly from both Virgil and Ovid in that in *their* poems' metamorphosis is always irreversible, while in *The Faerie Queene,* metamorphosis is sometimes irreversible (for example, the nymph turned to fountain in Book 2, or the fate of Malbecco) and sometimes reversible (Fra Dubio, Grill, though he chooses otherwise).[34]

Fra Dubio, in contrast to Myrrha and Daphne, who sought to be transformed to trees as acts of penance or escape, does not want to be a tree: "once a man, *Fradubio,* now a tree" (1.2.33). He has learned that he must wait until the ordained amount of time has passed in order to be released from his wooden prison. To find the human body bound in nature is for Spenser something deeply disturbing—a distortion of human form, a deformation that shows physically that human form has been abandoned internally—but the deformation of Fra Dubio also emphasizes that the reformation must take place. Nature is no saving arena of refuge here, and the narrative promises a temporal return to Fra Dubio (a promise not fulfilled in the poem) rather than heading irreversibly in one direction. Spenser learned something about reversible and irreversible metamorphosis from Dante, for the Christian epic is designed to reveal precisely God's power to change "things as they are"—that is, to redeem fallen nature. The fact that this redemption—the promised "time and suffised fates" (1.2.43) for Fra Dubio—does not take place within the poem indicates an uncertainty in *The Faerie Queene* between the dominance of its political purpose and the allegiance to its Christian conclusions and consequences. "Things as they are" include both the fallen world so central to Protestant understandings of human morality and also the limitations of court society, where Spenser's poem was not as fully appreciated as he had hoped. It is helpful, then, to conclude by considering what function the fantasy of reversibility might have served in Elizabethan society, a fantasy suggesting that the origin in crime, transgression, or (for the Tudors) civil war can be altered, and a new beginning made. The presentation of reversible origin in Spenser clearly has its roots in his religious conviction (and in the precedent of earlier Christian epic), but perhaps it also serves this broader cultural purpose. Spenser's mythological origin tale about the fall, told in the Arlo Hill digression in "The Mutabilitie Cantos," takes place in Ireland. Here in the colonial setting, the change narrated in the tale *is* represented as irreversible, suggesting that Irish barbarism should be understood as "nature," as "things as they are":

Nath'lesse, *Diana,* full of indignation,
Thence-forth abandond her delicious brooke;
In whose sweet streame, before that bad occasion,
So much delight to bathe her limbes she tooke:
Ne onely her, but also quite forsooke
All those faire forrests about *Arlo* hid,
And all that Mountaine, which doth over-looke

The richest champian that may else be rid,
And the faire *Shure*, in which are thousand Salmons bred.

Them all, and all that she so deare did way,
Thence-forth she left; and parting from the place,
There-on an heauy haplesse curse did lay,
To weet, that Wolues, where she was wont to space,
Should harbour'd be, and all those Woods deface,
And Thieues should rob and spoile that Coast around.
Since which, those Woods, and all that goodly Chase,
Doth to this day with Wolues and Thieues abound:
Which too-too true that lands in-dwellers since haue found.

(*Faerie Queene* 7.6.54–55)

Spenser's divided feelings about Ireland are figured here in a temporal displacement: the beauty of the landscape, which the Arlo Hill digression and the entire Mutability Cantos suggest he felt quite keenly, is largely placed into the past once Diana utters her curse, while the present inhabitants are compared to wolves in the wildness. The curse is irreversible; the departure of Diana from Arlo Hill is absolute; and the English colonization of Ireland all the more necessary and itself made to seem irreversible. But the private story of the origins of sin or doubt in the individual—Fra Dubio, for instance— must never become an irreversible one, even if the return to original form can only be hoped for, predicted, but never made complete.

APPENDIX TO CHAPTER 13

The First Loon

Long ago there were two lovers, a brother and sister. All night long they would fondle and embrace on their sleeping skins. This did not please their parents, who said: You can love each other and be first cousins, but not, certainly not, brother and sister.

"But why can't I love my brother?" the sister asked.

"And why can't I love my sister?" asked the brother.

"Because it's unhealthy, that's why," their parents said.

Hearing this, they loved each other even more.

At last the *mistapeo** spoke out against them: "A brother and sister who are lovers, that will bring a bad winter and plenty of starving."

The boy was forced to go into hiding. But wherever he hid, near or far, he'd only need to sing and his sister would hear him. And then she would come running.

Several months passed and the girl gave birth to a baby boy. She was carrying it in her moss-bag when one of her older brothers said: "I hope a lynx bites out its heart!"

"How can you say such a nasty thing?" the girl asked.

"Because your baby is unhealthy, that's why."

The girl did not understand this at all. To her, the baby looked as healthy as any she'd ever seen.

Now the girl's brothers decided to do something about the father of this baby. Although he was their younger brother, he was bringing home shame on the family. The best way to get rid of this shame, they figured, was to get rid of the boy himself.

A while later the boy was singing for his sister. The girl put on her snowshoes and followed his song. The brothers tracked their sister all the way to the shore of Michikimau. And there, in the middle of the frozen lake, the boy was waiting.

"Look at the lovely baby I've brought you!" the girl exclaimed.

Just then one of the brothers shot an arrow directly into the baby's heart. "It's not lovely anymore," he said.

The boy knew they would try to shoot his heart, too. So he quickly sang a hole in the ice. He took off all his clothes and jumped into this hole. The next instant he was a loon, flying up out of the cold water. And as he flew, he cried mournfully, for his sweetheart would never come to him again.

"The First Loon" and "The Origin of Robins" from *Wolverine Creates the World: Labrador Indian Tales,* collected and retold by Lawrence Millman (Santa Rosa, Calif.: Capra Press, 1993). Reprinted courtesy of Lawrence Millman.

* *Mistapeo* means shaman.

The Origin of Robins

A man, Aiasheu, had a wife and son. One day he noticed some scratches on his wife's breast. "Who made those scratches, woman?" he demanded.

Replied his wife: "I snared a partridge. While I was getting it out of the snare, it scratched me."

"Those look like love scratches to me. Are you sure you haven't been sleeping with our son?"

"Certainly not!"

Yet the more Aiasheu thought about this, the more he believed it. Why were his wife and son always picking berries together? What did they do when he went out hunting? Hadn't he once seen the boy fingering his mother's thigh at a *mukoshan*?

Now he was convinced that his wife and son were sleeping together. He decided to take the boy on a little trip . . . a little trip from which he would not return.

Father and son paddled their canoe to an island. "There are some duck eggs on those rocks, boy," Aiasheu said. "Why don't you gather a few?"

After the boy had jumped out of the canoe and waded ashore, Aiasheu began paddling away. "I'm leaving you here," he yelled back to his son, "because you're been sleeping with your mother."

"That's not true!" the boy protested.

"Tell it to the wolves who'll be picking over your bones . . ."

Back in camp Aiasheu told his wife that the boy had drowned when their canoe had flipped over. It was fortunate that he, her husband, knew how to swim or he would have drowned, too.

Now the man started treating his wife very badly. He'd throw her out of the tent, with no clothes on, in the middle of winter. Or he'd feed her lemmings, saying that if foxes could eat lemmings, so could she. Or he'd simply beat her until she felt her body would break.

Several years passed. The woman had a dream about her son. He was alive, the dream said, and soon would appear at her tent with a *tabaskan** piled high with meat. She told her husband this dream, but his only response was to beat her. "Our son is dead," he said. "His bones have turned yellow by now."

"No," the woman replied. "He is alive. I have dreamed it so. And he will bring us meat."

Now Aiasheu was so angry with his wife that he pushed her into the fire. "Taste your own meat, woman, if you're so hungry," he told her.

Just then a young man emerged from the bush with a *tabaskan*. He dropped the lead and reached into the fire, pulling out the woman. After he'd done this, he pushed in Aiasheu.

---

* *Tabaskan* means sled.

"You are my son," Aiasheu screamed. "Please don't let me burn up!"

"I don't have a father anymore," the young man said, throwing a birch log onto the fire to make it burn faster.

The woman had some very bad burns on her chest and seemed to be in pain. The young man took pity on her, saying that she didn't have to be a human being anymore. He asked what creature she would like to be. "I would like to be a bird, my son," she said.

And all at once the old woman was flying up into the sky, with red feathers on her breast where she'd been burned.

That's how robins came into the world.

NOTES

1. Swann 1994 provides an important recent translation of Native American literature; see also Elder and Wong 1994. For more information on the storytelling traditions of the Labrador Indians, see Millman 1992, 1990, and 1987.

2. Throughout this essay, I will be referring to R. D. Williams's edition of Virgil's *Aeneid* and to Robert Fitzgerald's translation (New York: Random House, Vintage Books, 1983). This essay benefited from a careful reading by Denis Feeney, who is of course not to be blamed for its limitations.

3. This and future references to the *Odyssey* in English will be to Robert Fitzgerald's translation (Garden City, N.Y.: Doubleday, Anchor Books, 1961).

4. See Wofford 1992a, 136–146.

5. On the regress of narratives characteristic of efforts to define origin, see Guillory 1993, esp. 23–45.

6. See Quint 1993, 9 and passim, including especially pp. 248–267 (in chap. 6, "Tasso, Milton and the Boat of Romance"); and the opening chapter of Bellamy 1992.

7. See Hardie 1993, 1–18, on the way that epics strive for completion and totality but are never successful in reaching either.

8. See Williams 1972, 1: 395, 433.

9. I have relied on A. D. Melville's translation of Ovid's *Metamorphoses* (Oxford: Oxford University Press, 1986). For the Latin, I have used the Loeb edition, except for passages from books 6–10, for which I have used Anderson's edition and commentary (1972).

10. See Forbes Irving 1990 for a typology of early Greek myths that tell of metamorphoses. This account divides the transformation stories into those about (a) mammals; (b) birds; (c) plants; (d) stones; (e) springs and rivers; (f) islands; and (g) insects, reptiles and sea-creatures. Forbes Irving finds distinct story patterns to be typical of each kind of metamorphosis. Most important for my purposes here, Forbes Irving distinguishes between those metamorphoses that serve as aetiologies for a species and those that create one unique, often monstrous representative.

11. See Stinton 1976, 60–89, an account of this problem and the use of similar phrases ("they say") in classical literature. On the question of this kind of fictive truth claims in the ancient world, see Feeney 1993, 230–244.

12. See Forbes Irving 1990 for a catalogue of bird transformations involving various kinds of pollution, almost all sexual in some way or another. Forbes Irving sees bird transformation stories in Greek myth as being principally structured around an opposition between the house and the wilds, and the stories of pollution tend, therefore, to be stories that begin with a "family crime" (p. 107)—incest of various sorts, with related family murder; a few examples of sex with animals. "But these polluting crimes can generally be seen as outbreaks of wildness," Forbes Irving writes, "and it is the more general opposition of the wilds and human order that is the basic structure of these stories" (p. 109). See Forbes Irving, pp. 107–109.

13. The question of the extent to which metamorphosis tends to produce an unchanging nature—the species existing in the world as we know it, no longer subject to a metamorphic principle—is discussed with complexity in Barkan 1986. Barkan argues that Ovid's metamorphoses, at least, function to initiate the reader into an

understanding of "the metaphoric flow among separate categories of existence" (p. 31), and yet he also notes that some metamorphoses are "changes to end all change," and comments that "the natural world is one endpoint of transformation" (p. 79). In treating the changes that end all change, though, Barkan focuses mostly on the Roman aetiologies in Ovid's poem, showing how the poem tends to undermine covertly its proclaimed story that transformations all lead to the creation of Rome and Roman institutions. Throughout his influential account of Ovid, Barkan is interested in the tension between the metamorphic principle—which can at times wreak havoc in a human context, as when categories that define social order dissolve—and the principle of fixity, by which the individual is fixed in an essentialized and often "savagely reduced" version of his or her identity (p. 66). Barkan's account of the basic structure of an Ovidian metamorphosis is as follows:

> [The story] takes place in a context where individuals are assigned clear roles, so clear that they may be oppressive. The central figure in the story rebels, specifically attacking the clarity and discreteness of the surrounding categories. The essential metamorphosis comes as a direct result of this rebellion: it is not the hero's or heroine's change of physical shape . . . but rather the discovery that what seemed like rigid categories of family and society can dissolve, just as physical categories dissolve in metamorphosis. Once the categories are attacked, similar things are diversified into opposites and opposites are made identical. The central figure reaches a condition that transcends and contradicts all these categories. From that point it is a short step to literal metamorphosis, a condition that merely serves as a final punctuation mark for a narrative experience whose crucial metamorphosis has amounted to the dissolution of assumptions we live by (p. 59).

Barkan's emphasis on the dissolution of ordinary assumptions about differences between, say, the human and the wild, or between the sexes, is salutary, and an essential feature of stories of origin is precisely that the narrative events that precede the creation of the world as we know it tend to involve transgressions of that world. It is still useful to note, though, how that "final punctuation mark" serves even in Barkan's metamorphic theory as a stabilizing and fixing closure to the story.

14. See Myers 1994 for a discussion of Ovid's poetry in relation to the genre of the *aetion,* and especially Myers's useful account of the way the first and last of Ovid's amatory tales serve as a framing device for the narrative.

15. On the frequency with which trees are used as comparisons for human growth and beauty in the metamorphoses associated with Greek myth, see Forbes Irving 1990, 134.

16. My understanding of the account of Daphne and Apollo has been immeasurably increased by having studied the story with Denis Feeney. See Feeney 1991, 205–224; see also p. 216 on the associations of Apollo and Augustus, and p. 219: "The emphasis on the constitutional facts of Roman cult has its corollary in the politically coloured anthropomorphism which infuses the epic descriptions of deities in action. . . . The preoccupation with such systems of analogy is something we have been familiar with since the actions centering on the poem's first simile, in which Jupiter was compared to Augustus." Feeney is discussing the more extended analogy in the poem between Augustus and Jupiter, but part of his point is that the absolute, irrational, and tyrannical behavior of the gods may often comment on what imperial power felt like to those on whom it was exercised.

17. See Barkan 1986, 66, for an account of how a metamorphosis is "an escape from entrapment into a higher condition where the blurred categories are no longer meaningful."

18. For the tension between elegy and epic in Ovid's two accounts of the rape of Persephone, where the origins of the world as we know it are located specifically in rape, see Hinds 1987, 115–134. On the frequency of rape in accounts of origins, see Wofford 1992b and Jed 1989.

19. From the note in the Melville translation, p. 383.

20. On the Greek sources of the Philomela story, see Forbes Irving 1990, 248–249. Forbes Irving comments on the extent to which in many of these accounts the transformation tends to be a form of escape, even when the existing species is marked or signed with the events of the narrative: "Since they are describing every day facts of nature and since the present birds are no longer really the original transformed people these birds will tend to be less alarming than the unique freaks created by transformation into an animal; also the positions of these transformations at the end of their story, and the fact that they will last forever, removes any sense of urgency about the heroes' behaviour or state of mind as birds, and produces a perhaps artificial sense of serenity about their new state. They are now free from any further human tragedy, in comparison with which neither the suffering of birds nor any further evil that they do among each other needs to be taken too seriously" (p. 112). See also Barkan 1986, 65, on the way in which for criminals against the natural order (such as Tereus) metamorphosis is "not a punishment but rather a definition of the extreme state into which they have brought themselves and a relief from the agony of those extremes."

21. Anderson 1972, 236.

22. For all references to "The First Loon," see the appendix, where the story is reproduced in full, and see Millman 1992.

23. Many indigenous origin tales do include precisely the kinds of detailed part-to-part analogy that impress readers of Ovid (her arms became branches, etc.). See, for one example that involves extensive analogy, the Tahitian tale "Tangaroa, Maker of All Things":

"But his anger was not finished, and so he took his backbone for a mountain range and his ribs for the ridges that ascend. . . . He took his fingernails and toenails for the scales and shells of fishes in the sea. Of his feathers he made trees and shrubs to clothe the land."

(Elder and Wong 1994, 40)

24. As Millman (1992) reminds us in his note to the story, Michikimau, the setting of the ending of the story, was a lake sacred to the Innu, which vanished in 1963 when the Churchill Falls Hydro Project was constructed. The tale is a tale of loss in more than one sense.

25. For all references to "The Origin of Robins," see the appendix, where the story is reproduced in full, and see Milliman 1992. This tale was told to Millman by Thomas Pastitshi, Utshimassits.

26. See Puttenham 1970, bk. 3, chap. 19, pp. 236–238.

27. See Murnaghan 1987 for a discussion of how the romance motifs such as this rejuvenation reverse epic temporality.

28. See Wofford 1992a, 112–113, for a more extended discussion of exactly how much Aeneas sees here and what he knows.

29. See Feeney 1991, 48–49, on the anthropomorphism of the gods in Homeric commentaries, and pp. 134–137 on the way that this anthropomorphism in the *Aeneid* signals that the gods are fictive. Feeney observes that "the gods of the *Aeneid* may be 'figures', 'tropes,' 'symbols', but only as Aeneas is a figure or a trope. Neptune and Juno need the same fictive energy to be creators and channellers of meaning as does Aeneas. If we accept that the gods are figural, symbolic, in that they refer to areas of meaning beyond themselves, we need not then feel baffled at their 'unnecessary' colour and force" (pp. 136–137). In a private communciation, Feeney also noted that "the anthropomorphic representation of angry deities had been criticized and scrutinized for centuries—it is not an ultimate explanation or cause but a metaphor always."

30. On the centrality of the repetition compulsion in Virgil and Renaissance epic, see also Bellamy 1992, a psychoanalytic study of the problem of origins in the epic tradition.

31. All quotations from Spenser's *Faerie Queene* are from A. C. Hamilton's edition (London and New York: Longman, 1977). See Guillory 1983 for Spenser's use of fountains as markers of an origin that has always been literary; and Quint 1983 for the topos of the fountain or spring as image for literary source. On the connections of Spenser's fountain to Ovid's aetiologies in the myth of Hermaphroditus and elsewhere in the *Metamorphoses*, see also Silberman 1987.

32. Contrast the opening of book 4 of Lucretius's *De Rerum Natura*: "A pathless country of the Pierides I traverse, where no other foot has ever trod. I love to approach virgin springs [*intregros . . . fontis*], and there to drink." Thanks to Denis Feeney for this reference.

33. For an account of this problem see Wofford 1992a, 262–281 (the section entitled "The Cause Was This").

34. I necessarily (because of limitations of scope in one essay) skip over here the Christian tradition of allegorizing metamorphosis, and most notably Dante, but we might briefly note that the metamorphoses in the *Inferno* (for instance, in the Wood of the Suicide) are also irreversible, a critical problem in the poem (where the fact that the damned cannot be saved is understood as a way of explaining how the sinners in the *Inferno* repeatedly and eternally make again the sinful choice that caused them to lose human form in the first place).

WORKS CITED

Barkan, Leonard.
    1986.   *The Gods Made Flesh: Metamorphosis and the Pursuit of Paganism.* New
                Haven: Yale University Press.
Bellamy, Elizabeth J.
    1992.   *Translations of Power: Narcissism and the Unconscious in Epic History.*
                Ithaca, N.Y.: Cornell University Press.
Boas, George, and Arthur O. Lovejoy.
    1980.   *Primitivism and Related Ideas in Antiquity.* New York: Octagon Books.
    [c. 1935]
Elder, John, and Hertha Wong, eds.
    1994.   *Family of Earth and Sky: Indigenous Tales of Nature from around the World.*
                Boston: Beacon Press.

Feeney, Denis C.
1993.   "Towards an Account of the Ancient World's Concepts of Fictive Be-
         lief." In *Lies and Fiction in the Ancient World,* edited by Christopher Gill
         and T. P. Wiseman, 230–244. Exeter: University of Exeter Press.
1991.   *The Gods in Epic: Poets and Critics of the Classical Tradition.* Oxford:
         Clarendon Press.
Forbes Irving, P. M. C.
1990.   *Metamorphosis in Greek Myths.* Oxford: Clarendon Press.
Guillory, John.
1983.   *Poetic Authority: Spenser, Milton, and Literary History.* New York: Co-
         lumbia University Press.
Hardie, Philip.
1993.   *The Epic Successors of Virgil: A Study in the Dynamics of a Tradition.* Cam-
         bridge: Cambridge University Press.
Harris, Joel Chandler.
1974   *Uncle Remus: His Songs and Sayings.* Rev. ed. by A. B. Frost. New York:
[1880]. Grosset and Dunlap.
Homer.
1961.   *The Odyssey.* Translated by Robert Fitzgerald. Garden City, N.Y.: Dou-
         bleday, Anchor Books.
Hinds, Stephen.
1987.   *The Metamorphoses of Persephone: Ovid and the Self-Conscious Muse.* Cam-
         bridge: Cambridge University Press.
Jed, Stephanie.
1989.   *Chaste Thinking: The Rape of Lucretia and the Birth of Humanism.* Bloom-
         ington: Indiana University Press.
Millman, Lawrence.
1992.   *Wolverine Creates the World: Labrador Indian Tales Gathered and Retold by
         Lawrence Millman.* Santa Barbara: Capra Press.
1990.   *Last Places: A Journey in the North.* Boston: Houghton Mifflin.
1987.   *A Kayak Full of Ghosts: Eskimo Tales Gathered and Retold by Lawrence Mill-
         man.* Santa Barbara: Capra Press.
Murnaghan, Sheila.
1987.   *Disguise and Recognition in the "Odyssey."* Princeton: Princeton Univer-
         sity Press.
Myers, K. Sara.
1994.   *Ovid's Causes: Cosmogony and Aetiology in the "Metamorphoses."* Ann Ar-
         bor: University of Michigan Press.
Ovid.
1986.   *Ovid's "Metamorphoses."* Translated by A. D. Melville. Oxford: Oxford
         University Press.
1972.   *Ovid's "Metamorphoses," Books 6–10.* Edited by William S. Anderson.
         Norman: University of Oklahoma Press.
1956.   *Metamorphoses.* Translated by F. J. Miller. Loeb Classical Library. Cam-
         bridge, Mass: Harvard University Press.
Puttenham, George.
1970   *The Arte of English Poesie.* [1586]. Kent, Ohio: Kent State University
[1906]. Press.

Quint, David.
1993.   *Epic and Empire: Poetics and Generic Form from Virgil to Milton*. Princeton: Princeton University Press.
1983.   *Origin and Originality in Renaissance Literature: Versions of the Source*. New Haven: Yale University Press.

Silberman, Lauren.
1987.   "The Hermaphrodite and the Metamorphosis of Spenserian Allegory." *English Literary Renaissance* 17: 207–223.

Spenser, Edmund.
1977.   *The Faerie Queene*. Edited by A. C. Hamilton. London and New York: Longman.

Stinton, T. C. W.
1976.   "'Si credere dignum est': Some Expressions of Disbelief in Euripides and Others." *Proceedings of the Cambridge Philological Society* n.s. 22: 60–89.

Swann, Brian, ed.
1994.   *Coming to Light: Contemporary Translations of the Native Literatures of North America*. New York: Random House, Vintage Books.

Virgil.
1983.   *The Aeneid*. Translated by Robert Fitzgerald. New York: Random House, Vintage Books.
1972–1973. *The Aeneid*. Edited by R. D. Williams. 2 vols. London: Macmillan; New York: St. Martin's Press.

Wofford, Susanne.
1992a.   *The Choice of Achilles: The Ideology of Figure in the Epic*. Stanford: Stanford University Press.
1992b.   "The Social Aesthetics of Rape: Closural Violence in Boccaccio and Botticelli." In *Creative Imitation: New Essays on Renaissance Literature in Honor of Thomas M. Greene*, edited by David Quint, Margaret W. Ferguson, G. W. Pigman III, and Wayne A. Rebhorn, 189–238. Binghamton, N.Y.: Medieval and Renaissance Texts and Studies.

14

Walcott's *Omeros*

The Classical Epic
in a Postmodern World

Joseph Farrell

With his plays drawn from Greek mythology and his evocative epic hymn to the
Caribbean, *Omeros*, Nobel laureate Derek Walcott has forced many to rethink
the relationships between archaic Greek society and the contemporary world.
Joseph Farrell, known especially for his work on classical epic, takes up a debate as to whether *Omeros* can be considered an epic at all, and suggests that in
forcing us even to ask this question, Walcott demands that we reassess the position and assumed supremacy of Western literary epic. In demonstrating the
complex relationship of *Omeros* to the tradition of classical epic, Farrell reveals
the contingencies of that tradition and the richness of Walcott's poem as a work
that straddles both epic and novel, classical and modern, scribal and oral.

Let me begin with an anecdote.

I have a daughter who is a student in the Philadelphia public school system. Like any other big-city school system, ours has its problems, but so far
they have seemed manageable. If nothing else, trying to negotiate the school-
district bureaucracy provides parents with a rich store of strange experiences
that we enjoy sharing with one another. This particular story concerns race.
Again like most cities, Philadelphia has had to cope with the problem of seg-
regation by race and has chosen to address the problem in schools not by
busing, but by establishing a voluntary desegregation program. Schools in
the "deseg" program receive extra funding from the central district and consequently have more instructional and support staff, enrichment programs,
and so forth. Parents choose whether to participate in the program and designate in order of preference the schools they would like their child to attend. The children are selected by lottery and are assigned to a school on
the basis of their number and their race: almost everything depends on
whether the school you want needs more white, black, Asian, or Hispanic
children in that particular year. The year we applied marked the first time
that the aspirations of anyone in our family had so explicitly been tied to his
or her race.

My daughter's name is Flannery—not the most common name, and when
a child who bears it encounters another, their common name creates a spe-

cial bond. One of the Flannerys we know is further distinguished by the fact that she is also a twin and that she and her brother Schuyler have one white and one black parent. It is their experience with the deseg system, a parental war story, that I want to recount. Because race is the only criterion for admitting a child to a deseg school, the district requires interested parents to specify their child's race, and to do so in terms that are, literally, black and white: they recognize nothing in between. Flannery and Schuyler's parents balked at this. To identify their children as either black or white would go against everything that they stand for, both in their marriage and in the absolutely interracial identity that they cherish in their children. But a choice had to be made. When they simply refused, the bureaucrat in charge of the interview, who had no doubt been through this before, sighed wearily and said: "Well, I guess we're just going to have to subject them to the eyeball test." The parents were too astonished to protest before the children were sized up by the bureaucrat, whose job at that moment was simply to determine the race of the children by his own judgment about the color of their skin. And in a decision that could have been scripted by Solomon, but more likely by Kafka, he found that one of the twins was black and the other was white.

Derek Walcott has been subjected repeatedly to the literary-critical equivalent of this test and indeed invites such scrutiny by the way in which he thematizes his own racially mixed ancestry.[1] As he wrote over thirty years ago in the often-quoted poem "A Far Cry from Africa,"

> I who am poisoned with the blood of both,
> Where shall I turn, divided to the vein?
> I who have cursed
> The drunken officer of British rule, how choose
> Between this Africa and the English tongue I love?
> Betray them both, or give back what they give?
> How can I face such slaughter and be cool?
> How can I turn from Africa and live?[2]

Years later in "The Hotel Normandie Pool," the theme returns:

> And I, whose ancestors were slave and Roman,
> have seen both sides of the imperial foam,
> heard palm and pine tree alternate applause
> as the white breakers rose in galleries
> to settle, whispering at the tilted palm
> of the boy-god Augustus. My own face
> held negro Neros, chalk Caligulas;
> my own reflection slid along the glass
> of faces foaming past triumphal cars.[3]

The motif of racial indeterminacy presents itself throughout Walcott's poetry in other registers as well: the linguistic register, in which English threat-

ens to occlude the Creole dialects of St. Lucia; the literary-historical register, in which Walcott speculates on his storyteller's craft in its relation to that
of the Caribbean "man of words" and to that of Shakespeare, to name but
two of his many models; the religious register, in which St. Lucia's Catholic
culture contrasts with Walcott's own Methodist upbringing, while both Christian traditions exist in dialogue with the folk religion of the common people and with the animism of the islands' ancient inhabitants; and in many
other registers. One of these others is the one on which I will focus, the
generic register; for the debate (if I may call it that) over the genre of *Omeros*
shares with these other questions the twin motifs of dichotomy and indeterminacy in ways that cast a strong and useful light on the poem and on the
concept of genre itself.

To begin, even characterizing discussion of the poem's genre as a debate
is an overstatement. Diverging opinions there have been, but little dialogue.
Classicists like Mary Lefkowitz, Oliver Taplin, and Bernard Knox and Eurocentric comparatists like George Steiner have expressed little doubt about
the poem's epic character.[4] But Sidney Burris, while hailing *Omeros* as a
"sprawling new poem" of "herculean ambition," pointedly avoids using the
word "epic," calling *Omeros* a Caribbean "national *narrative*."[5] Similarly, long-
time students of Walcott and of West Indian literature generally have been
chary of the epic label. It is true that Robert Hamner, one of the world's
foremost experts on Walcott, has not shied away from it.[6] But John Figueroa,
perhaps the dean of West Indian literary studies and a former teacher of Walcott's, in what was probably the first scholarly commentary on the poem,
stated flatly and preemptively: "*Omeros* is not an epic."[7] Similarly Patricia Ismond, another distinguished West Indianist and Walcott specialist, finds
Omeros informed by a lyric rather than an epic sensibility.[8] Finally, I should
mention that this is the tack taken by Walcott himself, who has said: "I do
not think of it as an epic. Certainly not in the sense of epic design. Where
are the battles? There are a few, I suppose. But 'epic' makes people think of
great wars and great warriors. That isn't the Homer I was thinking of; I was
thinking of Homer the poet of the seven seas."[9]

This last remark points to the different ways in which critics have viewed
the poem's relationship to the *Iliad* and the *Odyssey*. Eurocentric critics have
been quick to identify the poem's "debt" to Homer as its essential distinguishing characteristic; Taplin perhaps goes farthest in this regard.[10] Burris,
in contrast, predicts that "commentators on *Omeros* . . . will understandably
busy themselves in tracking down the Homeric parallels in Walcott's poem,"
but argues that this will be "a particularly ill-fated approach because part of
the poem's task, its attempt to recreate the original authenticity of Walcott's
Caribbean culture, lies in its deliberate deflation of analogy."[11] The most important antecedents of *Omeros*, Burris suggests, are to be found in Walcott's
own dramatic works and in another quasi-Homeric work of great generic in-

determinacy, Joyce's *Ulysses*.[12] Figueroa goes even farther, stating that "Walcott's poem is not an imitation of either the *Iliad* or the *Odyssey*. . . . The point of the use of Homer lies elsewhere," that is, in his metaphorical or allegorical significance "as the great creator," especially of poetic language, and "as the Blind Seer," himself a wanderer held in no great honor whose suffering has gained him an acute understanding of the nature of things, even as a kind of poetic savior who rescues Walcott's Narrator from the sins that have beset other poets.[13] But this Homer is, finally, a symbol of "the foreign in West Indian culture, especially . . . the non-African foreign," an element that is itself in need of redemption: for Figueroa, the value of a poem like *Omeros* "is a question not so much of what influences are at play"—of whether the poem merits a place in the apostolic succession of Homeric imitators—but of "the quality of what is made" out of these influences, whether they bear the authentic stamp of Homeric originality.[14]

There has thus been considerable anxiety among critics and on the part of the poet himself about the generic affinities of *Omeros*. One may conjecture that many of those who hail the poem as an epic do so without much interest in genre theory, but rather out of a desire to honor Walcott for what is indeed a remarkable achievement. In general most critics appear to regard the entire issue of genre as unfortunate, any choice among the available categories being difficult if not impossible for most readers to make. Despite the difficulty, however, critics raise the issue as one that is somehow necessary to confront, even if some can manage only an equivocal solution, like that of the reviewer who described the poem as, "if anything," a novel in verse.[15] Any uncertainty raised by the epic pretensions of *Omeros* stems from the obvious fact that the poem does not conform rigidly to the generic expectations that most readers bring to classical European epic poetry. In a way, this attitude is preferable to its opposite, which regards *Omeros* as unproblematically an epic in the Homeric tradition. The poem is, without question, about problems of belonging, concerning itself with the dubious prospect that any of us might find real comfort in a sense of belonging to some putatively homogeneous group. The problem of literary categorization is thus merely a special case of one of the poem's central themes; but it gains point from the fact that epic has been perceived—particularly European epic in the classical tradition—as, to use Bakhtin's term, the "monologic" genre par excellence and as the antithesis of the most thoroughly open and dialogic genre, which Bakhtin terms the novel.[16]

With respect to the assessment of postcolonial literature, the critical discourse of epic poetry acquires a racist tinge. Ultimately, I believe, it is the notion that the European epic speaks with the voice of the accumulated authority of generations of white imperialist culture that leads many readers to deny *Omeros* any meaningful association with the epic genre, while in the open polyphony of novelistic genres they find a quality better suited to the Cre-

olization of language, the racial and literary miscegenation, that characterize the poem. The debate clearly goes far beyond mere taxonomy and becomes a political battle for Walcott's racial identity and ethnic soul: is the author of *Omeros* "really" the white Walcott descended in blood from men of
Warwickshire and in ink from the bard of Avon, or is he the black descendant of slaves whose history and language have all but disappeared from the
official record, a man whose story can be told only in novelistic opposition
to the epic culture that seeks to co-opt him as its own spokesman? In this light,
it becomes clear that the epic element in *Omeros* threatens to reopen an old
debate over Walcott's relationship to the European and African elements in
his personal heritage and in the culture of the West Indies as a whole.[17]

In this essay I would like to make two responses to those critics who feel
compelled to deny that *Omeros* is an epic poem. First, to base such a denial
on a desire to claim *Omeros* as an *Afro*-Caribbean poem ignores those contemporary studies in world epic that go well beyond the literary tradition
defined by European poets such as Homer and Milton. Second, to distinguish
the poem from its predecessors in the canonical epic tradition on the basis
of its capacity to celebrate alterity is to ignore the European epic's capacity
for self-questioning and for radical reinterpretation of its own generic roots.

Let me expand upon both points.

AFRICA AND THE EPIC

Those critics who are embarrassed by the possibility that *Omeros* might be
taken for an epic, and hence as a white man's poem, are, no doubt unknowingly, endorsing an untenable and extremely reactionary view of what epic
poetry is in its racial and world-cultural dimensions. Such a view, to be sure,
has been maintained by a number of "authoritative" discussions of epic as a
world genre; but these discussions can easily be shown to be deeply, if unwittingly, implicated in a racist discourse of shocking naiveté.

The idea that the African nations were actually incapable of producing
an epic literature was articulated, not perhaps for the first time, but with
embarrassing clarity, by Maurice Bowra in his 1952 study *Heroic Poetry*.[18] In
surveying the heroic poetry of a wide variety of world literatures, Bowra
noted the close relationships between poetry of praise or of lamentation
and the heroic poetry with which he was concerned, but observed that the
two former categories "exist in some societies where heroic poetry is lack-
ing." He ascribes this lack to an "inability to rise beyond a single occasion to
the conception of a detached art." The examples he cites are from Africa—
specifically, from Uganda and Ethiopia—and he concludes his discussion
with these words: "Though these poems, and many others like them, show a
real admiration for active and generous manhood, they come from peoples
who have no heroic poetry and have never advanced beyond panegyric and

lament. The intellectual effort required for such an advance seems to have been beyond their powers."[19] It is extremely depressing to observe how often these and similarly demeaning cultural stereotypes leap to Bowra's mind as he discusses the literary achievements of African peoples. Characteristic is the presumption that heroic verse represents a later and more developed stage of the panegyric and lament that Bowra finds in Africa, the idea that a literary culture must progress from these early stages toward a true heroic literature, and that heroic poetry calls for a degree of intellectual abstraction of which Africans are not, in his view, capable; rather, the poetry that they do produce is notable for its "simple and primitive" qualities, its "expression of an immediate and violent excitement." Bowra's views, which strike us today as ignorant and insulting, are fully representative of literary scholarship in his day, and he was far from alone in believing that epic was simply not an African genre. A similar opinion was voiced in 1970, this time on purely formal grounds rather than as a judgment on the intellectual capacities of the African artist, by the influential folklorist Ruth Finnegan.[20] But by that time the tide had begun to turn, and since then considerable work has been done both to make known the existence of an epic literature among a number of African peoples and to study its particular qualities.

The procedure followed by many studies of the African epic is double. Scholars like Isidore Okpewho and John William Johnson aim to show, on the one hand, that the African epic is recognizable as epic on the same terms as canonical European specimens, and, on the other hand, that it displays certain distinctive characteristics as a primarily oral and performative rather than literary genre.[21] For this reason Africanists have an important role to play, first and self-evidently, in the comparative study of oral epic as a phenomenon of world literature, but also, to the extent that research into oral poetry has revolutionized the study of the Homeric poems, in the effort to reinterpret the canonical tradition of European epic that boasts of its Homeric ancestry. One consequence of this activity is that the African epic has been subjected to some of the same questions that had begun to be asked both of the archaic Greek epic and of its putative modern European analogues, principally, poetry of the South Slavic epic tradition recorded and studied by Milman Parry and Albert Lord.[22] It can now be seen that the African material stands in more or less the same relationship to texts like the Homeric *Iliad* and *Odyssey* as does the Slavic material, even if one reaches the conclusion that the Homeric poems are by comparison only vestigially oral performances that have traveled some considerable way down the road from performance to literary fixedness. For instance, when Okpewho, in order to illustrate oral poetry's tendency to strive for immediate effect by means of humor, compares the grim humor shown by the narrator of the *Kambili* epic ("The old sandle man's head was cut off at his neck. / Big trouble has begun in Jimini! / The little man fell flopping about like a tramp in the cold")[23] to Patroclus's ill-timed and entirely out-of-character jeering at the Trojan Cebriones, whom he has just killed, it is clear that what Okpewho regards as a typical and even normative procedure for the Mandingo poet is present, but nevertheless comparatively rare in Homer.[24] If we are unconvinced by this particular analogy, however, other examples come to mind: the Homeric narrator's ironic aside concerning the bargain struck by Glaucus, who exchanges his golden armor for Diomedes' bronze (*Iliad* 6.234–236),[25] or perhaps Odysseus's observation to his host and principal listener, Alcinous, that his story is getting rather long, and it might be time simply to stop and go to bed (*Odyssey* 11.328–384). This exchange occurs about halfway through the hero's narrative of his adventures since the Trojan War and, not incidentally, about halfway through the poem as a whole. When Alcinous refuses to hear of any delay in the completion of the tale, we may take his reaction as the oral poet's script for his ideal audience, who should be as eager for the rest of his story as Alcinous is for that of Odysseus.[26]

Passages like these are admittedly not very common in our *Iliad* and *Odyssey*—or perhaps they tend to be overlooked by readers unaccustomed to finding such elements in epics of the European canon. But despite Homer's distance from actual oral performance, comparative study establishes without question the ultimately oral and performative character of Homeric epic and in this way aligns the *Iliad* and the *Odyssey* with modern world epic as against the remainder of the ancient, medieval, and early modern tradition of "classicizing" European epic in the Homeric tradition—such as the *Aeneid, La Divina Commedia, Os Lusíadas, Paradise Lost,* and so forth. This is a crucial point, I suggest, because the scholarly discovery of an African epic linked to Homer by virtue of its being the product of an oral-epic performance culture actually parallels one of the dominant conceits of literary apologia in *Omeros*—namely Walcott's construction of Homer not as a participant in an exclusively European scribal culture, but as a singer of folktales whom one might find just as readily in an African or Afro-Caribbean context as in that of archaic Greece.

For Walcott, the Creole culture of the Caribbean is preeminently an oral culture. In the poem "Cul de Sac Valley" he contrasts this culture with the scribal culture in which he works, calling Creole "a tongue they speak in, but cannot write."[27] He imagines himself as a poet-carpenter, creating a work that images perfectly his Caribbean homeland:

> as consonants scroll
> off my shaving plane
> in the fragrant Creole
> of their native grain;
>
> from a trestle bench
> they'd curl at my foot,

C's, R's, with a French
or West African root

from a dialect throng-
ing, its leaves unread
yet light on the tongue
of their native road.
("Cul de Sac Valley"
1.13–24)

But as he catches the fresh scent from a stand of trees in the landscape he wishes to represent—trees designated in French Creole as *bois canot, bois campêche*—his dream of honestly representing that landscape is shattered as he imagines the trees "hissing" at him with reproach:

What you wish
from us will never be,
your words is English,
is a different tree.
(1.33–36)

Here the poet's language and his status as a member of the scribal culture distance him from the oral culture of his Creole home.

The motif of Caribbean culture as grounded in orality is basic to Walcott's thinking on language. His play *O Babylon!* concerns the cultural and political ideals of a Rastafarian community in Kingston, Jamaica. In a note on the play, Walcott writes of the Jamaican spoken dialect in its pure form as unintelligible except to Jamaicans, and thus in need of translation to any outsider; and "within that language itself," he writes, "the Rastafari have created still another for their own nation. . . . [They] have invented a grammar and a syntax which immures them from the seduction of Babylon, an oral poetry which requires translation into the language of the oppressor," and goes on to observe: "To translate is to betray."[28]

This confession pertains in the first instance to the author's project of representing an oral culture in a scripted play; but it sheds a painful light on his effort to write a West Indian poetry at all, and particularly to write it in English. Such an effort must be fatally flawed from the start because any English poem, any written work, stands at an extra degree of separation from its subject as compared with Creole utterance. It possesses the quality not so much of an original composition as of a translation—and, thus, as a betrayal.

What is crucial, however, is one's response to the recognition of this betrayal. If there is a division between English and Creole, between scribal and oral cultures, between Europe and Africa, there is also a relationship to be negotiated. It is this insight that makes place for the craft of translation, a space that is inevitably, necessarily *there*.

Translation is, however, an transitive process: if Creole must be translated into English, the converse is also true. If European colonialists bring foreign categories of intellection to the interpretation of Caribbean realities, it is equally possible to translate European culture into West Indian terms; and this latter type of translation, while it is, given the asymmetrical power relationship between the European colonialists and the islanders, less common than the first, shares with all forms of translation the impossibility of leaving the "original" unchanged. The decision to translate Homeric epic into West Indian terms cannot but change one's perception of Homer. Thus Walcott's characterization of Caribbean dialects as "oral poetry" finds its parallel in Walcott's refusal to cede Homer to the scribal culture of European colonialists.

This is no casual theme in *Omeros* (or, indeed, in Walcott's work as a whole), but a central problem to which the poem constantly and broodingly recurs. The theme is sounded first in the image of Seven Seas, a blind old man identified by the poem's Narrator with Omeros (1.2.2–3). Seven Seas spends some of his days sitting in the No Pain Cafe, observed by its proprietor, Ma Kilman: "Sometimes he would sing . . . But his words were not clear/They were Greek to her. Or old African babble" (1.3.2).[29] It is Seven Seas who, like a prophet, discloses to Philoctete the meaning of Achille's unusual, overnight absence from port: he has journeyed to Africa in search of "his name and his soul" (2.29.2).

This equivalency between Greek and "old African babble" involves an approximation of Homer's oral poetry to elements in West Indian speech that must remain, even to many West Indian listeners, inarticulate and at best partially understood. This motif finds its parallel in other contexts. When, for example, in the Narrator's interview with Homer himself the ancient poet declares that "a drifter/is the hero of my book," the Narrator surprises him by rejoining: "I never read it," which he then qualifies: "not all the way through."[30] For the reader alive to the poem's engagement with literary antecedents, it is a puzzling moment.[31] I take this reply as rejecting what is implied when Homer refers to his *Odyssey* as a "book." The passage thus indicates that Homer is not to be understood exclusively as the representative, nor *Omeros* as the product, of European scribal culture; for, after denying that he has ever "read" Homer "all the way through," the Narrator declares his debt to the oral tradition, going on to insist:

> "I have always heard
> your voice in that sea, master, it was the same song
> of the desert shaman, and when I was a boy
>
> your name was as wide as a bay, and I walked along
> the curled brow of the surf; the word 'Homer' meant joy,
> joy in battle, in work, in death, then the numbered peace

of the surf's benedictions, it rose in the cedars,
in the *laurier-cannelles*, pages of rustling trees.
Master, I was the freshest of your readers."[32]

This emphasis on Homer as an oral poet of the sea and of nature, one whose
poetry finds its analogue not in literature but in the unwritten landscape and
seascape of St. Lucia, in the quotidian experience of a growing boy, constructs
a Homer very different from his Virgilian and Miltonic progeny, one who
resembles much more the Slavic and African epicists recovered by folklorists.
If this Homer can be encountered at all through reading, it can only be a
partial encounter—"not all the way through"—involving not just the leaves
of a book but also "the pages of the trees."[33]

In this respect research into the existence and oral performative character of the African epic and the establishment of a link between these traditions and those that produced the songs of Homer in a sense substantiates
Walcott's imaginative characterization of Homer, in one of many avatars
within *Omeros*, as Seven Seas, the wizened old storyteller of St. Lucia who embodies the lore and wisdom of the island people and whose ultimate roots
are in Africa.

EPIC AS A DIALOGICAL GENRE

My second main point concerns the way in which most students of literature
have been taught to conceive of the European epic. It is clear that the study
of world epic in the twentieth century represents a major challenge to traditional definitions of the genre based on the European canon. In addition,
it can easily be shown that these traditional definitions are wholly inadequate to describe even poems like the *Aeneid* and *Paradise Lost*. A good deal
of the modern theoretical discourse that concerns itself with epic—and I
am thinking here primarily of the classic formulations, descended from
Schiller, of Hegel, Lukács, Auerbach, and Bakhtin—shows a pronounced
tendency to employ a discursive caricature of the genre as a foil for making clearer the less strictly defined, formally and culturally heterogeneous,
and in short "open" characteristics of other genres, especially the novel.[34]

This discursive strategy has resulted in a number of pernicious literary-
historical misconceptions, not least of which is the absurdly one-dimensional
idea of the epic genre that many students of literature regard as axiomatic.
Thus while the epic, when viewed from a multicultural perspective, may prove
to be many things, in the classical tradition of European literature it has been
accorded a privileged place among the most elevated genres. Among its attributes, along with a tone conforming to its elevated matter, are *authority*,
or the idea that the stories told by the epic narrator are objectively true; *transcendence*, or the idea that the authority and truth of the epic narrative are

wholly independent of any historical or cultural contingency; and *original-ity*, the idea that epic is in some sense a source of subsequent culture, particularly as the literary embodiment of a nation's character.

If we define the European epic as necessarily possessing characteristics such as these, it is easy to see why some readers would hesitate to regard *Omeros* as representing the genre. Its tone is seldom elevated, nor is much of its matter especially dignified. The narrative voice, though sure in a technical sense, is personal (in many passages explicitly autobiographical), uncertain (readier to ask questions than to provide answers), idiosyncratic (prone to seemingly uncontrolled punning), uncomfortable with the mantle of authority. The narrative itself is often untrue in any conventional sense: the Narrator does not really speak with his dead father or with Homer himself; Achille does not really sail to his ancestral Africa; Denis Plunkett is in fact neither the father nor the descendant of the obscure midshipman who bore the same surname and who died in the Battle of Les Saintes. It is also clear that the nationalism of this epic is far from embracing the imperialist ideology of previous epics. Walcott's St. Lucia is consistently represented as a remnant and a victim of empire, while as one among many Caribbean islands, the formerly contested possession of rival empires now, left to fend for itself, seems both an unlikely subject for a triumphalist national epic and an unlikely heir to the epic tradition handed down from Greece, Rome, and Christendom in general.

If there were any doubt that *Omeros* is a deliberate nonepic, it would seem to be dispelled by a pair of passages that occur near the end of the poem. In the first, Walcott imagines what a conventional epic description of St. Lucia might have looked like:

> "In the mist of the sea there is a horned island
> with deep green harbours where the Greek ships anchor
>
> ....
>
> It was a place of light with luminous valleys
>
> under thunderous clouds. A Genoan wanderer
> saying the beads of the Antilles named the place
> for a blinded saint. Later, others would name her
>
> for a wild wife. Her mountains tinkle with springs
> among moss-bearded forests, and the screeching of birds
> stitches its tapestry. The white egret makes rings
>
> stalking its pools. African fishermen make boards
> from trees as tall as their gods with their echoing
> axes and a volcano stinking with sulphur
>
> has made it a healing place."
>
> (*Omeros* 7. 57.1)

The style of this passage, its beauty notwithstanding, might strike the reader as absurd and hence sheerly parodic in the usually unpretentious linguistic context of *Omeros*, with its stretches of plain dialogue, its Creole, its occasional obscenities. But there is no mockery here. The passage is uttered first by Omeros himself, who observes the Narrator weeping like a boy:

> and he saw how deeply I had loved this island.
> Perhaps the oarsman knew this, but I didn't know.
> Then I saw the ebony of his lifted hand
>
> And Omeros nodded: "We will both praise it now."
> But I could not before him. My tongue was a stone
> at the bottom of the sea, my mouth a parted conch
>
> from which nothing sounded, and then I heard his own
> Greek calypso coming from the marble trunk,
> widening the sea with a blind man's anger.

Omeros then sings the first two lines of the song quoted above. The Narrator continues:

> and the waves were swaying to the stroke of his hand,
> as I heard my own voice riding on his praise
> the way a swift follows a crest, leaving its shore.

They sing the remaining stanzas together, until the Narrator informs us:

> My voice was going
> under the strength of his voice, which carried so far
> that a black frigate heard it, steadying its wing.

The concentration of literary motifs in this passage—its elevated tone; the appearance, in the fact that both Omeros and the Narrator are on a boat, of the classical conceit by which composing poetry is figured as sailing (to say nothing of allusions to specific literary voyages, like that of Dante and Virgil across the Styx); Omeros's vatic knowledge of the Narrator's love, unsuspected by himself, for his native land; the response of the waves and of the frigate bird to the Orphic power of Omeros's song; the blending of the poets' voices; and the younger poet's inability to sing before hearing the voice of the elder— all represent a departure from the "normal" (if one can speak of a norm) narrative style of the poem up to this point. Through this departure and in the distance it takes us from the poem's usual stylistic procedures we can measure the gap between *Omeros* and other epics of the Homeric stripe.

A second passage not long after this one accomplishes something similar, but in a less striking way. The poem's final chapter begins as follows:

> I sang of quiet Achille, Afolabe's son,
> who never ascended an elevator,
> who had no passport, since the horizon needs none,

never begged nor borrowed, was nobody's waiter,
whose end, when it comes, will be a death by water
(which is not for this book, which will remain unknown

and unread by him). I sang the only slaughter
that brought him delight, and that from necessity—
the slaughter of fish, sang the channels of his back in the sun.

I sang our wide country, the Caribbean Sea.
Who hated shoes, whose soles were as cracked as a stone,
who was gentle with ropes, who had one suit alone,

whom no man dared insult and who insulted no one,
whose grin was a white breaker cresting, but whose frown
was a growing thunderhead, whose fist of iron

would do me a greater honor if it held on
to my casket's oarlocks than mine lifting his own
when both anchors are lowered in the one island.

                                              (*Omeros* 7.64.1)

Such a passage is literally perverse, turned backwards, alluding in the poem's
final chapter to the conventional opening of a canonical epic. Indeed, one
can easily read the first line of the chapter as an allusion to the opening lines
of the *Iliad*, but an allusion that systematically inverts virtually everything in
its source:

μῆνιν, ἄειδε, θεά, Πηληϊάδεω Ἀχιλῆος
οὐλομένην

                                              (*Iliad* 1.1–2)

"Sing, goddess, the baleful anger of Peleus' son, Achilles." Every departure
from the Homeric model speaks eloquently of the vast difference in perspective between the two poems. In naming his hero, Walcott rejects the universal form Achilles in favor of the dialectal variant Achille, local Creole by
way of colonial French. By including the patronymic he underlines the theme
of cultural rift; for while Achilles and Peleus share membership in a single
Hellenic culture, the very names of Achille and Afolabe represent the victimization of Africans in the Americas at the hands of the European slave
trade. The epithet "quiet" is of course unimaginable for any Homeric hero.
Finally, in "I sang" two crucial reversals occur. First, in the change of tense
and mood from Homer's forward-looking "sing" ἄειδε is figured the dislo-
cation, as mentioned above, of the epic invocation from the poem's beginning to its end. Second, and more tellingly, Homer's "goddess" θεά, the Muse,
disappears: the poet has no need to petition divinity for his song but, mortal and fallible though he may be, sings on his own authority. For some readers it is this, more than anything else, that places *Omeros* outside the bounds

of the epic genre. "*Omeros* is not an epic," writes Figueroa, "and it hardly touches on the gods."[35] And indeed, it is in passages like this that we squarely confront Burris's "deliberate deflation of analogy."

If the European epic is what the theorists tell us it should be, then clearly *Omeros* is no epic. But those theorists are wrong. Certainly the idea that epic is a closed, authoritative genre, objective in its regard of the heroic past, and so on is a significant discursive construct that evidently answers some deep-seated cultural longing on the part of readers brought up on European literature. But a discursive construct it is, and its usefulness in describing or understanding an actual epic poem is limited at best. The discourse on the epic is, to be sure, one of the longest-lived and most powerful elements of literary investigation in the West. The fact is, however, that there has always been a counter tradition of reading epic as more open to pluralities of interpretation than the conventional view of the genre would seem to allow, and such interpretations have recently become a dominant feature of the critical discussion. From ancient allegoresis of the Homeric epics, which refuses to take the poems at face value, to romantic readings of Satan as the hero of *Paradise Lost*, to New Critical readings of the *Aeneid* as a deeply divided, grimly brooding meditation on the costs of empire, practical critics have always shown great acuity and resourcefulness at reading behind the objectivity and transcendence that we have all been taught to find in epic to the cultural anxieties and historical contingencies reflected and refracted within what poses as the inevitability of epic narrative.[36] It is in general I think fair to say that the rigid conception of epic that I have been outlining is by and large the province of theorists, who find such a construct useful for their own discursive purposes, and of nonspecialists, who are by definition not very interested in the epic; while the excellent work that any number of connoisseurs have done illustrates that an acceptance of alterity is a basic constitutive feature of the European epic from its inception. To deny that *Omeros* is an epic on the grounds that it is something "other" than the *Iliad* or *Paradise Lost* is to misunderstand the development of European epic as badly as Bowra misunderstood the existence of African epic.

But if *Omeros* does not conform to the expectations of theorists and nonspecialists, it does not fail to satisfy them. Walcott's ironic handling of the generic conventions of classical epic poetry is in my view more convincingly read as a logical extension of the epic genre's capacity to reinvent itself through inversion, opposition to epic predecessors, and ironic self-reflexion. To return briefly to the end of the poem: by announcing his subject here rather than at the beginning of the poem, the Narrator inverts normal epic procedure. While this particular stratagem is, I believe, an innovation, it is of a piece with the kind of striving for novelty that one finds throughout post-Homeric epic. That is to say, it is precisely the kind of innovation, commonly identified with Greek poetry of the Hellenistic period, but found everywhere in Virgil, Camões, and Milton as well, whereby either adherence to epic convention or imitation of a particular epic model is pointedly varied in such a way as to force rethinking about fundamental aspects of the genre.[37] This capacity has come to be seen as a central characteristic both of individual poems (e.g., Virgil's internal dialogue between the voices of celebration and lament, and his reduction of the hero and his enemy to a single pattern) and of the tradition as a whole (e.g., Milton's recasting of the classical pagan hero as a demon to be surpassed and defeated by a new, Christian hero possessed of qualities diametrically opposed to those of his prototype and foe).[38] Indeed, two recent studies of the European epic argue convincingly that the genre can be understood only in dialectical terms. For David Quint, the dialectic takes shape over time, with each instantiation of epic narrative finding its place on a continuum that lies between a wholehearted commitment to the celebration of triumph and a dissenting point of view that consistently takes the side of a defeated resistance. For Susanne Wofford, the epic poem is dialectical in its very structure: in the simile, the epic figure par excellence, the genre attempts to correlate its heroic ideology with the (largely antithetical) values of the external world.[39] Over time, Wofford argues, the genre develops various strategies for negotiating this disjunctive relationship, which nevertheless remains apparent to the reader and plays an essential role in constituting the epic. Both Quint and Wofford thus present views of the epic that are profoundly at odds with received opinion concerning the closed, monologic nature of the genre; and, what is more, their ideas, while developed and expressed with great energy and uncommon insight, are by no means eccentric when considered in relation to the bulk of contemporary critical work on the European epic. Indeed, one might say that their work marks an important stage in theoretical work on the epic and a signal that in this field theory has finally begun to catch up with practice.

Thus the polyglossia of *Omeros* does not just flout epic convention or render allusion to the classical epics merely parodic or unimportant, but actually continues the epic tradition of questioning and self-questioning engagement on the part of the poet with his predecessors. Placing at the end of the poem a passage that the "rules" of the genre tell us should come at the beginning is a formal instance of the capacity for inversion and reinvention that is itself a property of the epic genre. We may also take it as a signal that more substantive forms of inversion and reinvention are under way as well.

Once we realize this, it becomes clear that my earlier summary of a hypothetical argument in which I adduced this passage to prove that *Omeros* is no epic is itself open to drastic revision. To begin with, I called "Achille" a "dialectal variant" of "Achilles," the "universal" name for the greatest of heroes. This position is correct within the confines of a discourse that regards epic as the literary embodiment of a unitary, undifferentiated "European" culture; but a modest amount of philological inquiry reveals what is wrong with this perspective. "Achilles" happens to be the form that the name takes in English as well is in Latin, and it is through Latin that the form acquires its apparent universality. In fact, though, this form is, like "Ulysses" for "Odysseus" and "Hercules" for "Herakles," a Roman corruption of the Greek "Akhilleus." In other words, it is itself a dialectal variant. It is clear that the poem invites precisely this kind of scrutiny; consider its title, which designates the master poet of the tradition it engages not as the spuriously universal Latinate "Homer" (< Latin "Homerus"), but by the Greek "*Omeros.*" Indeed, even here we cannot claim that the Greek form represents a fixity or an authenticity that can pass for universality; for it is not the form that an ancient Greek would have used, Ὅμηρος [i.e., HO-me-ros], but modern Greek as spoken to the Narrator by a Greek woman and transcribed without regard for the conventions of the written Greek language.[40] It is the sound of the word that captivates the Narrator, who supplies it with his own idiosyncratic, aural etymology:

> I said "*Omeros,*"
> and *O* was the conch-shell's invocation, *mer* was
> both mother and sea in our Antillean patois,
> *os,* a grey bone, and the white surf as it crashes
>
> and spreads its sibilant collar on a lace shore.
> Omeros was the crunch of dry leaves, and the washes
> that echoed from a cave-mouth when the tide has ebbed.
>
> The name stayed in my mouth.
>
> (*Omeros* 1.2.3)

The Greek word is "derived" from elements of the French Creole dialect spoken, not written, on the islands and from the natural sounds of the Caribbean environment.[41] We may find in the apparent chronological inversion that derives Greek from French a parallel to the formal device of ending an epic with a formula normally used for beginnings, though in the sounds of the natural environment the Narrator finds a linguistic source that is indeed older than language itself. What is more important is to recognize in the "demotion" of Greek to a derivative status relative to the primacy of "our Antillean patois"—itself a tellingly ironic formulation in a poem written chiefly in English—a motif repeated in at least two other central conceits of the poem with much broader thematic significance.

The first of these conceits, which descends from the idea of *translatio imperii,* involves the unending succession whereby formerly enslaved and colonized peoples become oppressors in their own right. The motif first appears in the early poem "Ruins of a Great House," of which Rei Terada writes: "Walcott places the British conquest of St. Lucia at the end of an originless chain of conquests including the Roman colonization of Britain."[42] *Omeros* neatly extends this motif, beginning with the ancient Athenian democracy—"its *demos* demonic and its *ocracy* crass"[43] —that enslaved its fellow Greeks who inhabited the islands of the Aegean in what began as a defensive league against Persian invasion but ended as the Athenian Empire. Then Roman enslaved Greek and appropriated Greek culture as a symbol of empire, passing this iconography of power on to other enslaved peoples destined to gain empires of their own. The British Empire in turn established colonies throughout the New World and, with its fellow European powers, enslaved and exterminated the inhabitants of that world—virtually, in the case of the North American Iroquois and Sioux, completely in the case of the Antillean Aruacs and Caribs—and thereby created a fresh need for slaves, supplied by Africa, whose descendants remain oppressed by a pervasive racism particularly in the contemporary United States.[44] But even the enslaved and the oppressed are not free from complicity. A shocked Achille witnesses a slaving raid on his ancestral village carried out by another African tribe.[45] The warlike Caribs had been responsible for wiping out the peaceful Aruacs, while a regiment of freed North American slaves—the Buffalo Soldiers of the United States Ninth Cavalry—advanced the cause of white imperialism by carrying out the final defeat of the Sioux.[46] "All colonies inherit their empire's sin."[47]

· For our purposes a second motif is perhaps even more important. I refer to the figure of lineage or paternity in *Omeros* and in epic narrative generally.

In *Omeros* paternity is a far from simple matter. Denis Plunkett grieves because he will die without an heir, and in an act that is half pedantry and half unrestrained imagination he makes himself the "father" of a young midshipman also named Plunkett, who, he discovers, died serving under Admiral Rodney in the Battle of Les Saintes 200 years before the story of *Omeros* takes place. Imagining this young man as his son does not prevent Plunkett from claiming him as an ancestor as well, by a crazy logic based on the fact that, as Plunkett will do, the young midshipman also died without leaving an heir. The Narrator of the poem stands in a similarly ambiguous relationship to his father, who died at an age younger than that of the Narrator, who thus figures himself as "older" than his father as he tells the story of *Omeros*.[48] Achille experiences a hallucination that takes him to Africa, where he converses with people whom he imagines as his ancestors; and as the poem ends he prepares to raise Helen's child, who may be his own son or else that of his departed friend and rival, Hector. In all these instances the relationship of fathers to sons is deeply problematized, the basis of the relationship questioned: is it primarily a biological matter, or one dependent on empathy, imaginative sympathy, mutual interest, and acceptance, or even an act of will asserting itself over reason? Is the vector of the relationship always one that follows the arrow of time from father to son, or does the son engender the father from whom he wishes to inherit?

This is, I submit, one of the central problems of the European epic from its inception. The heroes of the *Iliad* are obsessed with their own ancestry and are bent on proving that they measure up to the standards set by their forebears. Telemachus's coming of age involves meeting his long-lost father for the first time in his life. Aeneas must transform himself from the dutiful son of a doomed race to the progenitor of the greatest empire in world history. Satan rebels against the appointed succession of the Father by the Son, so that Adam, fatherless himself, becomes the begetter of humankind in general. It is difficult not to see in the career of the European epic an ideal instantiation of the Oedipal warfare that for Harold Bloom constitutes the driving force behind all literature.[49] But the epigonal work can never overcome its own belatedness and derivative status. For epics such as these, genealogy— not just that of the hero, but that of the poem itself—becomes all important: by virtue of claiming legitimate descent from Homer, these epics attempt to take the place of Homer as originary texts in their own right. But on grounds of originality it is clear that the principal European epics are compromised by their membership in a clearly defined literary tradition stretching back to Homer: by virtue of this fact, they can never be original as Homer is.

By renewing this aspect of the epic tradition *Omeros* makes of itself a paradigm for the contemporary individual's relationship to the various cultural legacies that he or she inherits or wishes to claim. In a limited way, the poem can thus be read as an allegory of our own relationship to classical culture, or to the immigrant culture of our personal ancestors, or even of groups to which we feel or imagine a sympathetic connection rather than an ethnic or biological one. The central reflection of this arrangement is the relative lack of authority and control that Walcott's Narrator exerts over his story, in sharp contrast to the objectivity and truth that are conventionally ascribed to the epic poet. Walcott's Narrator is thus not so far removed from his reader, in that both are in the position of needing to piece together fragments of a broken past in order to make sense of their existence and experiences.

Thus *Omeros* presents the reader with a litmus test, or rather, with the illusion of such a test; for, like the bureaucrat of the story with which I began, any reader who seeks to apply such a test to this poem can only fail. There is in *Omeros* no black or white, but only black and white. Its roots are not in Europe or Africa, but necessarily in both Europe and Africa. Consequently, it is not epic or novel, but only epic and novel. This, however, it can only be if its relationship to classical epic, however we may choose to problematize this relationship, as well as to the epics of groups traditionally ignored by the canonical European epic tradition, is fully acknowledged and integrated into our reading. This is only one of the reasons that we should celebrate this remarkable poem, which is after all still new to us, still in many ways uncanny and unfamiliar—for its ability to make us see our own past anew, to force us to reflect upon our own ancestry, and to understand our own heritage— racial, intellectual, and cultural—both as it is and as we would have it be.

NOTES

1. For a brief bibliography and survey of the critical tradition, see Marowski and Matuz 1987, 414–423.

2. In this paper I cite from Walcott 1986 (*Collected Poems, 1948–1984*) unless otherwise noted. The passage in question may be found on p. 15. The poem originally appeared in 1956, according to Irma E. Goldstraw's indispensible bibliography (1984, 5), and was subsequently included in Walcott 1962, 18.

3. Walcott 1986, 443. The poem originally appeared in *The New Yorker* in 1981 (Goldstraw 1984, 39) and, later that year, in the collection *The Fortunate Traveller* (New York, 1981), 63–70.

4. Lefkowitz 1990, 1, 34–35; Knox 1991, 3–4; Taplin 1991, 213–226; Steiner 1993, 13–16.

5. Burris 1991, 559 (my emphasis).

6. Hamner 1993b, 19; cf. the introductory remarks in Hamner 1993a, 10–12.

7. Figueroa 1991, 211.

8. Ismond 1991, 10–11.

9. Quoted by Bruckner 1990, reprinted. in Hamner 1993a, 396–399. Walcott's remarks stress the importance to him of the novelists Rudyard Kipling, Joseph Conrad, and Ernest Hemingway as models for *Omeros*. See also Brown and Johnson 1990, 209–233; White 1990, 14–37.

10. "*Omeros* is profoundly Homeric and undoubtedly epic"; see Taplin 1991, 213–226.

11. Burris 1991, 560.

12. On dramatic elements in *Omeros*, see Burris 1991, 561–564. Burris calls *Ulysses* "the work that will in all likelihood emerge as the most generous sponsor of *Omeros*" (p. 561).

13. Figueroa 1991, 203–205. On p. 205 he observes that St. Lucy, the patron saint of the island, was herself a blind seer. Blindness and compensatory insight is a recurring theme in Walcott's work, one with special relevance to the figure of the poet. In "Cul de Sac Valley" the poet images himself as an Oedipus questioned by a row of Sphinxes (Walcott 1986, 13).

In this essay I will use the capitalized form "Narrator" to indicate the character in *Omeros* who narrates the poem and represents the figure of the poet himself; the lowercase form indicates the implied singer of whatever poem happens to be under discussion.

14. Figueroa 1991, 206.

15. Leithauser 1991. Cf. Figueroa 1991, 197: "The poem [is] much more a novel than an epic, while never losing its lyrical fire."

16. The argument is spelled out most clearly in Bakhtin's essay "Epic and Novel" (Bakhtin 1981, 3–40).

17. The question of Walcott's influences, which has been prominent in criticism of his work since the beginning, came to be viewed in terms of cultural allegiance as Walcott's European influences were found by some less relevant to the Africanist West Indian political consciousness of the 1960s and 1970s than the work of other writers, particularly Edward Brathwaite. The literature comparing the two writers is quite large: representative works include Lucie-Smith 1968; Drayton 1970; James 1970;

[Anonymous] "How Far are Derek Walcott and Edward Brathwaite Similar?" 1974; Collier 1979; King 1980.As Walcott's interest in African themes, particularly in plays such as *Dream on Monkey Mountain* and *O Babylon!*, came to be appreciated, the question of his cultural allegiances became less urgent. Further, with Walcott's rise to international stature he has come to be compared with poets such as Joseph Brodsky and Seamus Heaney, and one result of appearing in such company before an international audience is that his Caribbean identity seems hardly in doubt. Significantly, the West Indian writer with whom he is most often contrasted nowadays is not Brathwaite, but V. S. Naipaul, with whose dismal judgment upon postcolonial culture, particularly in the West Indies, Walcott (1974) took exception.

18. Bowra 1952, 1–11.

19. Ibid.

20. Finnegan 1970, 108ff. Finnegan, however, is not concerned, as Bowra is, with the capacity of Africans to produce heroic literature so much as with the technical question of whether their heroic literature is in verse.

21. Of crucial importance was the publication of the Sundiata epic (Niane 1960; Pickett 1965 (English translation). On the poem, see Miller 1990, 87–101. Other important scholarly investigations of African epic include Okpewho 1979; Knappert 1983; William Johnson 1980.

22. On the work of Parry and Lord on this tradition, see Lord 1960.

23. *Kambili*, vol. 1 of *The Songs of Seydou Camara*, trans. Charles S. Bird, Mamadou Koita, and Bourama Soumaoro (lines 505–507); cited by Okpewho 1979, 205–206.

24. A more apt comparison might have been between other instances of interaction between poet and audience in contemporary performative epic and passages in our *Iliad* and *Odyssey* that are best explained as "local variants," that is, as versions of the story suited to performance in some specific setting that somehow found their way into what eventually became the "canonical" text. Such an explanation has been advanced in the case of the episode involving Aeneas in *Iliad* 20, which may ultimately owe its existence to a ruling dynasty that claimed descent from the hero: see Kirk 1991, 298–301, with further references. An even stronger case can be made for the prominence of the Athenian contingent in the Catalogue of Ships in that Athens was not a great power either at the time when the events of the *Iliad* putatively occurred or at the time when a recognizable version of the poem was first coming into existence; yet the Athenian tyrant Peisistratus played some role, one that may have been both extensive and decisive, in the canonization of the text of Homer that has come down to us. On this particular problem see Kirk 1985, 178–180, with further references. On the phenomenon in general, see Svenbro 1976, 5–73.

25. This passage has a long history of interpretation, much of which finds the humorous element misplaced. See Kirk 1990,190–191, with further references.

26. With this motif we may compare contemporary performances of North African epic: see the Dwight Reynolds's essay in this volume: "Problematic Performances: Overlapping Genres and Levels of Participation in Arabic Oral Epic-Singing."

27. Walcott 1987, 10.

28. Walcott 1978, 155–156. This passage is quoted at greater length and discussed in Terada 1992, 93–94.

29. Seven Seas performs, for instance, at a party held at the café in honor of a political candidate (2.20.1). Ma Kilman's eventual role as Philoctete's healer un-

derlines the assonance between her name and that of Machaon, surgeon to the Greek forces in the *Iliad*, as Burris points out (1991, 561), citing the equivalence as an example of Walcott's "slapstick disregard" for his Homeric parallels. Burris's rather facile reaction ignores the fact that the character of Ma Kilman, a "gardeuse, sybil, obeah-woman" (1.10.2), antedates *Omeros* and indeed is first presented not as Walcott's creation, but as "found object" of St. Lucian folk culture, appearing first in a Creole song included and translated in "Sainte Lucie," secs. 4–5 (Walcott 1986, 314–319, first published in the collection *Sea Grapes* as long ago as 1976). The connection with Machaon would appear to have been forged or "discovered" some time after the poet's initial acquaintance with the figure. I would add that the hand of the poet is more clearly visible in the character's connection with the No Pain Cafe, which takes its name from that of νηπενθής (*nēpenthēs*), "[allowing] no pain," a drug administered by Helen to her husband, Menelaus, and to their guests, Telemachus and Peisistratus, so that they might discuss the war at Troy and the difficult homecomings of the Greeks who fought there without succumbing to grief. Thus Ma Kilman herself is a type of Helen in her odyssean, as opposed to her iliadic, manifestation.

30. *Omeros* 7.56.3.

31. The theme of alleged gaps in the author's reading recurs, again with respect to the sources of *Omeros*, but this time involving the *Aeneid* as well as the *Odyssey*, in White 1990, 16–35. The problem is addressed with great insight by Fuller (1992, 517–538). One thinks of Yeats's striking way of naming the inspiration of his life's work: "the half-read wisdom of daemonic images" ("Meditations in Time of Civil War" 7.40, in Yeats 1983, 206).

32. *Omeros* 7.56.3.

33. The theme of a natural language heard or even read in landscape is prominent throughout Walcott's work. See for instance the excellent observations of Terada 1992, 152, 164–165, 167, 171–174.

34. The locus classicus for this line of discourse is Friedrich Schiller's essay *Über naive und sentimentalische Dichtung* (1795–1796). It continues in G. W. F. Hegel's *Ästhetik* of 1835 (on which see Bowie 1990, 140–142), Georg Lukács's *Theorie des Romans* (1920), Erich Auerbach's *Mimesis* (1953), and Bakhtin's "Epic and Novel" (1941; not widely known in this country before the Emerson and Holquist translation of 1981). It is fair to say that the influence of these thinkers on the study of the novel and its relationship not only to epic but to premodern literature in general has been decisive, but in many ways far from constructive.

35. Figueroa 1991, 211; cf. *Omeros* 7.56.3: [Narrator] "The gods and the demigods aren't much use to us."/"Forget the gods," Omeros growled, "and read the rest."

36. On ancient allegoresis of Homer, see Lamberton 1986, with further references. On *Paradise Lost*, see Newlyn 1993. For a convenient survey of twentieth-century trends in Virgilian criticism, see Harrison 1990, 1–20.

37. This particular type of intertextuality goes by the convenient name *oppositio in imitando*. There is a considerable literature on this phenomenon, most of it known, unfortunately, only to specialists. For a brief survey with references, see the introduction to Farrell 1991, 3–25. As a convenient illustration of the effect produced by this type of writing, consider the Narrator's observation that Achille's "end, when it comes, will be a death by water/(which is not for this book)" (*Omeros* 7.64.1). The

point being imitated is Tiresias's prophecy in the Homeric *Odyssey* that the hero's death will occur far from the sea (*Odyssey* 11.134–136). The imitation *e contrario* not only redefines the meaning of death at sea according to the values of a new poetic universe but actively enlists the contribution of a whole range of previous independent imitators of the *Odyssey*, from Dante, whose Ulisse does in fact contradict Homer by dying a watery death (*Inferno* 26.85–142), to Kazantzakis, whose importance to Walcott as a mediator of Homeric and meta-Homeric traditions awaits further exploration, and Eliot, particularly of course in *The Waste Land*, to mention only these.

The phenomenon of *oppositio in imitando* parallels what Harold Bloom has famously figured as the belated poet's struggle for originality in the face of an oppressive weight of tradition in *The Anxiety of Influence* (1973) and subsequent studies, but differs by focusing largely on the impersonal forces of generic development rather than on the psychological trope of the Oedipus complex. A further parallel may be found in the work of those scholars who have attempted to define the role of the individual poet-singer working within a tradition of oral composition and performance: e.g., Nagler 1974; Austin 1975.

38. On this aspect of the *Aeneid*, see Putnam 1988, 151–201. On Milton's Christian revision of pagan heroism, see Fish 1967.

39. See Quint 1993; Wofford 1992. See the review of both Quint and Wofford in Farrell 1993.

40. The poem thus privileges orality over literacy: the modern spelling is identical to the ancient, but the rough breathing mark is vestigial since the initial *H* sound has disappeared (Walcott uses the *H* only at 3.30.2). Thus Walcott's transliteration of Homer's Greek name into Roman characters as "Omeros" ironically represents more accurately than standard modern Greek orthography not only the absence of the *H* sound, but also the fact that the first and second *O* sounds (represented in Greek by omicron and omega, respectively) no longer differ in quantity, as they did in the ancient language, but actually sound identical. In fact, to say even this is too simple in view of the multiplicity of ancient conventions of spelling and pronunciation and the modern distinction between Katharevousa and Demotike. But my main point is, I think, clear.

41. Note that it is clearly an inhabited or personified environment: a conch shell sounds only when blown like a horn; leaves may crunch under human footsteps or from other causes; and the mouth of the cave quickly becomes the Narrator's mouth.

42. Terada 1992, 60. "Ruins of a Great House" originally appeared in 1956, then in Walcott 1962 (the collection *In a Green Night: Poems, 1945–1960*), and most recently in Walcott 1986 (*Collected Poems*), 19–21.

43. *Omeros* 5.41.1.

44. *Omeros* 5.41.2–3.

45. *Omeros* 3.27.1.

46. "Buffalo Soldiers" was the name given by the Southwest and Plains Indians to the troops who served between 1866 and 1891 as the Ninth and Tenth Regiments of the United States Cavalry, all of them African-Americans. The troops evidently accepted the name as a badge of honor, and the Tenth incorporated a bison into its regimental emblem (Leckie 1967, 25–26). The Ninth's involvement in the U. S. government's response to the Ghost Dance movement among the Sioux in 1890–1891

was the last significant campaign of the Buffalo Soldiers (Leckie, pp. 25–26). The narrative of this episode in *Omeros* occurs in what may be the most elliptical part of the poem. It begins when Achille, fresh from his hallucinatory voyage to Africa, remembers hearing the Bob Marley song "Buffalo Soldier" at a party the previous night and imagines himself a member of that troop (*Omeros* 3.31.1). The tale is related sporadically in the thirteen chapters that flow through the Narrator's experiences living in Boston and, especially, traveling to the Great Plains (a trip explicitly likened to Achille's dream of Africa at 4.34.2) and in passages related from the perspective of Catherine Weldon, a Boston woman who lived with Sitting Bull at the time of the Ghost Dance. This thread of narrative ends with book 5. Achille himself, in the reverie induced in him by Marley's music, is imagistically associated with the destruction of the Sioux nation and of the Aruacs (3.31.1).

In a similar way, Achille's ancestor, the Afolabe who first acquired the name Achilles from Admiral Rodney himself, helped the British forces position a cannon for the defense of St. Lucia against a French assault (2.14.3). By this act this Achilles unwittingly takes the part of the British Empire, which would ultimately gain political control over the island, against the nation that would leave so great a stamp on the island's culture, particularly its language and religion, in the time of his descendants.

It is possible, although *Omeros* does not do so, to document the converse phenomenon, the complicity of American Indians in the enslavement of blacks: see Abel 1992. And, to complete this brief typological survey of racial oppression, see Koger 1985.

47. *Omeros* 5.41.2.

48. "Now that you are twice my age, which is the boy's/which the father's?" "Sir,"— I swallowed—"they are one voice" (1.12.1).

49. Bloom 1973.

WORKS CITED

Abel, Annie Heloise.

1992   *The American Indian as Slaveholder and Secessionist.* Reprint. Lincoln:
[1915].   University of Nebraska Press.

Anonymous

              "How Far Are Derek Walcott and Edward Brathwaite Similar? Is It Impossible for the Caribbean to Choose between the Two, If So, Which Way Should They Choose and Why?"1974. *Busara* 6.1: 90–100.

Auerbach, Erich.

1953.   *Mimesis.* Translated by Willard R. Trask. Princeton: Princeton University Press. First published in 1946.

Austin, Norman.

1975.   *Archery at the Dark of the Moon: Poetic Problems in Homer's "Odyssey."* Berkeley and Los Angeles: University of California Press.

Bakhtin, Mikhail.

1981.   *The Dialogic Imagination: Four Essays.* Edited by Michael Holquist and translated by Caryl Emerson and Michael Holquist. Austin: University of Texas Press.

Bloom, Harold.
1973.   *The Anxiety of Influence: A Theory of Poetry.* London, Oxford, and New
         York: Oxford University Press.
Bowie, Andrew.
1990.   *Aesthetics and Subjectivity from Kant to Nietzsche.* Manchester: Manches-
         ter University Press.
Bowra, C. M.
1952.   *Heroic Poetry.* London: Macmillan.
Brown, Robert, and Cheryl Johnson.
1990.   "Thinking Poetry: An Interview with Derek Walcott." *The Cream City
         Review* 14.2: 209–233.
Brown, Stewart, ed.
1991.   *The Art of Derek Walcott.* Chester Springs, Pa.: Dufour Editions.
Bruckner, D. J. R.
1990.   "A Poem in Homage to an Unwanted Man." *The New York Times*, 9 Oc-
         tober, pp. 13, 17. Reprinted in Hamner 1993a, 396–399.
Burris, Sidney.
1991.   "An Empire of Poetry." *The Southern Review* 27: 558–574.
Collier, Gordon.
1979.   "Artistic Autonomy and Cultural Allegiance: Aspects of the Walcott-
         Brathwaite Debate Re-examined." *The Literary Half-Yearly* (Mysore)
         20.1: 93–105.
Drayton, Arthur D.
1970.   "The European Factor in West Indian Literature." *The Literary Half-
         Yearly* 11.1: 71–95.
Farrell, Joseph.
1993.   Review of *Epic and Empire,* by David Quint, and *The Choice of Achilles,*
         by Susanne Wofford. *Bryn Mawr Classical Review* 4: 481–489.
1991.   *Vergil's "Georgics" and the Traditions of Ancient Epic: The Art of Allusion
         in Literary History.* New York and Oxford: Oxford University Press.
Figueroa, John.
1991.   "*Omeros.*" In *The Art of Derek Walcott,* edited by Stewart Brown, 193–213.
         Chester Springs, Pa.: Dufour Editions.
1987.   "Cul de Sac Valley." In *The Arkansas Testament.* New York: Farrar, Straus
         and Giroux.
1949.   *Epitaph for the Young.* Barbados: Advocate Co.
Finnegan, Ruth H.
1970.   *Oral Literature in Africa.* Oxford and London: Clarendon Press.
Fish, Stanley.
1967.   *Surprised by Sin: The Reader in "Paradise Lost."* London: Macmillan; New
         York: St. Martin's Press.
Fuller, Mary.
1992.   "Forgetting the *Aeneid.*" *American Literary History* 4: 517–538.
Goldstraw, Irma E.
1984.   *Derek Walcott: An Annotated Bibliography of His Works.* New York and Lon-
         don: Garland.

Hamner, Robert D., ed.
    1993a.   *Critical Perspectives on Derek Walcott.* Washington, D.C.: Three Conti-
               nents Press.
    1993b.   *Derek Walcott.* Updated ed. New York: Twayne.
Harrison, S. J., ed.
    1990.   *Oxford Readings in Vergil's "Aeneid."* Oxford: Clarendon Press.
Ismond, Patricia.
    1991.   "Walcott's *Omeros*—A Complex, Ambitious Work." *Caribbean Contact*
               18.5: 10–11.
James, Louis.
    1970.   "Caribbean Poetry in English—Some Problems." *Savacou* 2: 78–86.
Johnson, John William.
    1980.   "Yes, Virginia, There is an Epic in Africa." *Research in African Litera-
               tures* 11.3: 308–326.
King, Bruce Alvin.
    1980.   "Walcott, Brathwaite, and Authenticity." In *The New English Literatures:
               Cultural Nationalism in a Changing World.* New York and London:
               Macmillan.
Kirk, G. S., ed.
    1991.   *The Iliad: A Commentary.* Vol. 5, *Books 17–20*, edited by Mark Edwards.
               Cambridge: Cambridge University Press.
    1990.   *The Iliad: A Commentary.* Vol. 2, *Books 5–8.* Cambridge: Cambridge Uni-
               versity Press.
    1985.   *The Iliad: A Commentary.* Vol. 1, *Books 1–4.* Cambridge: Cambridge Uni-
               versity Press.
Knappert, Jan.
    1983.   *Epic Poetry in Swahili and Other African Languages.* Leiden: E. J. Brill.
Knox, B. M. W.
    1991.   "Achilles in the Caribbean" *The New York Review of Books* 7: 3–4.
Koger, Larry.
    1985.   *Black Slaveowners: Free Black Slave Masters in South Carolina, 1790–1860.*
               Jefferson, N.C.: McFarland Press.
Lamberton, Robert.
    1986.   *Homer the Theologian: Neoplatonist Allegorical Reading and the Growth of
               the Epic Tradition.* Berkeley: University of California Press.
Leckie, William H.
    1967.   *The Buffalo Soldiers: A Narrative of the Negro Cavalry in the West.* Norman:
               University of Oklahoma Press.
Lefkowitz, Mary.
    1990.   "Bringing Him Back Alive." *The New York Times Book Review,* 7 Octo-
               ber: 1, 34–35.
Leithauser, Brad.
    1991.   "Ancestral Rhyme." Review of *Omeros,* by Derek Walcott. *The New Yorker,*
               11 February: 91–95.
Lord, A. B.
    1960.   *The Singer of Tales.* Cambridge, Mass.: Harvard University Press.
Lucie-Smith, Edward.
    1968.   "West Indian Writing," *The London Magazine* 8.4: 96–102.

Lukács, Georg.
1971.   *The Theory of the Novel.* Tranlsated by Anna Bostock. Cambridge, Mass.:
           M.I.T. Press. Originally published as *Theorie des Romans* (1920).
Marowski, Daniel, and Roger Matuz.
1987.   "Derek Walcott." *Contemporary Literary Criticism* 42: 414–423.
Miller, Christopher L.
1990.   *Theories of Africans: Francophone Literature and Anthropology in Africa.*
           Chicago: University of Chicago Press.
Nagler, Michael.
1974.   *Spontaneity and Tradition: A Study in the Oral Art of Homer.* Berkeley and
           Los Angeles: University of California Press.
Newlyn, Lucy.
1993.   *"Paradise Lost" and the Romantic Reader.* Oxford: Clarendon Press.
Niane, D. T.
1965.   *Sundiata: An Epic of Old Mali.* Translated by G. D. Pickett. London:
           Longman. Originally published as *Sundjata, ou l'épopée mandingue*
           (Paris: Presence Africaine, 1960).
Okpewho, Isidore.
1979.   *The Epic in Africa: Toward a Poetics of the Oral Performance.* New York:
           Columbia University Press.
Putnam, Michael C. J.
1988   *The Poetry of the "Aeneid": Four Studies in Imaginative Unity and Design.*
[1965].   Reprint. Ithaca, N.Y.: Cornell University Press.
Quint, David.
1993.   *Epic and Empire: Politics and Generic Form from Virgil to Milton.* Prince-
           ton: Princeton University Press.
Steiner, George.
1993.   "From Caxton to *Omeros.*" *Times Literary Supplement* 27: 13–16.
Svenbro, Jesper.
1976.   *La parole et le marbre: Aux origines de la poésie grecque.* Lund: Student-
           litteratur.
Taplin, Oliver.
1991.   "Derek Walcott's *Omeros* and Derek Walcott's Homer." *Arion* 3, 1.2:
           213–226.
Terada, Rei.
1992.   *Derek Walcott's Poetry: American Mimicry.* Boston: Northeastern Uni-
           versity Press.
Walcott, Derek.
1990.   *Omeros.* New York: Farrar, Straus and Giroux.
1986.   *Collected Poems, 1948–1984.* New York: Farrar, Straus and Giroux.
1978.   *The "Joker of Seville" and "O Babylon!"* New York: Farrar, Straus and
           Giroux.
1974.   "The Caribbean: Culture or Mimicry." *Journal of Interamerican Studies
           and World Affairs* 16.1: 3–13. Reprinted in Hamner 1993a, 51–57.
1962.   *In a Green Night: Poems, 1948–1960.* London: Jonathan Cape.
White, J. P.
1990.   "An Interview with Derek Walcott." *The Green Mountain Review* n.s. 4.1:
           14–37.

Wofford, Susanne Lindgren.
   1992.   *The Choice of Achilles: The Ideology of Figure in the Epic.* Stanford: Stanford University Press.

Yeats, W. B.
   1983.   "Meditations in Time of Civil War." In *The Poems: A New Edition,* edited by Richard J. Finneran. New York: Macmillan.

CONTRIBUTORS

Margaret Hiebert Beissinger is Lecturer in the Department of Slavic Languages and Literatures at the University of Wisconsin-Madison. She is author of *The Art of the Lăutar: The Epic Tradition of Romania* (New York: Garland Press, 1991) as well as articles on Romanian and South Slavic oral traditions and literature. Her current research interests include gender issues in Balkan oral poetry.

Elaine Fantham is Giger Professor of Latin at Princeton University. She is author of commentaries on Seneca's tragedy *The Trojan Women* and book 2 of Lucan's *Civil War, Comparative Studies in Republican Latin Imagery* (Toronto: University of Toronto Press, 1972); and, most recently, *Roman Literary Culture from Cicero to Apuleius* (Baltimore: Johns Hopkins University Press, 1996). She is coauthor with H. Foley, N. Kampen, S. Pomeroy, and A. Shapiro of *Women in the Classical World: Image and Text* (Oxford and New York: Oxford University Press, 1994 and 1995).

Joseph Farrell is Professor of Classical Studies at the University of Pennsylvania. He is the author of *Vergil's "Georgics" and the Traditions of Ancient Epic* (New York: Oxford University Press, 1991) and *Latin Language and Latin Culture* (Cambridge: Cambridge University Press, forthcoming). His current research includes a study of the idea of the classic as it developed in antiquity and as it functions within modern theoretical discourse. He is also director of The Vergil Project, a collaborative, WWW-based resource for learning, teaching, and research about Virgil.

Joyce Burkhalter Flueckiger is Associate Professor of Religion at Emory University. She is the author of *Gender and Genre in the Folklore of Middle India* (Ithaca, N.Y.: Cornell University Press, 1996) and coeditor of *Oral Epics in India* (Berkeley: University of California Press, 1989) and *Boundaries of the Text: Performing the Epics in South and Southeast Asia* (Ann Arbor: University of Michigan, 1991). Currently, she is writing an ethnographic study on a female Muslim folk healer in South India.

Andrew Ford is Associate Professor of Classics at Princeton University. He is author of *Homer: The Poetry of the Past* (Ithaca, N.Y.: Cornell University Press, 1992) and numerous articles on Greek poetics and literary history in such journals as *Arion* and *Common Knowledge* and in *The New Companion to Homer* (Leiden: E. J. Brill, 1997). He is currently writing a book-length study of the origins of literary criticism in classical Greece.

Thomas M. Greene is Frederick Clifford Ford Professor Emeritus of English and Comparative Literature at Yale University. His publications include *The Descent from Heaven: A Study in Epic Continuity* (New Haven: Yale University Press, 1963); *The Light In Troy: Imitation and Discovery in Renaissance Poetry* (New Haven: Yale University Press, 1982), which received the Harry Levin Prize from the American Comparative Literature Association and the James Russell Lowell Prize from the Modern Language Association; and *The Vulnerable Text: Essays on Renaissance Literature* (New York: Columbia University Press, 1986). He is also the author of numerous articles, chiefly on early modern literature, and is the coeditor of a volume on literary theory. Greene is a Fellow of the American Academy of Arts and Sciences and received the Medal of the Collège de France in 1989. He is currently the organizer and manager of a theater company that produces plays in Connecticut high schools about ethical dilemmas.

Philip Hardie is a University Lecturer in Classics at the University of Cambridge and a Fellow of New Hall. He is the author of *Virgil's "Aeneid": Cosmos and Imperium* (Oxford: Clarendon Press, 1986); *The Epic Successors of Virgil: A Study in the Dynamics of a Tradition* (Cambridge: Cambridge University Press, 1993); and *Virgil, Aeneid IX,* Cambridge Greek and Latin Classics (Cambridge: Cambridge University Press, 1994). He is currently completing a commentary on Ovid's *Metamorphoses*, books 13–15, and is preparing a book on fame and rumor from Homer to Pope.

Sheila Murnaghan is Associate Professor of Classical Studies at the University of Pennsylvania. She is author of *Disguise and Recognition in the "Odyssey"* (Princeton: Princeton University Press, 1987) and coeditor of *Women and Slaves in Greco-Roman Culture: Differential Equations* (London: Routledge, 1998). She works on Greek epic and tragedy, gender in classical Greece, and the classical tradition.

Gregory Nagy is the Francis Jones Professor of Classical Greek Literature and

Professor of Comparative Literature at Harvard University. He is the author of *The Best of the Achaeans: Concepts of the Hero in Archaic Greek Poetry* (Baltimore: Johns Hopkins University Press, 1979), which won the American Philological Association's Goodwin Award of Merit in 1982. His other publications include *Comparative Studies in Greek and Indic Meter* (Cambridge, Mass.: Harvard University Press, 1974), *Greek Mythology and Poetics* (Ithaca, N.Y.: Cornell University Press, 1990), *Pindar's Homer: The Lyric Possession of an Epic Past* (Baltimore: Johns Hopkins University Press, 1990), *Poetry as Performance: Homer and Beyond* (Cambridge: Cambridge University Press, 1996), and *Homeric Questions* (Austin: University of Texas Press, 1996). His special research interests are archaic Greek literature and oral poetics, and he finds it rewarding to integrate these interests with teaching, especially in his course for Harvard's Core Curriculum, "The Concept of the Hero in Greek Civilization." He is currently chair of Harvard's Classics Department.

Dwight F. Reynolds is Associate Professor of Arabic Language and Literature in the Department of Religious Studies at the University of California, Santa Barbara. He is the author of *Heroic Poets, Poetic Heroes: The Ethnography of Performance in an Arabic Oral Epic Tradition* (Ithaca, N.Y.: Cornell University Press, 1995), coeditor of *Musical Narrative Traditions of Asia* (special issue of *Asian Music*, 1995), editor of *Arabic Autobiography* (special issue of *Edebiyat: Journal of Middle Eastern Literatures*, 1997), and editor of *Interpreting the Self: Autobiography in the Arabic Literary Tradition* (forthcoming). He is currently completing a comparative study of premodern Arabic and European autobiographies.

William Sax is Senior Lecturer in Religious Studies at the University of Canterbury in Christchurch, New Zealand. He is the author of *Mountain Goddess: Gender and Politics in a Himalayan Pilgrimage* (New York: Oxford University Press, 1991) and editor of *The Gods at Play: Līlā in South Asia* (New York: Oxford University Press, 1995). He is currently writing a book on Himalayan ritual performances of *Mahābhārata*.

Susan Slyomovics is the Geneviève McMillan-Reba Stewart Professor of the Study of Women in the Developing World and Professor of Anthropology at the Massachusetts Institute of Technology. She is the author of *The Merchant of Art: An Egyptian Hilali Oral Epic Poet in Performance* (Berkeley: University of California Press, 1987) and *Memory and Architecture: Arab and Jew Narrate the Palestinian Village* (Philadelphia: University of Pennsylvania Press, forthcoming) as well as numerous articles on theater and performance in the Middle East and North Africa.

Jane Tylus is Associate Professor of Comparative Literature at the University of Wisconsin-Madison. She is author of *Writing and Vulnerability in the Late Renaissance* (Stanford: Stanford University Press, 1993) and of numerous articles on Renaissance culture, literature, and theater. She is currently completing a book entitled *Pastoral Gossip: Shakespeare, Lope, Guarini* and beginning another on the relationship between religious and humanist norms of imitation in early modern Europe and the Americas.

Susanne Lindgren Wofford is Professor of English at the University of Wisconsin-Madison. She is author of *The Choice of Achilles: The Ideology of Figure in the Epic* (Stanford: Stanford University Press, 1992). She is editor of *Hamlet: A Case Study in Contemporary Criticism* (Boston: Bedford Books, 1994) and of the New Century Views volume *Shakespeare: The Late Tragedies* (Englewood Cliffs, N.J.: Prentice-Hall, 1994). She has published articles on Shakespeare, Spenser, Boccaccio, and Botticelli and is currently at work on two book projects, one entitled *Epic and Origin* and the other *Theatrical Power: Mimesis and Contagion on the Shakespearean Stage.*

INDEX

Abrahams, Roger, 54, 71
abstraction, philosophical, 93, 100
Abū Zayd. *See under* Arabic epic
academic interest in Indian epic, 144, 145–47
achievement, affective cost of, 192–93, 216–17
Achilles: funeral, 205–6; laments for Patroclus, 206, 207, 210–12, 213; shares grief with Priam, 191–92, 193, 212
Acis, 104 n. 54
Actaeon, 101 n. 20
Adler, Mortimer, 239
Aeneas: destabilization, 95; and Dido, 97–100, 114, 197–98, 224; displacement, 109, 113, 116; dream-vision of Hector, 94; in Hades, 191, 195, 197–98; and lineage and paternity, 287; and universal/local tendencies, 109, 116–17
Aesop, fables of, 41
aetiology. *See* origin tales; origins
Africa, 23, 24, 274–79, 289 n. 21
Ahir caste, 136
Ahl, Frederick M., 90, 231
ainos (riddling discourse), 34–35, 39–40, 40–42
Akashvani (All India Radio), 144–45
akhos ("grief"), Homeric use, 23
Alcaeus, 49 n. 46
Alcmaeon of Croton, 47 n. 16
Alecsandri, Vasile; *Dumbrava roşie* (The red oak grove), 71, 80, 81

Aletes, 228
alētheia/muthos opposition, 26
Alexandrian scholarship, 45
Alexiou, Margaret, 204, 221
Alha Kand (Indian epic), 132, 149 n. 17
alienation. *See* displacement
Allecto (Fury), 94–95, 97, 98, 124
allegory and allegoresis, 10, 14, 33–53, 89–107; *ainos*, 34–35, 39–40, 40–42; *allēgoria*, 38, 40; Derveni papyrus, 33, 39–40; and elitism, 41, 42, 43–44, 44–45, 119–20; and etymology, 35, 36, 37, 38; and fables, 41; and fixation, 89, 99–100; Hesiod, 36; Homeric allegoresis, 34, 35–38, 42, 43, 45, 92, 283; *huponoia*, 38–39, 40, 45; early Italian, 33–53; Latin epic, 45, 90, 95–97; lexical evidence, 38–42; and metamorphosis, 92, 98, 267 n. 34; origins, 35–38; personification allegory, 89, 95–97; preSocratics, 33, 39–40; as social performance, 46; Spenser, 45, 257–58; subversive function, 14; Theagenes, 34, 35–38, 42, 45; uses, 42–46
All India Radio (Akashvani), 144–45
allusion, 90
Amata, 197, 224
ambiguity, verbal, 10, 12, 56, 103 n. 40. *See also* punning; wordplay
American Indians. *See* Native American oral tradition